Rhetoric and Composition

A SOURCEBOOK FOR TEACHERS AND WRITERS

Rhetoric and Composition

A SOURCEBOOK FOR TEACHERS AND WRITERS

Third Edition

Edited by

Richard L. Graves

Professor of English Education
Auburn University

BOYNTON/COOK PUBLISHERS

HEINEMANN

PORTSMOUTH, NH

BOYNTON/COOK PUBLISHERS
A Division of
HEINEMANN EDUCATIONAL BOOKS, INC.
361 Hanover Street
Portsmouth, NH 03801-3959
Offices and agents throughout the world

Third edition
©Copyright 1990 by Boynton/Cook Publishers, Inc.
First edition ©Copyright 1984 by Boynton/Cook Publishers, Inc.

Library of Congress Cataloging-in-Publication Data

Rhetoric and composition: a sourcebook for teachers and writers/
    edited by Richard L. Graves. — 3rd ed.
       p.   cm.
    Includes bibliographical references.
    ISBN 0-86709-267-X
    I. Graves, Richard L. (Richard Layton), 1931–
PE 1404.R48   1990
808'.042—dc20   90-40515
                                    CIP

Cover design by Jenny Greenleaf.
Interior design by Vic Schwarz.
Cover photo by Dan Gair.

Printed in the United States of America
10   9   8   7   6   5   4   3   2   1

CONTENTS

Preface

When Bob Boynton asked me to consider editing a third edition of *Rhetoric and Composition: A Sourcebook for Teachers and Writers,* I was both pleased and perplexed. It is deeply gratifying to know that other teachers have found this book useful, but it also is a huge job to try to make sense out of a discipline as diverse as ours. The school-based teaching of writing stretches from kindergarten through graduate school and in the process touches a broad diversity of teaching and learning concerns. On one hand, there is the elementary teacher whose young charges are just beginning to learn to hold a pencil, and on the other the college teacher, wondering whether the latest theory of poststructural criticism has any relevance to the teaching of writing. Each in her heart of hearts believes that she is the "real" teacher of writing, but each also senses a common bond with writing teachers everywhere. This third edition celebrates that common bond, the thread that runs through the lives of all teachers of writing and provides a deep kind of coherence in spite of the superficial differences.

The purpose of this edition is the same as that of the first, which was published over fourteen years ago: to provide a resource "for practicing and prospective teachers—from elementary school through graduate school—who are (or will be) involved in the most challenging task in the educational enterprise, helping others learn how to write." Challenging, yes, but also satisfying, I would add. The two books, however, are not very much the same. During the intervening years the discipline has experienced a great amount of growth and change. I realized early on that if I am to be honest as an editor, honest to myself and to the profession, then I must set aside personal tastes, cherished friendships, warm thoughts, preconceived opinions, and other barnacles collected over the years. I must, to the best of my ability, come to this task with an open mind, to search out the best and most representative writing about the teaching of writing. I have ruthlessly stuck to the credo, and despite my reluctance in dropping several favorite pieces, I am not only surprised with the result but, I confess, shamelessly delighted with it.

My optimism comes chiefly from what I sense as the general good health of a growing discipline. Since its "birth" in 1963 (Stephen North; Robert Connors , Lisa Ede, Andrea Lunsford; John Schilb; and others all point to that date) the discipline has, like a river, made several changes. During the early years, one of our major concerns was understanding our past. In order to gain recognition among its peers, a discipline must have a sense of its history. During those years, considerable attention was focused on understanding Greek and Roman rhetoric, its impact on Western civilization for over 2000 years, and its eventual decline. Perhaps no book has been more influential in our growth than Edward Corbett's *Classical Rhetoric for the Modern Student,* which is now in its third edition. In its scholarly synthesis of classical rhetoric, Corbett's work not only provided a sound foundation for the discipline but spawned countless articles in professional journals, research studies, and sessions at professional conferences as well.

Then during the seventies a second major thrust occurred, a concern for the teaching of writing. Whereas other disciplines tend to view knowledge as an end in itself, ours has a strong utilitarian emphasis, with teaching and learning at its center. Two key publications fired this enthusiasm, Janet Emig's *The Composing Processes of Twelfth Graders,* which was published in 1971, and Mina Shaughnessy's *Errors and Expectations,* which came out in 1977. These and other influential works, such as those by James Moffett, Ken Macrorie, Donald Graves, Peter Elbow, Linda Flower, James Britton, Donald Murray and so many others, have taught us that the teaching of writing is not like teaching in other academic disciplines. As a consequence, a new pedagogy has emerged, focusing on the writing process and response to writing, particularly within the context of the workshop format. In the past, the stereotypical English teacher was Inspector Javert, absolutely committed to the task of upholding the law of grammar and punishing transgressors. Fortunately, that stereotype is dying (or retiring), and a more vibrant concept of the teacher of writing is taking its place: the Renaissance man or woman, bright, articulate, energetic, effective, open, but above all, compassionate.

Now, some thirty years later, a new thrust appears to be emerging. Having developed a solid sense of its past and confident in its teaching, the discipline is reaching out to strengthen its core. It is beginning to draw from other disciplines—from literature and literary criticism, linguistics, philosophy, psychology, sociology, in short, from any place the human mind can reach. In the process of absorbing information from other places and assimilating it to itself, the discipline continues to grow and flourish.

There will, of course, continue to be excellent historical studies and breakthroughs in the learning process. But, to continue the metaphor of the river, some of these may occur in quiet eddies, still and calm at the edge, rather than in the main channel where the current is stronger.

There are two major organizational changes in this edition. First, the section on pedagogy has been recast as "Stories from the Writing Classroom" and moved closer to the front of the book. When student writing is at the center of the writing classroom, then there is less, or perhaps even no, need for what we think of as traditional methodology. The second change is that the sections on the sentence and the paragraph have been combined into one section on style. Because of the wealth of excellent material available, the present edition focuses on the teaching and learning of writing and on new perspectives which hold promise for influencing the direction of the discipline. Articles which emphasize the history of the discipline have not been included.

The reader might also note a sequential, "front-to-back" quality in this edition. The first part of the book is directed toward the beginning teacher, the latter portion toward the experienced teacher or the graduate student. A certain amount of teaching experience is necessary to comprehend some of the ideas presented in the last section, "New Perspectives, New Horizons."

Early in the planning stages of this edition, I asked a number of people from around the country to identify articles which have been most useful to them. Their responses have been extremely helpful, to say the least. Some not only filled out the questionnaire but sent bibliographies, xeroxed copies of works, and provided helpful comments. I am grateful for all the comments, notes, good ideas, and just plain common sense which I received during the editing process.

Among those who responded are Hugh Agee, Bob Bain, Lynn Bloom, Laura Brady, Lil Brannon, Tom Brennan, Don Cunningham, Frank D'Angelo, Jim Davis, Theresa Enos, Anne Ruggles Gere, Dorothy Grimes, I. Hashimoto, Paul Kameen, Terry Ley, Richard Lloyd-Jones, Carolyn Matalene, Marian Mohr, Lyn Zalusky Mueller, Keith Miller, Tom Nash, Elizabeth Cowan Neeld, Gretchen Niva, Twila Yates Papay, Gordon Pradl, David Roberts, Mike Rose, Dennis Rygiel, Bob Shafer, John Simmons, Fred Standley, Patricia Stock, Isabelle Thompson, Ann Trousdale, Lynn Troyka, Susan Villaume, Betty Jane Wagner, Tom Waldrep, Barbara Walvoord, Sam Watson, Ed White, Harvey Wiener, Lisa Williams, and Bill Wolff.

It goes without saying how much I appreciate the wise counsel of Bob Boynton, the perfect editor, who has made some sound suggestions about this edition but has given me the freedom to make the final decisions.

Throughout this whole endeavor my wife Eloise has been encouraging, supportive, and patient. I am deeply appreciative of her good humor and constant support, not just during the past few months but over our many years together.

PART ONE

Introduction

"...Except he come to composition, a man remains un-put-together, more than usually troubled by the feuds within, and therefore a little more addicted to those without."

Robert B. Heilman

This section emphasizes the idea that writing is a difficult though deeply satisfying activity, the pinnacle perhaps of all intellectual growth and development. The teacher of writing, however, must understand not only the power of writing itself but the ways in which the behavior of the teacher influences student attitudes about writing and ultimately competence in writing. During the past two decades the role of the teacher of writing has undergone a significant transformation. In this section, the reader is introduced to the idea of "teaching writing as a process" as that idea has been interpreted by the major journals of the National Council of Teachers of English—*Language Arts, English Journal, College Composition and Communication,* and *College English,* plus an NCTE ERIC publication.

In the lead essay Maxine Hairston argues that the transformation of the teaching of writing is broad and extensive. Drawing on the work of the history of science scholar Thomas Kuhn, Hairston shows that the transformation now occurring is so deep and profound that it defies analysis by traditional methods. When a paradigm shift occurs, basic assumptions about a way of knowing are brought into question. Although Hairston's influential essay was published almost a decade ago, it continues to be widely discussed and quoted within the profession.

One of the reasons behind this transformation is our deepening understanding of the nature of writing itself. In the past in American schools, writing has been taught primarily as a surface skill or as the avoidance of error, but R.D. Walshe explains how "humanity's second greatest invention" is vastly more than that. Drawing on the work of John Dewey, Walshe explains how *learning* is central in the teaching of writing. Walshe concludes with a good description of the writing-to-learn classroom.

Contrasts between the old ways and the new paradigm are delineated in the article "Myths of Writing" by Frank Smith. A nationally recognized scholar

1

in the field, Smith rebuts twenty-two broadly held myths about the nature of writing, "concluding with a grand myth about who is able to teach writing." Smith's final conclusion is powerful and could well be adopted by writing teachers everywhere: "Anyone who hopes to teach children how to write must 1) demonstrate what writing does, and 2) demonstrate how to do it."

In the ERIC document "Language Across the Curriculum" Christopher Thaiss shows how writing can be used as a way of learning not just in English classes but in all academic disciplines. A large number of teachers from social sciences, math, science, as well as art, physical education, music, and other areas are discovering how writing can improve the quality of learning in their fields of study.

The concluding essay in this section, "Competing Theories of Process: A Critique and a Proposal," argues that the writing-as-process movement has several faces. The author, Lester Faigley, describes three views of process—the expressive, the cognitive, and the social. His synthesis argues for the general value of the movement and the ways in which each of the three views contributes to the whole. "These questions are not mere matters of ivory-tower debate," he writes. The teaching of writing, Faigley reminds us, occurs in a real world populated by people with everyday problems—staying well, finding a job, paying bills. If our work as teachers of writing produces any benefits, it must somehow find its place in that world.

The Winds of Change:
Thomas Kuhn and the Revolution in the Teaching of Writing

In 1963, the University of Chicago Press published a book titled *The Structure of Scientific Revolutions*, written by Thomas Kuhn, a University of California professor of the history of science. In the book Kuhn hypothesizes about the process by which major changes come about in scientific fields, and conjectures that they probably do not evolve gradually from patient and orderly inquiry by established investigators in the field. Rather, he suggests, revolutions in science come about as the result of breakdowns in intellectual systems, breakdowns that occur when old methods won't solve new problems. He calls the change in theory that underlies this kind of revolution a *paradigm shift*. I believe we are currently at the point of such a paradigm shift in the teaching of writing, and that it has been brought about by a variety of developments that have taken place in the last 25 years.

Briefly, Kuhn's thesis in *The Structure of Scientific Revolutions* is this.

When a scientific field is going through a stable period, most of the practitioners in the discipline hold a common body of beliefs and assumptions; they agree on the problems that need to be solved, the rules that govern research, and on the standards by which performance is to be measured. They share a conceptual model that Kuhn calls a paradigm, and that paradigm governs activity in their profession. Students who enter the discipline prepare for membership in its intellectual community by studying that paradigm.

But paradigms are not necessarily immutable. When several people working in a field begin to encounter anomalies or phenomena that cannot be explained by the established model, the paradigm begins to show signs of instability. For a while, those who subscribe to the paradigm try to ignore the contradictions and inconsistencies that they find, or they make improvised, *ad hoc* changes to cope with immediate crises. Eventually, however, when enough anomalies accumulate to make a substantial number of scientists in the field question whether the traditional paradigm can solve many of the serious problems that face them, a few innovative thinkers will devise a new model. And if enough scientists become convinced that the new paradigm works better than the old one, they will accept it as the new norm.

College Composition and Communication, 33 (February 1982), pp. 76-88. Copyright © 1982 by the National Council of Teachers of English. Reprinted with permission.

This replacement of one conceptual model by another one is Kuhn's *paradigm shift.* He cites as classic examples the astronomers' substitution of the Copernican model of the solar system for the Ptolemaic model and the development of Newtonian physics. Such shifts are usually disorderly and often controversial, and the period in which they occur is apt to be marked by insecurity and conflict within the discipline.

Kuhn believes that because these shifts are so disruptive, they will occur only when the number of unsolved problems in a discipline reaches crisis proportions and some major figures in the field begin to focus on those unsolved problems. But even with mounting evidence that their conceptual model doesn't work, supporters of the traditional paradigm resist change because they have an intellectual and sometimes an emotional investment in the accepted view. They particularly resist abandoning the conventional textbooks that set forth the precepts of their discipline in clear and unqualified terms. Those texts, as Richard Young points out in his essay, "Paradigms and Problems: Needed Research in Rhetorical Theory," are usually so similar that one way to discover the traditional paradigm of a field is to examine its textbooks.[1]

Finally, however, most of the resistance to the new paradigm will dissipate when its advocates can demonstrate that it will solve problems that the traditional paradigm could not solve. Most of the new generation of scholars working in the field will adopt the new model, and the older practitioners will gradually come around to it. Those who cling to the old paradigm lose their influence in the field because the leaders in the profession simply ignore their work. When that happens, the paradigm shift is complete, and the theory that was revolutionary becomes conventional.

This summary of Kuhn's book is sketchy and too simple, but I think it accurately reflects the key points in his theory. When he developed the theory, he considered only the so-called hard sciences, particularly chemistry, astronomy, and physics. He did not claim or even suggest that his model for scientific revolution could or should apply to social sciences or the humanities, where research is not done in laboratories and usually does not involve measurements or formulas. Nevertheless, I believe that composition theorists and writing teachers can learn from Thomas Kuhn if they see his theory of scientific revolutions as an analogy that can illuminate developments that are taking place in our profession. Those developments, the most prominent of which is the move to a process-centered theory of teaching writing, indicate that our profession is probably in the first stages of a paradigm shift.

The Current-Traditional Paradigm and Its Proponents

In order to understand the nature of that shift, we need to look at the principal features of the paradigm that has been the basis of composition teaching for several decades. In "Paradigms and Patterns" Richard Young describes it this way:

The overt features . . . are obvious enough: the emphasis on the composed product rather than the composing process; the analysis of discourse into description, narration, exposition, and argument; the strong
concern with usage . . . and with style; the preoccupation with the informal essay and research paper; and so on.[2]

Young adds that underlying the traditional paradigm is what he calls the "vi-
talist" attitude toward composing: that is, the assumption that no one can
really teach anyone else how to write because writing is a mysterious creative
activity that cannot be categorized or analyzed.

In an article in the Winter, 1980, *Freshman English News* James Berlin
and Robert Inkster ascribe other features to the conventional paradigm. Bas-
ing their conclusions on an analysis of repeated patterns in four well-known
and commercially successful rhetoric texts, they add that the traditional
paradigm stresses expository writing to the virtual exclusion of all other
forms, that it posits an unchanging reality which is independent of the writer
and which all writers are expected to describe in the same way regardless of
the rhetorical situation, that it neglects invention almost entirely, and that it
makes style the most important element in writing.[3]

I would make three other points about the traditional paradigm. First,
its adherents believe that competent writers know what they are going to say
before they begin to write; thus their most important task when they are
preparing to write is finding a form into which to organize their content.
They also believe that the composing process is linear, that it proceeds systematically from prewriting to writing to rewriting. Finally, they believe that
teaching editing is teaching writing.

It is important to note that the traditional paradigm did not grow out
of research or experimentation. It derives partly from the classical rhetorical
model that organizes the production of discourse into invention, arrangement, and style, but mostly it seems to be based on some idealized and orderly vision of what literature scholars, whose professional focus is on the
written product, seem to imagine is an efficient method of writing. It is a
prescriptive and orderly view of the creative act, a view that defines the successful writer as one who can systematically produce a 500-word theme of
five paragraphs, each with a topic sentence. Its proponents hold it *a priori;*
they have not tested it against the composing processes of actual writers.

At this point some of my readers may want to protest that I am bela-
boring a dead issue—that the admonition to "teach process, not product" is
now conventional wisdom. I disagree. Although those in the vanguard of the
profession have by and large adopted the process model for teaching composition and are now attentively watching the research on the composing
process in order to extract some pedagogical principles from it, the overwhelming majority of college writing teachers in the United States are not
professional writing teachers. They do not do research or publish on rhetoric
or composition, and they do not know the scholarship in the field; they do
not read the professional journals and they do not attend professional meet-

ings such as the annual Conference on College Composition and Communication; they do not participate in faculty development workshops for writing teachers. They are trained as literary critics first and as teachers of literature second, yet out of necessity most of them are doing half or more of their teaching in composition. And they teach it by the traditional paradigm, just as they did when they were untrained teaching assistants ten or twenty or forty years ago. Often they use a newer edition of the same book they used as teaching assistants.

Out of necessity, apathy, and what I see as a benighted and patronizing view of the essential nature of composition courses, English department administrators encourage this unprofessional approach to the teaching of writing. In the first place, they may believe that they have so many writing classes to staff that they could not possibly hire well-qualified professionals to teach them; only a comparatively few such specialists exist. Second, most departmental chairpersons don't believe that an English instructor needs special qualifications to teach writing. As one of my colleagues says, our department wouldn't think of letting her teach Chaucer courses because she is not qualified; yet the chairman is delighted for her to teach advanced composition, for which she is far more unqualified. The assumption is that anyone with a Ph.D. in English is an expert writing teacher.

I think, however, that the people who do most to promote a static and unexamined approach to teaching writing are those who define writing courses as service courses and skills courses; that group probably includes most administrators and teachers of writing. Such a view, which denies that writing requires intellectual activity and ignores the importance of writing as a basic method of learning, takes away any incentive for the writing teacher to grow professionally. People who teach skills and provide services are traditionally less respected and rewarded than those who teach theory, and hiring hordes of adjuncts and temporary instructors and assigning them to composition courses reinforces this value system. Consequently there is no external pressure to find a better way to teach writing.

In spite of this often discouraging situation, many teachers who cling to the traditional paradigm work very hard at teaching writing. They devote far more time than they can professionally afford to working with their students, but because they haven't read Elbow or Bruffee they have no way of knowing that their students might benefit far more from small group meetings with each other than from the exhausting one-to-one conferences that the teachers hold. They both complain and brag about how much time they spend meticulously marking each paper, but because they haven't read Diederich or Irmscher they don't know that an hour spent meticulously marking every error in a paper is probably doing more harm than good. They are exhausting themselves trying to teach writing from an outmoded model, and they come to despise the job more and more because many of their students improve so little despite their time and effort.

But the writing teacher's frustration and disenchantment may be less important than the fact that if they teach from the traditional paradigm, they are frequently emphasizing techniques that the research has largely discredited. As Kuhn points out, the paradigm that a group of professionals accepts will govern the kinds of problems they decide to work on, and that very paradigm keeps them from recognizing important problems that cannot be discussed in the terminology of their model. Thus teachers who concentrate their efforts on teaching style, organization, and correctness are not likely to recognize that their students need work in invention. And if they stress that proofreading and editing are the chief skills one uses to revise a paper, they won't realize that their students have no concept of what it means to make substantive revisions in a paper. The traditional paradigm hides these problems.

Textbooks complicate the problem further. As Kuhn repeatedly points out, the standard texts in any discipline constitute a major block to a paradigm shift because they represent accepted authority. Many, though certainly not all, of the standard textbooks in rhetoric and composition for the past two decades have been product-centered books that focus on style, usage, and argumentation; Sheridan Baker's *The Practical Stylist* and Brooks and Warren's *Modern Rhetoric* are typical examples. When Donald Stewart made an analysis of rhetoric texts three years ago, he found that only seven out of the thirty-four he examined showed any awareness of current research in rhetoric. The others were, as he put it, "strictly current-traditional in their discussions of invention, arrangement, and style."[4] And textbooks change slowly. Publishers want to keep what sells, and they tend to direct the appeals of their books to what they believe the average composition teacher wants, not to what those in the vanguard of the profession would like to have.

Signs of Change

Nevertheless, changes are under way, and I see in the current state of our profession enough evidence of insecurity and instability to suggest that the traditional prescriptive and product-centered paradigm that underlies writing instruction is beginning to crumble. I think that the forces contributing to its demise are both theoretical and concrete and come from both inside and outside of the profession. Changes in theory probably started, in the middle 1950's, from intellectual inquiry and speculation about language and language learning that was going on in several fields, notably linguistics, anthropology, and clinical and cognitive psychology. To identify and trace all these complex developments would go far beyond the scope of this article and beyond my current state of enlightenment. I can only touch on some of them here.

Probably one of the most important developments to affect writing theory was the publication of Noam Chomsky's *Syntactic Structures* in 1957. His theory of transformational grammar, with its insistent look at the rules by which language is generated, caused a new focus on the process by which language comes into being.* The publication of Francis Christensen's essays on the generative rhetoric of the sentence and the paragraph in the early 1960's also stimulated new interest in the processes by which writers produce texts. Certainly the tagmemicists also provoked a fresh look at the act of writing when they urged writers to generate ideas by thinking about subjects from a dynamic, three-faceted perspective. And when the humanistic psychologist Carl Rogers began to criticize behaviorist psychology just as Chomsky had criticized behaviorist theories of language, he probably hastened the shift away from the product-response evaluation of writing.

A major event that encouraged the shift of attention to the process of writing was the famous Anglo-American Seminar on the Teaching of English, held at Dartmouth College in the summer of 1966. In the final report of this gathering of eminent educators from Britain and the United States, the participants deëmphasized the formal teaching of grammar and usage in the classroom and emphasized having children engage directly in the writing process in a non-prescriptive atmosphere.

So the intellectual climate conducive to this change has been developing for more than two decades. Of course, if these shifts in theory and attitudes were the only forces that were putting pressure on the traditional approach to teaching writing, revolution in the profession would probably be long in coming. But other concrete and external forces have also been putting pressure on writing teachers. These teachers are plagued by embarrassing stories about college graduates who can't pass teacher competency tests, and by angry complaints about employees who can't write reports. And the professors agree. Their students come to them writing badly and they leave writing badly. Handbooks won't solve their problems, and having them revise papers does no good.

Worse, just at this time when they are most disheartened about teaching writing, large numbers of English professors are beginning to realize that most of them are going to be teaching a lot of writing to a lot of students from now on. The prospect is grim, so grim that the English departments at Harvard and the University of Michigan have given up and turned the bulk of their composition teaching over to specialists outside the departments. But most professors can't do that, and instead they feel insecure and angry because they know they are teaching badly. In Kuhn's terminology, their methods have become anomalous; the system that they have always depended on no longer seems to work.

But why should the paradigm begin to break down just now? After all, as Richard Young points out, thousands of people have learned to write by the trial-and-error method of producing a text and having it criticized. Why shouldn't that slow, but often effective, method continue to work most of the time? Once more, I think, Kuhn has the answer. He says, "One need look no further than Copernicus and the calendar to discover that external condi-

---

*I am indebted to my colleague Stephen Witte for bringing this development to my attention.

tions may help to transform a mere anomaly into a source of acute crisis."[5] I believe that the external conditions which have hastened the crisis in the teaching of writing are open admissions policies, the return to school of veterans and other groups of older students who are less docile and rule-bound than traditional freshmen, the national decline in conventional verbal skills, and the ever larger number of high school graduates going on to college as our society demands more and more credentials for economic citizenship. Any instructional system would come close to collapse under such a strain, and our system for teaching writing has been particularly vulnerable because it has been staffed largely by untrained teachers who have had little scholarly interest in this kind of teaching.

Following the pattern that Kuhn describes in his book, our first response to crisis has been to improvise *ad hoc* measures to try to patch the cracks and keep the system running. Among the first responses were the writing labs that sprang up about ten years ago to give first aid to students who seemed unable to function within the traditional paradigm. Those labs are still with us, but they're still giving only first aid and treating symptoms. They have not solved the problem. Another *ad hoc* remedy took the form of individualized instruction, but it has faded from the scene along with computer-assisted instruction. The first was too costly and too isolated, the second one proved too limited and impersonal. And the experiments with expressive writing also turned out to be *ad hoc* measures, although for a while they seemed to have enough strength to foreshadow a paradigm shift. Sentence combining, I predict, will prove to be another *ad hoc* measure that serves as only a temporary palliative for serious writing problems.

All these remedies have proved temporarily or partially useful; none, however, has answered the crucial question: what is the basic flaw in the traditional paradigm for teaching writing? Why doesn't it work?

The Transition Period

Someone who cares has to ask that question before the revolution can start because, as Kuhn points out, "novelty ordinarily emerges only for the man who, knowing *with precision* what he should expect, is able to recognize that something has gone wrong."[6] In the teaching of composition, the essential person who asked that question may not have been a man, but a woman, Mina Shaughnessy. In her book *Errors and Expectations*, Shaughnessy describes the educational experience that made her, a professor at a prestigious university, stop to ask, "What went wrong?"

In the spring of 1970, the City University of New York adopted an admissions policy that guaranteed to every city resident with a high school diploma a place in one of its eighteen tuition-free colleges, thereby opening its doors not only to a larger population of students than it had ever had before . . . but to a wider range of students than any college had probably ever admitted or thought of admitting to its campus. . . .
One of the first tasks these students faced when they arrived at col-

lege was to write a placement essay. . . . Judged by the results of these tests, the young men and women who were to be known as open admissions students fell into one of three groups: 1. Those who met the traditional requirements for college work, who appeared from their tests . . . to be able to begin at the traditional starting points; 2. those who had survived their secondary schooling . . . and whose writing reflected a flat competence; 3. [those] who had been left so far behind the others in their formal education that they appeared to have little chance of catching up, students whose difficulties with the written language seemed of a different order from those of other groups, as if they had come, you might say, from a different country.

   . . . The third group contained true outsiders, . . . strangers in academia, unacquainted with the rules and rituals of college life, unprepared for the sorts of tasks their teachers were about to assign them. . . .

Not surprisingly, the essays these students wrote during their first weeks of class stunned the teachers who read them. Nothing, it seemed, short of a miracle was going to turn such students into writers. . . . To make matters worse, there were no studies nor guides, nor even suitable textbooks to turn to. Here were teachers trained to analyze the belletristic achievements of the ages marooned in basic writing classrooms with adult student writers who appeared by college standards to be illiterate.[7]

Relying on their previous experience with selectively-admitted students at the City University, Shaughnessy and her colleagues thought they knew what to expect from "college writers." The shock of facing a kind of writing that fit no familiar category, that met no traditional standards, forced Shaughnessy, at least, to recognize an anomaly. If these students had come through schools in which writing had been taught with standard textbooks and standard methods, then one had to conclude that the method and the textbooks did not work, at least not for a substantial and important group of students. The question was, "Why?"

To find the answer, Shaughnessy analyzed the placement essays of 4000 students and over a period of five years worked at trying to get at the roots of their problems and devise a way to overcome them. Eventually she became persuaded

   . . . that basic writers write the way they do, not because they are slow or non-verbal, indifferent to or incapable of academic excellence, but because they are beginners and must, like all beginners, learn by making mistakes. . . . And the keys to their development as writers often lie in the very features of their writing that English teachers have been trained to brush aside with a marginal code letter or a scribbled injunction to "Proofread!" Such strategies ram at the doors of their incompetence while the keys that would open them lie in view. . . . The work [of teaching these students to write] must be informed by an understanding not only of what is missing or awry, but of *why this is so.*[8] (italics added)

Shaughnessy's insight is utterly simple and vitally important: we cannot teach students to write by looking only at what they have written. We must also understand *how* that product came into being, and *why* it assumed the form that it did. We have to try to understand what goes on during the internal act of writing and we have to intervene during the act of writing if we want to affect its outcome. We have to do the hard thing, examine the intangible process, rather than the easy thing, evaluate the tangible product.

Although Shaugnessy was not the first investigator to try to move behind students' written products and find out how those products came into being—Janet Emig and Charles Stallard had both done limited studies at about the same time as Shaughnessy, and James Britton and his colleagues in Great Britain were working on a very ambitious study of the development of writing abilities—she was the first to undertake a large-scale research project whose goal was to teach the new students of the seventies to write. Her example, her book, and her repeated calls for new research in composition have undoubtedly been important stimuli in spurring the profession's search for a new paradigm.

Others in the profession have also given impetus to the search. In 1968 a journalist and professor named Donald Murray published a book called *A Writer Teaches Writing,* in which he suggests that if we want to teach students to write, we have to initiate them into the process that writers go through, not give them a set of rules. He insists that writers find their real topics only through the act of writing. In fact, Murray may have originated the admonition, "Teach Writing as a Process not Product" in a 1972 article by that title.[9] A resurgence of interest in classical rhetoric in the seventies also sparked interest in a new approach to the teaching of writing. The books by rhetoricians Richard Weaver and Edward P. J. Corbett provided the theoretical foundations for the view that writing can not be separated from its context, that audience and intention should affect every stage of the creative process. When this premise became widely accepted at major universities—for example, the University of Iowa and the University of Texas—it inevitably put strains on the old product-centered paradigm.

Another major influence on the teaching of writing across the nation has come from California's Bay Area Writing Project, initiated in 1975. A cardinal principle of that project has been the revolutionary thesis that all writing teachers should write in order to understand the writing process first-hand. When teachers began to do so, the traditional textbook model for writing inevitably came into question. And as spin-offs of the Bay Area Writing Project have proliferated across the country, largely funded by grant money donated by agencies and foundations alarmed about the writing crisis, a growing number of teachers are changing to process-centered writing instruction.

The Emerging Paradigm

But the most promising indication that we are poised for a paradigm shift is that for the first time in the history of teaching writing we have specialists who are doing controlled and directed research on writers' composing processes. Sondra Perl of Herbert Lehman College of the City University of New York and Linda Flower and John Hayes of Carnegie-Mellon University are tape recording students' oral reports of the thoughts that come to them as they write and of the choices they make. They call their investigative strategy "protocol analysis," and they supplement it with interviews and questionnaires to put together composite pictures of the processes followed by working writers. Sharon Pianko of Rutgers University has done a study in which she matched groups of traditonal and remedial writers, men and women writers, and 18-year-old and adult writers and compared their composing habits. Nancy Sommers of New York University has done a study comparing the revising practices of college freshmen and experienced professional writers, and Lester Faigley and Stephen Witte of the University of Texas now have a federal grant to do a more comprehensive study on revising. (An article based on this study appeared in the December, 1981, issue of *CCC*.) Lee Odell of Rensselaer Polytechnic Institute and Dixie Goswami are currently involved in a federally-funded study of the practices of writers in business.

From these and other studies we are beginning to find out something about how people's minds work as they write, to chart the rhythm of their writing, to find out what constraints they are aware of as they write, and to see what physical behaviors are involved in writing and how they vary among different groups of writers. So far only a small amount of data has been collected, and the inferences we can draw from the studies are necessarily tentative. As Linda Flower puts it, because we are trying to chart and analyze an activity that goes on largely out of sight, the process is rather like trying to trace the path of a dolphin by catching glimpses of it when it leaps out of the water. We are seeing only a tiny part of the whole process, but from it we can infer much about what is going on beneath the surface.[10]

What are we finding out? One point that is becoming clear is that writing is an act of discovery for both skilled and unskilled writers; most writers have only a partial notion of what they want to say when they begin to write, and their ideas develop in the process of writing. They develop their topics intuitively, not methodically. Another truth is that usually the writing process is not linear, moving smoothly in one direction from start to finish. It is messy, recursive, convoluted, and uneven. Writers write, plan, revise, anticipate, and review throughout the writing process, moving back and forth among the different operations involved in writing without any apparent plan. No practicing writer will be surprised at these findings: nevertheless, they seriously contradict the traditional paradigm that has dominated writing textbooks for years.

But for me the most interesting data emerging from these studies are those that show us profound differences between the writing behaviors of skilled and unskilled writers and the behaviors of student and professional writers. Those differences involve the amount of time spent on writing, the amount of time preparing to write, the number of drafts written, the concern for audience, the number of changes made and the stages at which they are made, the frequency and length of pauses during writing, the way in which those pauses are used, the amount of time spent rereading and reformulating, and the kind and number of constraints that the writers are aware of as they work. This kind of information enables us to construct a tentative profile of the writing behaviors of effective writers; I have sketched such a profile in another paper, not yet published.

From all this activity in the field, the new paradigm for teaching writing is emerging. Its principal features are these:

1. It focuses on the writing process; instructors intervene in students' writing during the process.
2. It teaches strategies for invention and discovery; instructors help students to generate content and discover purpose.
3. It is rhetorically based; audience, purpose, and occasion figure prominently in the assignment of writing tasks.
4. Instructors evaluate the written product by how well it fulfills the writer's intention and meets the audience's needs
5. It views writing as a recursive rather than linear process; pre-writing, writing, and revision are activities that overlap and intertwine.
6. It is holistic, viewing writing as an activity that involves the intuitive and non-rational as well as the rational faculties.
7. It emphasizes that writing is a way of learning and developing as well as a communication skill.
8. It includes a variety of writing modes, expressive as well as expository.
9. It is informed by other disciplines, especially cognitive psychology and linguistics.
10. It views writing as a disciplined creative activity that can be analyzed and described; its practitioners believe that writing can be taught.
11. It is based on linguistic research and research into the composing process.
12. It stresses the principle that writing teachers should be people who write.

Portents for the Future

I believe that important events of the recent past are going to speed the revolution and help to establish this new paradigm in the nation's classrooms.

First, the University of Iowa's Writing Institute, which received a $680,000 grant from the National Endowment for the Humanities to train freshman composition directors, has this year completed its work and sent out forty administrators for writing programs who will almost certainly base those programs on the new model. They are bound to have a profound influence on their institutions.

Second, graduate programs in rhetoric are rapidly increasing across the country. The last count in the Spring, 1980, *Freshman English News* showed that fifty-three institutions have added graduate rhetoric courses since 1974, and that was not a complete list. Enrollment in these programs is climbing because students realize that English departments now offer more jobs in rhetoric and composition than in any other specialization. Most of these programs are going to produce young professionals who have been taught by scholars who know recent research and are committed to the new paradigm: Richard Young, Ross Winterowd, Joseph Comprone, James Kinneavy, Andrea Lunsford, Elizabeth Cowan, Linda Flower, to name just a few. When these new graduates go into English departments where the traditional paradigm prevails, they are certain to start working for change.

Third, in many schools, even graduate assistants who are in traditional literary programs rather than rhetoric programs are getting their in-service training from the rhetoric and composition specialists in their departments. They are being trained in process-centered approaches to the teaching of composition, and when they enter the profession and begin teaching lower-division writing courses along with their literary specialities, they are most likely to follow the new paradigm. And, more and more, the methods courses for high-school teachers are also being taught by the rhetoric specialists; that change will have a profound effect on secondary school teaching.

Fourth, we now have process-based texts on the teaching of writing. Shaughnessy's *Errors and Expectations* is well known and widely used. It has been joined by Irmscher's *Teaching Expository Writing* and Neman's *Teaching Students to Write*. The authors of both these latter books incorporate research findings and recent developments in the profession into their philosophies of and methodologies for teaching writing.

Fifth, college composition textbooks are changing. Along with their traditional books, most publishers are now publishing at least one process-oriented, rhetorically-based writing text. Several are now on the market and more are forthcoming, most of them written by scholars and teachers who are leaders in the profession. Moreover, many major publishing houses now retain well-known composition specialists to advise them on manuscripts. The publishers sense change in the wind and realize that the new crop of well-informed and committed writing program directors who will be taking over are going to insist on up-to-date textbooks. The change will even reach into some high schools because one large company has hired one of the country's leading rhetoricians to supervise and edit their high school composition series. Many others will probably follow their example.

But no revolution brings the millenium nor a guarantee of salvation, and we must remember that the new paradigm is sketchy and leaves many problems about the teaching or writing unresolved. As Kuhn points out, new paradigms are apt to be crude, and they seldom possess all the capabilities of their predecessors. So it is important for us to preserve the best parts of earlier methods for teaching writing: the concern for style and the preservation of high standards for the written product. I believe we also need to continue giving students models of excellence to imitate.

Kuhn contends that "the transition between competing paradigms cannot be made a step at a time, forced by logic. . . . Like the gestalt switch, it must occur all at once (though not necessarily in an instant) or not at all."[11] He says, however, that, "if its supporters are competent, they will improve it [the paradigm], explore its possibilities, and show what it would be like to belong to the community guided by it."[12] I see this last opportunity as the challenge to today's community of composition and rhetoric scholars: to refine the new paradigm for teaching composition so that it provides a rewarding, productive, and feasible way of teaching writing for the non-specialists who do most of the composition teaching in our colleges and universities.

Notes

[1] Richard Young, "Paradigms and Problems: Needed Research in Rhetorical Invention," *Research in Composing,* ed. Charles Cooper and Lee Odell (Urbana, IL: National Council of Teachers of English, 1978), p. 31.

[2] Young, p. 31.

[3] James A. Berlin and Robert P. Inkster, "Current-Traditional Rhetoric: Paradigm and Practice," *Freshman English News,* 8 (Winter, 1980), 1-4, 13-14.

[4] Donald Stewart, "Composition Textbooks and the Assault on Tradition," *College Composition and Communication,* 29 (May, 1978), 174.

[5] Thomas Kuhn, *The Structure of Scientific Revolutions,* Second Edition (Chicago: University of Chicago Press, 1970), p. x.

[6] Kuhn, p. 65.

[7] Mina Shaughnessy, *Errors and Expectations* (New York and London: Oxford University Press, 1977), pp. 1-3.

[8] Shaughnessy, p. 5.

[9] Donald Murray, "Teach Writing as a Process not Product," *The Leaflet,* November 1972, pp. 11-14 (the New England Association of Teachers of English).

[10] Linda Flower and John Hayes, "Identifying the Organization of the Writing Processes," *Cognitive Processes in Writing,* ed., Lee W. Gregg and Erwin R. Steinberg (Hillsdale, NJ: Lawrence Erlbaum Associates, 1980), pp. 9-10.

[11] Kuhn, p. 150.

[12] Kuhn, p. 159.

The Learning Power of Writing

R.D. WALSHE

Writing has been undervalued for so long that I feel like proposing this Learning Pledge to be chanted in school assemblies across the country at the start of every day:

> I PROMISE throughout this day's learning to handle with respect and pleasure humanity's greatest invention, language, and in particular, when I reach for a pen or sit at a word-processor, to remember that I am about to use humanity's second greatest invention, writing, with which I will take language from the invisible mind and make it visible on paper where I can work on it with full attention until it becomes the best thinking, the best learning, of which I am capable.

But friends tell me this won't persuade everyone, so I'll try instead to make out a case for the value of writing in human affairs and its high potential for lifting the quality of learning.

Humans do most of their effective thinking with language. For many thousands of years they manifested their thinking-languaging *competence* in oral societies, without help from courses in "thinking skills" or "speech skills" but simply by developing such skills through use.

The Amazing Invention

Then, between 3000 BC and 1000 BC, came the invention of writing. Whereas humans have a playful facility for inventing languages and have invented a great number, they could only come up with about half a dozen writing systems, all fiendishly difficult. Luckily for us the Greeks brilliantly tidied up one of those systems in the first millennium BC by devising a way to add the mysterious vowel sounds to the more obvious consonants, and so they constructed the first relatively simple alphabet, from which our twenty-six letters derive.

That achievement—and one should not hesitate to use superlatives for it like incredible or miraculous—made possible the first writing that ordinary men and women rather than specialist scribes could manage. It prompted the beginning of schooling, the first system of primary schools to initiate the young into this now accessible craft of writing and, of course, reading. The potential for mass literacy had entered the world.

English Journal, 76 (October 1987), pp. 22-27. Copyright © 1987 by the National Council of Teachers of English. Reprinted with permission.

How important was (and is) this invention? "Recorded history," says Robert Claiborne, "begins with the birth of writing; in most societies, so do science and philosophic thought" (19); and the orientalist, Robert D. Biggs, adds emphatically, "Among all the revolutionary creations of man, writing ranks as the supreme intellectual achievement" (cited in Claiborne 6). Which puts in interesting perspective, surely, creations such as the steam engine, the internal combustion motor, the computer, and space vehicles.

The question we need to ask of history is: What exactly was the nature of the change that writing brought into human affairs?

Writing took humanity's thinking-languaging competence and put at its disposal a technology which enabled thought to operate much more deeply than it normally does during conversation or inward reflection. This opened new vistas for learning.

New Learning Potential

I want to focus on just two of many remarkable new learning potentials brought into human affairs by writing:

Writing as the Great Collector of Ideas. Only writing can collect and store all the ideas that arise from reflecting, talking, researching. What it collects can then be made available as reading to curious minds—whence, the birth of the book and libraries.

Writing as the Great Clarifier of Thinking. Writers take thoughts from the invisible mind and make them visible on paper. They can then contemplate this objectified thought and revise it till it becomes the best thinking of which they are capable. (Cf. Walshe [142-44], which lists thirty attributes of writing as a mode of learning.)

These two attributes are enough to establish that indeed the invention of writing introduced a huge potential for learning into human culture. Yet writing is so commonly undervalued that we are surprised when some thinker feels obliged to speak up for its importance.

Karl Popper, for instance, says in his autobiography that learning to read and write are "the major events in one's intellectual development" (12). And the Russian educator Vygotsky, after taking a profound look at "the prehistory of written language," says that

> ...writing has occupied too narrow a place in school practice as compared to the enormous role that it plays in children's cultural development. The teaching of writing has been conceived in narrowly practical terms.... We need only try to imagine the enormous changes in the cultural development of children that occur as a result of mastery of written language and the ability to read—and of thus becoming aware of everything that human genius has created in the realm of the written word. (105, 166)

Features of Learning-through-Writing

What are the features of the learning that is promoted during the writing occasion?

First, there are the elemental aids-to-thinking that cluster around the physical act of writing, especially four which promote concentration: *handling,* the manipulation of the pen; *depicting,* the forming of letters, spellings, punctuation marks; *restating,* the shaping of selected inner-speech; *scrutinizing,* the continual reading back before writing on.

But they are only the beginning. More widely, writing frees the writer from social distraction and allows time to think again, choosing thoughts and words carefully. Still more widely, the writer has access to powers which can be consciously used to lift the quality of the thinking to high levels: the potential for long preparation, and, once a draft is achieved, the limitless potential for pondering, cutting, extending, putting aside, returning, revising again, and so on until the piece is right. So writing can become *a deeper kind of thinking than is otherwise possible.*

I see this as a view of thinking and learning at its best. It is the writing process used intelligently, and it is the equal of any model of thinking applauded by our culture. The chart on p. 20, "Learning at Its Best," compares the major models that have contributed over centuries to the humanities, sciences, and technologies. Several inferences can be made from it:

- These four great processes parallel one another so closely as to point to an inescapable conclusion: all are offspring of a common parent, the human potential for "creative process."

- Insofar as cognitive theory cannot draw a line between thinking and learning, or learning and problem-solving, or problem-solving and scientific inquiry, all four processes can be viewed as learning behaviors.

- And insofar as the artistic, scientific and problem-solving processes share a common flow of thought and action with the more recently understood writing process, writing is seen to be offering to every classroom the same *thinking-learning power* which students are ready to admire as the source of the great achievements of our culture in the arts, sciences, technologies.

These descriptions of writing—"offspring of the creative process," "learning behavior," "flow of thought and action"—reveal the shortsightedness of the widespread instrumental view which limits writing to the tool marking the page, the tedious service-skill of scribing ideas supposedly arrived at by pure thinking before the writing begins. On the contrary, writing is a process of thinking-out. So, for the engaged mind, it becomes the occasion or experience or adventure of learning.

Process Determines Product—and Learning!

With so many references to "process," we need to think about its relevance to our understanding of learning. This notion of process is a master theme running through twentieth-century thought. Early in the century, physicists demonstrated that nature, despite appearances, is at bottom not things but processes. That insight moved through all the sciences and some of the humanities before it began to register with writing teachers from the mid-sixties on. In Australia, some of us picked up an early understanding of writing-as-process around 1970, giving us a base from which to criticize shortcomings in the traditional ways we had been teaching.

Morris West says language is "a hollow vessel which can be filled with wine, or water, or poison." The "process" idea was wine to us. In Sydney a Teachers Writing Group formed to do what was then novel: write ourselves and discuss what happens when teachers join their students in writing; also, share our experiences of *prewriting* and *drafting* and *revising* and notice how these so-called stages often overlap. When we harangued our colleagues, some responded with our excitement but others, alas, carried the idea into effect without enthusiasm—our wine was water to them. Later, as principals or inspectors urged the idea on teachers, a mechanical version of process would sometimes result, with children marched lockstep through rigidly separated stages, a new "process" tyranny to take the place of the traditional "product" tyranny—poison!

How, then, to prevent such reduction of the rich idea of "process" to a three-stage formula?

I want to propose a fresh perspective on "process," helped by some thought-provoking synonyms which I assoicate with John Dewey, America's great educational thinker.

All his life, Dewey was fascinated by what he called the ends-and-means problem in education. There you have useful synonyms: *ends* are products, *means* are processes. He theorized at length on the means or processes by which human ends—aims, goals, purposes, plans, ideals—might be achieved. He was acutely aware that while it is easy to conceive an intended end, something can no less easily go astray in the attempt to achieve it. Why, for instance, do writers so often conceive an attractive ending only to find that the story takes off in a different direction, determined by the means, the unfolding events? (Dewey 27-37)

Dewey looked deeply into means, increasingly terming them "intermediate acts," another useful synonym. But he felt dissatisfied with his efforts to show a right relationship of means to the preconceived ends. At length, fate stepped in to help him. A bad back led him to an innovative posture therapist, Matthias Alexander, an Australian who had spent seven years devising a technique. Dewey not only felt vastly improved at Alexander's hands but was boggled by the unified theory and practice of the technique (Jones chapter 11).

Learning at Its Best

	Problem: ↑	Investigate ↑↓	Get Insights ↑↓	Express ↑↓	Refine ↑↓	Announcement	Reaction ↓
ARTISTIC PROCESS	**Experience** Feel challenged Decide on project	**Absorption** Engagement Study/research 'Imagining'	**Illumination** Inspiration or revelation/ 'flash'	**Drafting** e.g. in painting, prelim. sketching or 'roughing'	**Developing** Working out Crafting 'Finishing'	**Communication** Show to intimates Exhibit widely	**Response** Appreciation Criticism Evaluation
SCIENTIFIC PROCESS	**Problem** Define as question Plan the inquiry	**Observation** Exploratory stratagems Data collection	**Illumination** e.g. methodical generalization; or inspiration	**Hypothesis** Draft precisely	**Experiment/test** Verification or falsification Final writing	**Publication** Perhaps first to associates, then more widely	**Response** Acceptance or criticism
PROBLEM-SOLVING PROCESS	**Problem/puzzle** Define as question Plan the inquiry	**Investigation** Collect data Review alternatives Think laterally	**Illumination** 'Ah-ha' insights	**Formulation** of best solution	**Checking** Error elimination Critical review	**Report** Demonstration Performance	**Response** Appreciation Criticism Evaluation
WRITING PROCESS	**Experience** Decide to write Define writing-aim Early broad plan	**Pre-writing** Idea-recollection Research Brainstorming	**Illumination** 'See a pattern' 'Limit the subject' 'Get a lead'	**Drafting** Plan, or further brainstorming; then first draft	**Revision** Self-editing Redrafting Proofreading	**Publication** Show to another Read to others Circulate widely	**Response** Appreciation Criticism Evaluation

Comments on the chart, "Learning at Its Best":

(a) In life, the writing process is seldom separated neatly into the theoretical "stages" which the chart needs to use for discussion purposes. When a real process flows, the "stages" blur and overlap.

(b) In the classroom, learning-through-writing will sometimes take a "full process" form and sometimes use only parts of the process.

(c) Apart from its process forms, learning sometimes takes relatively mechanical forms, including simple reception, imitation, conditioning, rote/repetition/drill.

(d) A limitation of the chart is its almost exclusive concern with verbal thinking/learning. It omits attention to feeling/emotional influences; and it does not treat the six non-linguistic "intelligences" analyzed by Howard Gardner in his *Frames of Mind* (New York: Basic, 1983), viz., the logico-mathematical, spatial, musical, body-kinesthetic, intrapersonal, and interpersonal.

Alexander explained that as to "ends," he preferred the livelier compound *end-gaining,* and as to "means," the *means-whereby*—more useful synonyms! If I might oversimplify his views, they would go like this. Once you have conceived a desired end or product, don't overconcentrate on it, don't become an obsessive, impatient end-gainer; instead, emphasize the means-whereby, the process. The end must yield pride of place in present-time consciousness to the series of "intermediate acts." Each of these needs to become in its turn a sort of provisional end or product, to which full attention should be given. So, for writing, the working out, say, of an initial plan becomes work on a worthwhile product; the construction of a lively "lead," similarly; this paragraph...and so on. *Product is what process makes it.* It follows that quality of product depends on earnestly attending moment by moment to the means-whereby.

That makes writing a thinking-out, a discovery procedure. Learning at its best! It is what James Joyce meant when he somewhere said, "It is in the writing that good things come out." What come out are only partly ideas from the conscious mind; more importantly there are ideas that occur to us with the surprise of insight. The act of writing has cast its spell. We speak of it as "concentrating"; but it includes the opening up of a creative source that lies behind the everyday mind. And if this process has led us to a product different from the one we preconceived, so be it. It will have extended our understanding, our learning.

There are, of course, forms of writing which are simply informational and can be predicted in detail, like some business letters; but what I'm saying is relevant to the great range of inquiry and problem-solving and imaginative writing which is characteristic of the school as a distinct discourse community striving for excellence through learning-at-its-best.

Ideas for Reinvigorating "Process"

The Dewey-Alexander insight, "value the means-whereby," has all sorts of messages for reinvigorating the process idea, both as process-of-writing and process-of-learning-through-writing.

1. The notion of "process" must not be degraded to three cookbook steps between a topic and a product. There can be no recipes for how-to-write. Rather, "process" is a term and an idea which point to a whole engagement of the mind with some problem or experience that needs to be worked through in detail in the course of the writing, with each detail accorded full attention.

2. Except in broad theory, there is no such thing as THE process of writing; there are only processes, each different from the others, as individuals write to discover the means-whereby of their particular pieces. In the same way, the biologist Sir Peter Medawar, in his *Limits of Science,* says there is no such thing as THE scientific method, only a multiplicity of "exploratory stratagems" (51).

3. Because THE process exists in theory only, obviously the teacher's role is not to teach a generalized version of it but to help students explore their own way to a confident control of what is loosely termed "my individual process." This, more exactly, is the attitude that, "I can bring the process notion to any problem and work my way to an effective piece of writing." It is a confidence that has time to develop across all the years of writing-well-taught, K–12.

4. Time is vital, time to think through every "intermediate act." This may seem to state the obvious. But secondary schools in particular suffer from the "coverage problem," the need to cover all the subject matter set forth in well-meaning but over-loaded syllabuses. If that means rushing everything, then there is no useful learning. (An obvious cause of much poor essay writing, for instance, is insufficient time not only for drafting but also for wrestling with the problem in the pre-drafting period and for the revising of the draft.)

5. Experienced writing teachers learn to value the invisible aspects of the writing process as much as the visible. They know that writing is not just the pen on the page; it often begins long before the pen is taken up; it can proceed during spells when the pen is thrown down in frustration; and it may even continue after the product is apparently completed, perhaps prompting another start, a change of direction, a new product.

6. Writing is never only writing. As deep and careful thinking, it draws on all kinds of resources. Not only on memory but on reading, research and note-making, on talking things over, and on insights that come with waiting,

incubating. At its best it is a collecting, connecting, clarifying discovery process.

7. Classroom writing can usually have two faces: learning-to-write and writing-to-learn. In a sense they are interacting subprocesses which make up the writing process, for there is usually a *craft effort* to express clearly and a *deepening understanding* that comes through grappling with information.

8. Behind the learn-to-write and write-to-learn subprocesses, an even larger achievement is maturing. The student, whatever the curriculum or grade, is *learning how to learn:* how to engage thoughtfully with a problem, wrestle with it, make discoveries, compose these discoveries, and refine them.

From these close-up remarks about process, I want to shift to a long-shot look at a classroom in which writing-to-learn would flourish.

The Write-to-Learn Classroom

But first let's recall in stereotype the traditional *tell'm, drill'm and test'm* classroom, with its didactic teacher who saw children as by nature unwilling learners and who periodically imposed a "composition" to be written at a single sitting, with little or no discussion. No mention was made of revising, except for "proofreading" at the end; nor was there any one-to-one conversation between teacher and pupil. Mechanical and grammatical correctness, with neatness, was the desired product. The pupils almost all disliked writing and avoided it when they could.

By contrast, the write-to-learn classroom is engendered in the principle that humans are natural learners. As Frank Smith says, "It is the business of the brain to learn—basically the brain does nothing else" (163). From kindergarten, children are treated as having an inborn drive to learn, reserves of knowledge worth recalling, and experiences worth articulating with the help of writing.

- *The Teacher,* no longer a lecturer, has moved from the upfront position and now circulates among the students as guide, stimulator and commentator, sometimes writing with them, trading writing experiences with them, and continually promoting the value of writing, both for its usefulness in the day's learning and for the central role it will occupy throughout lifelong education.

- *The Student,* as this teacher well knows, has walked into the classroom with a tremendous potential for thinking and learning, which writing can incomparably tap, but only if the student can be won to enjoying and valuing writing and reading. The only hope of achieving this is to encourage writing and reading about experiences which are worth thinking deeply about, not formal exercises or skill-drills, not parts but wholes, which bring the satisfactions of an imagination engaged, insights realized, and meaning composed for conveying to others.

- *The Classroom,* in order to become its own interested "discourse community," assumes a workshop form, in the sense of generating and discussing problems, feeling challenged to explore some of them deeply, working out answers with the collecting-and-clarifying help of writing, and then submitting to the critical appraisal of colleagues. Everyone here is a writer, a reader, a talker, a thinker. It is collaborative learning: the students work variously as individuals or partners or small groups, occasionally as a whole class, with a good deal of teacher-with-student and student-with-student conferencing.

- *The Craft,* that is, the striving for quality which develops in this atmosphere, does so on the foundation of frequent writing itself, writing every day and perhaps several times a day, so long as it doesn't become oppressive. Such regular writing looks after the principle that, fundamentally, we learn-to-write-by-writing, developing this aspect of our thinking/languaging/learning competence by using it. The writing across the K–12 years develops the conciseness, connectedness and clarity that distinguish good writing from the copiousness characteristic of speech. And the workshop community, as it becomes increasingly informed and critical, sets up its own pressures for adherence to the conventions of standard written English and the features of one form of writing or another—it does not fail to attend to the so-called "skills."

This picture of *teacher, student, classroom,* and *craft* as writing workshop is broadly adaptable to writing in any year and on any subject.

It also leaves room for teachers to experiment within its framework by trying out any of the many special emphases and approaches now current in the teaching of writing; such as, moving strongly through *talk* to writing; using *models* from reading, literature, subject areas; fostering *drama* as an entree to writing; encouraging the many splendid uses of *journal* writing; emphasizing *prewriting* preparation, or *revision* as a constant throughout the process, or *audience* (and persuasion) as the chief concern of writing; exploring *register,* the appropriateness of ideas and language to situation; catering to the needs of *reluctant writers;* promoting a modern understanding of *genre* conventions; experimenting with writing in *bilingual* contexts; and continuing to see a place for the *strong stimulus* method of the "creative writing" that arose in the 1960s.

Tremendous Potential

This paper has argued that the potential for lifting the quality of learning through writing-well-taught is tremendous:

That neither in the past nor today has the potential been more than marginally sensed, except by all too rare individuals.

That the best learning in most school subjects is an act of composing carried out by the learner, with writing offering itself as the most consistently deep means of composing that is readily available.

That, insofar as any curriculum worth the name should strive to make its subjects mutually reinforcing, no strand of curriculum can equal writing with its universally available learning power—which is why the program encapsulated in the slogan *writing across the curriculum* needs to be seen as the present best frontier of educational advance.

That, finally, even if the greatest computer in the world could present us with the most up-to-date and relevant set of school subjects, they would not solve the individual student's most essential problem, which is to *learn self-reliance in learning,* unless such a curriculum places writing at the heart of its enterprise: writing, in its concentrating, collecting, connecting, clarifying roles, which can carry human thinking-learning ability to its highest levels and so realize at last on a mass scale the promise that entered the world via Greece with the "incredible, miraculous" alphabet.

References

Claiborne, Robert. *The Birth of Writing.* New York: Time-Life International, 1974.

Dewey, John. *Human Nature and Conduct.* New York: Modern Library, 1930

Jones, Frank Pierce. *Body Awareness in Action.* New York: Schocken, 1976.

Medawar, Sir Peter. *The Limits of Science.* New York: Harper, 1984.

Popper, Karl. *Unended Quest.* Glasgow: Fontana/Collins, 1976.

Smith, Frank. *Writing and the Writer.* New York: Holt, 1982.

Vygotsky, L.S. *Mind in Society.* Boston: Harvard UP, 1978.

Walshe, Robert D. *Every Child Can Write.* Sydney: Primary English Teaching Association, 1981.

Myths of Writing

FRANK SMITH

Whether writing should be considered to be as natural as speech for anyone to learn and to practice may be the subject of debate. My own view is that every child who can talk has the capacity to learn to write and also to seize upon its possibilities with enthusiasm. But in any case, I think there can be little debate that writing as children are expected to learn and to practice it in many classrooms is a highly unnatural activity, reflecting (or creating) some basic misconceptions about the nature of writing and about the manner in which proficient writers usually write.

Not all teachers harbor all or even many of these misconceptions. Nevertheless I believe they are sufficiently egregious both in school and out to warrant their exposure and examination. Many of the misconceptions constitute handicaps in their own writing as well as in their efforts to teach children how to write.

I shall present and briefly discuss a collection of twenty-one misconceptions—Smith's myths—which I acquired in the course of a recent exploration of writing (Smith 1981b). For display purposes I shall organize my collection into sets of myths about the nature of writing, about how writing is learned, and about how it is practiced, concluding with a grand myth about who is able to teach writing.

Myths about the Nature of Writing

1. *Writing is for the transmission of information.* Reality: Two major functions of writing—to create experiences and to explore ideas—are obscured if not ignored by the contemporary "information processing" approach to literacy (Rosenblatt 1980). Children may not have much new knowledge to convey to other people, but they will use all forms of language, including writing, if they become aware of its potential to create worlds of experience and of ideas which they can explore personally, enjoy, and perhaps subsequently share with others. A danger of the information transmission myth is that it focuses attention on how texts are presented from the point of view of a reader (usually one very touchy about minor points of spelling and punctuation) rather than on what the act of writing can accomplish for the developing thought of the writer. The writer is overlooked.

Language Arts, 76 (October 1981), pp. 792-798. Copyright © 1981 by the National Council of Teachers of English. Reprinted with permission.

2. *Writing is for communication.* Reality: Writing can of course be used for communication, but this is scarcely its only or even major value, certainly not for children. The writer is always the first reader and may often be the only one (for diaries, journals, notes, and more extended texts written for the writer's own exploratory or other purposes). Of course, children often like to *show* what they write—until they become self-conscious about their expression, neatness, punctuation or spelling errors—but the purpose of this social act is to share their delight or to demonstrate how clever they are, rather than to communicate information. A similar personal motivation is not absent among adults who have their own written creations prominently displayed on staffroom notice boards or in professional journals.

3. *Writing involves transferring thoughts from the mind to paper.* Reality: Writing can create ideas and experiences on paper which could never have existence in the mind (and possibly not in the "real world" either). Thoughts are created in the act of writing, which changes the writer just as it changes the paper on which the text is produced. Many authors have said that their books know more than they do; that they cannot recount in detail what their books contain before, while, or after they write them. Writing is not a matter of taking dictation from yourself; it is more like a conversation with a highly responsive and reflective other person. Some reasons why writing is so potent in permitting writers to form and develop ideas they might otherwise not have are considered in the following discussion of myths #4 and #5.

4. *Writing is permanent, speech ephemeral.* Reality: Speech, once uttered, can rarely be revised, no matter how much we might struggle to unsay something we wish we had not said. But writing can be reflected upon, altered, and even erased at will. This is the first great and unique potential of writing— that it gives the writer power to manipulate time. Events that occurred in the past or that may occur in the future can be evaluated, organized, and changed. What will be read quickly can be written slowly. What may be read several times need be written only once. What will be read first can be written last. What is written first need not remain first; the order of anything that is written can be changed. Such control over time is completely beyond the scope of spoken language or of thought that remains "in the head."

5. *Writing is a linear, left-to-right process.* Reality: Writing can be done in several places and directions concurrently, and is as easily manipulated in space as it is in time. Texts can be constructed from writing done on separate pieces of paper, in notebooks, on index cards, or on chalk boards at the same time that a main draft is being produced. Words and lines can be moved around on a page just as pages themselves can be reshuffled into different sequences. Writing is a plastic art.

6. *Writing is speech plus handwriting, spelling and punctuation.* Reality: Every kind of text has its own conventions of form and expression quite different from any kind of speech. The relevant models for writing are how other people write, not how they speak. Spelling, punctuation, capitalization, paragraphing, indentation, word dividing, neatness, and so forth are necessary

aspects of the *transcription* required to make written language manifest, though what is sufficient for a writer to produce and explore written experiences and ideas is by no means as detailed or demanding as the intricacy of transcription required by a reader. The transcription aspects of writing need not in fact be done by the writer; they can be looked after by a secretary. For all writers, undue concern with transcription can interfere with *composition,* the creative and exploratory aspect of writing which is of course its major value to the writer.

7. *A writer is a special kind of person.* Reality: There is no evidence that writers are any more intelligent, sensitive, talented, dedicated, disciplined, or persevering than people who do not write. Writers come from no exclusive kind of background. Some come from large families, some from small; some from rich, others from poor; some have literate parents, others the reverse; some received family encouragement, others did not. There is only one difference between writers and people who do not write—*writers write.* This unique difference may be because writers have some rare and as yet undiscovered gene for writing, though I doubt it. An alternative is that all children are born capable of learning to write at least as well as they learn to talk, but that something goes wrong. What goes wrong could be related to some of the myths that follow.

Myths about How Writing Is Learned

8. *Learning to write precedes writing.* Reality: Both reading and writing can only be learned in the course of reading and writing. Writing may need years of practice to make it fluent and facile (for most of us this "learning to write" continues all our lives), but the fluency and facility come with writing, not with repetitive and separate exercises and drills. The only difference between children learning to write and more proficient adults is that children need more help—they can write less by themselves. They need their own writing to be done for them just as they need other people's writing to be read to them. Unless children try to write and receive help in writing, they will have no motivation for attending to "writing" exercises and instruction, they will find such instruction incomprehensible, and they will not read in ways that will help them learn to write. A disastrous consequence of the "learn now, write later" myth is that the "secretarial" transcription aspects of writing are emphasized before the learner has a chance to experience or even understand the composition aspect of being an author. Even as a means of becoming a secretary, this approach is still not an efficient way to learn.

9. *Writing is learned from instruction.* Reality: Not even such transcription skills as spelling, punctuation or capitalization can be learned from lectures, from reading about them, or from drills. Spelling is too complex to be learned from rules or by memorizing word lists (Smith 1981*a*; in more detail in Smith 1981*b*). And the "rules" of punctuation and capitalization tend like all grammatical explanations to be circular—"Begin every sentence with a capital

letter," "What is a sentence?" "Something that begins with a capital letter." Formal instruction in grammar is necessarily restricted to conventional niceties like subject-verb agreement, which do not constitute a comprehensive or even comprehensible system for enabling anyone to get thoughts on paper. The easiest way to learn to write is to see something you would like to say (or would like to be able to say) being written.

10. *Writing is learned by writing.* Reality: No one writes enough, especially at school, to have enough mistakes corrected to learn to write by trial and error. Not even the transcription aspects of writing could be learned in this way, let alone all the subtleties of style and expression. The only source of knowledge sufficiently rich and reliable for learning about written language is the writing already done by others. In other words, one learns to write by reading. The act of writing is critical as a *basis* for learning to write from reading; the desire to write ourselves provides an incentive and direction for learning about writing from reading. But the writing that anyone does must be vastly complemented by reading if it is to achieve anything like the creative and communicative power that written language offers.

11. *Most classrooms are reasonable places in which to expect children to learn to write.* Reality: Most professional writers could not write with the physical and psychological constraints under which many children are expected to learn to write in school. Children who attempted to behave the way most adults find it necessary to behave while writing would probably not be permitted to stay in the classroom. Much of this discrepancy can be attributed to the following myths (unless the myths themselves have been created to justify the conditions existing in many classrooms).

Myths about the Act of Writing

12. *You must have something to say in order to write.* Reality: You often need to write in order to have anything to say. Thought comes with writing, and writing may never come if it is postponed until we are satisfied that we have something to say. Like every other reference to "writing" in this article, this assertion of "write first, see what you had to say later" applies to all manifestations of written language, to letters and memoranda as well as to short stories and novels, to poems, plays, and film scripts as well as to diaries, journals, term papers, research reports, and notes for ourselves and for others.

13. *Writing should be easy.* Reality: Writing is often hard work; it requires concentration, physical effort, and a tolerance for frustration and disappointment. The fact that writing is a demanding activity should not discourage anyone from writing, especially children. Many satisfying activities require physical effort and are not necessarily easy, especially in the learning. Children are not strangers to the idea that worthwhile ends may require effort and concentration, which they frequently display in their "play." Only work which seems to have no point or productive outcome is aversive.

14. *Writing should be right the first time.* Reality: Something all experienced writers know that seems to have been concealed from many teachers is that writing generally requires many drafts and revisions to get ideas into a form that satisfies the writer, and that a separate editorial polishing is required to make the text appropriate for a different reader. Part of the power of writing is that it does not have to be right the first time, that drafts can usually be modified or even thrown away. In a few situations, usually contrived ones like examinations, writing may have to be right the first time. But ability to write in this way requires special practice and is the result of considerable experience. Only through freedom to write provisionally most of the time can the facility be developed of producing first drafts in a form reasonably presentable to a reader.

15. *Writing can be done to order.* Reality: Once again, every experienced writer knows that writing is often most reluctant to come when it is most urgently required, yet quite likely to begin to flow on inconvenient or impossible occasions. Writing to order is not an ability that develops independently of writing in a more spontaneous and unpredictable manner, nor should it be expected to take priority over such writing.

16. *A fixed period of "prewriting" can or should be distinguishable before any writing act.* Reality: the fact that it is difficult to write to order or to be right the first time does not entail that a fixed period of "prewriting time" exists that should be allocated before writing can be expected to occur. On the one hand, much of what is written involves a whole lifetime of preparation—of experiencing, reading, reflecting, and arguing. It is only from a transcription point of view that an author can say that work began on a particular text at a particular time, even if that was the time when a decision to write was made or formal research begun. And many relevant ideas for what we might propose to write come to us when we are not thinking specifically about what we propose to write, perhaps when we "daydream" or when we are supposed to be thinking about something else. On the other hand, writing itself can be prewriting. As we draft one part of a text, we reflect upon what we might write next or upon what we have written already. The act of writing does not break itself down into neatly identifiable and manageable "steps," rather it is a part of all our existence.

17. *Writing is a sedentary activity.* Reality: Little of the reflective or preparatory aspects of writing can or need be performed at a desk, and even the transcription of writing is sometimes more comfortably performed standing up or against a wall. The traditional notion of the writer quietly working at the desk is romantic and unrealistic.

18. *Writing is a silent activity.* Reality: Writing frequently involves making noise, not only to exchange ideas (or feelings) with other people, but to give vent to expressions of exhilaration or frustration. As with myths #15 and #17, the image of a writer attentive to his muse in garret or cell (the stereotype is usually sexual as well as behavioral) is sentimentalized and unrealistic.

19. *Writing is a solitary activity.* Reality: Writing in general often requires other people to stimulate discussion, to provide spellings, to listen to choice phrases, and even just for companionship in an activity which can be so personal and unpredictable that it creates considerable stress. And especially when writing is being learned there is often a great need for and advantage in people working together on a letter, poem, or story. The ability to write alone comes with experience, and is not always easy or necessary.

20. *Writing is a tidy activity.* Reality: Truly creative (or difficult) writing spreads itself all over the writing surface and all over the floor. Writing is messy; it can involve scissors, paste, transparent tape, paper clips, staplers, pens and papers of many colors and more than one working surface (not all necessarily horizontal).

21. *Writing should be the same for everyone.* Reality: All writers have idiosyncracies. Some write best in the morning, some in the evening; some with pen or pencil, some with typewriter or tape recorder; some only in silence, others only in company; some systematically, others irregularly. Most writers have very strong preferences about writing with a particular kind of instrument on a particular kind of paper in particular locations at particular times with particular kinds of physical and psychological support, holding to these supports with a tenacity verging on superstition. But then superstition is a characteristic of all high-risk occupations. Steeplejacks and astronauts have their rabbits' feet. Writers put themselves on the line and undertake enterprises without knowing what the outcome will be. Inconvenient though it might often be, writing behavior may have to be idiosyncratic if it is to be engaged in at all.

The Grand Myth about Who Can Teach Writing

22. *People who do not themselves enjoy and practice writing can teach children how to write.* Reality: Anyone who hopes to teach children how to write must 1) demonstrate what writing does, and 2) demonstrate how to do it. A "teacher" who dislikes or fears writing will demonstrate that writing is to be disliked or feared, just as a teacher who is only seen writing comments on children's work, reports for parents, or notes and exercises for classroom activities will demonstrate that writing is simply for administrative and classroom purposes. Children will learn what they are taught (Smith 1981a), and a teacher who perceives writing as a tedious chore with trivial applications will teach just those things.

For most of the myths I have collected I have not attempted to present a means for their eradication. My general feeling (or hope) is that recognition of the myth should be sufficient for most teachers to avoid falling victim to it. But for the myth of who can teach writing I want to offer a practical suggestion.

The assertion is that children will learn to write and to enjoy writing only in the presence of teachers (or other adults) who themselves write and enjoy writing. If some teachers do not have these necessary characteristics, then more might be done to bring people who do have them into the classroom, not just the professionals like local authors and journalists but anyone who enjoys writing letters, poetry, or short stories (just as athletic coaches and assistants do not need to be professional athletes themselves, though they are expected to understand and enjoy the sport).

But an additional and even more desirable solution would be for all teachers to learn to become at least moderately keen and competent writers. And for this they should not themselves turn to the exercises and "how to do it" books any more than they should try to educate their own pupils in this way. Teachers should learn the way children should learn, in the mutual effort of writing with a purpose—the primary initial purpose being one's own joy and satisfaction with what is written—and in the delight of reading widely from a writer's perspective. The easiest way for teachers to learn these things in order to teach children in this way is to learn them *with* children, to share the writing activities with the children themselves. In this way, teachers and children alike should be best able to avoid the tyranny of all the myths of writing, and in the process discover that writing is a natural, attainable, enjoyable, and highly productive way of spending one's time.

References

Rosenblatt, Louise. "What Facts Does This Poem Teach You?" *Language Arts* 57 (1980): 386-394.
Smith, Frank. "Demonstrations, Engagement and Sensitivity: A Revised Approach to Language Learning." *Language Arts* 58 (1981a): 103-112.
——————— . *Writing and the Writer*. New York: Holt, Rinehart & Winston, 1981b.

Language Across the Curriculum

CHRISTOPHER THAISS

"Language across the curriculum" means basically two things. First, it means that gaining power in all the modes of language—writing, reading, speaking, and listening—must take place in every school course and at every school level, if this growth is to be deep and substantial. This meaning rejects the notion that the diverse uses of language are best learned in specific "skills" courses in, for example, English or speech. Second, "language across the curriculum" stresses the interrelationship of the modes: one learns to write *as* one learns to speak *as* one learns to read and listen. Each ability, therefore, improves to the extent that all are exercised. This second meaning rejects the teaching of, for example, writing or reading in relative isolation from the other. Ultimately, these two meanings of language across the curriculum come together in a third: the inseparableness of language, thinking, and learning. If we do not apply the full range of our language resources to our learning of any subject, then we stifle thought, conscious and unconscious, and so deprive ourselves of more than the most superficial understanding.

History and Theory

Language across the curriculum is hardly a new idea. Teachers in every age have seen that learning flourishes in rich environments that regularly challenge students to manipulate ideas through writing and through talk between teacher and student, parent and child, peer and peer. Furthermore, it has probably never been doubted that the ability to communicate is profoundly connected to the desire to share and acquire knowledge. After all, teachers and textbook writers at all levels have tried to make language instruction "interesting." Model essays, speech and discussion topics, and even workbook sentences—all are presumably chosen (though not always successfully) to excite the wonder and curiosity of the student. Nevertheless, the very fact that so much has been done to fabricate a learning context for language instruction shows that language across the curriculum, if not a new idea, was for a time submerged. Clearly, school curricula became divided—for various reasons—into "content" and "skills" courses, and educators created the circumstances out of which language across the curriculum would have to reemerge as a fresh concept.

Much credit for this resurgence belongs to the British Schools Council Project in Writing Across the Curriculum, which from the mid-1960s onward

Published 1984 by ERIC/RCS. Used with permission.

studied how writing—and talk—were learned and used in schools throughout the United Kingdom. In a series of books (e.g., Britton 1970, and Martin et al. 1976), the Schools Council Project reported that the vast majority of school-based talking and writing was not "genuine communication," in which one person tries to convey new knowledge to another, but was mere giving back of information to the teacher in the role of judge. This "bogus" communication not only limited drastically the student's use of language, but produced dull, inauthentic responses. Conversely, when students were encouraged to write for audiences who would be interested in learning something new from the student (for example, readers of the school newspaper), researchers found the writing more lively and engagement with the topic more intense. Likewise, in language-rich classes, such as science labs where teams of students freely conversed in order to solve problems raised by an experiment, scripts showed that the give-and-take sparked varied language uses, including speculation and argument, plus the desire to repeat experiments or try new ones in order to answer new questions.

In the United States, Janet Emig (1977) reinforced the Schools Council conclusions by bringing to bear on the issue of language and learning the discoveries of linguistics and cognitive psychology. Vygotsky (1962), Kelly (1969), Bruner (1971), and Jaynes (1977) had found close correlation between verbalizing, in speech and writing, and the ability to assimilate perceptions. Particularly important was the recognition that language itself, whether read or heard, could be understood only if the individual translated the messages of others into his or her own words. Thus, conviction of the usefulness of language as a tool of learning grew.

Meanwhile, research on written composition began giving overwhelming evidence of the importance of talk in the development of writing ability. Britton (1967, 1975), in conceptualizing writing as a "process," defined "expressive writing," a form nearest to talk, as the matrix out of which more sophisticated written communication necessarily developed. He and other members of the Schools Council Project, as well as Moffett (1968), gave examples of classrooms in which the cultivation of many forms of discourse led to writing that showed fluency and awareness of audience. Writers such as Macrorie (1977) and Elbow (1973) demonstrated that talk *about* writing, especially within small groups of writers, could spark livelier, more coherent writing. Further studies of the speaking-writing connection have been brought together by Kroll and Vann (1981).

Implications for Teaching: Faculty Training

One meaning emphatically *not* implied by language across the curriculum is that the content area teacher must also become a specialist in the teaching of speech, a specialist in the teaching of writing, and so forth. What is required is that teachers look for ways to increase or vary the language experience that will help students understand and explore the subject matter of the course. As language-across-the-curriculum workshops continually demonstrate, teachers in every field are already creating language-rich environments. Most of their techniques can be applied rather easily by their colleagues (Fulwiler and Young 1982, Griffin 1982, Thaiss 1983).

Typically, these ideas and practices are disseminated through in-service workshops or institutes. Beginning in the 1970s, federal, state, and local sponsorship of faculty training programs, particularly at the college level, has encouraged language across the curriculum to proliferate in the United States, with special emphasis on the uses and improvement of writing. For K-12 teachers, leadership in language across the curriculum has been taken by the 102 sites of the National Writing Project, which has expanded its in-service network to include teachers in all fields. Summer seminars sponsored by the National Endowment for the Humanities at Beaver College (Penn.) have also contributed to the colleges-schools liaison in writing across the curriculum.

In the cross-curricular course conducted by the National Writing Project sites, faculty training occurs in two reinforcing ways: (1) NWP-trained teachers from different fields, for example, history and physics, conduct presentations on successful language-across-the-curriculum practices in their classrooms; and (2) class members practice writing-and-speaking-to-learn techniques, such as learning logs and focused small-group discussions, throughout the semester. Many such courses are set up for the faculty of a single school, to insure the continuing exchange of ideas and often to initiate schoolwide curriculum reforms. Though the contributions of language arts and English specialists are almost always important in these faculty-training programs, whether in colleges or schools, most programs are geared toward developing an inter-disciplinary focus, with ongoing leadership coming from diverse departments.

Implications for Teaching: Techniques

In accordance with writing-process theory and the pioneering British research, the most successful language-and-learning practices tend to promote relatively unpressured expression, emphasizing techniques that encourage imagination and intuition. Journals and logs, small-group projects, teacher-student dialogues, and role playing are popular devices. Traditional content-area assignments such as research papers and laboratory reports are reinterpreted in terms of process theory, so that the research paper may become an "I-Search" project (Macrorie 1980), with significant expressive writing and classroom interaction, while the lab report may be divided into steps—method, observations, analysis—with each successive portion discussed by class groups.

Student journals of various types have been particularly powerful, and popular, learning tools. Regular writing to record or to analyze speculatively has long been practiced by professionals in many fields; thus, teachers tend to take readily to this form of instruction. In process terms, journals (often called learning logs, reader response logs, or any of a number of other names) encourage and teach expressive writing. Entries can also become the basis for more formal papers, when students' writing is carried through revision and editing stages. As a learning tool, the journal provides ample practice for translation of reading assignments or lectures, as well as labs and other kinds of experience, into the writer's own words; thus the journal can improve reading and listening comprehension (Wotring and Tierney 1982).

Journals are also adaptable to more- or less-structured learning situations. Teachers can make the journal an open-ended daily or weekly assignment, or they can use the journal for speculative answers to specific study questions. Some teachers ask students to sharply focus their entries on analysis of reading, lectures, or experiments; others want their students to exploit the journal's power as an emotional, psychological release (Progoff 1975). Many use the journal with entries voluntarily read aloud in class, as a spur to class discussion, while other teachers maintain a separate "journal dialogue" with each student in writing (Staton 1984).

The teacher's response to and evaluation of journals, as of other popular language-across-the-curriculum devices, is crucial to their effectiveness. The Schools Council research gave early evidence that expressive writing, like oral brainstorming, would fail if teachers did not continually nurture students' risk taking in analysis or speculation. Using the journal as a facts quiz or marking entries for mechanical errors would defeat its purpose. Guarding students' privacy, by allowing them to withhold certain entries and by never demanding that students read entries aloud, also seems essential. On the other hand, since teachers often find expressive forms new to their students, it is important to show students how to make the most of the freedom to interpret and imagine that these forms offer them.

Implications for Curriculum Change

In most schools and colleges with language-across-the-curriculum programs, change has meant more variety in how language is used and learning accomplished. Where language across the curriculum has affected school programs, this change has taken such forms as increases in team-taught courses, cooperative relationships among sections of English and sections of other subjects, or the use of "writing intensive" courses in content areas to fulfill composition requirements. In some instances it has meant the full interweaving of all language instruction into the learning of such subjects as history, art, mathematics, and science. Full applications of language across the curriculum have been most smoothly undertaken in schools with a history of interdisciplinary planning and in the all-subjects classroom in the elementary grades. In whatever setting it occurs and however deeply it affects structure, language across the curriculum promotes the fruitful, invigorating exchange of perspectives and methods among teachers who all too often have been strangers across the curricular walls.

References

Britton, James. *Language and Learning*. Harmondsworth, England: Penguin, 1970. ED 052 217.

——————— , ed. *Talking and Writing*. London, England: Methuen, 1967.

Britton, James, Tony Burgess, Nancy Martin, Alex McLeod, and Harold Rosen. *The Development of Writing Abilities, 11-18*. London, England: Macmillan Education, 1975. ED 144 049.

Bruner, Jerome. *The Relevance of Education*. New York: Norton, 1971.

Elbow, Peter. *Writing Without Teachers*. New York: Oxford, 1973.

Emig, Janet. "Writing as a Mode of Learning." *College Composition and Communication* 28, no. 2 (May 1977). EJ 162 045.

Fulwiler, Toby, and Art Young, eds. *Language Connections: Writing and Reading Across the Curriculum*. Urbana, IL: National Council of Teachers of English, 1982. ED 218 667.

Jaynes, Julian. *The Origin of Consciousness in the Breakdown of the Bicameral Mind*. Boston, Mass.: Houghton Mifflin, 1977.

Kelly, George. "The Language of Hypothesis." In *Clinical Psychology and Personality: The Selected Papers of George Kelly*, edited by Brendan Maher. New York: John Wiley, 1969.

Kroll, Barry M., and Roberta J. Vann, eds. *Exploring Speaking-Writing Relationships: Connections and Contrasts*. Urbana, Ill.: National Council of Teachers of English, 1981. ED 204 794.

Macrorie, Ken. *Searching Writing*. Rochelle Park, N.J.: Hayden, 1980.

——————— . *Telling Writing*. 3rd ed. Rochelle Park, N.J.: Hayden, 1980.

Martin, Nancy, Pat D'Arcy, Bryan Newton, and Robert Parker. *Writing and Learning Across the Curriculum, 11-16*. London, England: Ward Lock, 1976. ED 161 064.

Moffett, James. *Teaching the Universe of Discourse*. Boston, Mass.: Houghton Mifflin, 1968. ED 030 664.

Progoff, Ira. *At a Journal Workshop*. New York: Dialogue House, 1975.

Staton, Jana. "Thinking Together: Language Interaction in Children's Reasoning." In *Speaking and Writing, K-12*, edited by Christopher Thaiss and Charles Suhor. Urbana, Ill.: National Council of Teachers of English, 1984.

Thaiss, Christopher, ed. *Writing to Learn: Essays and Reflections on Writing Across the Curriculum*. Dubuque, Iowa: Kendall/Hunt, 1983.

Vygotsky, Lev S. *Thought and Language*. Edited by Gertrude Vakar, translated by Eugenia Hanfmann. Cambridge, Mass.: MIT Press, 1962.

Wotring, Anne, and Robert Tierney. *Two Studies of Writing in High School Science*. Berkeley, Calif.: University of California, 1981.

Competing Theories of Process:
A Critique and a Proposal

The recognition of the study of writing as an important area of research within English in North America has also led to a questioning of its theoretical underpinnings. While the teaching of writing has achieved programmatic or departmental status at many colleges and universities, voices from outside and from within the ranks question whether a discipline devoted to the study of writing exists or if those who teach writing simply assume it exists because they share common problems and interests. The convenient landmark for disciplinary historians is the Richard Braddock, Richard Lloyd-Jones, and Lowell Schoer review of the field in 1963, a survey that found a legion of pedagogical studies of writing, most lacking any broad theoretical notion of writing abilities or even awareness of similar existing studies. Contemporary reviewers of writing research point out how much happened in the years that followed, but no development has been more influential than the emphasis on writing as a process. For the last few years, Richard Young's and Maxine Hairston's accounts of the process movement as a Kuhnian paradigm shift have served as justifications for disciplinary status. Even though the claim of a paradigm shift is now viewed by some as an overstatement, it is evident that many writing teachers in grade schools, high schools, and colleges have internalized process assumptions. In the most optimistic visions, writing teachers K–13 march happily under the process banner. Slogans such as "revising is good for you" are repeated in nearly every college writing textbook as well as in many secondary and elementary classrooms. Paradigm, pre-paradigm, or no paradigm, nearly everyone seems to agree that writing as a process is good and "current-traditional rhetoric" is bad. It would seem, therefore, that any disciplinary claims must be based on some shared definition of process.

The problem, of course, is that conceptions of writing as a process vary from theorist to theorist. Commentators on the process movement (e.g., Berlin, *Writing Instruction*) now assume at least two major perspectives on composing, an *expressive view* including the work of "authentic voice" proponents such as William Coles, Peter Elbow, Ken Macrorie, and Donald Stewart, and a *cognitive view* including the research of those who analyze composing processes such as Linda Flower, Barry Kroll, and Andrea Lunsford. More

College English, 48 (October 1986), pp. 527-542. Copyright © 1986 by the National Council of Teachers of English. Reprinted with permission.

recently, a third perspective on composing has emerged, one that contends processes of writing are social in character instead of originating within individual writers. Statements on composing from the third perspective, which I call the *social view,* have come from Patricia Bizzell, Kenneth Bruffee, Marilyn Cooper, Shirley Brice Heath, James Reither, and authors of several essays collected in *Writing in Non-academic Settings* edited by Lee Odell and Dixie Goswami.

Before I contrast the assumptions of each of these three views on composing with the goal of identifying a disciplinary basis for the study of writing, I want to raise the underlying assumption that the study and teaching of writing *should* aspire to disciplinary status. In a radical critique of education in America, Stanley Aronowitz and Henry Giroux see the development of writing programs as part of a more general trend toward an atheoretical and skills-oriented curriculum that regards teachers as civil servants who dispense pre-packaged lessons. Here is Aronowitz and Giroux's assessment:

> We wish to suggest that schools, especially the colleges and universities, are now battlegrounds that may help to determine the shape of the future. The proliferation of composition programs at all levels of higher education may signal a new effort to extend the technicization process even further into the humanities.... The splitting of composition as a course from the study of literature, [sic] is of course a sign of its technicization and should be resisted both because it is an attack against critical thought and because it results in demoralization of teachers and their alienation from work. (52)

While I find their conclusions extreme, their critique provokes us to examine writing in relation to larger social and political issues. Unlike most other Marxist educational theorists, Aronowitz and Giroux do not present a pessimistic determinism nor do they deny human agency. They allow for the possibility that teachers and students can resist domination and think critically, thus leaving open the possibility for a historically aware theory and pedagogy of composing.

I will outline briefly the histories of each of the dominant theoretical views of composition, drawing on an earlier book by Giroux, *Theory and Resistance in Education,* for a critical review of the assumptions of each position.[1] In the concluding section of this essay, however, I reject Aronowitz and Giroux's dour assessment of the study of writing as a discipline. Each of the theoretical positions on composing has given teachers of writing a pedagogy for resisting a narrow definition of writing based largely on "correct" grammar and usage. Finally, I argue that disciplinary claims for writing must be based on a conception of process broader than any of the three views.

The Expressive View

The beginnings of composing research in the mid-1960s hardly marked a revolution against the prevailing line of research; in fact, early studies of composing issues typically were isolated pedagogical experiments similar to those described by Braddock, Lloyd-Jones, and Schoer. One of these experiments was D. Gordon Rohman and Albert Wlecke's study of the effects of "prewriting" on writing performance, first published in 1964. Rohman and Wlecke maintained that thinking was different from writing and antecedent to writing; therefore, teachers should stimulate students' thinking by having them write journals, construct analogies, and, in the spirit of the sixties, meditate before writing essays. Young cites the Rohman and Wlecke study as one that helped to overturn the current-traditional paradigm. What Young neglects to mention is that Rohman and Wlecke revived certain Romantic notions about composing and were instigators of a "neo-Romantic" view of process. Rohman defines "good writing" as

> that discovered combination of words which allows a person the integrity to dominate his subject with a pattern both fresh and original. "Bad writing," then, is an echo of someone else's combination which we have merely taken over for the occasion of our writing.... "Good writing" must be the discovery by a responsible person of his uniqueness within his subject. (107-08)

This definition of "good writing" includes the essential qualities of Romantic expressivism—integrity, spontaneity, and originality—the same qualities M. H. Abrams uses to define "expressive" poetry in *The Mirror and the Lamp*.

Each of these expressivist qualities has motivated a series of studies and theoretical statements on composing. We can see the influence of the first notion—integrity—in the transmission of Rohman and Wlecke's definitions of "good" and "bad" writing. In 1969 Donald Stewart argued that the unified aim for writing courses should be writing with integrity. He illustrated his argument with a student paper titled "Money Isn't as Valuable as It Seems" that contained a series of predictable generalities. Stewart criticized the student not for failing to support his generalizations but because he "doesn't believe what he is saying. Worse yet, it is possible that he doesn't even realize he doesn't believe it" (225).[2] The problem with using integrity as a measure of value is obvious in retrospect. Not only is the writer of the paper Stewart reproduces bound by his culture, as Stewart argues, but so too are Stewart's criticisms. Stewart's charges of insincerity are based on the assumption that the student is parroting the anti-establishment idealism of the late sixties. Conversely, career-oriented students of today are so unlikely to write such a paper that if one started an essay with the same sentences as Stewart's example ("Having money is one of the least important items of life. Money only causes problems and heartaches among one's friends and self."), a teacher likely would assume that the student believed what she was saying, no matter how trite or predictable.

Because the sincerity of a text is finally impossible to assess, a second quality of Romantic expressivism—spontaneity—became important to the process movement primarily through Peter Elbow's *Writing without Teachers,* a book that was written for a broad audience, and that enjoyed great popular success. Elbow adopted Macrorie's method of free writing, but he presented the method as practical advice for writing spontaneously, not as a way of discovering "the truth." Elbow questioned Rohman and Wlecke's separation of thinking from writing, a model he maintained led to frustration. Instead, Elbow urged that we

> think of writing as an organic, developmental process in which you start writing at the very beginning—before you know your meaning at all—and encourage your words gradually to change and evolve. Only at the end will you know what you want to say or the words you want to say it with. (15)

Elbow chose the metaphor of organic growth to describe the operations of composing, the same metaphor Edward Young used to describe the vegetable concept of genius in 1759 and Coleridge borrowed from German philosophers to describe the workings of the imagination (see Abrams 198-225). Coleridge contrasted two kinds of form—one mechanical, when we impress upon any material a predetermined form, the other organic, when the material shapes itself from within. Coleridge also realized the plant metaphor implied a kind of organic determinism. (Tulip bulbs cannot grow into daffodils.) He avoided this consequence by insisting upon the free will of the artist, that the artist has foresight and the power of choice. In much the same way, Elbow qualifies his organic metaphor:

> It is true, of course, that an initial set of words does not, like a young live organism, contain within each cell a *plan* for the final mature stage and all the intervening stages that must be gone through. Perhaps, therefore, the final higher organization in words should only be called a borrowed reflection of a higher organization that is really in me or my mind. (23)

Elbow's point is one of the standards of Romantic theory: that "good" writing does not follow rules but reflects the processes of the creative imagination.

If writing is to unfold with organic spontaneity, then it ought to expose the writer's false starts and confused preliminary explorations of the topic. In other words, the writing should proceed obliquely as a "striving toward"—a mimetic of the writer's actual thought processes—and only hint at the goal of such striving. The resultant piece of writing would then seem fragmentary and unfinished, but would reveal what Coleridge calls a progressive method, a psychological rather than rhetorical organization, unifying its outwardly disparate parts. On the other hand, insofar as a piece of writing—no matter how expressive—is coherent, it must also be mimetic and rhetorical. At times Wordsworth and to a lesser extent Coleridge seem to argue that expressivism precludes all intentionality—as if such meditations as Wordsworth's "Tintern Abbey" and Coleridge's "This Lime-Tree Bower My Prison" weren't carefully *arranged* to seem spontaneous. Peter Elbow's solution to the dilemma of spontaneity comes in *Writing with Power,* where he discusses revision as the shaping of unformed material.

A third quality of Romantic expressivism—originality—could not be adapted directly to current theories of composing because the Romantic notion of originality is linked to the notion of natural genius, the difference between the poet who is born and the poet who is made. The concept of natural genius has been replaced in contemporary expressive theory with an emphasis on the innate potential of the unconscious mind. More limited statements of this position recommend teaching creative writing to stimulate originality.[3] Stronger statements come from those expressive theorists who apply the concept of "self-actualization" from psychoanalysis to writing. Rohman says teachers "must recognize and use, as the psychologists do in therapy, a person's desire to actualize himself" (108). The implication is that personal development aids writing development or that writing development can aid personal development, with the result that better psychologically integrated people become better writers. (Case histories of twentieth-century poets and novelists are seldom introduced in these discussions.) In an essay on meditation and writing James Moffett extends the self-actualization notion introduced by Rohman, saying "good therapy and composition aim at clear thinking, effective relating, and satisfying self-expression" (235).

Giroux, however, would see Moffett's essay as emblematic of what is wrong with the expressive view. Although Giroux grants that expressive theory came as a reaction against, to use his word, the "technicization" of education, he contends the result of the quest for "psychic redemption" and "personal growth" is a turning away from the relation of the individual to the social world, a world where "social practices situated in issues of class, gender, and race shape every day experience" (219). For Giroux, the expressive view of composing ignores how writing works in the world, hides the social nature of language, and offers a false notion of a "private" self. Before I defend the expressive position against Giroux's attack, I will move on to the cognitive view where Giroux's strongest criticisms center.

The Cognitive View

In addition to promoting expressive assumptions about composing, Rohman and Wlecke helped inspire research that led to the current cognitive view. Several researchers in the late sixties were encouraged by Rohman and Wlecke's mention of *heuristics* and their finding that students who were taught "pre-writing" activities wrote better essays. More important, Rohman and Wlecke's proposal of three linear stages in the writing process stimulated research in response. In 1964 Janet Emig first argued against a linear model of composing, and she redoubled her attack in her 1969 dissertation, later published as an NCTE research monograph. Emig was among the first writing researchers to act on calls for research on cognitive processes issued at the influential 1966 Dartmouth Seminar on English. She observed that high school writers, in contrast to standard textbook advice of the time, did not use outlines to compose and that composing "does not occur as a left-to-right, solid, uninterrupted activity with an even pace" (84). Instead, Emig described composing as "recursive," an adjective from mathematics that refers to a formula generating successive terms. While the term is technically misapplied, since writing processes do not operate this simply, the extent to which it is used by other researchers attests to Emig's influence. Another measure of Emig's influence is that denunciations of Rohman and Wlecke's *Pre-writing, Writing, Re-writing* model became a trope for introductions of later articles on composing.

In a recent consideration of Emig's monograph, Ralph Voss credits her with developing a "science consciousness' in composition research" (279). Emig appropriated from psychology more than the case-study approach and think-aloud methodolgy. Her monograph is a mixture of social science and literary idioms, with one sentence talking about a "sense of closure," the next about "a moment in the process when one feels most godlike" (44). Emig's work was well received because writing researchers wanted to enter the mainstream of educational research. For example, Janice Lauer began a 1970 article directing writing researchers to psychologists' work in problem solving with the following sentence: "Freshman English will never reach the status of a respectable intellectual discipline unless both its theorizers and its practitioners break out of the ghetto" (396). Emig provided not only a new methodology but an agenda for subsequent research, raising issues such as pausing during composing, the role of rereading in revision, and the paucity of substantial revision in student writing. Her monograph led to numerous observational studies of writers' composing behavior during the next decade.[4]

The main ingredient Emig did not give researchers was a cognitive theory of composing. When writing researchers realized Chomsky's theory of trans-formational grammar could not explain composing abilities, they turned to two other sources of cognitive theory. The first was cognitive-developmental psychology, which James Britton and his colleagues applied to the developing sense of audience among young writers. Britton argued that children as speakers gain a sense of audience because the hearer is a reactive presence, but children as writers have more difficulty because the "other" is not present. Consequently, a child writing must imagine a generalized context for the particular text in all but the most immediate writing situations (such as an informal letter). Britton condemned most school writing assignments for failing to encourage children to imagine real writing situations (see *Development* 63-65). Other researchers probed the notion of developmental stages in writing. Barry Kroll adapted Jean Piaget's concept of *Egocentrism*—the inability to take any perspective but one's own—to explain young children's lack of a sense of audience. He hypothesized, like Britton, that children's ability to *decenter*—to imagine another perspective—develops more slowly in writing than in speaking. Andrea Lunsford extended Piaget's stages of cognitive development to college basic writers, arguing that their tendency to lapse into personal narrative in writing situations that call for "abstract" discourse indicates they are arrested in an "egocentric stage."

The second source of cognitive theory came from American cognitive psychology, which has spawned several strands of research on composing. Many college writing teachers were introduced to a cognitive theory of composing through the work of Linda Flower and John R. Hayes. Flower and Hayes' main claims—that composing processes intermingle, that goals direct composing, and that experts compose differently from inexperienced writers—all have become commonplaces of the process movement. Less well understood by writing teachers, however, are the assumptions underlying Flower and Hayes' model, assumptions derived from a cognitive research tradition. Flower and Hayes acknowledge their debt to this tradition, especially to Allen Newell and Herbert A. Simon's *Human Problem Solving,* a classic work that helped define the aims and agenda for a cognitive science research program. Newell and Simon theorize that the key to understanding how people solve problems is in their "programmability"; in other words, how people use "a very simple information processing system" to account for their "problem solving in such tasks as chess, logic, and cryptarithmetic" (870). The idea that thinking and language can be represented by computers underlies much research in cognitive science in several camps, including artificial intelligence, computational linguistics, and cognitive psychology. Newell and Simon's historical overview of this movement credits Norbert Wiener's theory of *cybernetics* as the beginnings of contemporary cognitive science.[5] The basic principle of cybernetics is the *feedback loop,* in which the regulating mechanism receives information from the thing regulated and makes adjustments.

George A. Miller was among the first to introduce cybernetic theory as an alternative to the stimulus-response reflex arc as the basis of mental activity. In *Plans and the Structure of Behavior,* Miller, Eugene Galanter, and Karl Pribram describe human behavior as guided by plans that are constantly being evaluated as they are being carried out in a feedback loop. They theorize that the brain—like a computer—is divided into a *memory* and a *processing unit.* What Miller, Galanter, and Pribram do not attempt to theorize is where plans come from. To fill in this gap, Newell and Simon add to the feedback loop an entity they call the *task environment,* defined in terms of a goal coupled with a specific environment. Newell and Simon claim the resulting loop explains how people think.

If we look at the graphic representation of the Flower and Hayes model in the 1980 and 1981 versions, we can see how closely the overall design follows in the cognitive science tradition. The box labelled *Writing Processes* is analogous to the central processing unit of a computer. In the 1980 version, diagrams representing the subprocesses of composing (*planning, translating,* and *reviewing*) are presented as computer flowcharts. Like Newell and Simon's model of information processing, Flower and Hayes' model makes strong theoretical claims in assuming relatively simple cognitive operations produce enormously complex actions, and like Emig's monograph, the Flower and Hayes model helped promote a "science consciousness" among writing teachers. Even though cognitive researchers have warned that "novice writers cannot be turned into experts simply by tutoring them in the knowledge expert writers have" (Scardamalia 174)), many writing teachers believed cognitive research could provide a "deep structure" theory of *the* composing process, which could in turn specify how writing should be taught. Furthermore, the Flower and Hayes model had other atttractions. The placement of *translating* after *planning* was compatible with the sequence of invention, arrangement, and style in classical rhetoric. It also suited a popular conception that language comes after ideas are formed, a conception found in everyday metaphors that express ideas as objects placed in containers (e.g., "It's difficult to put my ideas into words").[6]

Giroux's response to the cognitive view of composing can be readily inferred. To begin, Giroux would be highly critical of any attempt to discover universal laws underlying writing. Writing for Giroux, like other acts of literacy, is not universal but social in nature and cannot be removed from culture. He would fault the cognitive view for collapsing cultural issues under the label "audience," which, defined unproblematically, is reduced to the status of a variable in an equation. He further would accuse the cognitive view of neglecting the content of writing and downplaying conflicts inherent in acts of writing. As a consequence, pedagogies assuming a cognitive view tend to overlook differences in language use among students of different social classes, genders, and ethnic backgrounds.

At this point I'll let Giroux's bricks fly against my windows and use an article on revision I wrote with Steve Witte as a case in point. In this study Witte and I attempt to classify revision changes according to the extent they affect the content of the text. We apply a scheme for describing the structure of a text developed by the Dutch text linguist, Teun van Dijk. What seems obviously wrong with this article in hindsight is the degree to which we assign meaning to the text. Now even van Dijk admits there are as many macrostructures for a text as there are readers. Although our conclusions criticize the artificiality of the experiment and recognize that "revision cannot be separated from other aspects of composing," the intent of the study still suffers from what Giroux sees as a fundamental flaw of cognitivist research—the isolation of part from whole.

The Social View

The third perspective on composing I identified at the beginning of this essay—the social view—is less codified and less constituted at present than the expressive and cognitive views because it arises from several disciplinary traditions. Because of this diversity a comprehensive social view cannot be extrapolated from a collection of positions in the same way I have described the expressive and cognitive views of composing. Statements that propose a social view of writing range from those urging more attention to the immediate circumstances of how a text is composed to those denying the existence of an individual author. My effort to outline a social view will be on the basis of one central assumption: human language (including writing) can be understood only from the perspective of a society rather than a single individual. Thus, taking a social view requires a great deal more than simply paying more attention to the context surrounding a discourse. It rejects the assumption that writing is the act of a private consciousness and that everything else—readers, subjects, and texts—is "out there" in the world. The focus of a social view of writing, therefore, is not on how the social situation influences the individual, but on how the individual is a constituent of a culture.

I will attempt to identify four lines of research that take a social view of writing, although I recognize that these positions overlap and that each draws on earlier work (e.g., Kenneth Burke). These four lines of research can be characterized by the traditions from which they emerge: poststructuralist theories of language, the sociology of science, ethnography, and Marxism.

In the last few years, writing researchers influenced by poststructuralist theories of language have brought notions of discourse communities to discussions of composing. Patricia Bizzell and David Bartholomae, for example, have found such ideas advantageous in examining the writing of college students. Those who believe that meaning resides in the text accuse any other positon of solipsism and relativism, but concepts of discourse communities provide an alternative position, offering solutions to difficult problems in interpretative theory. Reading is neither an experience of extracting a fixed meaning from a text nor is it a matter of making words mean anything you want them to in *Alice in Wonderland* fashion. Ambiguity in texts is not the problem for humans that it is for computers—not so much because we are better at extracting meaning but because language is social practice; because, to paraphrase Bakhtin, words carry with them the places where they have been.

This view of language raises serious problems for cognitive-based research programs investigating adults' composing processes. For instance, Bizzell criticizes the separation of "Planning" and "Translating" in the Flower and Hayes model. Even though Flower and Hayes allow for language to generate language through rereading, Bizzell claims the separation of words from ideas distorts the nature of composing. Bizzell cites Vygotsky, whom many cognitive researchers lump together with Piaget, but whose understanding of language is very different from Piaget's. Vygotsky studied language development as a historical and cultural process, in which a child acquires not only the words of language but the intentions carried by those words and the situations implied by them.

From a social perspective, a major shortcoming in studies that contrast expert and novice writers lies not so much in the artificiality of the experimental situation, but in the assumption that expertise can be defined outside of a specific community of writers. Since individual expertise varies across communities, there can be no one definition of an expert writer. David Bartholomae explores the implications for the teaching of college writing. He argues that writing in college is difficult for inexperienced writers not because they are forced to make the transition from "writer-based" to "reader-based" prose but because they lack the privileged language of the academic community. Bartholomae's point is similar to Bizzell's: when students write in an academic discipline, they write in reference to texts that define the scholarly activities of interpreting and reporting in that discipline. Bartholomae alludes to Barthes' observation that a text on a particular topic always has "off-stage voices" for what has previously been written about that topic. Thus a social view of writing moves beyond the expressivist contention that the individual discovers the self through language and beyond the cognitivist position that an individual constructs reality through language. In a social view, any effort to write about the self or reality always comes in relation to previous texts.

A substantial body of research examining the social processes of writing in an academic discourse community now exists in the sociology of science. Most of this research has been done in Britain, but Americans Charles Bazerman and Greg Myers have made important contributions (see Myers' review article in this issue of *CE*). Research in scientific writing displays many of the theoretical and methodological differences mentioned at the beginning of this section, but this literature taken as a whole challenges the assumption that scientific texts contain autonomous presentations of facts; instead, the texts are "active social tools in the complex interactions of a research community" (Bazerman 3). In the more extreme version of this argument, which follows from Rorty and other pragmatists, science itself becomes a collection of literary forms. Writing about the basis of economics, Donald McCloskey calls statistics "figures of speech in numerical dress" (98). He goes on to say that "the scientific paper is, after all, a literary genre, with an actual author, an implied author, an implied reader, a history, and a form" (105). In contrast, current British research understands a dialectical relationship between external reality and the conventions of a community. A good introduction to this field is Nigel Gilbert and Michael Mulkay's 1984 book, *Opening Pandora's Box.*[7]

A third line of research taking a social view of composing develops from the traditon of ethnography. Ethnographic methodology in the 1970s and 1980s has been used to examine the immediate communities in which writers learn to write—the family and the classroom. These researchers have observed that for many children, the ways literacy is used at home and in the world around them matches poorly with the literacy expectations of the school.[8] The most important of these studies to date is Shirley Brice Heath's analysis of working-class and middle-class families in the Carolina Piedmont. Heath found that how children learn to use literacy originates from how families and communities are structured. Another line of research using ethnographic methodology investigates writing in the workplace, interpreting acts of writing and reading within the culture of the workplace (see Odell and Goswami for examples).

Finally, I include Marxist studies of literacy as a fourth social position on composing. The essential tenet of a Marxist position would be that any act of writing or of teaching writing must be understood within a structure of power related to modes of production. A Marxist critique of the other social positions would accuse each of failing to deal with key concepts such as class, power, and ideology.[9] Giroux finds discourse communities are often more concerned with ways of excluding new members than with ways of admitting them. He attacks non-Marxist ethnographies for sacrificing "theoretical depth for methodological refinement" (98). Indeed, much Marxist scholarship consists of faulting other theorists for their lack of political sophistication.

Toward a Synthesis

At the beginning of this essay I quoted Aronowitz and Giroux's conclusion that the spread of writing programs and, by implication, the process movement itself are part of a general movement toward "atheoretical" and "skills-oriented" education in America. Now I would like to evaluate that claim. If process theory and pedagogy have up to now been unproblematically accepted, I see a danger that it could be unproblematically rejected. Process theory and pedagogy have given student writing a value and authority absent in current-traditional approaches. Each view of process has provided teachers with ways of resisting static methods of teaching writing—methods based on notions of abstract form and adherence to the "rules" of Standard English. Expressive theorists validate personal experience in school systems that often deny it. Cognitive theorists see language as a way of negotiating the world, which is the basis of James Berlin's dialogic redefinition of epistemic rhetoric (*Rhetoric and Reality*). And social theorists such as Heath have found that children who are labelled remedial in traditional classrooms can learn literacy skills by studying the occurrences of writing in the familiar world around them (see *Ways with Words*, Chapter 9).

But equally instructive is the conclusion of Heath's book, where she describes how the curriculum she helped create was quickly swept away. It illustrates how social and historical forces shape the teaching of writing—relationships that, with few exceptions, are only now beginning to be critically investigated. If the process movement is to continue to influence the teaching of writing and to supply alternatives to current-traditional pedagogy, it must take a broader conception of writing, one that understands writing processes are historically dynamic—not psychic states, cognitive routines, or neutral social realtionships. This historical awareness would allow us to reinterpret and integrate each of the theoretical perspectives I have outlined.

The expressive view presents one of two opposing influences in discourse —the unique character of particular acts of writing versus the conventions of language, genre, and social occasion that make that act understandable to others. The expressive view, therefore, leads us to one of the key paradoxes of literacy. When literacy began to be widespread in Northern Europe and its colonies during the eighteenth and nineteenth centuries, it reduced differences between language groups in those countries and brought an emphasis on standard usage. But at the same time linguistic differences were being reduced, individuals became capable of changing the social order by writing for a literate populace (witness the many revolutionary tracts published during the nineteenth century). Furthermore, modern notions of the individual came into being through the widespread publication of the many literary figures and philosophers associated with the Romantic movement and the later development of psychology as a discipline in the nineteenth century. Current technologies for electronic communications bring the potential for gaining access to large bodies of information from the home, yet at the same time these technologies bring increased potential for control through surveillance of communication and restriction of access. People, however, find ways to adapt technologies for their own interests. In organizations where computer technologies have become commonplace, people have taken advantage of opportunities for horizontal communication on topics of their choice through computer "bulletin boards," which function like radio call-in programs. For example, on ARPANET, the Department of Defense's computer network linking research facilities, military contractors, and universities, popular bulletin boards include ones for science fiction, movie reviews, and even a lively debate on arms control. How the possibilities for individual expression will be affected by major technological changes in progress should become one of the most important areas of research for those who study writing.

In a similar way, historical awareness would enhance a cognitive view of composing by demonstrating the historical origins of an individual writer's goals. The cognitive view has brought attention to how writers compose in the workplace. Many writing tasks on the job can be characterized as rhetorical "problems," but the problems themselves are not ones the writers devise. Writing processes take place as part of a structure of power. For instance, Lee Iacocca's autobiography reveals how writing conveys power in large organizations. Iacocca says he communicated good news in writing, but bad news orally. Surely Iacocca's goals and processes in writing are inseparable from what he does and where he works, which in turn must be considered in relation to other large corporations, and which finally should be considered within a history of capitalism.

Some social approaches to the study of discourse entail historical awareness, but a social view is not necessarily historical. The insight that the learning of literacy is a social activity within a specific community will not necessarily lead us to a desirable end. Raymond Williams observes that the term *community* has been used to refer to existing social relationships or possible alternative social relationships, but that it is always used positively, that there is no opposing term. Yet we know from the sad experiences of the twentieth century that consensus often brings oppression. How written texts become instruments of power in a community is evident in the history of colonial empires, where written documents served to implement colonial power. Some of the earliest recorded uses of writing in Mesopotamia and ancient Egypt were for collecting taxes and issuing laws in conquered territories. Written documents made possible the incident George Orwell describes in "The Hanging"— an essay frequently anthologized but rarely analyzed in writing classes for its political significance. Furthermore, in the effort to identify conventions that define communities of writers, commentators on writing processes from a social viewpoint have neglected the issue of what *cannot* be discussed in a particular community, exclusions Foucault has shown to be the exercise of power.

These questions are not mere matters of ivory-tower debate. The preoccupation with an underlying theory of the writing process has led us to neglect finding answers to the most obvious questions in college writing instruction today: why college writing courses are prevalent in the United States and rare in the rest of the world; why the emphasis on teaching writing occurring in the aftermath of the "literacy crises" of the seventies has not abated; why the majority of college writing courses are taught by graduate students and other persons in nontenurable positions. Answers to such questions will come only when we look beyond who is writing to whom to the texts and social systems that stand in relation to the act of writing. If the teaching of writing is to reach disciplinary status, it will be achieved through recognition that writing processes are, as Stanley Fish says of linguistic knowledge, "contextual rather than abstract, local rather than general, dynamic rather then invariant" (438).

Notes

[1] Giroux directly criticizes "romantic" and "cognitive developmental" traditions of teaching literacy in *Theory and Resistance in Education*. Bruce Herzberg has extended Giroux's critique to particular composition theorists.

[2] Even more strident attacks on cliches and conventional writing assignments came from Ken Macrorie, who damned "themes" as papers "not meant to be read but corrected" (686), and from William Coles, who accused textbook authors of promoting "themewriting" by presenting writing "as a trick that can be played, a device that can be put into operation...just as one can be taught or learn to run an adding machine, or pour concrete" (134-42).

[3] For example, Art Young advocates having students write poems, plays, and stories in writing-across-the-curriculum classes. During the 1920s and 1930s, there were numerous appeals to incorporate creative writing into the English curriculum; see, for example, Lou LaBrant.

[4] For a bibliographic review of cognitive studies of composing, see Faigley, Cherry, Jolliffe, and Skinner, chapters 1-5.

[5] Wiener used the term *cybernetics*—derived from the Greek word for the pilot of a ship—as a

metaphor for the functioning mind. He claimed as a precedent James Watt's use of the word *governor* to describe the mechanical regulator of a steam engine. Wiener's metaphor explained the mind as a control mechanism such as an automatic pilot of an airplane. For a historical overview of cybernetics and the beginnings of cognitive science, see Bell.

[6] Reddy discusses some of the consequences of the "conduit" metaphor for our understanding of language.

[7] Gilbert and Mulkay provide a bibliography of social studies of scientific discourse on 194-95.

[8] Heath includes an annotated bibliography of school and community ethnographies in the endnotes of *Ways with Words*.

[9] Richard Ohmann's *English in America* remains the seminal Marxist analysis of American writing instruction.

References

Abrams, M.H. *The Mirror and the Lamp*. New York: Oxford UP, 1953.

Aronowitz, Stanley, and Henry A. Giroux. *Education Under Siege*. South Hadley, MA: Bergin, 1985.

Bartholomae, David. "Inventing the University." *When a Writer Can't Write*. Ed. Mike Rose. New York: Guilford, 1985. 134-65.

Bazerman, Charles. "Physicists Reading Physics: Schema-Laden Purposes and Purpose-Laden Schema." *Written Communication* 2 (1985): 3-23.

Bell, Daniel. *The Social Sciences since the Second World War*. New Brunswick, NJ: Transaction, 1982.

Berlin, James. *Rhetoric and Reality: Writing Instruction in American Colleges, 1900-1985*. Carbondale: Southern Illinois UP, 1987.

——————— . *Writing Instruction in Nineteenth-Century American Colleges*. Carbondale: Southern Illinois UP, 1984.

Bizzell, Patricia. "Cognition, Convention, and Certainty: What We Need to Know about Writing." *PRE/TEXT* 3 (1982): 213-43.

Braddock, Richard, Richard Lloyd-Jones, and Lowell Schoer. *Research in Written Composition*. Urbana: NCTE, 1963.

Britton, James, Tony Burgess, Nancy Martin, Alex McLeod, and Harold Rosen. *The Development of Writing Abilities (11-18)*. London: Macmillan, 1975.

Bruffee, Kenneth A. *"Collaborative Learning and the 'Conversion of Mankind.'"* *College English* 46 (1984): 635-52.

Coleridge, Samuel Taylor. "On Method." *The Portable Coleridge*. Ed. I.A. Richards. New York: Viking, 1950. 339-86.

Coles, William, Jr. "Freshman Composition: The Circle of Unbelief." *College English* 31 (1969): 134-42.

Cooper, Marilyn M. "The Ecology of Writing." *College English* 48 (1986): 364-75.

Elbow, Peter. *Writing without Teachers*. New York: Oxford UP, 1973.

——————— . *Writing with Power*. New York: Oxford UP, 1981.

Emig, Janet. *The Composing Processes of Twelfth Graders*. NCTE Research Report No. 13. Urbana: NCTE, 1971.

——————— . "The Uses of the Unconscious in Composing." *College Composition and Communication* 16 (1964): 6-11.

Faigley, Lester, Roger D. Cherry, David A. Jolliffe, and Anna M. Skinner. *Assessing Writers' Knowledge and Processes of Composing*. Norwood, NJ: Ablex, 1985.

Faigley, Lester, and Stephen P. Witte. "Analyzing Revision." *College Composition and Communication* 32 (1981): 400-14.

Fish, Stanley. "Consequences." *Critical Inquiry* 11 (1985): 433-58.

Flower, Linda, and John R. Hayes. "A Cognitive Process Theory of Writing." *College Composition and Communication* 31 (1980): 365-87.

Foucault, Michel. *Power/Knowledge: Selected Interviews and Other Writings, 1972-1977*. Ed. Colin Gordon. New York: Pantheon, 1980.

Gilbert, G. Nigel, and Michael Mulkay. *Opening Pandora's Box: A Sociological Analysis of Scientists' Discourse*. Cambridge: Cambridge UP, 1984.

Giroux, Henry A. *Theory and Resistance in Education*. South Hadley, MA: Bergin, 1983.

Hairston, Maxine. "The Winds of Change: Thomas Kuhn and the Revolution in the Teaching of Writing." *College Composition and Communication* 33 (1982): 76-88.

Hayes, John R., and Linda Flower. "Identifying the Organization of Writing Processes." *Cognitive Processes in Writing: An Interdisiciplinary Approach*. Ed. Lee Gregg and Erwin Steinberg. Hillsdale, NJ: Lawrence Erlbaum, 1980. 3-30.

Heath, Shirley Brice. *Ways with Words*. New York: Cambridge UP, 1983.

Herzberg, Bruce. "The Politics of Discourse Communities." Paper presented at the Conference on College Composition and Communication, New Orleans, March 1986.

Iacocca, Lee. *Iacocca: An Autobiography*. New York: Bantam, 1984.

Kroll, Barry M. "Cognitive Egocentrism and the Problem of Audience Awareness in Written Discourse." *Research in the Teaching of English* 12 (1978): 269-81.

LaBrant, Lou. "The Psychological Basis for Creative Writing." *English Journal* 25 (1936): 292-301.

Lauer, Janice. "Heuristics and Composition." *College Composition and Communication* 21 (1970): 396-404.

Lunsford, Andrea. "The Content of Basic Writers' Essays." *College Composition and Communication* 31 (1980): 278-90.

Macrorie, Ken. "To Be Read." *English Journal* 57 (1968): 686-92.

McCloskey, Donald N. "The Literary Character of Economics." *Daedalus* 113.3 (1984): 97-119.

Miller, George A., Eugene Galanter, and Karl Pribram. *Plans and the Structure of Behavior*. New York: Holt, 1962.

Moffett, James. "Writing, Inner Speech, and Meditation." *College English* 44 (1982): 231-44.

Myers, Greg. "Texts as Knowledge Claims: The Social Construction of Two Biologists' Articles." *Social Studies of Science* 15 (1985): 593-630.

——————— . "Writing Research and the Sociology of Scientific Knowledge: A Review of Three New Books." *College English* 48 (1986): 595-610.

Newell, Alan, and Herbert A. Simon. *Human Problem Solving*. Englewood Cliffs, NJ: Prentice-Hall, 1972.

Odell, Lee, and Dixie Goswami, eds. *Writing in Nonacademic Settings*. New York: Guilford, 1985.

Ohmann, Richard. *English in America: A Radical View of the Profession*. New York: Oxford UP, 1976.

Reddy, Michael J. "The Conduit Metaphor." *Metaphor and Thought*. Ed. Andrew Ortony. Cambridge: Cambridge UP, 1979. 284-324.

Reither, James A. "Writing and Knowing: Toward Redefining the Writing Process." *College English* 47 (1985): 620-28.

Rohman, D. Gordon, "Pre-Writing: The Stage of Discovery in the Writing Process." *College Composition and Communication* 16 (1965): 106-12.

Rohman, D. Gordon, and Alfred O. Wlecke. "Pre-Writing: The Construction and Application of Models for Concept Formation in Writing." U.S. Department of Health, Education, and Welfare Cooperative Research Project No. 2174. East Lansing: Michigan State U, 1964.

Scardamalia, Marlene, Carl Bereiter, and Hillel Goelman. "The Role of Production Factors in Writing Ability." *What Writers Know: The Language, Process, and Structure of Written Discourse.* Ed. Martin Nystrand. New York: Academic, 1982. 173-210.

Stewart, Donald. "Prose with Integrity: A Primary Objective." *College Composition and Communication* 20 (1969): 223-27.

Voss, Ralph. "Janet Emig's *The Composing Processes of Twelfth Graders:* A Reassessment." *College Composition and Communication* 34 (1983): 278-83.

Williams, Raymond. *Keywords: A Vocabulary of Culture and Society.* New York: Oxford, 1976.

Young, Art. "Considering Values: The Poetic Function of Language." *Language Connections.* Ed. Toby Fulwiler and Art Young. Urbana: NCTE, 1982. 77-97.

Young, Richard. "Paradigms and Problems: Needed Research in Rhetorical Invention." *Research on Composing: Points of Departure.* Ed. Charles R. Cooper and Lee Odell. Urbana: NCTE, 1978. 29-47.

Joseph Alkana, Andrew Cooper, Beth Daniell, Kristine Hansen, Greg Myers, Carolyn Miller, and Walter Reed made helpful comments on earlier drafts of this essay.

PART TWO

Stories from the
Writing Classroom

"Their story, yours, mine—it's what we all carry with us on this trip we take, and we owe it to each other to respect our stories and learn from them."

William Carlos Williams as told to Robert Coles

The stories in our lives are a remarkable source for growth and understanding. In the teaching of writing, stories are especially important, first because writing itself is personal, and second because the general pull of our culture is toward abstraction rather than story. Teachers tend to overlook the value of story as a rich storehouse for learning, turning instead to methodology, professional jargon, the adoption of a teacher persona, and other impersonal means that sometimes stand between teacher and student and inhibit the learning process. Included in this section are stories from writing teachers at all grade levels, for stories somehow transcend age and other superficial kinds of difference. The college teacher can learn much from the elementary teacher, and vice versa. There is something personal and compelling in all these stories, something that invites us to learn and grow.

Although the stories in this section have theory embedded in them, it is the story itself which seems most compelling. A story has several advantages over a theoretical statement. For example, the story provides a richer context than a description of theory. It provides a "feel" or "flavor," something of the human dimension purposefully omitted in the abstraction. The story occurs at a deeper, more primal level, and it has the power to speak directly to another—at its own level and on its own terms. Stories may be described as "raw" data, but an even better description would be "pure" or "uncontaminated" data. In the story, we see the original events, before someone else has drawn conclusions or made assumptions, a process which itself is open to bias and error. There is, of course, a place for theory, but story has its place too. This section is an eloquent reminder of the power of story and its ability to communicate in ways which theory doesn't understand.

In the opening essay, "On Stories and Scholarship," Richard Murphy not only provides a rationale for using story but weaves marvelous examples of stories from his own experience throughout the account. "The irony of my argument," he laments, "is that I am making it at all. I should just use this space to tell a story...." His argument is compelling and deserves close reading.

The legacy which Carol Avery describes is about Laura, a child in her first-grade classroom, but it is also about herself, the teacher, and about every other child in the class. Ultimately, it touches the life of the reader, thus spreading over many miles and through time. Following "Laura's Legacy" is a series of vignettes from *Writing in Trust,* a collection of teacher writing published by the Southeastern Educational Improvement Laboratory. Karen Rose, Alice Ackley, and Diane Price explore the joy and frustration in the teaching of writing.

At first glance, Nancie Atwell's story appears to be about the "Big Desk," but it is really about herself and the transformation she experienced as a teacher of writing. What it means to be an author, Atwell suggests, is to find your own subjects for writing, not look to the teacher to find them for you. Peggy Swoger, using the workshop approach with her ninth-grade special education students, gently encouraged them, "Tell me about your story." Scott, whose disability was diagnosed as Attention Deficit Disorder, responded, at first slowly, but by the end of the year he had shown four years of growth in reading and writing. Scott's breakthrough in learning is what teachers look for, and this moving account illustrates what makes it possible.

The next two stories come from the college classroom. Dick Harrington, the teacher, meets General Apache, the student, and in the process both lives are changed. The reader is encouraged to note the creative energy which this article reveals. The healing process is also evident in "A Prayer in Spring" by Nanette Mengel, who teaches in the University of North Carolina Evening College. Both of these accounts illustrate that the teaching of writing at its best involves personal transformation.

The concluding essay in this section is Robert Brooke's "Underlife and Writing Instruction," which won the distinguished Braddock award for 1987. Brooke's purpose is to show how the concept of underlife applies to the writing classroom, and in the process, he uses the techniques of story, particularly dialogue and personal example. Further, the concept itself is similar to what we think of as story. Brooke's work illustrates how story can inform our research efforts and tacitly argues that good research is not necessarily quantitative.

In his conclusion, Brooke touches on an idea that runs through all the articles in this section—the ways people change and grow in the writing classroom: "Writing, in short, is 'about' autonomy and action—to really learn to write means becoming a certain kind of person, a person who accepts, explores, and uses her differences from assigned roles to produce new knowledge, new action, and new roles."

On Stories and Scholarship

RICHARD J. MURPHY, JR.

In *The Making of Knowledge in Composition* (Boynton/Cook, 1987), Stephen North claims that we need to give credit again to a kind of knowledge that has in recent years been deprecated. According to North, this knowledge—what he calls "lore"—has a profound influence on all of us involved in composition studies. It is practitioner knowledge, the knowledge of teachers. Teachers need to defend it, and themselves, North says, "to argue for the value of what they know, and how they come to know it" (55).

This is the task I want to work toward here. These are notes toward a re-evaluation of teacher knowledge and of what I think is the most important form in which that knowledge is represented—stories.

Making Autobiography

Barbara Hardy says that human beings cannot keep from telling stories. Sleeping and waking we tell ourselves and each other the stories of our days: "We mingle truths and falsehoods, not always quite knowing where one blends into the other. As we sleep we dream dreams from which we wake to remember, half-remember and almost remember, in forms that may be dislocated, dilapidated or deviant but are recognizably narrative... [Stories are the] autobiography we are all engaged in making and remaking, as long as we live, which we never complete, though we all know how it is going to end" (*Tellers and Listeners,* Athlone, 1975, 4).

During a graduation party across the street last spring, I stood in my neighbor's kitchen drying dishes and talking with her about her son David's writing. She had recently read something he had written for one of his high-school teachers. She had found it almost unintelligible, full of what she called "gunk." When she asked him why he didn't just come out and say what he meant, David told her that his teachers don't want that. They want it all gunked up, he said. They want it indirect, hidden. "*Do* they?" she asked me suddenly, looking at me intently as if I knew. "Do they want *that?*" I said no as quickly as I could, and she went on: "Well, I didn't think so. I thought they wanted kids to make sense, but David was *sure*. No doubt in his mind at all. Bullshit. The kids know it's bullshit, and they think the teachers want it anyway."

College Composition and Communication, 40 (December 1989), pp. 466-472. Copyright © 1989 by the National Council of Teachers of English. Reprinted with permission.

I was drying the dishes and setting them on the kitchen table. She was putting them away. Thinking about David and David's teacher reminded me of Rhonda and me.

A student in one of my introductory composition courses, Rhonda had done some writing one day in class, open-ended writing, free, a memory trace. In it she suddenly happened on a moment from her childhood. She was rocking her little sister (the sister she never liked) in the front-porch rocker at their home in Buchanan, Virginia. Both girls were giggling gaily when the chair— and Rhonda's little sister—tipped off the porch into the yard. Everyone rushed out of the house and tried to comfort the fallen child. Even Rhonda looked concerned for her sister, asking if she was hurt, saying she was sorry it happened, patting her on the head. Soon it was clear that no real harm had been done. The chair was returned to the porch, and the girls were cautioned against rocking too close to the rail-less edge. But no one knew—not her sister, not her parents—what really happened: that she deliberately flipped her sister into the yard because she disliked her so.

When Rhonda called me over in class to ask me what she should do next, I suggested that she write more, that she go back through the incident, enlarge it, texture it, sharpen its meanings. I crouched down in the aisle next to her plastic and steel desk, balanced myself with my right hand on the edge of the desk top, and urged her to write more. What was it like to have a little sister you never liked? Why didn't you like her? What was it like to have her sitting in that chair and you rocking and hearing her squeals of delight? What was it like to be giggling so hard and then to hear yourself giggle, to be intent on rocking your sister and then to have the thought steal up on you that you could hurt her? What was it like to notice how the chair was edging slowly, almost imperceptibly, toward the side of the porch, and then to keep on rocking and laughing as it moved? I urged her to write more because already, in reading that first rush of memory, I could feel in it not only Rhonda's story but yours and mine as well, not the story of just one moment but of her whole childhood, perhaps of her whole life.

When I heard my neighbor describe her son's guess about what his teachers wanted, I began to imagine what Rhonda must have thought. I pictured her getting back to her dorm room in Stuart Hall and trying to tell her roommate about what had happened during English. About how her teacher liked what she wrote and told her to go on writing. About how she didn't really understand what he wanted her to do. "He told me to write more," she's likely to have said, "but I don't know...I wrote all there was to it already. I don't know what more there is to say. I guess I could put some other gunk in, but I don't know if it'll be what he wants."

This story of Rhonda and David, of high school and Freshman English, of kitchens and classrooms, has little in the way of data. It is based on no tape-recorded conversation, no protocols, and—because I did not keep copies of Rhonda's writing—no scripts. It has no systematic analysis, no findings, no conclusion even. To ask if it is valid or reliable is to ask an impertinent question. It is just a story of a teacher trying to think about his work, remembering some, making some up, trying to sort out the puzzle of his experience. It is very hard—even for him—to tell where memory ends and imagination begins.

In Book I of *The Prelude,* Wordsworth tells of a harrowing experience made up of both memory and imagination. Once, as a young boy, he stole a boat and rowed stealthily out onto a moonlit lake. It was an act, he says, "of troubled pleasure." The night was clear and silent, the lake beautiful, but the traces of the boy's movements were everywhere—in the voices of the mountain echoes that followed his oars, in the line of moonwashed pools that stretched out behind the boat as he rowed. He felt a wonderful exhilaration in his skill, in the speed and power with which he rowed through the stillness, but all the while he trembled with fear. Then he noticed something. Behind the small ridge under which the boy had found the boat, there was a huge cliff hidden from his sight when he was close to shore. As he rowed onto the lake, however, this cliff gradually came more and more into view. It seemed to rise up as he rowed. Wordsworth says that it seemed alive. We know the cliff was solid and inanimate, and the boy knew it too, but the more he rowed away from the edge of the lake the larger it loomed. The faster he rowed the more insistently it rose. All his guilt and fear amassed themselves in that mountain and strode after him, until finally he shrank, turned the boat, and crept back to where he had found it moored.

Memory and imagination are inseparable in this story; fact and fiction merge. The story is *about* their merging. Did the mountain live that night? Did the boy steal that boat? We cannot answer these questions; we probably do not ask them. The story invites us to enter lyrically into this moment of troubled pleasure and to re-experience the animation of a vast guilt. For days after that night, Wordsworth says, he was cut off from his ordinary world:

> No familiar shapes
> Remained, no pleasant images of trees,
> Of sea or sky, no colours of green fields;
> But huge and mighty forms, that do not live
> Like living men, moved slowly through the mind
> By day, and were a trouble to my dreams. (I.395—400)

The forms that move by day through our minds as teachers may not be huge and mighty, and they may not always be the trouble of our dreams, but they have a profound impact on our teaching. They are the stories by which, as teachers, we come to understand ourselves.

Teacher Knowledge

"Teacher knowledge" is a term developed recently by educational researchers to identify the subtle understanding that grows out of teacher practice. Our knowledge enables us to respond to the complex, specific, and dynamic demands of particular teaching situations. It combines knowledge of content, pedagogical skill, and what Lee Shulman calls the "wisdom of practice" ("Knowledge and Teaching," *Harvard Educational Review* 57 [February 1987]: 11). As such, teacher knowledge is not abstract or generalized, but embedded in actual school experience. According to Walter Doyle, "[W]hat teachers know about chunks of content, instructional actions, or management strategies is tied to specific events that they have experienced in classrooms" ("Curriculum in Teacher Education," Meeting of the American Educational Research Association, April 1988). Teacher knowledge is represented, then, in one of its most important forms in the stories we tell ourselves and perhaps our fellow teachers and students of moments of our teaching and learning, moments in which we were thrilled or troubled or surprised by the most complicated joy.

During the first class meeting one semester in Freshman English, I talked too much. I do not remember why. Usually I ask students the first day to interview and introduce each other to the rest of us, but that day I did something else, so it took me far longer than usual to learn their names. It was several weeks before I felt I had a fairly sure grasp of who was who, and even then some students eluded me.

The class met in the basement of Curie, the science building, a huge black lab table at the front of the room with two sinks and a couple of gas jets. The ceiling was a maze of pipes and heating ducts. She was the quietest student. She never spoke in class. The first three class days devoted to group reading of drafts, she was absent. She sat in the second row, in the fifth desk. Even when she was present she seemed absent. Our eyes never connected. When I looked over to her, she was always looking down, writing some note or other, picking paper scraps out of her notebook spiral.

She gave me her first and third essays to read and mark. I cannot remember what they were about. The second essay she brought to my office for a conference. The fourth essay she did not submit. The rest of her record is blank. On the twelfth of October, I received a form memo from the Dean, addressed to me and all her other teachers, informing us that she had withdrawn from the university. Almost our entire relationship, then, is bound up for me in that one conference in my office during which we talked about her second essay. I do not have a copy of her paper, but I remember it.

It was a letter to her grandfather who lived in northern California, a letter of thanks for the summer she had just spent with him. She was trying to explain why the visit was so important to her. Having grown up in the East, she had never seen the West Coast, never seen the grey, fog-bound Pacific. All summer she and her grandfather had lived together in his small house near the water. They had wandered along the beach, watched the weather and the shore birds, talked, permitted each other to sit alone in silence. She wanted him to know how much it had meant to her, that summer, and the feeling was practically beyond words.

She told me that she couldn't read the paper to her classmates. When she tried to read it aloud to me in my office, she was unable to make it all the way through. Coming to college had been hard for her, she said by way of explanation, far harder than she had thought it would be. But she wanted to send the letter to her grandfather; she had something to tell him that she wanted him to know. When she stopped reading, I read the rest aloud myself.

One day she was down on the beach alone. At the edge of the ocean, on a shelf of still wet sand she came upon a dying seal. She didn't know what to do. The seal's glistening body heaved, but otherwise it did not move. Its eyes were open. She knelt down next to it and waited. All day she waited there, watching. Once, when she reached her hand out and rested it on the fur of the seal's neck, she could feel its labored breathing in her fingers. She quickly pulled her hand away. Later she found that she could caress its side without feeling that she was making its work harder, so for a while she did that. Eventually the seal's eyes closed, and before the tide came back in its panting also stopped. She still sat there for a time. When she finally rose to dig a grave for the seal, her legs were sore and locked tight, so she stumbled in her awkward work. When she was done with the burial, she smoothed the sand with her hands and left the water to do the rest.

The reason she was writing this to her grandfather was that she had not told him about it at the time. She had made up some story about her day—she didn't know why, couldn't say even now, something about how she felt, well, *responsible* for that death—and now she wanted him to know the truth.

By the end of the fourth week of the semester, she had stopped coming to class. By the end of the fifth, she was gone.

Such a story reminds me that I am sometimes helpless as a teacher, that sometimes all I can do is sit by and watch. But I want to resist turning the story into a parable. If I try to say what its "point" is, I have to generalize the experience—her, me, the seal, the paper, and that mythic seashore where she knelt. If it can be analyzed into domains, if it can be reduced to findings or implications for research, I want to insist that it was not made to have any. It is a story, one fragment of my knowledge as a teacher.

Literary Scholarship

As we reconsider teacher knowledge, we need to distinguish such stories from case study. However much a case depends on rich description and narration, its meaning is propositional, a statement of abstract generalization. As Lee Shulman puts it in "Those Who Understand: Knowledge Growth in Teaching" (*Educational Researcher* [February 1986]: 4-14), "To call something a case is to make a theoretical claim—to argue that it is a 'case of something,' or to argue that it is an instance of a larger class" (11). The meaning of the stories we tell ourselves about our lives and work, on the other hand, is aesthetic. We recreate the past, selecting its particulars and making them vivid, in order to re-experience them imaginatively. The meaning of a case depends on its systematic construction—on the internal validity with which it is drawn from the data, reduced, analyzed, and interpreted. The meaning of the stories I think we should tell and value lies in their forceful representation of the experience of teaching and learning, in their believability, in their memorability. Case study aspires to science. Stories of teaching and learning aspire to poetry.

Jerome Bruner makes a parallel distiction between two different ways or modes of knowing. In "Narrative and Paradigmatic Modes of Thought" (*Learning and Teaching the Ways of Knowing,* Ed. Elliot Eisner, National Society for the Study of Education, 1985 97-115), Bruner claims that the two modes differ radically. Both are important ways of making sense of the world, and they complement one another. But they are irreducible, and the differences between them are so profound that the paradigmatic cannot be said to be the "refinement" or "abstraction" of the narrative. "Moreover," Bruner concludes, "there is no direct way in which a statement derived from one mode can contradict or even corroborate a statement derived from the other" (97-98).

The distinction Bruner makes here is a familiar one. James Britton contrasts poetic and transactional writing in *Language and Learning* (U of Miami P, 1970), arguing that "one 'has meaning' in a way the other does not— and *vice versa.* If we ask 'What does it mean?' of a piece of transactional writing, we shall not expect the same sort of answer as we expect when we ask it of a poem or a novel" (178). James Moffett puts it differently in *Teaching the Universe of Discourse* (Houghton, 1968), but he too claims that the narrative and the paradigmatic are irreducible. According to Moffett, "The essence of story is once-upon-a-time. Once. Unique and unrepeatable events—not 'recurring' events, as in science." (121).

We need to remember this distinction as we develop the argument for stories in the literature of composition studies. We need to keep in mind the peculiar power of narrative to shape and articulate what we know as teachers. Stephen North calls for a new understanding of teacher lore "such that other kinds of knowledge can *usefully* interact with it" (371), but in the interest of "useful interaction" we ought not to try to make stories into something else. The meanings and methods of the stories we tell ourselves are unlike those of any systematic mode of inquiry. Their value to us depends on this difference. A renewed appreciation of them, then, will require acceptance of their non-scientific, essentially literary character.

Story

The irony of my argument is that I am making it at all. I should just use this space to tell a story, but I have been afraid to. I have included some fragments—moments of memory, spots of time—but the argument has abashed me with its claim: that the stories we tell will be deeply valuable to us, that in telling them we will define ourselves and what we know, that in hearing them we will remember who we are and what teaching and learning have come to mean to us. Still, this characterization of stories does not describe their purpose so much as their effect. The *purpose* is the same as has always moved tellers and listeners—the pleasure of the story.

My youngest son Stephen is in the fifth grade. He had to do a report this year on Marco Polo, a written report and an oral presentation in front of the class. The report was due on Friday, so on Monday he rode his bike down to the public library, looked up two encyclopedia articles on Marco Polo, made photocopies of them, and brought them home. Tuesday and Wednesday he spent at the computer, typing what he titled the "1rst Draft" of his report.

We had some grief over this draft: he wanted to use the copies of the articles he had brought home (he kept calling them his "data"; "I can't write it without my data," he kept saying); but I wanted him to write it out at least once without looking at the articles, just the way he had told it to us in the car on the way home from K-Mart. And by the way, I told him, when you get all done with this, remind me to read you a poem about Kubla Khan, the emperor with whom Marco lived and worked. He waved this away with an OK and went on with his complaint.

"You're making me do it *your* way," he said.

"Yes," I said. "Now get to work. I'm trying to type. You type, too."

By the time his mom called from the National Reading Conference in Tucson where she was spending the week, he was reconciled to his work. He had almost a page, he told her happily, pointing at the screen as he talked into the phone. "This is my first draft," he told her. "I'm free-minding it."

Thursday night I showed him how to do the spellcheck and how to doublespace (his freckled face beamed when suddenly he had two pages, not one). Then we saved his file under a new name so he wouldn't lose the earlier draft.

"You mean I get to keep them both?" he asked, amazed.

When we printed out the final version, he was so excited by it that he kept thinking of people he wanted to give copies to—his teacher, of course, and one for himself and one for me and one for his sister and one for his brother in California.

At breakfast Friday morning, as he was reading it aloud to us over his cereal, he noticed a glitch. "That's not right," he said. "'*On* Marco and his father go back to Venice'? *That's* not right. It should be '*Then* Marco and his father go back.'"

Downstairs to the computer, load up the file, make the change, save it under a new name, draft three, no time to make extra copies now, but Stephen wants his teacher to see all three versions so he grabs them all for her and races for the school bus that's already honking at the corner.

The report was a success, he told me Friday afternoon. He was nervous in front of the class, and his teacher asked him to give his presentation twice, but she said it was *excellent,* an evaluation Stephen underlined in the air with his voice.

Then I read the poem to him.

> In Xanadu did Kubla Khan
> A stately pleasure dome decree:
> Where Alph, the sacred river, ran
> Through caverns measureless to man
>   Down to a sunless sea. (1-5)

I planned to give him all sorts of explanation, but at the last moment I decided just to read. No glosses on "athwart," "cedarn," "momently," or "Mount Abora." Just the poem, trying to revive within us its symphony and song. When I got to the end, Stephen said—his highest compliment—*"Cool."*

I think he meant it. As we went up the stairs from the basement to get some more stove wood, he said, "You know the part I like best? That part about the dome of sun and the caves of ice. *"Yeah,"* he said. "That was *cool."*

Laura's Legacy

May 8, 1987
We celebrate Mother's Day in our first grade classroom this Friday afternoon. The children perform a play for their mothers entitled "The Big Race," the story of the tortoise and the hare. Laura is the "turtle" who wins the race.

A few minutes later Laura reads aloud the book she has authored about her mother. The group laughs as she reads about learning to count with her cousins when she was three years old. Laura writes: "I was learning six. Then my Mom came in and asked what we were doing. I said, 'I'm learning sex!'" Laura's mother was delighted. The reading continues with a hilarious account of a family squabble between Mom and Dad over a broken plate. Laura concludes the anecdote, "So then I just went in and watched TV." Laura looks at me and smiles as she pauses, waiting for her audience to quieten before she goes on. I wink at her; I know she is thinking, "Wait till they hear the next part. It's the funniest of all." She reads about a llama spitting in Mom's eye on a visit to the zoo. Laura's way with words has brought delight to everyone. I remember a week earlier when Laura and I sat to type her draft and she said, "This is the best part. I put it last so that everyone will feel happy at the end."

May 9, 1987
Saturday night, around 11:45 P.M., a light bulb ignites fabric in a closet outside Laura's bedroom. Laura wakes. She cannot get through the flames and by the time firefighters reach her it is too late. Laura dies. No one else is injured.

May 11, 1987
The children and I gather on our Sharing Rug in the classroom on Monday morning. I have no plans. We start to talk. There are endless interruptions until Michael says, "Mrs. Avery, can we shut the door so people stop bothering us?" So Michael shuts the door. "Are you going to read us the newspapers?" they ask. "Is that what you'd like?" "Yes," comes the unanimous response. The children huddle close; a dozen knees nuzzle against me. I read aloud the four-paragraph story on the front page of the *Sunday News* that accompanies a picture of our Laura sprawled on the lawn of her home with firefighters working over her. I read the longer story in Monday morning's paper that carries Laura's school picture. We cry. We talk and cry some more. And then we

Language Arts, 65 (February 1988), pp. 110-111. Copyright © 1988 by the National Council of Teachers of English. Reprinted with permission.

read Laura's books—writings which Laura determined were her best throughout the year and which were "published" to become part of our classroom library. These books are stories of Laura and her family, stories with titles such as *My Dad Had a Birthday* and *When My Grandmother Came to My House.* Laura's voice comes through loud and clear with its sense of humor and enthusiasm. We laugh and enjoy her words. "Laura was a good writer," they say. "She always makes us laugh when we read her stories." Then Dustin says, "You know, it feels like Laura is right here with us, right now. We just can't see her."

A short time later we begin our writing workshop. Every child chooses to write about Laura this day. Some write about the fire, some write memories of Laura as a friend. I write with them. After forty-five minutes it is time to go to art and there are cries of disappointment at having to stop. We will come back to the writing. There will be plenty of time. The last five weeks of school will be filled with memories of Laura as we work through our loss together. The children will decide to leave her desk in it's place in the room because, "It's not in our way and anyway, this is still Laura's room even if she's not really here anymore." Laura's mother and little brother will come in to see us. On the last day they will bring us garden roses that Laura would have brought. Laura will always be a part of us and none of us will ever be the same.

In the days immediately following Laura's death and in the weeks since then certain thoughts have been rattling around in my head: I'm so glad that I teach the way I do. I'm so glad I really knew Laura. I know that I can never again teach in a way that is not focused on children. I can never again put a textbook or a "program" between me and the children. I'm glad I knew Laura so well. I'm glad all of us knew her so well. I'm glad the classroom context allowed her to read real books, to write about real events and experiences in her life, to share herself with us and to become part of us and we of her. I'm grateful for a classroom community that nurtured us all throughout the year and especially when Laura was gone. Laura left a legacy. Part of that legacy is the six little published books and the five-inch-thick stack of paper that is her writing from our daily writing workshops. When we read her words, we hear again her voice and her laughter.

Three Stories from *Writing in Trust*

Who's Bright?

KAREN ROSE

Because he hadn't appeared in class at all in the three weeks since the semester had begun, I dropped his name from the roll and recommended that he be dropped from the course. Three days later as I sat in my office grading student compositions, I imagined I heard—and then realized I really had heard—a faint, feathery tapping on the door. I glanced up to see who had responded to the impatient "Come in!" I'd shouted over my shoulder and saw the most windblown, disheveled figure I ever could have imagined.

"Oh, no. I couldn't. I was responsible for the two pepperoni pizzas in the back seat."

His tennis shoes were caked with dried mud of varied hues, and one shoelace was held together by two filthy knots. One leg of his jeans looked like new, navy denim; the other was faded and worn to a fuzzy softness. His camouflage Army jacket, pockets bulging with who-knows-what treasures, was buttoned all the way to his throat like a child's winter car coat. Topping the broad expanse of his black, featureless face was Medusa hair, twisted, curled, and cowlicked in a thousand different directions.

His almost invisible eyes finally found mine as he mumbled through barely moving lips, "Miss Rose? I'm Bright."

Dear God, I thought, which of my friends has set this up. Choking back my laughter, I decided I'd play along. "Are you really? What make you think so?"

"Ma'am?"

"Bright. What makes you think you're so bright?"

"That's my name. I'm George Bright. From your 7:50 freshman comp. class?"

Ah, the invisible Mr. Bright I'd so recently stricken from my roll.

"Oh, George," I gushed, trying to cover my embarrassment. "You haven't

Writing in Trust: A Tapestry of Teachers' Voices, edited by Sam Watson; Research Triangle Park, North Carolina: Southeastern Educational Improvement Laboratory, 1989. Reprinted by permission of the publisher and the editor.

made it to class a single time in over three weeks, so I've dropped your name from the class roll."

"That's why I'm here, Miss Rose. My adviser told me I should come and explain that I'm an unusual case."

No kidding! Unusual seemed such a mild word!

"I've just gotten out of the hospital," he went on to explain as he rummaged through his jacket pockets and finally landed on a crumpled ball of paper. Unfolding it and trying to press the wrinkles out of it with a hand whose fingernails were caked with what looked like automotive grease, he went on.

"Was there for six weeks. I was in an accident. Hit by a train."

This was going too far. Did my friends honestly believe that I was so gullible I'd fall for this?

George thrust the fingerprint-covered letter into my hands, and there on the letterhead stationery was verification of his story. According to the doctor who'd treated him, George had been struck by a train, had sustained extensive injuries, and had been hospitalized for almost six weeks.

"You're not kidding, are you, George?"

"Nope. It's the truth. My car stalled on the tracks and I was hit."

"And you just sat there? You didn't leave your car and run for your life?"

George, it seemed, worked for a local pizza delivery company and had been imbued, through a series of harsh lectures and company pep talks, with the understanding of his professional responsibility to his pizzas and his store manager. This manager intimidated and bullied him mercilessly, so—naturally —when George's car stalled on the railroad tracks, he had felt it his obligation to guard with his life the pizzas he was preparing to deliver. After all, he couldn't risk being yelled at by his boss, could he?

I laughed at and pitied George Bright for years, amazed that anybody with any degree of sense could so fear an authority figure. It's frightening, I thought to myself, to realize how easily the George Brights of this world can be intimidated and used. Why don't they learn to stand up for themselves?

About four years after George had passed through my office, I was teaching in another school system where, as the new principal made it clear, the faculty was expected to participate in all facets of school life. For no additional benefits or compensation, we were to sell tickets at football, soccer, basketball, and baseball games; organize the prom and assorted school dances; serve on scholarship, reaccreditation, hospitality, and advisory committees; and attend workshops on improving our communication, writing, and listening skills. And we were to teach, individually, each of the 150 students who came our way every day.

Like the rest of the faculty, I complained, I groused, and I did as I was told. After all, I was reminded whenever I hesitantly offered an unsolicited opinion, there were "fifteen qualified teachers lined up, ready and willing" to take my job. I would do as I was told, or else!

I was, as I had been assigned, selling tickets at a basketball game late in the winter that year. Sitting in the tiny unheated ticket booth that opened to the arctic February air, I angrily berated myself. Why was I doing this? Why was the principal making us do so many extra things that we didn't have time to grade papers or prepare for classes? Why wasn't somebody telling him how unfair it all was?

In mid-complaint, I glanced up at a figure crossing the parking lot and walking toward the gym. Spotlighted in the dim glow of the parking lot lights, the figure—wearing worn jeans and a camouflage jacket topped with Medusa hair—approached closer and closer.

It didn't matter that the man who bought the ticket wasn't really George. All I'd needed was that momentary glimpse of George's ghost to recall the impatience and pity I'd felt years earlier for the teenager who couldn't say no to authority.

The words I'd said then with such a sense of superiority echoed through my mind and slapped me in the face.

"What makes you think you're so bright?"

I never sold tickets at another game.

How Important to Publish

ALICE ACKLEY

At a football game, a student I had taught nearly nine years before brought his wife and child over to meet me. What did he remember most about having me as a teacher? He remembered the time his below-grade-level class had written some haikus in class and I had typed them up and run them off. To my amazement, he pulled a battered copy of his poem out of his wallet. He said he had carried it with him since the day I handed it to him.

Some afternoons it was a trial when "Jimmy" came by my room after school. He would ask about my health, my day at school, my plans for the evening, and then after much twisting around, out of his well-worn pea jacket, it would come, the poem he had written during the day at school. None of this could be hurried and he never came by unless he had a poem for me to read "if it's not too much trouble."

Slowly, I got to know him. His father was a brutal man, his mother was not of the highest moral fiber, his brothers and all but one sister had all dropped out of high school. During one two-month period in the winter, I found out later, his father had beaten him and thrown him out of the house. He lived in his car.

All through that period he was producing poems for me to read, poems about love and beauty in the world. Many of his poems ended up in the school literary magazine.

I knew there was something happening on the Friday he came by without a poem. "I just wanted to tell you I can't fight it no more. I've enlisted in the Army."

He called me three nights before I left for the workshop at Wildacres in the fall of 1987. Jimmy, the dropout, has published two books of poetry in Japan in Japanese; another book of his poems has been published in the Philippine language, too. Jimmy has completed two years of college in Japan, going when he wasn't on duty, and is out of the service and planning to go to college to become a teacher. I asked him why he thought he had broken the mold for his family. "I think it was seeing my poem published with my name beside it."

Notes from a Writing Teacher in Late Spring

DIANE PRICE

Writing to learn took on new meaning for me and my students last spring. My own journal writing revealed not only evidence of the students' movement toward new self-awareness, but my own as well.

First Week

MONDAY—Debbie came into my class today hugging the current issue of *Modern Bride.* I pointed to the magazine and said, "Interesting choice of reading material." She replied, "We're gonna get married Sunday-After-Graduation. Don't worry Mrs. Price, I'll go on to school."

I know this is a general-level English class, and I expect this will be the last formal education for many of them. But I had hoped Debbie would understand the promise of empowerment in continuing her education. She haunts me; the daily activities in my classroom seem so inconsequential. I also feel the indictment of Paul Simon's words, "When I look back on all the crap I learned in high school, it's a wonder I can think at all." Must remember to make lesson plans.

TUESDAY—Today, for Debbie, we wrote in our journals, "Where I will be ten years from now." The boys wrote of cars, boats, motorcycles, and wives that don't have careers. Or they wrote of fantastical endeavors: "I'm gonna be a movie star," or "a singer like Stevie Wonder." The girls wrote of fabulous careers that were turned down for husbands, babies, four-bedroom houses, beach homes, and several cars.

What a perception of the future! All in ten years. Ouch! I'll be 50. Oh, fiddle dee dee, I'll think about that tomorrow. Now, tonight, I feel like crying—

Why? For lost dreams? Theirs? Mine? For the loss of childhood? Lesson plans?

WEDNESDAY—Using yesterday's journal entry, each student compiled a personal list of "Desirables." These desirables could be a role, a relationship, or a material possession. One list was:

- owner of a radio station
- two-story, four-bedroom house
- three children
- wife (with a college degree, but who dosen't work)
- Mercedes
- beach house

I sent them out, tonight, to interview an "older person" about dreams and goals. What had that person wanted from life, and how does he or she feel about the success or failure of attaining those goals? I suggested finding an interviewee at the retirement home if there weren't any older people in their neighborhoods. Maybe this is the groundwork for a character sketch.

I am still troubled by their belief that these "Desirables" are attainable within ten years. I hope Debbie will go to the retirement home. There are a number of females there who never really had an occupation. Even if she hears what I want her to hear, will she listen?

THURSDAY—Those few students who had interviewed their older person helped those who felt less confident. Debbie hasn't done hers yet. We put twenty interview questions on the board; twelve were very good. The interview is to be completed by Monday.

How much longer will this sustain their interest?

FRIDAY—Discussed character sketches. Read a few; modeled writing some pieces on the board. Mary's description of Rosicky in *Neighbor Rosicky* was so good to use because of its simplicity. The students even got into the simile stuff—"mustache like a buggy rake," "back like an old turtle." I have thought of a reading assignment. Read one of the following books: *Of Mice and Men* or *The Member of the Wedding.* They will have two weeks to read. (If I do this with an advanced group, I would include in the list *The Great Gatsby* and *The Death of a Salesman.*) I am also assigning Reader Response Journals. These will be done as homework, but we will use them as springboards for discussion. I read aloud a short selection from their textbook, and we wrote a response. After sharing, and some more modeling, they still felt insecure.

Will they get the dream stuff in the novels? I think they're insecure because they don't believe in the validity of their responses to literature. They try to detach their feelings from literature and wait for me to supply the "right" response. But I feel good about our trying it. Monday, I think we'll go back to the list of "Desirables."

Second Week

MONDAY—This morning I was sharing what seems to be a developing unit of study with a vocational teacher. She gave me enough copies of the SELF-DIRECTED SEARCH for all my students to have a copy! When we finished, some students were shocked by their career/aptitude/interest cluster. It didn't jive with their list of "Desirables." But for others, it was support for their dreams. Character sketch drafts due Wednesday.

All I can say is, "God looks after teachers." I never thought that I would have such a stroke of luck. Maybe the key was sharing my struggle with the other professionals. Tomorrow, and Tomorrow, and Tomorrow creeps in with no lesson plans.

TUESDAY—I must be thinking about these classes in my sleep. When I opened my eyes this morning, I sensed the rightness of trying Ken Macrorie's "I-Search" with this career thing. Most of them want to use a career from their cluster on the SDS.

I am afraid of letting them research "any" topic, but I could learn how this method works if all the students are researching a career. I want to make sure they have a projected salary, a sense of the availability of a job, a list of institutions that would qualify them, and an interview with a person in their chosen profession. Debbie chose business administration. How many will research teaching?

Most students have selected a novel; few have begun. Some shared Response Journal entries. We completed the first steps of the "I-Search."

The more I use editing groups, the more I learn how to use them. Peer editors don't find every mistake. They are only teenagers, and their mistakes belong to them, also. I am astounded at the high level of interest in my classroom. But, they had better get busy on the outside reading. This research stuff is library activity, and I want that book read at home. The first steps of the "I-Search" went well—Maybe it will be OK. Library, tomorrow.

THURSDAY—I assigned a reading test for Monday on the first third of the novel. While we were in the library, several students needed conferences concerning their character sketches.

FRIDAY—Library. Several more conferences. Some students and I had an interesting discussion in the stacks. The term "fringe benefits" meant nothing to them. I explained insurance, death benefits, workers' compensation, expense accounts, and anything else I could think of. Finally, John said, "Oh yeah, it's like something your boss gives you that is extra, more than your salary. And it's better to have a job with some of them."

Third Week

MONDAY—Collected character sketches; they look good. Reading test: Assume the persona of Lennie or Bernice. Write a journal entry about your biggest problem. No time to go to the library.

TUESDAY—Library. Good reading test—for those who read. Debbie made 100; she is reading *The Member of the Wedding*.

WEDNESDAY—Library. Conferences about interviews.

I am amazed at the level of fear in my students that adults will not talk to them. I reinforced the initial steps to an interview and the idea that most people like to discuss their work.

THURSDAY—Library. Seems OK with the "I-Search." Thanks to the *Occupational Outlook Handbook*.

FRIDAY—Only a few days of research left. Assigned discussion groups on novels for Monday.

Fourth Week

MONDAY—Questions for Discussion Groups:

- What is the dream in your novel?

- Why did this dream develop?

- Did the dream come true? Why? Why not?

- Was the central character happy or sad? At the beginning? At the end?

- Were there any similarities in both books in the dreams and their outcomes?

- Were there any differences in the writing style used by the authors?

- After reading the novels, can your group write any generalizations (lessons) about life?

They didn't finish, and I had planned ten minutes in editing groups. I am really pleased with the "I-Search." This unit could be evolving into something that I may use again. It has been so accidental, I am almost afraid to trust it. But, it was very exciting to hear a student say to his group, "In that last scene where George kills Lennie, do you think Lennie sees heaven?"

TUESDAY—Continued discussion on the novels. Editing groups for the "I-Search" Monday.

My students are so excited. I must be doing something right. I can't bring myself to stop their discussion (which is often heated) with my lecture on symbolism, etc. Are they being cheated?

WEDNESDAY-FRIDAY—Library.

Fifth Week

MONDAY—Editing groups really polish students' work. Papers are due Thursday. Test on the novel will be Friday. I am so proud of their research that I will share some of it with the vocational teachers and my supervisor. I told the students what I would be doing with their work. I think I will test plot and character only. Their discussion has been so powerful—the test seems less important. I want to go back to the original set of "Desirables."

THURSDAY—Response journals were shared and discussed.

It is astounding how many of them cued in on the loneliness facet of each novel. Some responses were very good; others were so-so. But next time more students will be successful!

WEDNESDAY—First, we developed a composite list of "Desirables."

Each class generated a somewhat different list, but all included a house, two/three children, cars, wives that don't work in spite of years of preparation (why does that continue to amaze me?), and vacation homes. Some classes opted for big yearly vacations instead of a second home. I provided the monetary value for many of the items on the list. Next year, I will assign a "Desirable" to each group within the class and send them into the community —to banks, mortgage companies, day care centers, insurance agents, real estate offices. I believe the community research will be more powerful than my assuming the resident-expert role.

Then, I instructed the students to use the beginning salary according to their research and budget their money. We budgeted the money or tried to budget the money. In every single class, most of the students ran out of money before food and clothing. Several of them became very frustrated because of the constant revision of "Desirables." That budget is the key to their perception of the future, and they are working very hard at it. The bell rang, but homework is trying to balance the budget. I wish Debbie had been here today. I put off the "I-Search" until Friday, and the test will be Monday.

I don't know now where this unit is coming from, but I am ending one of the most powerful days I have ever had in the classroom. Each student has a personal stake in the budget that was the result of his or her own research. Each one sweated out success or failure. My role changed drastically; I was needed only when they were totally stumped and their friends couldn't provide the solution. Yet, the classroom was relatively quiet. But, it was electric with the energy of a combined purpose. When someone finally balanced the budget, we all cheered!

THURSDAY—We worked more successfully with the budgets. As I was walking around the room, Paul looked up at me and said, "This is why my Dad doesn't smile so much."

Why are my feelings so bittersweet? I feel good because Paul has made a real discovery about a human being named "Dad." I am sad because Paul has glimpsed some of the truth of adult lives. Did the money make the future real? I think from now on, my professional life will be dated from today. Our work has transcended anything else I have ever done. Why? Is it because the work began with a student—Debbie? Is it because I had a powerful response to Debbie's vision of the future? Is it because my life has not been a fulfillment of my adolescent dreams? Has it all been serendipity? Isn't all of life a happy accident?

FRIDAY—"I-Search" papers were taken up, discussion continued about budgets.

Sixth Week

MONDAY—Test on the novel. Some wrap-up discussion. Some of the students went to see the movies of these novels. I recommended to the librarian that we add *The Member of the Wedding* to our collection. Wednesday through Friday we will watch *Of Mice and Men*.

TUESDAY—Journal entry: What have I learned during the past few weeks?

During our discussion, Peanut said, "Mrs. Price, don't do this with seniors no more. It's too late for me. I would have took a math this year if I had known then what I know now. Do this with juniors; they have a chance to change before they graduate."

EPILOGUE—I know good advice when I hear it.

Everyone Sits at a Big Desk:
Discovering Topics for Writing

NANCIE ATWELL

For longer than I care to remember, students in my junior high English classes wrote a composition a week on the good, creative topics their good, creative teacher assigned. Every Monday I orchestrated a pre-writing activity, and every Friday I collected final drafts to read and grade, evaluating, I know now, based on how well each writer had guessed the scenario in my head. Students wrote narratives, poetry, persuasion, essays, journals, and all manner of dramatic writing. And from my perspective of the big desk at the front of the classroom, it looked as if real writing were going on out there. In fact, although some tasks were engaging, most were, plain and simple, exercises—what James Britton calls "dummy runs." Underneath the veneer of my assignment lurked some unexamined—and pretty faulty—assumptions.

I assigned topics because I believed most of my students wouldn't write without them. I assigned topics because I believed my structures and strictures were necessary for kids to write well. I assigned topics, when it came right down to it, because I believed my ideas were more valuable than any my students might possibly entertain. So decreeing topics wasn't just philosophical; it was political, too. Writing well became a matter of writing appropriately and convincingly about my ideas, and I chalked up ineffective or perfunctory responses to low ability or effort.

Lucy Calkins has written about the "underground curriculum" teachers often fail to acknowledge and tap. Sitting there at my big desk, developing new assignments and evaluating the results, I remained oblivious to the grade eight underground curriculum—my students' ideas, experiences, and expertise. I remained in charge.

When Students Discover Their Own Topics

Four years ago, a language arts curriculum committee on which I served decided to investigate how children acquire language. It was our good fortune that Susan Sowers was one of the consultants we looked to for answers.

Sowers, Donald Graves, and Lucy Calkins were then nearing the end of their second year as researchers-in-residence at Atkinson Academy, a public

English Journal, 74 (September 1985), pp. 35-39. Copyright © 1985 by the National Council of Teachers of English. Reprinted with permission.

elementary school in rural New Hampshire. Under a grant from the National Institute of Education, they spent these two years following sixteen first- and third-grade writers and their teachers, observing students *in the process* of composing to discover how children develop as writers. Susan brought to our curriculum committee meeting copies of reports from their study. She also brought her authority as a teacher and researcher, a wealth of knowledge—and patience. What she had to say was not what I wanted to hear.

Children in the Graves team's study learned to write by exercising all the options available to real-world authors, including daily time for writing, conferences with teachers and peers, and opportunities to draft, revise, and publish their writing; most significantly, they took responsibility for deciding what and why and for whom they would write.

Because the topics were their own, these young writers had an investment in their writing. They cared about content and correctness. They wrote on a range of topics and in a variety of modes wider than their teachers had dreamed of assigning. The writers and their writing flourished as teachers came out from behind their big desks to observe, listen to, and learn from their students.

I kept Susan at our school much later that day than she intended to stay, explaining the reasons her findings couldn't possibly apply to me and my students. All that week I continued to explain, to anyone who would listen, how Sowers had advocated topic anarchy. But on my free periods and in the evening, I read and reread the manuscripts she'd shared. And I saw through my defenses to the truth. I didn't know how to share responsibility with my students, and I wasn't too sure I wanted to. I liked the vantage of my big desk; I liked setting topic and pace and establishing criteria. I liked being in charge. If responsibility for thinking and planning shifted to my students, what would *I* do?

What I did, finally, was to put the question to my students: "Children in an elementary school in New Hampshire are choosing their own topics for writing. Could you do this? Would you like to?" Resoundingly, they said yes, and the underground curriculum surfaced.

Eighth graders began writing to satisfy genuine, individual needs, discovering that in-school writing can do something for them. They recreate happy times, work through sad times, discover what they know about a subject and learn more, convey and request information, apply for jobs, parody, petition, play, argue, apologize, advise, and, through contests and professional publication, make money.

My students do have ideas for writing. Over the past four years, I've seen the critical role that self-selected topics play in their involvement and growth as writers. These writers take chances, trying new subjects, techniques, and formats. They're more apt to revise, so their writing will do what they intend it to, and more careful in editing and proofreading so readers will attend to their meanings, not their mistakes. They seldom lose pieces of writing; they talk about their writing with parents and friends; they spend much of their own time writing and thinking about their writing; they identify themselves as authors; and "literature" becomes a term that embraces students' writing, too.

Most importantly, open topic choice allows young writers to tap their own, rich, personal and academic resources. As Pam, one of my students, explained it:

> I get to find out what's important for me, what I think and have to say. It might just be some little thing, but it's a thing a teacher wouldn't know about me that I think is important. It's boring when thirty students all write the same thing. It makes me not care about it and not want to do it...I want to tell people things in my writing. I can't do that when teachers tell me what to write about.

Pam describes the sense of authority that comes when she's truly an author, sitting at her own big desk. True authorship begins with a thought that eventually becomes words on the page about an individual's interests and concerns. This is the step I'd denied with my assignments—that struggle to discover and clarify what one thinks. In denying that step, I'd usurped my students' authority.

The methods Susan Sowers described to our committee had struck me as permissive, as a sure road to undisciplined and purposeless writing. This has proved not to be the case: open topics choice does not undercut structure. Instead, it holds students accountable for developing and refining their own structures and allows me to offer individual guidance within the context of each writer's intentions. I know now that one of my roles as writing teacher is, in conferences, to help students discover and act on their options.

Making and defending writing choices is part of what Tom Newkirk calls "the democratic gamble." I'm not advocating topic anarchy either; I am arguing for a redistribution of the power of ideas and a new kind of classroom seating plan. When students initiate writing by taking responsibility for finding out what they have to say, they all sit at the big desk.

A Writer's Environment

Students in primary grades have little trouble finding subjects for writing. At this stage, Graves writes, "Their voices boom through the print." Young children are playful about language and artwork; they write and draw primarily for themselves and tend not to be self-critical. Older students, inexperienced in writing about their own ideas, have two strikes against them: self-consciousness and a sense of audience that come naturally with age, leaving many kids wanting correctness and acceptance, and too many years on the receiving end of teachers' ideas and assignments, victims of what Graves terms "the teaching cycle that places young people on writer's welfare."

Faced with decisions about topics, secondary students may balk or complain. They may try to figure the teacher's new angle—what we're really after but won't say. Or they may freeze, suffering what one of my students called "a bad case of writer's blues." Given time and a conducive environment, these writers can rediscover their voices and ideas.

During last spring's evaluation conferences—quarterly interviews between each of my students and me about their growth and efforts as writers—I conducted some simple research. Students responded to two questions: what is your best piece of writing of this quarter and where did your idea for this piece come from? Their answers describe a writer's environment—the circumstances, arrangements, and provisions that enable students to discover and explore their own ideas for writing.

Time

Frequent time for writing—in their case, every day—is crucial to my students' topic selection.

Because they write regularly, they anticipate and plan for writing time. Mindy's comment is typical. "'Attic Prize' is my best piece. It's about a personal experience that was really funny, and it sounds just like what happened—the piece is funny, too. Right after it happened I thought, 'This is going to make a great piece.' And I went to bed that night thinking, 'Tomorrow, I've *got* to write that.'"

Mindy naturally spent her off-duty time planning her writing because she knew that in the next day's class she could write. In situations where students can't write every day, three writing days each week are enough for developing the habit of gathering and considering ideas for writing. And I think the three days should be regular and consecutive—e.g., every Monday, Tuesday and Wednesday—providing the sense of continuity and routine writers need.

Talk

Talking with others—parents, friends and me—also serves as a springboard for pieces of writing. My students identified three kinds of discussion that elicited ideas: informal conversations, interviews, and writing conferences.

Mike's best piece, "Busch Gardens," came about because of a conversation with his mother: "Mom and I were talking about Maryland and Busch Gardens, 'cause she'd gone with my class on a field trip there. I said, 'Hold on, Mom!' And I wrote it down on a piece of paper to remember it." Amanda's letter to the editor of a local newspaper also started with a conversation at home. Amanda said, "My mother pointed out the paper's mistake in printing the tournament scores and said, 'Is this something to write about' And I said, 'It sure is.'"

Parents became part of a cadre of interviewers helping students discover their ideas. Bert conducted and wrote a series of interviews with area artists after his father had interviewed him. "Dad said I should do something that interested me, something I really cared about. We talked about my interests. Since art is my field, I decided to focus on local artists, to see what I could learn." Mike, Amanda and Bert were sitting at big desks at home, too, where their writing provided a new context for talking about their ideas.

Other interviews that resulted in writing ideas were conducted in school, by me or other students. Blocked writers know one of their options is to ask for a topic conference, where the interviewer asks open-ended questions about the writer's ideas and experiences. For example, an interviewer might ask, "Tell me about your weekend, family, friends, neighborhood, likes and dislikes, jobs around the house, earliest memories, hobbies, skills, fears, problems that need solving, birthday, Christmas, favorite books, movies, poems, sports, subjects, etc." At first I made copies of questions available, but these sheets saw less and less use as, through writing and conferences, students and I came to know about each others' lives and concerns. Lance wrote "Happy Valentine's Day," about a job that had required him to miss school on a day he'd really wanted to be there, because he and I talked about his situation one day after school: "I was thinking of writing it before—because it was really on my mind—but your interest got me more interested in it as something important to think and write about."

Writing conferences, where students read their pieces aloud seeking help in the form of questions and comments, are another source of ideas for writing. In conferences, students hear the topics other writers are choosing. This is how Sandy explained the origins of her essay on the nature of friendship: "Other people were writing about friends. When Mindy read me her story of what we'd be like when we were older, she gave me the idea."

Reading

Students' success in taking responsibility for their writing eventually led me to give over similar responsibility for reading, a separate course which also meets daily. I read to them, and we read stories, plays and poems as a group, but the heart of the reading course is students' self-selected texts. They read, on average, thirty books each year, with two-thirds of each week's class time devoted to independent reading. The impact of others' writing on their own happens naturally as they discover what they like to read or try out themes and techniques of authors who impress them. For example, I think two of my eighth graders' most significant writing teachers are S.E. Hinton and Robert Frost.

Six students identified elements in their best pieces as being inspired by Hinton's novel *The Outsiders*—from topic (Damon's short story about a boy caught in a gang war) to technique (Tara "made a point" in her narrative "Beautiful Mountains" because she was so impressed by the themes she identified in *The Outsiders*).

Frost's poetry has a similar influence. "Nothing Gold Can Stay" served as a model for almost a dozen student poems, including these by Billy and Dede.

Beyond the Light

The sunset is so lovely,
    with its warm colors and bright glow.
I could sit and stare for hours
    at the elegant sight.

Then I shiver
    as a cold breeze blows—
to warn me of the night.
Dede Reed

Dawn

The lake sparkled
in the light of the moon.
Dawn was near—
it would be soon.
The clouds gave off a goldish light
and broke the silence of the night.

Now the dawn has come to be noon,
just like grown-up life—all too soon.
Bill Snow

Other students' published writing—and the opportunity for students to publish their writing—is another way that reading informs writing. My students have produced dozens of classroom magazines, anthologies by kids who choose to submit something in response to calls-for-manuscripts on various themes. David wrote "The Ski Flip" after the annoucement of a forthcoming sports story collection. Vicky's first piece of fiction was inspired by Justine's "A Night in the Life," which appeared in a class fiction volume. Mindy's poem about iceskating, published in one of our poetry anthologies, gave Phil the idea for his poem about feelings, entitled "What Are They?" It was Mindy's technique that caught Phil's interest: "I liked her poem a lot—the way it wasn't clear until the end what she was talking about. But she really gave it away, and I decided not to—to give clues but not too many."

Wide reading of both students and professional writing allows young writers to learn from others' subjects, styles, and formats. In turn, opportunities to *be* read evoke the desire to write and share one's writing. A student left this note on my desk the day after the publication of his class's first magazine:

Dear Ms. Atwell,

I enjoyed What Are Friends For? It was great reading stories written by *young adults* of my own age. I especially liked David's and Bert's pieces, David's because he told his feelings and bravery along with helpful details, and Bert's because of his wording and the techniques he used. I hope more books like this are written. If so, would you please inform me?
    Your friend,
    Willie

Willie submitted an essay to the next class magazine.

writing contests and magazines that feature student writing; to the address file I set up and they maintain; and to guides such as N.C.T.E's *All About Letters,* where Luanne, Carol and Leslie found inspiration and models for the resumés and cover letters they wrote in pursuit of summer jobs.

Finally, a variety of materials for writing can aid students in generating ideas: different weights, sizes, and colors of lined and unlined paper, blank booklets, ditto masters, poster paper, stencils, stationery and envelopes, stamps, a typewriter, and all kinds and colors of pens, pencils, and markers. These materials suggest formats beyond the white-lined-paper composition—correspondence, individual collections of poetry, notices and announcements, etc.

Materials

Several kinds of classroom resources see regular use as sources of ideas for writing. The most important are students' permanent writing folders. We save all of each eighth grader's writing, keeping it on file and accessible in the classroom. Sometimes previous pieces of writing suggest new ideas. Daniel's "A Trip Nowhere," his best piece,

> captured the way my friend Tyler and I are together. I got the idea from the first piece about Tyler, Gary and me that I wrote. I just thought of other things we'd done. It helps to look back at my writing folder.

Another helpful resource are sheets headed "My Ideas for Writing" where students can capture potential topics, jotting down ideas as they come. Students carry these lists in their daily or working folders. I've also taught writers how to brainstorm—how to generate, uncensored, as many ideas as possible and then see what's emerged as a topic possibility. Writers who have a range of ideas to choose from usually have strong feelings about topics they ultimately select.

My students can also look to writers' source books, for example, *The Writer's Market;* to a "Places to Publish" folder where we've gathered lists of writing contests and magazines that feature student writing; to the address file I set up and they maintain; and to guides such as N.C.T.E's *All About Letters,* where Luanne, Carol and Leslie found inspiration and models for the resumés and cover letters they wrote in pursuit of summer jobs.

Finally, a variety of materials for writing can aid students in generating ideas: different weights, sizes, and colors of lined and unlined paper, blank booklets, ditto masters, poster paper, stencils, stationery and envelopes, stamps, a typewriter, and all kinds and colors of pens, pencils, and markers. These materials suggest formats beyond the white-lined-paper composition—correspondence, individual collections of poetry, notices and announcements, etc.

Getting Started

After four years of unassigned topics, I'm still slightly panicked the first day of school—afraid that every student in each class will draw a "writer's blues" blank. It never happens. This tells me a lot about the ingenious topics I'd developed for so long at my big desk. It tells me more, though, about my ingenious students. I've started off our year together in one of two ways; they've proven equally successful.

The first is to ask students, in pairs, to take turns interviewing each other, using the list of open-ended interview questions I referred to earlier. Interviewers take notes on interviewee's "My Ideas for Writing" lists. I model an interview with one student, then he or she interviews me, before the pairs go to work. They have twenty minutes to storm each others' brains.

A second approach is one I learned from Mary Ellen Giacobbe. I describe the topics I considered the night before, lying awake anticipating the day's writing. I purposefully propose, then reject, topics too broad or subjects about which I know nothing, settling on a topic I know and care about and genuinely want to write about. I ask students to sit silently for three minutes, thinking as I thought the night before. Then they describe to a friend the ideas that came to mind. After three minutes, students change roles. (This tight timing focuses writers on the one task before them.) Finally, I bring the group together and ask six or eight volunteers to quickly describe the topics they discovered.

Whichever approach starts the class, the rest of the period is writing time. This is the crucial part of getting started—an expectation that everyone will write and the tacit acknowledgement that everyone has something to say. I transfer authority from the desk at the front of the classroom so my students can assume it; they do, taking their rightful places as true authors.

And I'm writing, too—out from behind my big desk, listening to young writer's voices and finding my own.

References

Calkins, Lucy McCormick, *Lessons from a Child*. Exeter, New Hampshire: Heinemann Educational Books, 1983.

Day, Robert and Gail Cohen Weaver. *Creative Writing in the Classroom: An Annotated Bibliography of Selected Resources*. Urbana, Illinois: National Council of Teachers of English, 1978, pp. 104-7 (information about magazines that publish student work and writing contests).

Graves, Donald H. *Writing: Teachers and Children at Work*. Exeter, New Hampshire: Heinemann Educational Books, 1982.

—————— . "Break the Welfare Cycle: Let Writers Choose Their Own Topics." In *fforum*, Patricia Stock, ed., Montclair, New Jersey: Boynton/Cook, 1983: 98-101.

Murray, Donald. "Questions to Produce Writing Topics." *English Journal* 69 (May 1980): 69.

—————— . *Write to Learn*. New York: Holt, Rinehart and Winston, 1984.

Simmons, Joan. "The Writer's Chart to Discovery." In *Understanding Writing: Ways of Observing, Learning and Teaching,* Thomas Newkirk and Nancie Atwell, eds. Chelmsford, Massachusetts: New England Regional Exchange, 1982: 57-62.

All about Letters. Urbana, Illinois. National Council of Teachers of English and the U.S. Postal Service, 1979.

Scott's Gift

PEGGY A. SWOGER

The urge to communicate must be as basic a need for humans as hunger and sex. I remember once a small, friendly girl approaching me on the sidewalk, smiling and gesturing to me. The child was mute, and I could see in the urgency of expression how desperately she wanted me to understand. Finally she tugged me down to her level and touched my necklace. "Oh, you like my necklace," I said. She smiled with delight at having communicated her thoughts and returned, contented, to her play.

Scott must have felt the same joy when he wrote on his self-evaluation after several weeks of writing workshop, "I feel good when I write." Scott was one of several learning-disabled students in my basic English class. Generally, I taught advanced and regular ninth-grade students, but this year I wanted to see how effective writing workshop would be for the basic writers. I set up the same class structure for my three gifted classes and basic class, hoping it would work equally well for all ability levels; for, if so, I could demonstrate that tracking of students is not necessary.

From the first day I had outside visitors to these classes, especially to Scott's first-period class. Nancie Atwell (1987) says in her book *In the Middle,* "Close your door and try it; open your door and share it." Well, my door never closed, and the students and I never tired of sharing our joy of writing.

Scott's Writing

That first day all fourteen of the students wrote on their own topics, but two of them needed extra prompting from me. When I said, "Now write three topics of your own on your topics list," Scott hunched over his clean paper and looked up helplessly at me. He is a tall, broad-shouldered boy, sixteen years old and going out for football. It is also his first year out of special-education classes, and he feels the pressure of "making it." His special-education teacher said that last year Scott became so depressed and withdrawn that they considered special counseling for him. He rarely tried to communicate; in fact, Scott's problems had always been complicated by his language and speech difficulties. He seemed not to be able to generate sentences, even orally.

English Journal, 78 (March 1989), pp. 61-65. Copyright © 1989 by the National Council of Teachers of English. Reprinted with permission.

Scott's mother told me about his efforts to cultivate friends. He invited a boy from his special-education class to go home with him after school. Scott offered his friend everything he could think of in the kitchen: "You want Coke? You want potato chips?" But after that, neither boy could think of anything to say. They sat around the living room in embarrassed silence, thinking of nothing to do. Will Scott ever be able to talk with people, the mother wanted to know; will Scott's progress this year continue? I could not answer her questions because this was my first time around the track, my first experience with the learning disabled.

Perhaps that was a blessing because I just accepted whatever they could do and praised it. If they did not perform, I waited, but I revisited each desk every day. "Tell me about your story," I would say while looking with interest into their eyes at the person somewhere within. Scott was shy, but his soft brown eyes said that he liked my visits to his desk. He stumbled over each word and started over repeatedly. After three days he had written three sentences (Figure 1).

After three weeks he had finished this story (Figure 2), which he punched into the computer one painful letter at a time. The importance of this first story

Figure 1. Hambone

When I first got Hambone, I was only 6 years old. I was so exicted when I got him. He was a Dalamiun dog.

Figure 2. Hambone

When I first got Hambone, I was only 6 years old. I was so exicted when I got him. He was a Dalamiun dog with spots un him. He weuld always slept in the dinning room. Then he got old and sick. One day we took him to the vect. We came home. Got him some medican at the vect. Then he jus went off. We couldn't find him anywhere, and we looked everywhere. The neibhurs looked everywhere but they didn't find him. This went on for one week.

Some kids found him and came to us. They found him neer this fence. He was lying dead with flys flying around him. He looked pretty gross. We lifted him up to the fence. I was pretty scared.

So then we got a shvle and dig a good hole for him very deep. Then we buiried him. It was a little sad. We knew he would die sometime. So we buirded him in that hole and we covered it up, Tom and me. We were pretty sad.

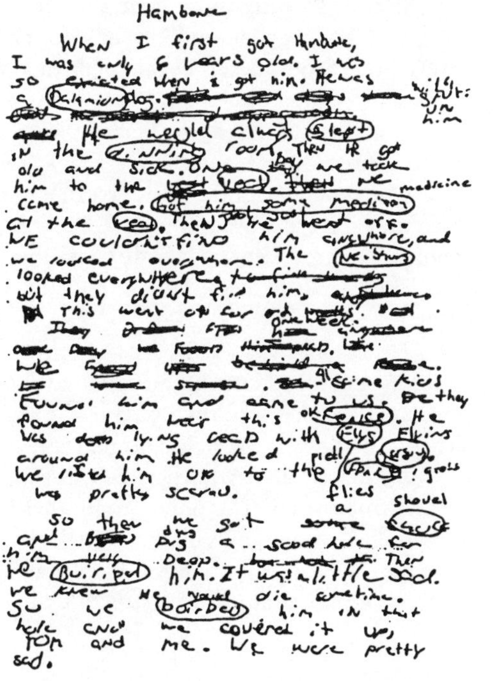

was not that, with help, he corrected most of the spelling and put periods in the right places. Instead, Scott, visualizing and reliving this experience of his earlier years, had touched a deep pool of emotions. Probably this had been his first realization of death and his first painful awareness of love. His special-education teachers were surprised and delighted at his expression of emotion, something they had never seen from him before.

With his first story published on the bulletin board, Scott was cooking. "What's your next story?" I asked. "Snow skiing," he announced, while already hunched over his paper and writing. As he read the first draft to me, he thoughtfully went back to his sentence: "I was real afraid of the mountain." He said, "I was real afraid of the *steep* mountain." Scott had entered the world of revision.

These two stories and a first draft of a visit to his grandmother's at the beach comprised his first nine-weeks' work. Both Kellogg Hunt's T-Unit analysis and Fry's readability level suggest that Scott's first published story equaled that of an average first grader. Carol Avery, a first-grade teacher visiting my classes, had made that comment about several of the papers on our bulletin board. "This is about what my first graders can do by the end of the year," she said. Carol observed Scott at work in the computer room. He was capitalizing every word, and she, a wonderful observer of children's learning, asked him why. "She told me to capitalize all the important words," he said as he gestured toward the aide in the computer room who had been helping him with the title of his story. "Every word was important to Scott," Carol commented.

It is interesting to me that although Scott seldom used language, he had language. It's like those millions of seeds and deep roots lying dormant until the rains come. Scott's desert began to bloom. I first noticed changes in his choice of words. He wrote "obnoxious," his first three-syllable word, when describing his two new puppies. No doubt he had picked up some of his mother's vocabulary in relation to those dogs.

One day, later in the year, he came to my desk and asked if there were two meanings of the word "hospital." He wrote: "The friend's sister had a lot of people over to celebrate Mardi Gras. I met a lot of them and they were very hospitable." Scott seemed to be noticing words. He needed words; he was a writer.

He also needed details. "Scott notices everything," his mother told me. His writing began to show this attention to detail. He wrote: "It was the first time I ate crawfish. You suck the inside of the head and eat the tail. It was very spicy." These details were certain to entertain his classmates.

By March, his syntactic structures and vocabulary indicated a growth of nearly three years. The only activity that will produce syntactic growth, critics of sentence combining said, was intellectual development. My teacher instincts told me that Scott's growth was intellectual; the more complex his thinking, the more complex grammatical structures he required to carry his message.

Scott's Reading

But what was happening with Scott's reading was even more phenomenal. Even Scott commented that his reading had improved. Each week he had time for two periods of sustained, silent reading in English class, and he had five periods a week in reading class. Scott read slowly, agonizing over the fact that he couldn't pass a simple five-question computer quiz on the books he finished. About a week before Christmas holidays, Scott finished *The Outsiders*. He loved it but, again, could not pass the multiple-choice quiz. He asked if he could write to me about the book. For the first time, with events organized for him already, he wrote with abandon. "Cutting loose," someone has called it. In two class periods Scott wrote three pages of readable prose. He enjoyed himself immensely.

His classmates suggested that he should read *Where the Red Fern Grows* because they wanted Scott to name his two new puppies Dan and Ann after those in this book. Scott selected three books to take home for the holidays. His mother exclaimed to me later, when she and I cried over his reading scores, "He was really reading all those books he carried up to his room!" In just eight months Scott's reading growth, measured by the Stanford Reading Diagnostic Test (Brown Level), moved from 2.8 to 7.3—over four years' growth!

As unbelievable as these scores were, they were not the best in the class. Scott's reading growth was fourth from the bottom of the class, and his

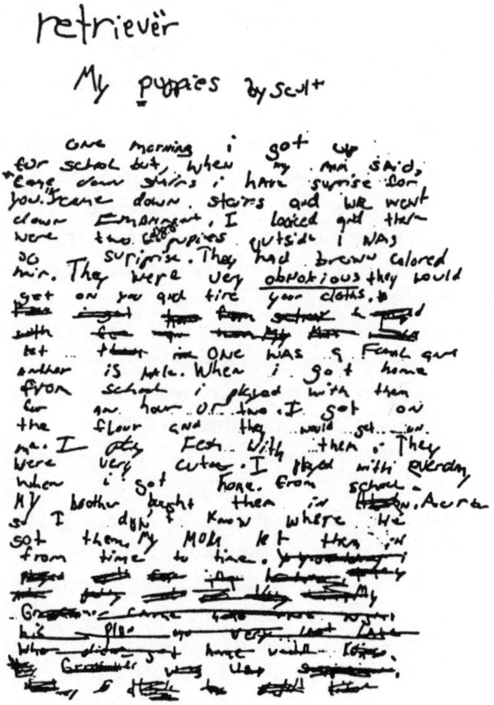

Figure 3. Retriever

My puppies by Scott

One morning i got up for school but, when my mom said, "Come down stairs i have suprise for you." I came down stairs and we went down in bhment. I looked and there were two pupies ouside i was so suriprise. They had brown colored hair. They were very obnoxious they would get on you and tire your cloths. One was a femal and another is male. When i got hom from school i played with them for an hour or two. I got on the flour and they would get on me. I play fesh with them. They were very cute. I played with everday when i got home. from school. My brother bought them in Aura so I don't know where he got them. My mom let them in time to time.

syntactic growth was about the same as that of his peers. The length of Scott's pieces doubled in words, but many of his classmates tripled their output. The top student, with an IQ of 100, moved from approximately the fifth to the ninth stanine in reading and from 9.8 to 11.0 in syntactic maturity. His first story was 98 words and his final one 716. On an average, the class members increased their essay length by 100 words. But none of them had as much to overcome as Scott.

Scott's disability had been diagnosed as Attention Deficit Disorder (ADD) with hyperactivity and speech difficulties. Paired with an IQ of 74, these are terrible hurdles. Scott could not have struggled harder if he had been wrestling Grendel's mother.

Scott's Growth: Some Lessons for Teachers

The question is, Why? What was happening here that had not happened before for these students? It is as though something clicked and suddenly written language made sense. The students made giant leaps, first in writing and then in reading, greater than I had ever seen before in my fifteen years of teaching. My instinct told me that the workshop approach worked because the students had the time and the freedom to work out of their own mental constructs. There were no assignments, no tests, no homework, nothing that the students had to see *My Way*.

Scott was telling his own story in his own way from what he knew. His mind was learning to "go around," to cope with the learning disability. Special-education teachers tell me there is no cure for a disability; the kid just learns to live with it.

Scott's efforts and successes surely must inspire us all. I would like to say to him the words of Beethoven: You, Scott, like all mankind, were "born with a divine spark; you deserve to be free." The fact that language was your liberator makes me realize as never before the importance of my job, of being called English teacher. You have unknowingly been both the writer and the teacher, showing us a way into your world, into your intellectual world. Your lesson is a rich tapestry, written as much by the patient silences between us as by your written and spoken words.

I know that you are ready to step out. Your mother told me, in a worried way, that for some time now you have been going to your room to stand in front of your mirror and talk to the person you see there. She seemed to think you do this out of loneliness, that your reflection is a kind of imaginary friend. She thought you might be "cracking up." But I think you are practicing as children do when they learn a new skill. You are using your language, listening to your voice, observing the movements of your lips as you form words. You are working on your speech, a speech that has always embarrassed you, to make it sound normal. You are practicing to enter that wonderful social whirl of the high-school hallway with the strutting jocks and the pretty girls; you are practicing to say "yes" the next time a girl asks you to a lead-out.

Some lessons seem obvious to me from Scott's experience. First, our students, even most of the handicapped, are little learning machines when, as Frank Smith says, they are learning what *they* need to know. Writing seems to be a catalyst, an ignition system to start up these learning machines. Scott and his classmates wrote every day in both English language class and reading class. Having school time to write and read in a community of learners is essential.

Next, we must, as language teachers, take advantage of the social purpose of language itself. Who taught language to the grunting cave dweller? We know that out of that basic drive to communicate, human beings have created language, our greatest invention. It happened naturally, out of daily needs and daily give-and-take. Language growth happens in a social context, and that is the only way it happens. If literacy is our goal, students need to be working and interacting purposefully in pairs and small groups.

Finally, perhaps no other children in our schools have had learning dissected into such small pieces as much as the learning disabled. We feed them like feeding crumbs to birds. Their natural learning has been stymied by contrived assignments, worksheets, and writing formulas. We must understand that the mind works naturally with whole pieces of discourse.

Let us sit at the feet of the learners and let them guide us into their worlds; let us trust and celebrate their potential by focusing on what they can do. Like Scott, these children have gifts to give us if we can learn to receive.

Writing about General Apache

DICK HARRINGTON

My poem "General Apache Talks with His Writing Teacher" is a true story though I can hardly portray the degree of pain and triumph of this man, this student, this Vietnam vet who in the war had come to be known as General Apache. He took developmental writing for two quarters, progressed to college composition, and then in midterm dropped his classes because the bullet lodged next to his spine had started to move. If it moved far enough away, the surgeons could take it out. If it moved closer, they might be powerless to stop paralysis. I phoned his home a while later and learned he is doing fine, working at the post office.

What's so special about him, given his history, is his capacity to make peace with the world and his tremendous desire to communicate his experience. Once while visiting Washington, DC, he paid a homeless man $20 for an inside tour of the streets. The next week he came to class with an article on the surprises of that afternoon. He'd thought he'd known just about everything about the streets because he'd lived there himself, but he'd been mistaken.

In the early days of developmental writing he seemed very quiet but industrious. Not more than five foot ten, he reminded me of a wiry NFL cornerback who always shows up where he's supposed to be. His shoulders were unusually broad, his arms muscular, his hands big. He walked with quiet grace.

I always sit down with my developmental students to talk and to listen. I don't want to miss that phrase or that look in the eye revealing an interest they might not yet be able to verbalize, especially to a teacher. After years of trying to think up stimulating assignments for the whole class, I now encourage students to satisfy course requirements with subjects of their own choosing, preferably subjects which, as Ken Macrorie is fond of saying, choose them. I get much more and better writing these days by learning what stimulates them to think and write.

I'd just finished conferring with a woman in her midtwenties who had told me she was interested in writing about alcoholism. Our conversation had revealed her great need to write the story of her husband's drunken rampage with his shotgun, threatening to kill her and the four kids as they huddled screaming behind the bed. She had seemed excited to learn I would guide her in writing that story.

Teaching English in the Two-Year College, 16 (October 1989), pp. 190-192. Copyright © 1989 by the National Council of Teachers of English. Reprinted with permission.

And so in the first days, I sat down with this vet and asked to see the list of subjects he might like to pursue. There weren't many items in his daybook because he felt reluctant. He was not used to a teacher sitting so close. As we talked, I was struck by his gentle directness. His head seemed to buzz with possibilities.

He wanted to write about his experience as a drug counselor for the children of Vietnam veterans; about his trip to *The Wall* after years of alcoholism, drug addiction and brawling; about the jungle itself at night; about misrepresentations of the war; about the chaos of a firefight. He'd been quite something in the war, often decorated. Afterward he'd been chosen, despite his physical impairment, to train officers how to fight and survive in jungle combat. He wanted to write it all "so people will understand what happened to guys."

We talked in class. We talked in my office. At first, of course, he was skeptical about me. I hadn't gone. I was a teacher, a Ph.D. What did I know? But somehow he began to trust that I listened to what he said. More important, I didn't judge him and I didn't fear him for having cut so many human throats. Not that he bragged. He talked with humility and grace about things that probably would have broken me. If there were old fashioned heroes in Vietnam, he was surely one. His unit twice took Hamburger Hill.

One day I sat down and asked, "What are you working on?" He said, "Special." I said, "What?" He said, "Special. All my life growing up, my momma and my grandmother and others always said I was special. The coaches said I was special. I was even special in Nam because everybody looked to me for what to do next. But when I come back, people spit on me and called me baby killer. For over 20 years I was lost in alcohol, nightmares, and I don't know what else. And then just the other day a young boy I was counseling told me I was a very special person. I'm writing about that. Special."

I wanted to write down the many things he told me about his life. As I began, the poem took shape. I worked on it for at least a month off and on. When I finally got up the nerve, I told him I'd written something about him that I wanted him to read. I admitted I was very nervous but I wanted him to come to my office. In the office I fidgeted, tried to explain, started to hand it to him, and pulled back again. At last I gave it up. He read it carefully, deliberately, which is his way, and then looked up with a kind of bashful smile. "That's me. That's my whole life right there. I wish I could find words to put things like you can."

I said with practice he would improve his own writing. I told him I appreciated his response and needed to ask him about the accuracy of one part. He'd told me everything else in the poem except the details of the throat cutting. I told him I'd never cut anyone's throat, so I'd had to imagine what it must be like. He said it was exactly as I'd described. Writing about it had made me feel I was forcing myself into one of his nightmares of reality, yet I felt I had to be true to what he'd done and had been. I guess part of me feared the throat-cutting passage might set him off, but it didn't perhaps because I didn't judge or shy from the act of deliberate killing.

Showing him this poem was one of the most liberating experiences of my life, and I want to share my experience with readers of *TETYC*.

I was just out of school
playing ball for Cincinnati
When my notice come.
Marines taught me to kill people
every kind of way,
sent me to Nam,
made me a bush rat.

In the monsoon jungle
on night patrol
I'd always take point.
The other guys would
follow after me,
listening for the VC's
gurgle when my knife
cut the jugular
and vocal cords.

Fisrt they just
called me Apache.
But I done the job so well
they got to calling me
General Apache.
When our time come
the whole outfit got surrounded.
AK-45 slug paralyzed me,
kept me laying almost a whole day
till the choppers come,
looking at my buddy's face,
his head spewing out brains.

I still dream about it.
That bullet still in me
here next to my spine.
Back in the States people'd ask,
"You really do all them
things they say you did?"

Tried out for the Reds,
but they cut me,
my arm being numb and all.
I got to drinking more
and looking for guys
that could fight me.

Instead of just jailing me again
one judge got me a shrink.
I went to The Wall in DC,
found each name,
thirty-five bush rats.
Didn't find my name.
Just stood there crying.

I do counseling myself now
with kids hooked on drugs and
    alcohol.
  Missed class yesterday,
up all night with a kid
wanting to kill his parents.
My own son, the oldest,
about to graduate from college.
Time to make something of me now.
When I start to remember
I don't sleep.
Some nights I feel
I got to have a drink.

I want you to help me
write it all down
so people will understand
what happened to guys.
Been flying round and round
on a plane since Nam
and now I know
it's about to land.

A Prayer in Spring

NANETTE V. MENGEL

I met her at registration. At the end of a battering day of wholesale academic advising in the Student Union, an intense young woman, a Registered Nurse in her mid-twenties, required all my tattered attention. Utterly unsmiling, with a marked accent that sounded like "Chicago" to me, her very blue eyes emblems of a driven soul, she drilled me closely. "What is Psychology 10? What does this Comparative Literature course include?" Gripping the wheel of self-responsibility, but against my hopes, she persistently eliminated all the possible courses except my own, Introduction to American Literature. I hoped against hope that she would end by giving her intensity to someone else. I concealed my own connection with the course until it was no longer possible. "I'll take English 28," she said. "O.K.," I confessed, "That's mine," and I imagined her disappointed to find after so much scrutiny that she would have a teacher as tired as I felt.

The next phase of our relationship was curiously on-and-off. When she came to class she invariably pressed for literal explanations. "What *did* Emily Dickinson mean by 'Experience is the Angled Road/Preferred against the Mind'?" But then she had alerted me that she must often miss class to work late shifts with the bloodmobile so that she could pay her tuition. I was surprised that her first paper, an explication which faltered in its treatment of imagery, was double the required length and that it was one of the best in the class.

She was, it seems, gathering her powers. When we got to T.S. Eliot, she made an appointment to see me during office hours because "The Love Song of J. Alfred Prufrock" had engaged her. His "lifestyle" troubled her, she said. It depressed her that Prufrock allowed himself to be stuck in a cityscape where the yellow fog "lingered upon the pools that stand in drains," and that his human encounters were bloodless. "What did Eliot mean by having his protagonist, in the middle of a party, wish himself 'a pair of ragged claws/Scuttling across the floors of silent seas'? Did Eliot think there was hope for Prufrock or not?"

When it was time for our class to read "The Waste Land," I did something I seldom do: I gave an unbroken lecture for an hour and a quarter. Suppressing my doubts about my own scholarship, being as careful and honest as I could, I outlined the situation in the poem's five sections, identified the sources and traced the development of its themes. How discouraging it was at the end when

College English, 47 (April 1985), pp. 376-378. Copyright © by the National Council of Teachers of English. Reprinted with permission.

my student remained after class to ask for an appointment the next day. "I want to ask you what 'The Waste Land' means!"

What a relief when she opened the conference by saying, "I don't want to ask you about 'The Waste Land' after all. Eliot was miserably unhappy when he wrote it, wasn't he? I want to write a paper comparing 'Prufrock' with Eliot's 'Journey of the Magi' because in his religious poetry, when he had recovered from his nervous breakdown, I can see him renewed. The Wise Men in that later poem, returning to their summer palaces and 'the silken girls bringing sherbet,' couldn't stand the old life any more. He does believe that one can be reborn, doesn't he?"

Her paper was strong indeed. She worked rigorously back and forth between generalizations and supporting evidence. At the bottom she attached a note: "Dear Ms. Mengel, Do you think I have what it takes to consider being an English major?" It was easy to say "Yes!"

Our next reading was Faulkner's *The Sound and the Fury,* whose difficult first chapter, narrated by the feeble-minded Benjy, called for a clarifying lecture. I felt competent as I explained that Benjy was loving and that there was a legible pattern in what he experienced. My student lingered after class. "It was Jason I liked," she said. "Especially toward the end of the novel." Undaunted by the fact that he is Faulkner's most vicious character, she added, "He is like me." And then, surprisingly, "He is out of place when he leaves his region."

It was hot in that evening classroom under glaring neon lights and I was ready to go home myself, but fatigue, like the fatigue on registration afternoon, stalled me when she talked, suddenly pouring out her distress. She came from "the north," worked an odd schedule, was required to draw blood from millworkers who contributed only for the relief a day off gave them from the boredom of their jobs, carpooled with older, small-town, southern nurses who, unlike her, had husbands and children and thought her strange when she tried to talk about what she was reading. As we finally made our way down the long hall and into the night where I was bound to be free, I knew that this person who did not want to let me go was nearly desperate. At the same time I knew she was strong.

After we left Faulkner to begin Robert Frost, I again found myself lecturing, distilling Lawrance Thompson's two-volume biography. Frost, who had been violent at times with his own children, was abused as a child in San Francisco by his own father. "Is it possible," my student asked, "for someone like that to break the cycle?" After class she confided that her own father had assaulted her and that in her whole family only her sister now remained a friend. Resisting the temptation to answer with empty reassurances, I asked her what she thought about her question. I simply didn't know.

And then at the end of April we met for the last time in what were to have been groups of two's and three's. As it happened my student came alone to her session, so we sat on a stone wall outside the English building where the leaves were newly green to read aloud and ponder Robert Frost's "A Prayer in Spring," which begins

Oh, give us pleasure in the flowers to-day;
And give us not to think so far away
As the uncertain harvest; keep us here
All simply in the springing of the year.

Oh, give us pleasure in the orchard white,
Like nothing else by day, like ghosts by night;
And make us happy in the happy bees,
The swarm dilating round the perfect trees.

We took it line by line, seeing what the poet said and how he said it. Remembering the disembodied, white and lovely dogwoods I had seen the previous evening, I understood freshly, "Like nothing else by day, like ghosts by night." She saw the way Frost's insistence on imperative forms—"give us," "give us," "make us"—gave way in the last stanza to blissful acknowledgment of the mercy of loving in present time: "For this is love and nothing else is love." We read it together as if for the first time. Frost's poetic action was recreating itself in us on that wall where my student said suddenly, "I see now. Frost could 'get over the fence.' It is possible to break out."

There were only a few minutes before I had another appointment. Aware that my student had made some kind of a home in Chapel Hill that she was sacrificing to return "north" to live with her sister so that she could be a full-time English major at another university, I asked her to read me the second poem I had assigned, "The Road Not Taken," about the two roads diverging in a yellow wood:

And both that morning equally lay
In leaves no step had trodden black.
Oh, I kept the first for another day!
Yet knowing how way leads on to way,
I doubted if I should ever come back.

I wanted her to know that I knew what she was doing and that I was with-her-not-being-with-her. "You do have 'what it takes,' you know." "Thank you," she said smiling, and seeing tears gather, she held out her hand to me, "Thank you for having confidence in me."

Underlife and Writing Instruction

ROBERT BROOKE

This article uses the sociological concept of underlife to explain several aspects of writing instruction. In sociological theory, "underlife" refers to those behaviors which undercut the roles expected of participants in a situation—the ways an employee, for example, shows she is not just an employee, but has a more complex personality outside that role.

In contemporary writing instruction, both students and teachers undercut the traditional roles of the American educational system in order to substitute more complex identities in their place. On the one hand, students disobey, write letters instead of taking notes, and whisper with their peers to show they are more than just students and can think independently of classroom expectations. On the other, writing teachers develop workshop methods, use small groups, and focus on students' own "voices" in order to help students see themselves as writers first and students second. Both sets of behaviors are underlife behaviors, for they seek to provide identities that go beyond the roles offered by the normal teacher-as-lecturer, student-as-passive-learner educational system.

These forms of underlife, moreover, are connected to the nature of writing itself. Writing, in the rich sense of interactive knowledge creation advocated by theorists like Ann Berthoff in *The Making of Meaning* and Janet Emig in *The Web of Meaning,* necessarily involves standing outside the roles and beliefs offered by a social situation—it involves questioning them, searching for new connections, building ideas that may be in conflict with accepted ways of thinking and acting. Writing involves being able to challenge one's assigned roles long enough that one can think originally; it involves living in conflict with accepted (expected) thought and action.

This article will explore student and teacher behavior in writing instruction as the underlife of the current educational system, and will suggest that the identities which may be developing for students in writing classrooms are more powerful for real academic success than the traditional identity of the successful student. It may be that the process of allowing a particular kind of identity to develop is what contemporary writing instruction is all about.

The Concept of Underlife

My understanding of "underlife" stems from Erving Goffman's books *Asylums* and *Stigma,* although the concept has long been accepted in sociology.

College Composition and Communication, 38 (May 1987), pp. 141-153. Copyright © by the National Council of Teachers of English. Reprinted with permission.

As presented in these books, the concept of underlife rests on three assumptions about social interaction. First, a person's identity is assumed to be a function of social interaction. Second, social interaction is assumed to be a system of information games. Third, social organizations are assumed to provide roles for individuals which imply certain kinds of identities. With these assumptions in mind, "underlife" can be understood as the activities (or information games) individuals engage in to show that their identities are different from or more complex than the identities assigned them by organizational roles. In this section, I will describe these assumptions and the concept of underlife that emerges from them.

Identity as Social Interaction. In *Stigma,* Goffman explains that we understand another person's identity as a product of (1) how they immediately appear to us through dress, bearing, accent, physical features, and the like; (2) what we know about their history; and (3) the stances they take towards the groups we assume they belong to. We may initially assume, for example, that the young man in the front row of a new class is a typical "fraternity boy" because of (1) his haircut, his polo shirt, and his brand name tennis shoes. As we get to know (2) his history, we may find out that he comes from a wealthy family, that his parents hope he will become a doctor, and that he struggles with this because he has a hard time keeping up his grades. We will also begin to get a sense of him as a unique individual when we find out (3) he is troubled by his relationship to his family, more interested in English than in medicine, and feels in conflict because he would like to drop medicine, reject the family, and go into graduate school, but also wants to marry his sorority sweetheart, keep the family fortune, and lead a "successful" life. We (and he) use all three forms of information in assigning to him a particular identity.

Information Games. The identity we assign such a young man is greatly determined, however, by the kinds of information he chooses to give us. If he dressed differently, we would see him differently. Perhaps if we knew more of his history we would see him in a different light. Perhaps we may think that his choice to tell us of his interest in English is a calculated choice, intended to get us to grade easier. The identity assigned an individual by other people is largely the product of the "information games" people play when interacting with each other. By what each person chooses to reveal about himself in each context, we develop a sense of that person's identity. Central to Goffman's conception of the human person, then, is a sense of the "information games" nature of interaction—people are assumed to attempt to develop the best defensible portrait for themselves in social interactions.

Organizational Roles. The kind of portrait a person can develop for herself, however, is a function of the organizations (businesses, families, clubs, hospitals, etc.) she operates in. As Goffman explains, social organizations are places where individuals are placed into certain roles. Appropriate activity in these roles carries with it implications about identity. In a school classroom, for example, prompt and accurate completion of tasks set by the teacher carries with it a "good student" identity, and a student who always complies pleasantly will be understood as smart, well-mannered, possibly a teacher's pet.

Underlife. Exactly because organizations offer definitions of identity, they also offer individuals the opportunity to respond to the definitions in creative ways. Because definitions of self exist in organizations, individuals can give information about how they see themselves by rejecting the definition offered. Institutional underlife is exactly such a case: actors in an institution develop behaviors which assert an identity different from the one assigned them.

In *Asylums,* Goffman studies the underlife of a major American mental hospital, and comes to the conclusion that underlife activities take two primary forms. First, there are *disruptive* forms of underlife, like those engaged in by union organizers, "where the realistic intentions of the participants are to abandon the organization or radically alter its structure." Second, there are *contained* forms of underlife, which attempt to fit into "existing institutional structures without introducing pressure for radical change" (199). Most forms of underlife are of the second kind—they work around the institution to assert the actor's difference from the assigned role, rather than working for the elimination of the institution. In the mental hospital, Goffman finds many examples of such contained underlife patterns, including identity jokes and challenges (where staff and inmates would kid each other about having attributes of the other class), attempts to "get around" established procedures (such as dumping dinner in the garbage and having a friend who works in the kitchen smuggle out a plateful of boiled eggs), and explicit attempts to express rejection of inmate status (like withdrawing from interaction with other patients, parodying psychological theory, claiming it was all a mistake, and engaging in violent behavior). The point of each of these behaviors, claims Goffman, is to show that one has a self different from the patient-self assigned by the hospital.

The prevalence of such behaviors throughout the hospital and other institutions leads Goffman to conclude that underlife behaviors are a normal part of institutional life. All members of the institution—staff, patients, technicians, janitors, doctors—engaged in such behaviors. Consequently, Goffman claims, institutional underlife must be understood as an activity closely related to individual identity. "I want to argue," he writes, "that this recalcitrance is not an incidental mechanism of defense but rather an essential constituent of the self" (319). For Goffman, looking at those activities through which individuals resist or reject the identity assigned them by institutions is a way of looking at how individuals form their sense of identity. No one but the complete fanatic completely associates herself with only one role—instead, the self is formed in the distance one takes from the roles one is assigned. In such an analysis, activities which aren't "on task" become as important as activities which are, for besides the task itself there is also always the formation of identity.

Underlife in a Writing Class

Underlife activities, as Goffman describes them, are the range of activities people develop to distance themselves from the surrounding institution. By so doing they assert something about their identity. Underlife allows individuals to take stances towards the roles they are expected to play, and to show others the stances they take. When the kinds of student behaviors normally seen as misbehavior are examined in writing classrooms, what appears is exactly this sort of constructive, individual stance-taking. It is exactly in these underlife behaviors that students are developing their individual stances towards classroom experience.

I would like to discuss several examples of underlife in the writing classroom from this perspective. The examples all come from a semester-long participant-observation study of a freshmen writing class in spring 1986. As a participant-observer, I was able to hear and record many behaviors I am unable to attend to while teaching my own courses. These behaviors include the private conversations students have with one another, the notes they write to themselves and then scratch out, the things they're writing when the teacher thinks they're taking notes, and other such activities. What surprised me was the extent and content of these activities—even in the most docile class hour, such activities are constantly going on, and (significantly) they are usually connected to the class activities in some way. The students are developing their own stances towards class activity, not whispering about unrelated subjects like parties and dates as I had always assumed.

In the classroom I observed, the students' underlife activities divided fairly cleanly into four major types, which I will discuss in order of frequency.

First, students tend to find creative uses for classroom activities and materials which are purposefully different from those the teacher intended. Usually, these creative uses show that classroom ideas could be used outside of class in ways more interesting to the students. During a class period devoted to using Young, Becker, and Pike's tagmemic matrix in *Rhetoric: Discovery and Change,* for example, two male students found ways of thinking about the subject that asserted their own interests. The teacher had brought in a bag of potatoes to serve as an example, and was having the class use the tagmemic matrix to explore "how many ways they could think about something as simple as a potato." While the class was discussing how a potato might change over time and in what contexts this change would be interesting, these students began a private discussion of how to ferment the potato to get vodka. When asked by the teacher what they were talking about, one of the two (looking nervous) explained that the process of fermentation was obviously a "change over time" and that this process was interesting "in the context of alcohol production." In this example, the students had openly ceased to participate in class, and seemed (from their giggles) to be "telling jokes" behind the teacher's back. But the content of their "jokes" was actually a way of applying the class concepts to their own late-adolescent interests in alcohol. Their retreat from class participation was a retreat which took a class concept with it, and which applied that concept in a highly creative and accurate way.

In the classroom I studied, this kind of creative use of classroom ideas was the most frequent form of underlife behavior. Most of the private conversations I heard applied a class concept to the students' world. In fact, particularly striking images or ideas frequently sparked several private conversations throughout the room. When the class discussed Annie Dillard's "Lenses," for example, a student pointed out Dillard's comparison of feeling disoriented to the shock of coming out of a really good movie and realizing you'd forgotten where you parked the car. Immediately, several private conversations started up throughout the room—the ones I could hear focused on how that feeling had happened to them too, in situations they could share with their peers.

To a teacher thinking only of how well her point is getting across, what seems to be going on in these cases is disruptive: students aren't paying attention, but are talking to one another about things that don't have to do with class. But to a teacher thinking about how students are using classroom information, these diversions should seem positive. In them, no matter how jokingly, students are actively connecting ideas in the classroom to their own lives outside the classroom, and are discovering ways in which classroom knowledge seems useful even when (or especially when) it isn't used for classroom purposes.

The second most frequent kind of underlife was student comments on the roles people were taking in the classroom, or the roles the classroom was asking them to take. Students, for example, frequently focused on the "gamesplaying" nature of student participation in college courses. Consider, for example, the following interaction which occurred during a small group discussion of a chapter from Margaret Laurence's *A Bird in the House:*

Mick: "You know, everyone in the story tries to make themselves seem better than they are, you know, but Vanessa finds out every one of them is worse than they seem. It's like *all* of them are lying."

Mel: "Good point. She [the teacher]'ll like that."

Chuck: "Yeah. Home run. Three strikes."

Mel: "(laughing): "Big bucks."

Chuck: "Yeah, big bucks, no whammies."

General laughter, and the conversation immediately turned to discussion of a TV game show called "Press Your Luck!" On this show, contestants played a form of roulette to get "big bucks," but lost everything if they landed on a "whammie." The whammies, incidentally, were animated cartoon characters which would ramble across the screen and devour the hapless contestant's earnings. The group's discussion (which went on for several minutes, the assigned task having been forgotten) focused on how "lucky" players had to be to win anything on "Press Your Luck!" and how in general the game was a rip-off—as a contestant, nine times out of ten you got to get humiliated for nothing.

What struck me most about this interaction was not that students were avoiding the official task, nor that they were avoiding my presence enough to feel comfortable avoiding the task, but that the interaction highlighted (and sprung from) a deep-rooted sense of their experience with classrooms. Their comments, and the quick shift from doing a classroom exercise to discussing a game show, pointed out that they thought of the classroom as a "games-playing" environment, where "points" accumulated "big bucks," where one might get "whammied," where you always had to "press your luck." They thought of themselves as contestants in a game of luck, nerves, and skill, in which those who scored the most points survived, and those who didn't went home humiliated. They were aware, in short, that the classroom environment demanded certain actions of them which were as formal and arbitrary as the actions demanded in games-playing. The purpose of their interaction was to show each other that they all recognized this, that they as individuals were different from the roles they were being asked to play, and that they were all aware of each other as fellow games-players.

As a consequence of this mutual recognition of each other as games-players, students frequently engaged in conversations about how to "get by" effectively in the classroom. Especially in the few minutes before class when the teacher was not yet in the room, students would openly discuss strategies they'd used to succeed in the classroom. One woman told another, for example, that she'd written in her journal (which the teacher would see) an entry describing how hard the last paper was to write and how long it took her because that was the sort of thing the teacher wanted—even though she'd actually written the paper in an hour and a half after midnight the night before. Similarly, students would often share the comments they received on papers, and discuss what in the papers might have sparked the teacher to make these comments. These conversations occurred especially when one student had done well on a paper, and another hadn't, as if the students were together trying to pinpoint what was expected of them for success in this classroom. In all these activities, it was clear that students were not immediately evaluating each other on their success and honesty in embracing the classroom roles, but were instead mutually helping each other to succeed in "getting by" in the classroom without losing themselves in its expectations.

Such "role-recognition" activities on the part of students seem very similar to the "identity jokes" Goffman found in the hospital he studied. The purpose for commenting on the roles that exist in the classroom is the same purpose for kidding a staff member for acting like an inmate—such comments show that the speaker is aware of and different from the roles assigned in the situation, that there is more to the speaker than that. The quantity of such comments in the classroom I studied suggests that students are highly aware of the roles the classroom asks them to play, and highly defensive of their differences from these roles.

A third major category of underlife activities involves evaluations of what is going on in the classroom. In these comments, students explicitly took a stance towards some aspect of the classroom, and evaluated it as good or bad. Often, these evaluations focused on their own performance:

> Chuck: Did you bring your paper?
> Ben: That damn thing—
> Chuck: Pretty "damn," huh?
> Ben: It's so "damn" I keep forgetting it.

or on the course materials:

> Jane: (holding up book): Did you think this was all right?
> Holly: Dumb.
> Jane: Dumb?
> Holly: I hated it. Let me read your journal.
> Jane: No, it's stupid.—No, don't take it.—Give it back. (whispers) Teacher! Teacher! (Teacher comes into the classroom, and both students straighten in their seats).

or on the day's activity:

> Nellie: (to those around her during potato description day): I can't believe this! (She closes her book and starts writing a letter to a friend).

These activities, also relatively common, allow the individual students to claim explicitly whether or not they accept the activity going on around them. Interestingly, most of these in-class comments expressed negative evaluations, even though formal student evaluations of the course showed most students thought this was the best writing course they'd ever taken. The purpose of these evaluative comments, it seems, is the same purpose as the other underlife activities—to assert one's fundamental distance from the classroom roles. Negative evaluations show that one can think independently; positive evaluations would show compliance with the course expectations. The purpose of such an evaluative comment has nothing to do with what the student really thinks of the class when comparing it to other classes. Instead, it has to do with asserting the student's ability to think in ways other than those expected in the classroom.

The last major category of underlife activity involved those private activities whereby an individual divides her attention between the class activity and something else. The most common example of divided attention was reading the student newspaper while the teacher was beginning class, but more interesting examples occurred. In this class, students were required to turn in a one-page journal entry every day—in a typical class period, four or five students could be observed writing their journals. Sometimes they would write these in such a way that the teacher would think they were taking notes. Sometimes they would write them as they were participating in small group discussions. In each case, however, they would be dividing their attention between the journal page and the activity that the teacher had set up. Both activities, of course, were connected to class demands; what was rebellious about writing the journal in class was that it took full and undivided attention away from the prescribed activity in the classroom.

The point of all these underlife activities is clearly to distance oneself from the demands of the classroom while hopefully remaining successful within it. All would be considered examples of "contained" underlife by Erving Goffman. The point is not to disrupt the functioning of the classroom, but to provide the other participants in the classroom with a sense that one has other things to do, other interests, that one is a much richer personality than can be shown in this context. All these activities, in short, allow the student to take a stance towards her participation in the classroom, and show that, while she can succeed in this situation, her self is not swallowed up by it. The interesting parts of herself, she seems to say, are being held in reserve.

Underlife and the Writing Teacher

If student underlife within the writing classroom is "contained" underlife, then the writing teacher's position can only be considered "disruptive." Students merely try to gain a little psychic distance from the roles they must inhabit in the classroom, but writing teachers clearly see themselves as engaged in the process of changing classroom roles. In fact, many writing teachers explain their position as one of "struggle" against the prevailing educational institution because the goals of writing are finally different from the goals of traditional education. Adrienne Rich, for example, claims in "Teaching Language in Open Admissions" that her goal of helping underprivileged writers find ways of writing powerfully in their own contexts comes into conflict with large social institutions which would prefer these individuals remained inarticulate. Mike Rose's article, "The Language of Exclusion," describes the writing teacher's plight, aware of the importance of writing for learning and thinking on the one hand, but forced by institutional administrators to test, remediate, and exclude students because of their poor writing "skills" on the other, and claims teachers must strive for the first while combating the second. In "Reality, Consensus, and Reform," Greg Myers shows how wanting to teach writing as a freeing process has historically been in conflict with (and undercut by) the ideological purposes of the educational institution, and argues that writing teachers need to recognize that "our interests are not the same as those of the institutions that employ us, and that the improvement of our work will involve social changes" (170). Similarly, Pamela Annas' "Style as Politics" shows how, for writers who are disadvantaged within the current social structure, writing is always a complex political act of finding language to express other possibilities than those offered by the current sociopolitical climate, and that this finding of language is in conflict with the standards of accepted writing. In each case, these writing teachers feel themselves to be after something different from what the traditional education system produces—instead of traditional "good students," they want students who will come to see themselves as unique, productive writers with influence on their environment.

They would like their students to see themselves as writers rather than as students, and their pedagogical changes are attempts to facilitate this shift in roles. Writing teachers change the classroom to help students extend their identities.

Writing teachers, however, are more likely to speak of "voice" than of "identity," for the first is a rhetorical concept and the second a sociological concept. But the two are very closely related, since both have to do with the stance an individual takes towards experience. In writing theory, a writer's "voice" is most often described as the unique stance she takes towards experience, and the unique way she relates herself to her context. In sociological theory, as we have seen, "identity" develops out of the individual's stance towards experience and out of the way she relates herself to the roles assigned her in the context. The ideas are closely connected: when a writing teacher worries about her student's "voice," she is also worrying about her student's "identity."

In writing classrooms, "voice" is often felt to be the paradox that prompts pedagogical change—as teachers, we want students to write in their own voices, but how can they when we *assign* them to? And how can their voices really be their own when they are evaluated by us? Knoblauch and Brannon explain in their *Rhetorical Traditions and the Teaching of Writing:*

> How can teachers hope to encourage engaged writing, particularly given the fact that classroom composing is, to a degree, inevitably artificial since the impulse to write comes from outside the writers? . . . Any school writing alters the normal circumstances in which a writer takes initiative to communicate to some reader, and in which the reader is interested in the substance of that particular text but not especially interested in the writer's overall ability or continuing maturation. (108)

If our goal as writing teachers is to enable students to see themselves as and to act as writers, then our role as teachers making assignments and evaluating their performance can only get in the way. In the classroom, students write to comply with our demands—they don't write because they see themselves as writers. The need for writers to develop their own voices is the central place where writing pedagogy comes into conflict with itself. If students really are to develop their own voices, they will need to ignore the requirements set for them by outsiders and write instead as they want—they would need, in short, to engage in a kind of underlife in relation to the classroom.

What's at stake, it seems, is a part of their "identity"—we would like them to think of themselves as *writers* rather than as *students*. We would hope they see purposes for writing beyond the single purpose of getting us to give them good grades. We would like them to take initiative to communicate with readers, to use writing to help better their world, to use writing to help them understand their world. Instead, we worry that they may see themselves only as games-players, as individuals forced to play the student role and who consequently distance themselves from that role as anyone working in an organization does. As writing teachers, we want them to *own* their writing, rather than attributing it only to the classroom—rather than claiming it's only a game we play in class.

If we wish them to see themselves as writers, we must help both them and ourselves to see our interaction in writing classrooms as cut from a different mold than "regular" classrooms. The roles must be different.

In fact, it is exactly such problems with classroom roles that lurk behind current calls to change writing pedagogy. The range of such suggested changes is staggering. Janet Emig's "Non-Magical Thinking" and Peter Elbow's *Writing Without Teachers* both argue that the teacher should become "a writer among writers," and that the first requirement of the writing teacher is that she must write herself, often and in many modes. Knoblauch and Brannon's *Rhetorical Traditions* suggests changing the structure of the classroom to a "writing workshop" where students and teacher can really talk to one another "as members of the same community of learners" (111). Donald Murray's *A Writer Teaches Writing* argues for one-on-one conferences between writer and teacher, in which the teacher takes a secondary place to the writer's own talk about her work and acts mainly as a fellow writer-editor and not as a teacher. Alongside these suggestions for classroom reform are powerful indictments of the traditional writing classroom for being teacher-centered rather than student-centered, focused on the product rather than process, being oppressive rather than liberating.

The whole call for pedagogical shift is most powerfully a call for a shift in the identity roles offered in the classroom. In other words, although we haven't clearly articulated it, the organizing assumption of composition instruction, in theory and practice, is that the primary function of the composition classroom is to foster a particular identity or stance towards the world. Writing teachers want to produce writers, not students, and consequently we seek to change our pedagogy to allow the possibility of the writer's identity.

Conclusion: Writing, Autonomy, and Action

The reasons writing teachers seek to alter normal classroom practice and the reasons students express their distance as individuals from classroom roles thus seem intimately connected: both have to do with a concern for the student's identity. Neither writing teacher nor student is content to rely on the expected roles of teacher and student. Both want there to be more to the self, and both show this desire—the student by distancing herself from classroom expectations, the teacher by structuring the course so that normal classroom expectations are only partly in effect.

What is at stake, in other words, is who the individuals in the classroom will be. Student underlife primarily attempts to assert that the individuals who play the role of students are not only students, that there is more to them than that. It is thus a *contained* form of underlife, a form which (as Goffman would say) attempts to exist within the existing structure without introducing too much friction. But writing teachers would have students go further—they would have students see themselves as writers, as people who use the processes writing offers to explore, question, and change elements of their social lives. Writing instruction is thus a *disruptive* form of underlife, a form which tries to undermine the nature of the institution and posit a different one in its place.

When we look at writing instruction from the perspective of underlife, it appears that the purpose of our courses is to allow students to substitute one kind of underlife for another. Instead of the naive, contained form they normally employ, we're asking them to take on a disruptive form—a whole stance towards their social world that questions it, explores it, writes about it. We ask them to stand apart from the roles they normally play, and instead to try exploring what they normally think and what they'd normally do through writing. We would like them to become distanced from their experience, and consider it. As their underlife behavior shows, they are of course already distanced, already posing as "different from" the roles they play every day. They *are* different from these roles. But they aren't conscious of how they are different, and how they work to maintain their difference. And that, it seems, is what writing instruction tries to do—get them to become conscious of their differences from their normal roles, get them to accept that they are different, get them to explore and write out of these differences. Writing, finally, asks individuals to accept their own underlife, to accept the fact that they are never completely subsumed by their roles, and instead can stand apart from them and contemplate. Writing instruction seeks to help the learner see herself as an original thinker, instead of as a "student" whose purpose is to please teachers by absorbing and repeating information.

It is in this desire to shift roles, from student to writer, from teacher-pleaser to original thinker, that writing instruction comes into greatest conflict with the existing educational system, and also has the most to offer to it. For the shift begun in writing classrooms is a shift that would improve education in other classrooms as well. If the student in a chemistry class grew to think of herself as someone who thinks in certain ways to solve certain problems rather than as someone who must "learn" equations to pass tests, then the student would begin to see herself as a chemist, and to act accordingly. In other words, if all our classrooms were to focus on fostering the identities of students as thinkers in our disciplines rather than merely on transmitting the knowledge of our fields, then students might easily see the purpose for these particular "information games." But for students to see themselves as chemists, or social scientists, or writers, they must first see themselves as more than just students in our classrooms, as real thinkers with power and ability in this area. To help students make this change, of course, would require just as far-reaching pedagogical changes in other areas as writing teachers have begun to make in theirs. It would need much that is now only offered in writing classes—small class size, student-directed projects, peer interaction, chances for revising work and ideas as the course progresses. In all these changes, writing teachers could lead the way. For the student's identity of writer as original thinker, as able to step ouside expectations and think creatively on one's own, may be the identity that would make the other identities possible, in the same way that the identity of "good student" (complete with study skills and time management behaviors) is now what makes traditional academic learning possible. Such a shift in education would be a far-reaching and beneficial shift, focusing on the identity and abilities of the student as an original thinker, rather than on the student's ability to comply with classroom authority.

Writing, in short, is "about" autonomy and action—to really learn to write means becoming a certain kind of person, a person who accepts, explores, and uses her differences from assigned roles to produce new knowledge, new action, and new roles. The concept of underlife shows us this process, a process at work in every classroom and at the core of our discipline. It suggests we think carefully about the identities we have, the identities we model, and the identities we ask students to take on, for the process of building identity is the business we are in.

References

Annas, Pamela. "Style as Politics." *College English* 47 (1985): 360-71.

Berthoff, Ann. *The Making of Meaning.* Upper Montclair, NJ: Boynton/Cook, 1983.

Dillard, Annie. "Lenses." *The Beford Reader.* Ed. X.J. Kennedy and Dorothy Kennedy. 2nd ed. New York: St. Martin's Press, 1985. 101-05.

Elbow, Peter. *Writing Without Teachers.* New York: Oxford UP, 1973.

Emig, Janet. "Non-Magical Thinking: Presenting Writing Developmentally in Schools." *Writing: The Nature, Development, and Teaching of Written Communication. Vol. II: Writing: Process, Development and Communication.* Ed. C.H. Frederiksen and J.F. Dominic. Hillsdale, NJ: Erlbaum, 1981. 21-30.

———. *The Web of Meaning.* Upper Montclair, NJ: Boynton/Cook, 1983.

Goffman, Erving. *Asylums: Essays on the Social Situation of Mental Patients and Other Inmates.* New York: Anchor, 1961.

———. *Stigma: Notes on the Management of Spoiled Identity.* Englewood Cliffs, NJ: Prentice-Hall, 1963.

Knoblauch, C.H., and Lil Brannon. *Rhetorical Traditions and the Teaching of Writing.* Upper Montclair, NJ: Boynton/Cook, 1984.

Laurence, Margaret. *A Bird in the House.* Toronto: Seal, 1978.

Murray, Donald. *A Writer Teaches Writing.* 2nd Ed. Boston: Houghton Mifflin, 1982.

Myers, Greg. "Reality, Consensus, and Reform in the Rhetoric of Composition Teaching." *College English* 48 (1986): 154-74.

Rich, Adrienne. "Teaching Language in Open Admissions." *On Lies, Secrets, and Silence: Selected Prose 1966-1978.* New York: Norton, 1979. 51-68.

Rose, Mike. "The Language of Exclusion." *College English* 47 (1985): 341-59.

Young, Richard, Alton Becker, and Kenneth Pike. *Rhetoric: Discovery and Change.* New York: Harcourt Brace Jovanovich, 1970.

PART THREE

Motivating Student Writing

"My first impetus to write came from a sixth grade English teacher who filled us with the feeling that writing was a good thing to do and that there was something noble about the English language."

Anonymous

The role of motivation in the writing process is enormous. It is a simple matter, for example, to teach someone the rules for using the comma, but how do you teach people to care? How does a teacher persuade young people to spend a significant part of each day writing? More important, how does a teacher lead them (if it is possible at all) to experience the kind of satisfaction that comes from writing well? Over and over, young people express their deep sense of boredom in the two-word epithet, "Who cares?" This section explores ways of helping them come to care about what they write.

Roughly speaking, motivation in the composition class may be classified into two types: *extrinsic,* which includes pictures, songs, field trips, posters, "gimmicks," and all kinds of rewards; and *intrinsic,* which focuses primarily on writing and the writer. Sometimes teachers use extrinsic motivation as a temporary measure—like the forms which hold wet concrete until it is cured. The essays in this section, however, all focus on intrinsic motivation, on leading the young writer to develop commitment, to care about what is being written, to feel a sense of ownership and authorship.

In the first essay, poet-teacher Jean Pumphrey describes how she moved her students away from "classroom writing" to more personally engaging work. The reader might observe that at the outset Pumphrey describes a personal conviction that has now become widespread in the profession—a dissatisfaction with the traditional approaches to teaching composition. The author goes on to explain, step by step, how she restructured her class to become a community of learners. The success of her method is revealed in an ironic student comment: "At one point I asked a student if the five-minute write-ins were helping him. 'No,' he replied, 'I want to keep writing.'"

In "Tapping Creative Potential for Writing," Gabriele Rico describes the popular clustering technique, which "helps writers learn to connect thoughts, feelings, ideas not connected before. It enables pupils to generate ideas, to structure them loosely, and to discover in them a tentative shape that allows writing to flow." Drawing on the "holistic, image-making, synthetic capabilities" of the brain, clustering is a gentle way for the writer to explore his or her own subconscious world and bring to light those subjects which are vitally important but elusive. As Rico suggests, this technique is useful across the grade levels and in many situations.

The central idea in "What I Learned from Verle Barnes: The Exploratory Self in Writing" is that teachers might extend their understanding of motivation by looking in some unlikely places. The great German mystic Meister Eckhart, for example, dwelt over and over in the concept of freedom, an idea whose awe-inspiring power is again being felt in the 1990s. The connections between freedom and creativity are so profound that the teacher of writing cannot afford to overlook them.

In "Focusing Twice Removed," Lesley Rex-Kerish shows how someone can find a subject for writing by making "a list of personal experiences that somehow changed you or your life so that you were not the same after they happened." The reader of this essay is spellbound as Linda, a student in the author's class, describes the experience of childhood rape. The author goes on to describe a series of steps which lead toward a completed piece of writing, and draws explicit connections between literature and good student writing.

"We must learn to accept and delight in the difference we find in our students," writes Donald Murray, "for surprise is the most significant element in writing." Murray argues that the writing teacher must not be so much the rigid planner as the astute listener, ever sensitive to nuance and innuendo in student writing. It comes, then comes again, then spreads, and the whole class becomes alive. "Writing and Teaching for Surprise" provides an eloquent description of an intangible but absolutely necessary ingredient for the successful writing class.

Alice Brand ("The Why of Cognition: Emotion and the Writing Process") says "that a realistic and complete psychology of writing must include affective as well as cognitive phenomena." Over the past two decades, a cognitive approach to teaching writing has been dominant, but it fails to account for the whole of the writing process. Brand calls for a balance in the teaching of writing, a balance between cognitive and affective concerns.

Teaching English Composition
as a Creative Art

JEAN PUMPHREY

If someone came up to you and said, "Go develop a sense of humor," I suppose you'd laugh if you had one, and go into a deeper depression if you didn't. This, I submit, is what happens all too often in the teaching of English composition. So much of what we say to students really amounts to "go write a good theme," and those who can, do; those who can't get depressed, frequently to the point of dropping out.

Even as there is too little meaningful teacher involvement in the process of writing, there is all too often too much involvement of the wrong kind. I think most teachers of composition will recognize the writing style which follows:

Each separate society is different from one another in their own way as individuals differ from each other. Every society is conditioned around what the people make it to be. The more people contained in a given area, the bigger the society and the greater the norms. And when you have these norms you can only do what is accepted by the people (who, of course, made up the norms) and if you violate the social expectations, you run into conflict.

If I seem to give too much credit to the author of this statement when I refer to her "style," I do not intend to. Credit must go to her teachers. I submit that no one writes this way naturally. Such a style of writing has to be learned. Few of us would like to think that this is what we're teaching, but when we stand outside the process, pushing the student too quickly into communicative language, leaping past the expressive function of language, I believe we are, unwittingly, teaching the style we then sit back and criticize.

Each fall we stagger under the barrage of such language from freshman college students. In an attempt to unscramble the student from such impossible "textbookeze," some may resort to a handbook, assuming the student is not ready for "great ideas" and must return to "go." Others may plead with or otherwise exhort the student to write in his own voice, write plainly about whatever he knows. "Write in your own voice," we tell him. "Pick a topic familiar to you, a theme you can support." We urge him to expose his private feelings. Surely that is something he knows something about. We tell him to give evidence, to be specific, to use examples, to be concrete, and, in

College English, 34 (February 1973), pp. 666-673. Copyright © by the National Council of Teachers of English. Reprinted with permission.

telling him, we are doing exactly what we are telling him not to do. It is not surprising that students should do as we do, not as we say. It is not surprising that they should learn more from *how* we teach than from what we teach.

The fact is that *no one,* in the decade of the seventies, is convinced by being told. Yet students and teachers go on telling with greater and greater embellishments as if extravagant rhetoric could obviate simple illustration. And we are all turned off, students and teachers alike.

The teacher, concerning himself primarily with the product rather than the process, grades in silence, grimly revising his transmogrifying comments. The student is expected to learn language by writing in silence, later by observing his "corrected" errors, often in contrast to an accomplished writer's "model essay." Alone in his study, suspecting somehow he is responsible, the teacher tries to devise means to help the student reorder his thoughts. Removed from the process, he is inclined to think in terms of form aside from content. Should he decide, in the name of Order or Expediency, to impose a pre-determined form upon his students' raw material, he runs the risk of alienating his students from language. Pleasure in language may be lost, and with it the opportunity to see writing as a process of discovery.

Much of the graceless language we are confronted with comes as a direct result of student attempts to put together too much too soon, using someone else's format. Much of this writing is simply a reflection of the degree to which the student has become alienated from language which should be as naturally his as love. Susanne Langer ("The Lord of Creation," *Fortune*, January, 1944) writes, "The process of transforming all direct experience into imagery or into that supreme mode of symbolic expression, language, has so completely taken possession of the human mind that it is not only a special talent but a dominant, organic need." If this be so, then why should writing be considered such an unpleasant task by so many students?

In the opinion of this writer, there can be no pleasure in language in the classroom so long as students write and teachers grade in painful isolation from one another. Yet teacher involvement in the process of writing has all too often meant interference, a dictating of form or content, a coming in with red pencil in hand, an approach which tends to separate teacher from student, form from content, and ultimately, student from language.

We need to get involved in the process together, all together, to mutually re-discover that language lives, that the word is alive, that writing is a process of discovery.

The sort of teacher involvement I am advocating brings teacher and students together in exploring the problems we all have in common when we try to write. It means sharing the pleasure we all can experience through writing. It means a shift in emphasis from teacher-student to student-peer evaluation, and an opening up of the classroom to let in real problems, as opposed to those artificially set up to "train" the student into logic or to "prepare" him for entrance into some other institution.

As a poet and as a teacher I have come to see the creative process as a process of scattering, then bringing together of various parts into a new whole. One does not know beforehand what form that whole will take, but that is how discoveries are made, and that is what makes writing, or any other creative act, exciting. It is the excitement of writing creatively which needs to be restored to the English classroom.

What follows is not a course description, but rather an attempt to illustrate some of the discoveries I and my students made while becoming involved together in the process of writing.

Attempting to illustrate a process is a little like trying to communicate a color in braille. I comfort myself with what I say to students: "All writing assignments are impossible. Though we can summon things to us with words (which is miracle enough), the word can never be the thing, and since writing is a process of selection, always we are compelled to leave things out, and to fear we have left the 'wrong' things out." With this *a priori* limitation in mind I shall try to illustrate the value of "spontaneous" writing in the classroom, and to show how certain techniques of fiction can be used to teach a multi-purpose writing skill to many who have become alienated from language, as well as to those who love language.

The class I refer to in the paragraphs which follow is a three unit freshman transfer composition class made up of students who placed themselves.

The class met three times a week. During the first week, after arranging our seats in a kind of circle, we began our discussion of writing. From the beginning we agreed that writing is a very complex and difficult task. I explained to the students that all of the writing assignments would be impossible; that I would not be looking for the perfectly executed assignment, but that I would be most concerned to see that each person had grappled in his or her way with the problem posed by the assignment. "What is it that makes writing so frustrating and so painful?" was the subject of the first of a series of five to ten minute write-ins designed to help students recover the excitement of using language expressively.

I suggested the students write on one side of the paper only, and with a smooth ball point pen. Much of the frustration connected with writing comes because the mind moves so much faster than the hand. Pencils move too slowly, and the process of erasing stops the forward movement. Often what has been erased turns out to be useful alter on. It is less frustrating and more productive to scratch out and later revise.

I wrote along with the students. This helped me to discover more about my own processes, and it served the purpose of encouraging the students, and of keeping me in closer touch with what was happening to them. I tried to make the most of my own "mistakes" to *reinforce* the idea that we were not aiming for perfection. Spelling, sentence structure, punctuation were all matters to be considered on a final draft, but not for now. Since we were not aiming for perfection the students were soon freer in their writing, and at the same time, less hesitant in reading aloud what they had written. Sometimes it was fun, sometimes serious, often it was both at the same time.

One student's response to the question "What makes writing so painful?" provoked a very serious and stimulating discussion. She wrote, "Writing is difficult because everything you write down is there forever. When you *say* something you get feelings back right away, and it's easier to know how to respond. But writing is stating something—not being able to take anything back."

We discussed whether or not it is true that we can't take back what we say in writing. We decided that although it is not true, most people act as if it were true. And that is part of what makes writing painful. We tend to write every moment as if every one of our words were to be published and immortalized. And so long as we are wondering "Am I saying the right thing? Am I saying it the right way?" that is the object of our concentration, and not the subject we are writing about. Our powers of observation are cut off to the extent to which we internalize a voice of authority which constantly demands a perfect product, even on a first draft. Our motto became "Write first, think later. Don't try to be the writer and the critic at the same time."

I asked the students to write the next assignment on white, unlined paper. This assignment was to write for five minutes without stopping, on any subject. Those who "couldn't find" a subject were asked to write on just that. The aim was pure quantity. After five minutes we did a word count. The record was 193. The girl who won had written about being fired from her job. She had more than enough to say on that subject. The students "without subjects" began to realize that, in actuality, they had a great wealth of material. It was a question of tapping the source, the flow. Who hasn't failed at something? And, sadly, we always have much to say about our failures. We wrote for another five minutes to see if anyone could beat the record. No one did, but we discovered that no had had time to be bored or intimidated by the prospect of writing.

I asked the students to hold up their papers. Facing each other, they made the not so surprising observation that nearly everyone had written as though his paper were lined, and as though the object were, not to expand thoughts, but to conserve paper. Thereafter, continuing to use unlined paper, and resolving to be more expansive and wasteful, we placed the waste paper basket in the center of the room, and used it freely as we wrote.

Released from the bondage of spelling, punctuation, erasers, and lined paper we were free wheeling. The students themselves began to provide the in-class writing assignments. We wrote on all sorts of objects, both strange and commonplace, and often grappled with unanswerable questions. If a hungry student began furtively to peel an orange so that the pervasive smell of rind reached us long before the sight of the orange, we wrote about that. Nothing was irrelevant, and thus much of the attention, the best concentration, which ordinarily goes out the window or toward some other "distraction," was caught and held.

The next planned assignment was to "put the classroom on paper" the way a novelist or short story writer puts a room into a sentence or a paragraph. After we had written for five minutes I asked the students what problems they were encountering. By this time they were aware of the great number of possibilities, angles of vision, open to the writer in describing any object or scene. The problem, they said, was where to begin. As we analyzed this problem it became clear the real problem was not where to begin, but *to begin*. The discovery that they could find so much to say had stopped them. We discussed writing as a process of selection. Selecting means making decisions, and the more importance we attach to each decision the more painful and difficult it becomes. The tendency to attach undue importance to each decision is minimized once the distinction between a first draft and a finished piece is clearly realized.

Gradually the students came to realize that it is more effective, more efficient, and less painful to write three drafts rapidly, each time adding and/or subtracting detail, rather than painstakingly attempting a polished, all inclusive piece the first time through. I suggested they concern themselves, not absolutely, but generally, with *what* they have to say on a first draft, with the *order* in which they say it on a second draft, and with *how* they say it on a third draft.

Constantly we *tell* students to revise, revise, but not until they have been through the process, not once, but a number of times, do they clearly see the value of what we are telling them. This is partly because students are all too inclined to treat a first draft like a final draft; to approach it at the last minute, and with great intensity, until they exhaust themselves half way through. Perhaps this is because teachers themselves have tended to ask for "first drafts" while looking for neatly structured outlines, perfect sentence structure, precise punctuation, and perfect spelling. For whatever reason, most students initially rebel at the thought of going through, what seems to them, the very tedious process of writing a second or third draft.

Too often, I think, teachers have acted under the fear or the assumption that students, left to their own devices, will write sloppy, disorganized papers. One has only to leave them to their own devices to discover that students are no more resistant to the mind's need for order than the rest of us, and that their desire for order is, in fact, very great. It then becomes the function of the teacher, not to leap in with a magic formula five paragraph theme to assure the student of what will please him, the teacher, but rather to help the student through the wilderness of his own thought, to encourage him to use language expansively until he discovers what it is he wished to give order to. Free of any pressure to pre-order his thoughts, the student can then experience the excitement of seeing form evolve out of content as his scattered thoughts come together into a new whole.

By the time the students caught on to the advantage of writing freely and of doing several drafts, we were already into more sophisticated assignments related to their reading of literature. Thus far I have mentioned only in-class writing assignments and related discussion. The students were, at the same time, reading short stories and poems outside of class. The first few out-of-class writing assignments simply required the students to react in a personal way, positively or negatively, to the literature assigned. Gradually the in-class and out-of-class assignments came together. For example, having attempted to put a room on paper ourselves, we examined the way writers of fiction accomplish this.

One in-class assignment was to write from memory a description of a character from one of the stories. We then went through the story line by line listing all concrete details in order to determine what had been left out, or perhaps of greater interest, what had been added, by each of us. The next out-of-class assignment was to describe a person so everyone in the class would either like or dislike him. As we reacted to each description it soon became clear that the most convincing pieces of writing were those in which the writer paid close attention to concrete detail, attempting to show rather than tell. Increasingly the students grew to trust one another to evaluate and criticize constructively. Their writing improved as they continued to write for an audience beyond themselves or their teacher.

At one point I read the students the first few pages of Kafka's *The Metamorphosis*, up to the point where Gregor's mother calls to him from the other side of the door. I then asked the students to finish the story as they saw fit. This led to some hilariously funny writing, but they were able to see the limitless possibilities which confront, and at the same time offer themselves to the writer of fiction. We discussed how and why Kafka might have made certain decisions as he wrote, and how writing decisions in general are made. We played with the idea of a metamorphosis, trying to decide how other characters we had encountered would have reacted had each, like Gregor, found himself transformed into an insect. Or what if Gregor had turned into an antelope instead of an insect? The students could readily envision many variations on a single theme. Perhaps the most important discovery they made while tackling this assignment was how much easier it is to write when one has hold of a plot or a theme interesting enough to be self-propelling.

The next step was to prepare for a longer, more formal, out-of-class paper. I suggested possible themes, but recommended that the students develop their own. They were free to write a formal essay or to try writing a short story. The only requirement was that the paper must relate to the literature assigned. A short story, for example, could be modeled on Kafka's *The Metamorphosis*.

I asked the students on a Friday to bring in a statement of theme for Monday. Though they had been quite good about doing assignments, when Monday came, less than two thirds of the students had done the assignment. I asked how much time each of them had spent worrying about the assignment in the midst of weekend activities. That was another matter. One girl estimated she had spent as many as twelve hours worrying about, not doing the assignment. I suggested we take five minutes to write a statement of theme. In five minutes the student who had spent twelve hours worrying about the assignment had written a statement satisfactory to me. She had given herself a far more difficult assignment than I had because she unconsciously assumed, despite all indications to the contrary, that she would be held to her statement, tied to this one decision. Instead of writing a state-ment of theme she was attempting to write the entire paper in her head—a little like trying to put a puzzle together in one's head without looking at the pieces. I pointed out that an initial statement of theme should be simply a tool to explore with, and added, somewhat didactically, "He who post-pones the assignment, does it a hundred times."

Next I asked those who had statements to begin their first drafts. I reminded them that a first draft would simply amount to getting the pieces of the puzzle out on the table. I suggested they write only one set of ideas or images per page on one side of the page in order to achieve greater mobility when the time came to put their ideas back together in new form. Those who did not yet have a statement of theme I asked to write for five minutes at a time on several potential themes suggested by other students. When a student found something he wanted to continue writing on, I suggested he pursue that.

Though not every student found his theme that day, nearly everyone discarded a few dead ends. One by one the students were discovering that they had themes of their own, and could develop them. I wanted them to understand, also, that certain themes, unanswered questions, run through our entire lives, and that in writing a single paper, one only begins to tap a major theme.

Increasingly the students were coming to find they did not want to stop writing after five or ten minutes, that writing for "five" minutes was a good way to begin, a way to get past that time just prior to writing when the mind rebels. At one point I asked a student if the five minute write-ins were help-ing him. "No," he replied, "I want to keep writing."

Before the papers were due the students brought them into class for criticism. I suggested they divide into groups of three so that each student would have an audience of two. Each student read his paper aloud and was given general criticism. Then I asked them to exchange papers and to make specific comments in writing. I asked that the papers be typed, not just be-cause a typed paper makes a better impression on the reader, but because I am convinced that typing a paper improves the quality of writing. The pen may be friendlier in the beginning, but typing a paper finishes it.

Despite student enthusiasm and the opportunity for much criticism beforehand, the papers were not all A's, and I would have been happier had I not had to put a grade on some of them. Some of the students had a problem with sentence structure until the very end, and I do not mean any-where to imply that some of them would not have benefited from a gram-matical approach. I will say that much of the rough sentence structure I encountered in the beginning had become smoother by the end of the course. I could particularly see a change in the writing of those who began with the sort of cramped style so evident in the piece of student writing first quoted in this paper. "Correcting" such writing is nearly impossible, and any attempt to do so is likely to produce more pain than anything else. It is not enough to *tell* such a student to be concrete, to give examples. She needs to discover the examples she needs by learning to explore ideas freely through writing.

I was generally pleased with the final papers the students turned in and also with the improvement I could see in their in-class writing. But more than that I was pleased to hear some of them say they were, for the first time, enjoying writing, that they were even beginning to write letters! I was pleased, not because I think learning must always be "fun," but because I know that one does more of what one enjoys and by doing more, one becomes better, and so enjoys doing more. A new and positive cycle is begun. Writing is, and always will be, one of the most diffiucult of human endeavors. This we understood and accepted from the beginning. The discovery, for some of the students, was that writing could be pleasurable and rewarding. . . .

The greatest problem I encountered throughout the course was that of evaluation. I postponed grading by making comments rather than corrections on the short out-of-class papers. In making comments I tried to re-enforce the positive, rather than emphasize errors. In addition, I told the students that I would, at any time, accept a paper to be graded, should anyone wish to know where he stood grade-wise. This worked for the better students who were more readily able to move from expressive to communicative language. But one semester is hardly enough time for the weaker student to make such a transition. It would have been better had these students been allowed to continue writing expressively without having to "get it altogether" for a grade. The course would have been more effective for all concerned, and more readily adaptable to individual needs, had it been offered on a credit, no-credit basis.

It could be asked at this point "Where and how will the student learn his basic grammar, his spelling and punctuation?" It is by no means my intent to discount this very real and valid concern. I can only say that if the student has not acquired his basic English in twelve years of schooling, it would be presumptuous to think that as college teachers we have the magic to teach him all this in one or two semesters. But we can, by *allowing* him to find pleasure in language, by encouraging him to expand his thoughts until they become interesting to him, help him to find the motivation to pursue the more mechanical aspects of language.

On the last day of class I asked the students to write for five minutes in response to the following question: "Has your attitude toward writing changed at all since the beginning of the semester?" I think the following anonymous response best illustrates how writing can be a process of discovery.

Not really—If I have a good topic I get interested—If I don't it's just another assignment—I've always enjoyed writing when I'm interested in the subject. I've become a lot more critical of my writing. I guess my attitude has changed—I now feel that what I write must be a total expression of me—rather than just writing to fulfill the assignment—True, I am writing to fulfill this assignment but I'm also saying things I mean rather than a lot of the bullshit I'm capable of producing.

Tapping Creative Potential for Writing

GABRIELE LUSSER RICO

What would happen if you wrote *round* on the board and asked your class to write something about it? Many teachers would get dictionary-type definitions, cliched rhymes, or fragments of stories. A few pupils might struggle to come up with even one sentence, and a few might produce a fresh complete piece of writing. Would these results satisfy you? Probably not. You'd want every child to enjoy the pleasure that comes with sharing his or her own thoughts—and to enjoy writing so much that concern for quality follows naturally. Encouraging children's natural writing ability may be easier than you'd guess. What's important is understanding how to help children draw on their natural need to make patterns out of their experience, tapping the pleasure of creating their personal whole through language. Clustering is a nonlinear brainstorming technique that can get kids started. It involves a circled stimulus word, like *round,* and an open receptivity to words and phrases that come to mind. It helps writers learn to connect thoughts, feelings, ideas not connected before. It enables pupils to generate ideas, to structure them loosely, and to discover in them a tentative shape that allows writing to flow.

Like many teachers, I used to require my pupils to write in journals. I hoped writing in journals would stimulate the flow of ideas. But results were largely disappointing, often degenerating into mundane, diary-like entries without beginning or end, such as "I wish I were at the beach today instead of school. I'm hungry. After school I have to do chores at home, ugh...." Clustering, because it taps associations that generate patterns of ideas rather than such sequential thinking, does not produce this shallow, uninteresting rattling off of events. Clustering is based on what we know from brain research. The left brain has primarily logical, linear, syntactic capabilities; the right brain has holistic, image-making, synthetic capabilities. Of overriding importance for writing is that the talents of both hemispheres be brought into play, each in its own time.

Any effective writing effort moves from a whole—no matter how vague or tenuous—to the parts, then back to a more clearly delineated whole. Clustering focuses on that initial whole by eliciting associations and metaphors from the clusterer's mental storehouse until some of them begin to shape themselves into a whole, giving the writer a sense of direction.

A good part of this article first appeared with the title "Tapping the Right Brain for Writing Ideas" in *Prime Areas,* the journal of the British Columbia Primary Teachers' Association. Vol. 30, No. 3. Spring 1988, pp. 20-25. Reprinted with permission.

As the stimulus word echoes through the right brain, it is like a magnet, picking up images, certain feelings and emotional nuances, lines of songs or poems, similar rhythms, whatever an individual's pattern-seeking right brain perceives as related. The technique temporarily blocks the critical censorship of the analytic left brain and allows the synthesizing right brain to make flashlike, nonlinear connections. As each child clusters around a stimulus word, the encircled words rapidly radiate outward until a sudden shift takes place—a sort of "Aha!"—signaling an awareness of that tentative whole, a focus and direction that allows each child to begin writing. This moment is like watching clouds, and seeing just clouds, then suddenly seeing a horse or a duck or your neighbor's profile. It is a moment of pattern recognition.

Children need to know that not everything from the cluster is used, and some things may be changed. A stimulus word filtering through a child's personal experiential sieve will always generate writing expressive of the child's unique consciousness. That is the essence of natural writing: expression unique and authentic to each child; each child's own voice heard in words written on the page.

Consider one experience I had with a group of Grade 2s and 3s given the stimulus word *round*. Every youngster wrote with a clear relationship to the concept of roundness, and each vignette was different from the others. Some thought of bicycle tires, M & Ms, and a cat curling up to go to sleep. Notice the differences in these writing samples that originally appeared in *Writing the Natural Way:*

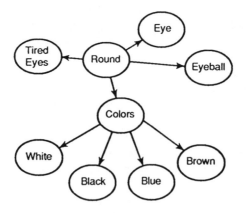

An eyeball has two circles in it. One circle is blue or brown or green. You and I know that everyone has one color in each eye, but there is also black and white. The pupil of the eye is black of course. The eyeball, not the colored part and not the pupil, is white. Sometimes your eye is bloodshot. Maybe it is because you have not had much sleep.

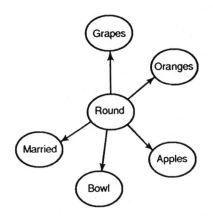

Once there was an apple and an orange that fell in love. But their fathers didn't let them get married. But they wanted to so badly they even threatened to jump into a bowl of fruit and get eaten by the humans. Then they threatened to lie down in the middle of the street and get run over and they did it and that was the end of that and the two fathers jumped into a bowl of fruit and they got eaten and nobody lived happily ever after.

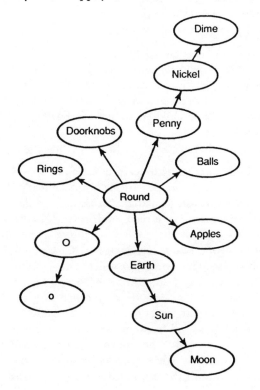

What is Round?
Round is a ball bouncing high in the air.
Round is a flea that crawls up in your hair.
Round is the earth that we're now standing on.
Round is the sun that goes up at dawn.
Round is an apple that blooms in the spring.
Round is a beautiful emerald ring.
Round is a planet up in space.
Round is a necklace made out of a shoelace.
Round is the super small moon.
Round is the head of a big baboon.
Round is a log floating down the stream.
Round is a pie topped with whipped cream.
Round is a little o.
Round is a tangerine that had a friend cow.
Round is a dime, a penny, a nickel.
Round is the end of a pickle.
Round is the doorknob that sits on a door.
Round is a table that stands on the floor.
Round is a tummy of a boy.
Round is the middle of a toy.
And that's all of this round tale.
Goodbye, see ya after my bottle of ale!

The first writer produces clear expository prose for one so young. The second writer illustrates a wild prose for one so young, and the third a fine attunement to the natural rhythms of language, with the repetition of *round* as the cohesive factor. The only change I made in these samples of writing was to correct the spelling to allow children to see the power of their narratives instead of their errors.

Here are some tips for introducing cluster writing into your classroom:

1. Tell pupils that they are going to learn to use a tool that will enable them to write more easily and more powerfully, a tool similar to brainstorming. To loosen up conformist thinking, discuss how different people see different shapes in a cloud or a piece of driftwood. Explain that children have personal associations that each can capture in writing.

2. Encircle a word on the board, say, *energy,* and ask pupils, "What do you think of when you see that word? Just watch, I'm going to write whatever ideas come into my mind. I don't know what will happen." Then begin clustering yourself, writing ideas as they come to you. Flow with any current of connections that comes to mind. Write these rapidly, each in its own circle, radiating outward from the center in any direction they want to go. Connect each new word or phrase with a line to the preceding circle. When something different strikes you, begin again at the stimulus word and radiate outward until those associations are exhausted. Don't censor

yourself. The idea is to show yourself to be as open and receptive to your ideas as you'd like your pupils to be. When you finish your cluster, say something like, "See how many ideas are floating around in my head? I bet my ideas are different from each of yours, and each of yours from each other's. If you cluster by yourself, you'll have a set of connections as unique as your thumbprint."

3. Ask pupils to cluster a second word for themselves. Explain that they don't have to show this paper to anyone. Try a word like *afraid* or *help*. Before the children begin, tell them that clustering should take no more than two minutes. Ask them to be sensitive to the moment when they sense a direction of what to write about. Ask them to keep clustering until the "Aha!" shift signals that their mind is holding something they can shape into a whole. Tell the children they'll write a short, self-contained vignette in 10 minutes. Ask them to choose only what seems to fit from the profusion of choices in the cluster. Say that there's no need to force every idea in. Suggest that they use what feels comfortable and ignore the rest.

As pupils write, the only constraint is that they don't leave their vignettes unfinished. Ask them to consider a whole, complete thought or statement on a subject. When they finish, pupils should reread their work and make any improvements. Ask them to give their vignettes titles.

Writers will discover—even after the first time—that clustering is easy and nonthreatening. Because a cluster draws on primary impressions, yet stimultaneously on a sense of overall design, clustering actually generates structure, shaping one thought into a starburst of other thoughts, each related to the whole. Once children discover something to write about, or at least a sense of direction, they become so involved in expressing this direction that they worry less about how the parts fit together or what errors they might be making than about communicating the whole thought. That's why clustering often results in writing marked by increased coherence, fluency, and originality of images and metaphors.

Here's an example. Before clustering, one sixth grader wrote this sentence in response to the stimulus word *question*.

A question is a way to find out information.

Then the child tried clustering.

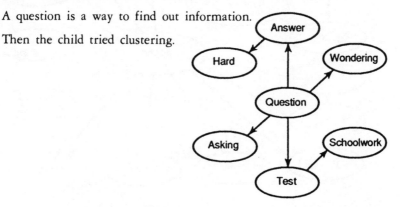

After clustering, the child wrote this.

In my world a question is a wondering. It comes upon you while you're doing schoolwork or something like that. It's an asking that you want to answer, but it isn't always easy. Then it seems to get harder and harder until you give up. You wonder about it for days, then you figure it out, but it's too late; you have already taken the test.

4. Because you want to encourage open receptivity to ideas and because children's writing is sometimes very personal, you'll want to be especially sensitive to privacy. Don't collect this first piece of writing. Instead, ask pupils to use it as their first entry in their writer's notebook. Cluster and write every day or two in the notebooks.

Recently, a Grade 1 teacher asked her pupils to cluster *round,* letting them know that, if they didn't know how to write a word, they could draw a picture. On the pages that follow I give you not only their original clusters but also their vignettes as they wrote them. In doing so, I emphasize three thoughts about learning and writing: 1) the children's thinking is richly imaginative at age six, 2) their connection-making ability is complex, and 3) correctness of spelling is, at this stage, secondary to the children's getting these riches on paper and feeling good about them.

Leslie's huge cluster ended up focusing on body parts, most of which possess aspects of roundness, followed by conjecture about how each part is *important,* a three-syllable word she didn't know how to spell. Because she was given permission to draw a line for words she could not spell, she managed to write a long, wondering, rather sophisticated vignette, ending with a thought about thinking.

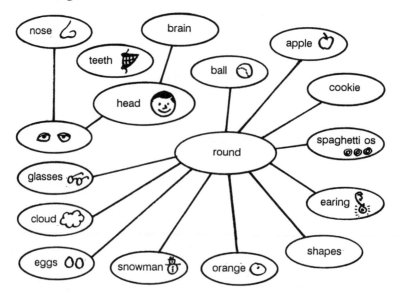

A head has eyes, nose, mouth and inside the mouth there are teeth and a tongue. The top of your head is your brain. Some people were glasses. The glasses belong on your eyes. And glasses are ver im _____ for your eyes. Your eyes sometimes need because you can't see to good. The mouth is very im _____ to because thats how you talk and eat. If you didn't have a mouth than you wouldn't be alde (able) to talk or eat. And your brain is very im _____ too so if you didn't have a brain you wouldn't be alde to think.

Leslie, Grade 1

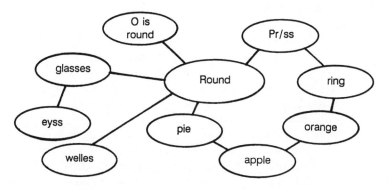

My eyes are round so is black berry pie that my mom makes. bubbles I blow in the bath tub there rill round! I like to eat apples and oranges I have lots of round things in my hous butens are ronud on my close. I like to have snowball fights with my sister snowbaulls are round!

Sarah, Grade 1

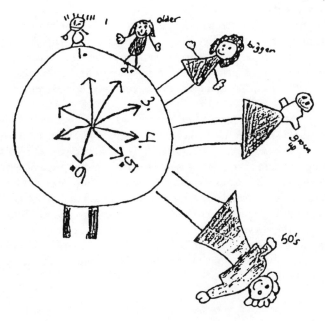

Once a lifetime you live as a child and get bigger and bigger. While your getting bigger you get older. Some people think you die and another hondred you comme back as something else. It's a rotatiun.

Kady, Grade 1

Sarah's vignette indicates concept learning. Since the concept is *roundness,* she describes a series of round things and elaborates about what she does with them. In her cluster, note the delightful spelling of *pearls* as "prlss." Despite the inverted spellings of "rilly" and "butens" and "close," we know exactly what she is telling us with evident relish. Look at her exclamation marks!

Kady's cluster turned into a clock with legs. Here is a six year old who in nine little lines has imagined the progression from birth to childhood through adolescence to adulthood, ending her visually clustered progression in the "50s," although her arrow designated "6," followed by unnumbered arrows, implies an ongoing cycle. Indeed, in her vignette, she echoes this cyclical awareness of life when she asserts: "it's a rotatiun."

The knowings in children's heads are nothing short of awesome. Let's enable children to draw these knowings out—the meaning of *educare*—by giving them power over their language. Writing allows children ownership of that power if we encourage them to risk without penalizing them. Focusing on correctness before children have learned that the expression of these emerging patterns is pleasurable confuses the means with the ends of writing; we may teach them the right notes, but they miss the melody.

For the first few weeks, schedule free time after cluster writing so that no child's writing has to be interrupted. But encourage children to finish in 10 to 15 minutes. It's important for them to realize that they can finish satisfactorily within a given time.

At the end of a few weeks, ask pupils to turn in their notebooks, after stapling down those entries they prefer to keep private. The children should also select a few entries to polish for you to grade. Self-selection not only creates the assurance of privacy needed for pupils to cluster freely but also reduces your workload, allows pupils choice, and asks them to reread and judge their own work.

5. Don't emphasize the mechanics until pupils have been clustering for a couple of weeks. Discuss what fun it is to know you can write about anything. Explain that, when you've created a special piece of writing, you want to make it as good as you can by looking for improvements in spelling and punctuation. Consider asking children to read their selected vignettes to each other in groups; then work together on corrections. Children often value what they have written so much that they'll pay much more attention to mechanics. Then, mechanics become more meaningful because the writing is already valuable to the child. Don't expect the clusters themselves to be intelligible.

Psychological Benefits of Clustering

- Allows students to experience a discovery process

- Is nonthreatening, enabling positive involvement in the learning process

- Honors what students already know, joining the known to the new to be learned

- Encourages the creation of patterns meaningful to students in a language that is theirs

- Creates a level of comfort that leads to writing/discussion/genuine learning

- Permits playfulness and stimulates curiosity and wonder

- Eliminates indecisiveness because a cluster breaks the ice by filling the page with associations

- Permits students to begin where they are, not where they "ought" to be

What Clustering Is

- It is a self-organizing process, allowing the clusterer to observe an emerging pattern in apparent confusion.

- It evolves into an organic thought structure from which the ensuing writing grows.

- It is a starting point for any class discussion, beginning with what students already know.

- It is an anxiety reducer, drawing, in short-hand fashion, on their knowings, opinions, feelings, images.

- It is a powerful tool for concept learning.

- It is a personal "centering" tool, allowing connections to spill out which might otherwise never emerge.

- It is a brain-compatible tool for overcoming resistance, inertia, and fear.

- It is a way of "drawing out" (educare) rather than "pounding in" (rote learning).

Clustering engenders and encourages expressive language at all ages and levels of proficiency. The more it is used, the more natural and comfortable it becomes and the more surprising the results. As pupils gain a sense of accomplishment in producing a cluster, they discover that they do have something to say after all. They also discover that writing begins to flow on its own if a sense of play is allowed to enter into the process. Such play makes contact with our natural potential for creating connections, for perceiving one idea related to another, for seeing the world whole.

* * *

If clustering is effective in tapping the images, patterns and feelings of children, it is even more so with adolescents and adults. Adults have a broader experiential base and greater resources in language. Yet despite their obvious advantages, adults tend to believe they have little to say—possibly because they are seldom asked to tap their rich potential. And the more their potential remains untapped and unused, the more inaccessible it becomes.

Clustering is a powerful and effective way to draw out the important themes lying dormant in our lives. Below are examples of adolescent and adult writers who have used clustering to engage their deeper thought processes, which in turn led to significant writing.

I. Junior high school student, Washington, D.C., demonstrating via her own story just how much she has learned in an Earth Science class.

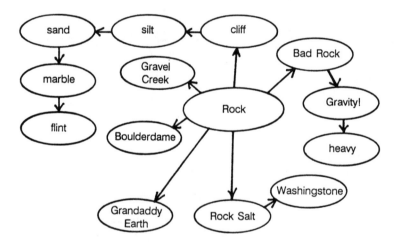

Chalk One Up for the Old Fossil

Hello, my name is Betty-Rock.* I come from the city of Washingstone, you know, the place right next to Crystal Slate. The College of Boulderdame is where I graduated from, and Gravel Creek is where I work at or did until this little girl picked me up and made me her pet rock. She reminds me of my sister so much that I named her after my sister, Limestone. Oh, well back to my story.

*Get it? "Bedrock"

Every member in my family from Mrs. Marble to Uncle Flint has kept the family secret of gravity. Only the Rock family, my family, including cousins Cliff, Silt, and Soil know what is gravity and now I am about to share this secret with you. Or should I? I don't know, this secret has been kept for 65 billion years. Oh, I know, let me go ask Grandaddy Earth. I'll be back quick as a sand pebble!

Queretta Simms

II. Adult, college

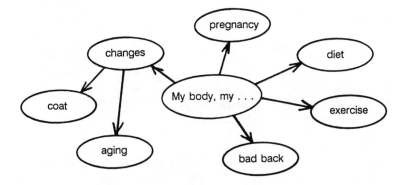

My body, my coat,
a new one for each season.
Thin and supple in my youth,
I put you on without a thought
that I might ever
                have to hang you up.
And now I wear a different coat;
it weighs upon my shoulders,
it is a little worn,
a bit stretched and sagging.
I am more careful now,
protective of the fabric.
I found a tear needing mending.
I want to make it through the winter.

Susan Chiavelli

III. Young adult, Vietnam veteran returning to college

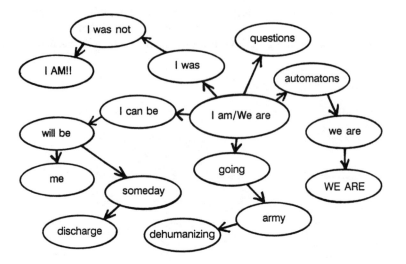

We are. We are. We are. From the day you enlist 'til the day you got out, that thought is beat into you: We are. The backbone of the military is teamwork. We are. The buddy system is always in effect. We are. "You're one of us now." We are. Power in numbers. We are. We are. We are.

There's no room for the individual in the military way of thought, no informalities, no friendliness. "Sgt. Ashworth, 558-86-2707, Sir!" You become a cog in the military machine. You have a job to do. Whether it's mopping the mess or killing a Commie, popping a picture or flying a fighter, towing a truck or moving a mountain; it doesn't matter. Just do as you are told. "Don't question me, boy, yours is to do, not to question."

But one can't help but question. "Do what you will with my body, but my mind is mine." The lone cry of the individual within the ranks of the military: "I am not a number—I'm a free man," or so you think. The most unnerving fact you must accept is that you are not a free man, but, instead, a military man. So what if your supervisor is an incompetent ass—he's been one for 18 years now and is not about to have some young recruit change his methods.

The one saving grace that helps the lone individual get through his tour of duty is the gradual realization that he is not alone. There are other individuals, too. You can spot one every now and then. I think it's something in the eyes— you can tell that there is something going on inside. They are mostly quiet— don't talk much with or about dedicated military personal (as the lifers prefer to be called). They just listen to themselves. "It'll be over eventually. This won't last forever. Someday you'll be able to tell all of these assholes to get bent and they won't be able to do a damn thing about it." The day comes for all. It always seems like an eternity, but it has a way of sneaking up on you, too. Every person has his discharge date stamped in his brain in indelible ink. It's impossible to forget (27 March '77). It's a prayer you say at night, a light at the end of the tunnel, the impossible dream that eventually comes true.

The I AM within you works its way towards the surface as discharge nears, as you become "short." You listen to your supervisors less, you listen to yourself more. You become more and more dependent upon yourself. The military has a way of making you dependent upon it. "Don't worry, we'll take care of it." "Don't worry about a thing, boy." "Trust us." We are. We are. We are.

But as discharge nears, it becomes a battle. WE ARE, WE ARE, WE ARE, i am. WE ARE, WE ARE. i am. WE ARE. i am. WE ARE. i am. WE ARE. I AM. WE ARE. I AM. WEAREIAM WE AREIAMWEAREIAMWEAREIAM. WE ARE. I AM. I AM. we are. I AM. I AM. I AM.

And finally you are—free once again. You're not the same—more cynical, much wiser, a little older, and much more appreciative of the fact that YOU ARE.

What I Learned from Verle Barnes:
The Exploratory Self in Writing

"I wonder how many of you—or anyone in the organization, for that matter—would like to go on a sea turtle patrol?"

I thought I had missed something. The occasion was the fall business meeting of the officers of the Southeastern Conference on English in the Two-Year College. The setting was a conference room in an Atlanta hotel. Sea turtles? Had my mind wandered momentarily?

"You see, the sea turtle is an endangered species. We need people to watch where they lay their eggs, and then put wire mesh around the eggs to protect them from predators."

"The island is uninhabited, just off the coast of Florida," he went on. "You can't imagine how beautiful it is, there in the Apalachicola Estuary. One of the best kept secrets of the Northern Hemisphere."

"Sorry, sea turtles are not on the agenda," the Chair reluctantly stated.

I didn't hear anything else about sea turtles until the following February at the annual convention, this one in Jackson, MS. There on the program under the general heading of "Creative Writing/Reading" was the title: "The Apalachicola Estuary: An Overview." The speaker was Woody Miley, Manager of the Apalachicola National Estuarine Reserve. Also at this same session was—you guessed it—Verle Barnes[1]: "Earth, Water, and Good Writing: The Making of a Natural History Book." I couldn't resist; I went to the session. In a little less than an hour I learned a lot about the Apalachicola Estuary, but even more important I re-learned a valuable lesson about the teaching of writing which I hope will remain with me for life. This lesson is so important and so profound that it touches the professional lives of writing teachers everywhere and determines in large measure how much our students learn. Yet it is so subtle that it is routinely overlooked and taken for granted. First, though, more about the estuary.

Apalachicola Estuary

From the session and from later conversations, I was able to piece together why Verle Barnes was so interested in the Apalachicola Estuary. In the early 1970s, while a graduate student in English at the University of Florida, he

Teaching English in the Two-Year College, 15 (February 1988), pp. 20-24. Copyright © 1988 by the National Council of Teachers of English. Reprinted with permission.

became interested in a series of articles appearing in the Gainesville and other newspapers. A battle was raging between the Corps of Engineers, who wanted to dam the Apalachicola, and a group of environmentalists who wanted the river to remain free flowing. Always something of an environmentalist himself, Verle followed the story throughout that spring, generally siding with those who wanted the river left as is. In order to see the situation firsthand, he decided on a memorable day in 1974 to visit the town where the river comes into the bay. Little did he realize that the experience would profoundly alter the rest of his life.

Friday, May 3, 1974: I come to the town of Apalachicola for the first time. You arrive from the east, along Highway 98, following the Gulf coast. You cross the bridge, and there's the town.

Clean in the morning sun. Hint of salt spray in the air. Old. Quaint. Unpainted but clean. Everything is slow. Time stands still.

To the left, across the bay, hazy in the morning sun, are the barrier islands. In the distance to the right are the fish houses and shrimp boats.

But here immediately before me is the river. The river joins the bay, fresh water and salt intermingling, and I am overwhelmed. Sunlight everywhere is mirrored on the surface. Sun and river and bay, and I am here, breathing slow. I see and understand this holy place.

It has been almost fifteen years since Verle first came to the Apalachicola. During that time he has spent many hours, many days, in the region, and even when he could not be there physically, his mind was filled with it. He has canoed the length of the river; spent time on the barrier islands which provide a haven for the endangered sea turtle; studied the estuary and surrounding flood plain; met local merchants, fishermen, townspeople; become acquainted with others who love the estuary with equal intensity; studied the plant and animal life of the region; speculated about the impact of hurricanes and other natural phenomena; read voraciously everything he could find about the history and ecology of the area. On several occasions he has conducted field trips, first with his jouralism students, taking them from eastern Tennessee to Florida to study and write about the Apalachicola, and then later with other faculty members to protect the sea turtle. On a trip last summer, one of the students, Torrey Fields, fell in love with the beauty of the region, and then later became Verle's wife.

It is only natural that a book should grow out of this long-standing love affair with the estuary. Just off press, the full citation is Verle Barnes, *Portrait of an Estuary,* Corpus Christi, Texas: Helix Press, 1987. The publication is a story in itself. The book was originally conceived in 1979 as a chronicle of the struggle between the Corps of Engineers and the environmentalists. Over the years, however, it evolved into what the title suggests, a portrait of the estuary. Finally, in the fall of 1986 a contract was signed with Helix, and the book became a reality.

The Lesson I Learned

As interesting as the estuary is, the lesson I learned most vividly is not so much about a place in Florida as it is about writing, and about teaching and learning. In all this, I have been eloquently reminded that the first lesson in teaching composition is that the writer must find his or her own subject. If young people do not care about what they are writing, if they do not own their work, or better, if their writing does not *possess* them, then it profits little to lecture on parallel structure or rhetorical strategy or whatever. If our students are ever to understand what writing really is, then they must come face to face with their own subjects. "A good subject is like a jewel buried in the bottom of the sea," I tell them. "You must dive deep, hold your breath, scrape away all the sand and mud and debris, take the jewel in your fingers, and bring it to the surface." I cannot give another person my subjects, for good writing has its origins and roots in the writer's soul. The kind of class I want is one where the discovery experience occurs routinely and where writing grows naturally out of that experience, taking its own direction, finding its own form, reaching its own audience.

What I really want is to bring Apalachicola into my classroom. That is, I want my students to discover a topic which captivates them in the same way the Apalachicola Estuary captivated Verle Barnes. I realize, of course, that Verle's experience is extraordinary and that my students may not experience anything with an equal intensity or that has such a long-standing effect. Still I want them to experience *some* of it. I want them to get perhaps a taste of it, to experience the quality of it directly.

This kind of discovery experience is not found in an English textbook. Indeed, the kind of experience I am describing is not an intellectual experience at all but rather an emotional response. It is not something you can put into a syllabus. You don't talk much about it, especially to department heads or deans or basic skills people. They wouldn't understand. But it's there, always in the back of your mind. You don't experience it directly but wait for it to happen. Perhaps you call it "creative energy," but it's not something you control directly. It's like an early morning fog. The more you try to capture it, the more it eludes you. So you lie back, and watch and wait for it to come, and then, Bingo! it happens. You sense its presence, nod silently, and pray that it becomes epidemic. Sometimes it does, but there are no guarantees.

What I am describing is not found in Aristotle or Quintilian or the standard writers, but rather in Carl Jung or Daisetz Suzuki or Meister Eckhart. More than likely they would phrase it this way: "The writer must become one with the subject." This concept of oneness or wholeness has been generally characterized by Walter T. Stace as "undifferentiated unity" and for centuries has permeated the literature of both east and west.

> Undifferentiated unity is necessarily thought of by mystics as being *beyond space and beyond time*. For it is without any internal division or multiplicity of parts, whereas the essence of time is its division into an

endless multitude of successive parts, and the essence of space is its division or parts lying side by side. Therefore the undifferentiated unity, being without any multiplicity of parts, is necessarily spaceless and timeless. Being timeless is the same as being eternal. Hence Eckhart is constantly telling us that the mystical experience transcends time and is an experience of "the Eternal Now." (25)

Being beyond time and space, this concept of undifferentiated unity is exceedingly difficult to explain. Once at the conclusion of a discourse on the topic, Eckhart told his audience, "If anyone does not understand this discourse, let him not worry about that, for if he does not find this truth in himself he cannot understand what I have said" (232). In other words, if you did not already understand it before I told you, you wouldn't understand it anyway. The clearest and perhaps most vivid illustration of the concept can be seen in a recent movie. The final scene of *Places in the Heart* is both breathtaking and puzzling. Because of the final juxtaposition of the characters, the viewer's sense of time and space is distorted. There is no dialogue, just music, and the viewer is left with a feeling of peace and wholeness. It is indeed a beautiful and gripping cinematic portrayal of what Stace calls "undifferentiated unity."

A classroom in which this kind of discovery experience happens is one in which there is much freedom. Not surprisingly, the idea of freedom occurs over and over throughout Eckhart's work. Eckhart's concept of freedom was revolutionary; at the time of his death, he was being tried by the Church for heresy. Although the following passage comes to us from a theological perspective, it takes little effort to see how the idea itself applies equally well in a pedagogical setting:

Some with attachment cling to prayers, to fastings, to vigils, and to all kinds of exercises and mortifications. Attachment to any of these deprives you of the freedom to serve God in this present now and to follow him alone in the light by which he instructs you what to do and what not to do, free and new in each now, as if you did not possess (anything), nor desire (anything), nor indeed could do anything else. (208)

Eckhart could just as easily have been talking about the creative process. As long as we rigidly follow preconceived rules or principles or guidelines or whatever, we will miss out on the opportunity to reach that level of excellence in our writing that comes through the freedom to create. When rules are foremost in our minds, then our primary concern is the fear of making a mistake. When rules are foremost, we find ourselves in a passive stance, like someone in a game of dodge ball. Our primary concern is reacting to someone else (in the composition class, to the teacher) rather than finding our own way. So the lesson of freedom is important in the composition class. It requires intelligence but also courage. When our students fully understand this, they will likely say, "It's scary."

But as important as freedom is, it must be tempered with discipline, or it will remain mushy and accomplish no good end. The important thing, I believe, is that discipline must grow naturally out of freedom, and not vice versa. It is only after our students have tasted the ecstasy of writing their own subjects that we can demand excellence. Only then will they understand and be willing to endure the tedious work of editing. This is why Verle persevered year after year to find a publisher. This is why no is never really No. This is the creative energy that motivates and compels the writer to do the difficult work that writing is.

Someday I hope to go out on that barrier island in the Apalachicola Bay and maybe even put wire mesh around turtle eggs. I'll think of Verle. I'll think of writing. I'll wonder if I can communicate to my students what Verle's experience communicated to me. Will my students have the courage to seek out those subjects buried deep and lying dormant within their own experience, to bring them to the surface, to look them full in the face and to write? I will listen to the waves, and wonder.

Note

[1] Verle Barnes teaches at Roane State Community College, Harriman, TN.

References

Barnes, Verle. *Portrait of an Estuary*. Corpus Christi: Helix Press, 1987.

Blakney, Raymond B. *Meister Eckhart: A Modern Translation*. New York: Harper, 1941.

Stace, Walter T. *The Teachings of the Mystics*. New York: Mentor Books, 1960.

Focusing Twice Removed

LESLEY REX-KERISH

"Before I read this I need to tell you that when I was seven I was raped." These words of warning were my freshman student's apprehensive introduction to her shocking account of being attacked by the neighbor's gardener's son. Taken completely by surprise, the class and I listened as she read the description she had been given ten minutes to write. Though its details were not particularly graphic, we were riveted. Her classmates were impressed and appalled by her open sharing. I was taken back by the unexpected intimacy of her subject. She had chosen to write about her rape knowing that she would be reading it to the rest of the class and that I would follow-up with questions. Bravado was not her intent; her hands shook, her voice quavered, and her eyes welled up as she recalled the experience. Later I asked her how she had been able to write about such a painfully personal experience. "You told us that the one experience we didn't want to face, the one we felt in the gut, was the one that could potentially yield the best writing," she said. "I wanted to start with something that could really be good."

As startling as it seemed to me then and as shockingly insensitive as it may sound now, this was exactly the kind of experience that I had wanted her to write about when I asked her to volunteer. The late Robert Kirsch, writer and literary critic, had advised his students to "write from the gut" when selecting their topics. I had found this advice invaluable and passed it on to my students. This quarter, as usual, I had fortuitously asked the right student to share her "gut-level" prose. I chose Linda because she was the first student to show up for class that day and because she was a self-possessed participant in class discussions. This was only the third week of classes, so I had had nine sessions with my students—not enough to find out who would be best suited for this type of public soul-baring. For indeed, that was really what I had asked for and hoped would happen. The exercise's success depended mainly upon the sensitivity and openness of the student guinea pig.

This barbaric sounding exercise was one that I used each quarter with my freshman literature students. It seemed to me that my students took for granted the insight and skill of published writers like E.B. White, George Orwell, and Joan Didion (the essayists with whom they were beginning the quarter). With typical freshman critical aplomb, they berated the themes, the style, and the tone of these professionals. For them, criticising a piece of literature meant

Freshman English News, 14 (Spring 1985), pp. 1-4, 8. Reprinted by permission of the publisher.

saying why they didn't like certain things, which meant identifying those elements which didn't fit their worldview, their experience, or their personal expectations for style and form.

I like to think that one of the reasons I am teaching literature, though certainly not the main reason, is to sophisticate my students' critical perceptions of literature. I spent quite some time pondering which word to use before I settled on "sophisticate," and even then I looked it up to make sure Webster thought it meant what I had intended. He said it means, among other things, to deprive of simplicity, to disillusion, to make worldly wise. That's what I was after. I wanted my students to see, appreciate, and absorb some of the wisdom they encountered in literature so that the rather simple view they have of themselves and of the world would expand—much like the f-stop on a camera opens to allow more incoming light. What I wanted was a perceptual and intellectual transformation from an f-stopless Kodak instamatic mentality to a Canon with its changeable f-stop aperture and compatible film speeds. As the Canon is more sensitive to the light, producing more perceptive photographs, changing snapshots into art, I wanted my student readers more sensitive and sensible. For this to occur, they needed to willingly open themselves up, which, as Webster points out, requires an initial disillusionment with their present view of the world. They had to be willing to endure self-questioning, uncertainty, and confusion to be receptive to the complexities of the human condition and the artistry with which it is portrayed in literature. They had to open themselves to the *affect* and the *effect* literature has on them: its power to lay hold of them, to impress them, and then to change them so they can truly see what literature has to say and the way in which it is said.

Dilation began the first day of class because my students arrived having read few engrossing essays and having written even fewer. Using the text *Eight Modern Essayists* (Wm. Smart; St. Martin's Press; 1980) we read and discussed a half dozen essays of three very different professional essayists which had come directly from the author's personal experiences, for example, E.B. White's "Walden," "Once More to the Lake," and "Death of a Pig"; George Orwell's "Shooting an Elephant," "How the Poor Die," and "Marrakech"; and Joan Didion's "On Morality," "On Going Home," and "Goodbye to All That." Far from being intimidated or even impressed by the professionals, the students were blasé. They had no idea of what was involved in writing an engrossing essay in the manner worthy of such critical attention. Pursuing my goal to sophisticate them, we read what the writers said about their own work, including the interesting comparison between Orwell's and Didion's respective renderings of "Why I Write." They listened to my laudatory analyses and strove to adopt the language and logic of the literary critic, but they were simply trying on the accoutrements of literary appreciation; they were not yet engaged closely in the text, not yet seeing it for themselves. While they were beginning to understand what they should be looking for and how they should be looking, they still had not read carefully and closely enough. Few of them could comprehend beyond a surface reading of the text that elicited the author's general meaning and intent. Of even more importance to the exercise I am presenting in this article was my observation that hardly any students had ever written an essay of the kind they were reading. They had not been asked to write about a critical personal experience that made the demands on their thinking and writing the professionals had made upon themselves. Another means of developing their appreciation had not been used. They couldn't understand what the essayists had accomplished by reading their texts, and, furthermore, they had not tried writing personal analyses themselves to find out what the professionals were up against to produce essays with power to engage, depict, and persuade.

I do not mean to suggest that their high school English teachers were remiss, though more often than not I find myself working with students who have written less than five essay length papers throughout their four years of high school. While I advocate the use of this exercise in high school, the level of analytical sophistication it could produce would probably be less than what I expect from my college freshmen. Nevertheless, in principle the effect should be the same: becoming more aware of the difficulties involved in personal analysis and more sensitive to the accomplishments of those who master it intelligently and artistically with written language.

I had other reasons for choosing this kind of writing assignment in place of the traditional literary analysis essay. I thought it would make my students more mature writers as well as more sophisticated readers. Indeed, my freshman writers preferred the view that they were in the process of maturing rather than suffering from inadequacies. With exercises like this, I intentionally shifted my teaching to promote their maturity, whereas my former approach was to inform them of what they had somehow missed learning and needed to acquire to catch up. Seeing them as the pupa still at work in the chrysalis and not the fully formed, but crippled, butterfly gave both of us more leverage to experiment and explore possibilities that would not have presented themselves before.

Reading and writing, the prospective and the introspective, aligned in a more meaningful and useful way for the students when they did the focusing exercise. First they read the mature thinkers and writers who used their significant personal experiences as the gist from which they dramatized, narrated, analyzed, and theorized about life. Their probing reflection spun persuasive essays with the dramatic immediacy of fiction and the convincing urgency of real life actions and issues. E.B. White's pig's death took on farcical and tragic proportions as he recaptured the events of the pig's passing. We tittered as he recounted his much interrupted telephone conversation with the vet, sniggered as he described his pet dog licking the suds from the pig's enema bag, and fussed along with White about the intimate bonds that are broken by death. Speculations about the implications of loss and unmet expectations continued to reverberate within us long after we had put the essay aside.

Next, I wanted my students to ponder the causes of these reverberations and attempt to duplicate them in a writing assignment. After pointing out the levels of abstraction which manifest in various discourse modes within each essay (e.g. recording, reporting, explaining, classifying, advising, speculating), I explained James Moffett's manner of depicting the relationship between a writer and his/her subject (*Universe of Discourse* p. 35). Having synthesized several of Moffett's writer-subject progressions into a single chart for my students, we practiced finding evidence in the texts of the various relationships the writers had with their subject matter.

Recording what is happening	Dramatization	Sensory on-going perceptual selection
Reporting what happened	Narration	Chronologic memory selection
Generalizing what happens	Exposition	Analogic of class inclusion and exclusion
Inferring what will, may, or could happen (or be true)	Logical Argumentation	Tautologic of trans-formation and combination

When they arrived, some of my students wrote almost entirely in the narrative mode; others were clinically analytical. None of them incorporated all modes in a single text. The dramatic impact and persuasive engagement of the professional essayists eluded them as long as they continued to write in a mode that restricted how they approached their subjects. I wanted them to write a three page essay incorporating a variety of abstraction levels so they might expand and play with the many relationships they could have with their subject matter.

To generate their first drafts, I led them through an exercise I adapted from one that Cherryl Armstrong, a member of the South Coast Writing Project, had published in one of their newsletters. She had observed Keith Caldwell's Bay Area Writing Project presentation of "Focusing" at the South Coast Writing Project's Summer Institute and written her slightly modified version. You could say that my exercise is "Focusing" twice removed, and probably bears little resemblance and relates only slightly to the exercise Caldwell developed. I was after more than focusing from my students' writing, although that was an essential starting place. I wanted them to work their thinking and writing from description that put the writer in the critical moment of a significant personal experience through the modes of narration and exposition to persuasion, stopping short of blatant argumentation. After several trials, I had honed the steps of the exercise and my methods of delivery to the point where, in hindsight, students remarked about how satisfying and engaging their writing had been. They were also more appreciative of what the authors they were reading had accomplished.

Nevertheless, at its start each exercise was another shot in the dark, and as such could miss entirely. Before class I asked one student, Linda, if she would mind volunteering to read a piece of personal writing to the rest of the class. I identified the topic, explaining that it would be a descriptive piece everyone would write according to my instructions which I would then question her about while the class looked on. The other class members, after seeing our model, would group in dyads and question each other. Our purpose was to model the questioning procedure for the rest of the class.

Linda agreed and, along with the class, began following my instructions to generate the first draft. First, make a list of personal experiences that somehow changed you or your life so that you were not the same after they happened. They do not have to be major events. They could be something that the rest of us might consider insignificant (e.g. E.B. White's pig's death). However, they should be events that caused a shift in your perception of yourself, of life, or of "reality." You were not quite the same after these events happened. Those vivid memories that frequently crop up, especially those that flashed in your mind as I was giving these instructions, are the ones you want to write down. After generating a list of four or five, select one that you would be willing to write about. The best choice is usually the one that gives you a gut reaction when you recall it, the one that you definitely do not want to write about. Those are the incidents from which previous students have produced their best writing. Hearing these instructions, Linda changed her topic to her rape.

Second, after getting a vivid mental picture of the incident, jot down the colors and sounds that seem to stand out. Perhaps there was a particular smell or feeling that you had at the time; what was it? List the people who were involved and their distinguishing characteristics. Be brief. Next, listen to the dialogue that occurred if there was one. Write down key snatches of dialogue that would unlock the whole conversation.

Third, writers have to decide where to begin and end the episode they will write about. They have to arbitrarily cut a manageable chunk out of the whole story which may have its beginnings in early childhood and still be re-verberating in their lives. However, they only want the most interesting piece, the part which is the context for the actual experience. Do this now: choose an appropriate manageable beginning and end for your experience. Remember that you are only writing a three page paper and not a novel. (When students find it difficult to arbitrarily choose a starting point, I suggest they proceed by saying, "Once I was _____ when _____ " which forces them into a storytelling mode.)

Fourth, draw a linear time line on your paper. Place the first action of your story's plot at the left end and the last action at the right. As you mentally recall the actions in between, fill them in on the time line. Again, don't try to include every action, only the ones significant to the plot. Survey the actions you've plotted and pick the critical moment, the exact moment at which students have said they "shifted," "cracked," "realized," "knew," "changed" or "decided." Put an X on the time line at that spot. I usually interrupt the instructions at this point to provide an example out of my own experience. I tell them a story, hastily plot the event for them on the board, and mark a big X at the strategic moment. I then wax dramatic and describe the crucial seconds in vivid detail, including my own physical and emotional conditions along with the action and color of the moment.

Shifting their attention back to their own critical moments, while trying to maintain the sense of significance and intensity that has developed in the room, I give the next direction. Fifth, as you keep that critical moment clear in your mind's eye, begin writing it down, describing it so completely that it provides a language photograph of that moment for the reader. It puts the reader in the moment and allows him/her to recreate your experience. Write for about ten minutes.

By this time all the students were writing vigorously in the emotional fervor of the moment. Unfortunately, limited by time, I had to drag most of them away from their papers after ten minutes, turning their attention to Linda. Drenched by the emotional recall of their own triggering moment, they were primed for Linda's recounting of the moment of her rape.

> He threw me down on the floor, forcing me with his body to lie down. He pushed up against me. I was only seven years old, but I had guessed what he was going to do to me. I knew I had to try to get away. He hit me in the face, punched me in the stomach so I couldn't move. He started touching me in ways that I _____ . He ripped off clothing and starting fondling me. At this moment I felt a horrible feeling of disgust. I could not believe he was doing this to me. I started screaming louder and louder. He told me to shut up or he would kill me. So I did. Then he raped me, a seven-year-old child, shivering, terrified under his weight.

On other occasions students have recounted witnessing deaths of loved ones and complete strangers, divorce announcements, all types of accidents, and incidents involving animals. They, like Linda, had often completely forgotten about the incident until recently and had not discussed the moment with a mental health professional. Often, a recent event had brought the earlier incident to their attention. After Linda finished reading I asked her one of several versions of the question I eventually repeated ten times: "So what?" I softened the stark effrontery of it by saying instead after a respectful pause, "So Linda, what do you want to say to us about your rape?" Struggling to a more objective view of the experience so she could go on with the exercise, she said in a whisper, "That it is terrible to be raped when you are seven years old." She had leapt immediately to the point she wanted to make. Now I had to lead her back to fill in the explanation she knew but had not put into words. My next question was obvious. "What is so terrible?" She replied, "The pain, the fear, and the disgust." Wanting to provide a narrative context for the description she had given us and the analysis and explanation that was to come I asked her, "What happened that created the pain, the fear, and the disgust?" She began a narrative recounting of the events surrounding the critical moment she had described. By saying, "Then what?" I urged her narrative on to give us a chronological context of what had happened. When she had given us enough narration I moved her on by asking, "So what?" She responded by shifting into prose that was analytical and advisory. As though she were talking to another seven year old, she analyzed her feelings and actions. For a long time she had been afraid of men, including her father. She went on to explain her present difficulties with intimate relationships. She did not like to be touched. Moving from emotional saturation to mental engagement, the class was beginning to see the enormity and complexity of what Linda had meant by "it's terrible."

Even though I had ended the exercise by thanking Linda for being such a powerful model and releasing the rest of the class to perform the same "so what" exercise with their partners, Linda did not want to stop. She wanted to explain more about the incident and ask the same question that the rest of the class asked after I dragged them away from their partners: How do we write this up? What do we do next? My instructions sent them off to find writing havens as the next class entered: Write about your significant personal experience in such a way that you include description that puts us in the moment, narration that gives us a context, explanation that reflects insightful analysis, and a touch of persuasiveness that is speculative but not argumentative. The power of your recreated moment and your accompanying explanation should move the reader to adopt your point of view, or at least accept its validity. This essay is not meant to be objectively and logically argumentative. By this I mean that we are not trying to construct a logical argument for or against an issue (in Linda's case, rape) which could stand alone if the writer's personal experience were removed. We are not working to remove the writer's subjective authority from the issue. Rather we are working to draw the reader into the writer's subjective frame of reference. We want to use the writer's emotional expression to entangle the reader's sensibilities, and in so doing persuade the reader to adopt the writer's point of view, putting the reader in the writer's position where she/he experiences the crisis through the writer's eyes.

As one would expect, Linda's first draft, while gripping in its reporting of a shocking moment, is not a well-written depiction. I directed Linda away from concerns about graceful writing on this first draft. A series of refining and polishing drafts would follow, but for now the exercise had another objective— to affect the class so that its members would relate to each other and their writing in a different manner. I wasn't disappointed. Linda's exercise did more than rivet the class's attention; it changed the working atmosphere, the kinds of writing the students would do, and their attitudes toward their work. From now on they would not write what James Britton calls "dummy runs." The stakes were much higher than simply completing the assignment. Linda had put her heart into the ring, and the others knew they had to follow her lead to produce writing the rest of us thought worth reading. They now expected more from themselves. They were challenged to find something truly meaningful to write about. Several students moaned that unfortunately nothing dramatic had ever happened to them, so they had nothing of equal value to write about.

Interestingly enough, these students, who thought they had lived uneventful lives, often wrote better essays for this assignment. Without the shocking impact of a significant crisis to rely upon, they had to wring more subtle and often sensitive significances out of their mini-traumas. Deeply reflective and perceptive essays were written about a decision to forgive a family member, the first shot on a hunting trip, and a father-daughter conversation.

Class members also expected more from each other—more openness, more personal commitment, more honesty, or else they felt disappointed. They were also more curious about each other. Effervescent and gregarious, Linda did not seem like a childhood rape victim. We carry stereotypes of how such people should look: withdrawn, anxious and tentative. If Linda had such a secret, what about the others? Was their jocularity a cover for equivalent psychic traumas?

At the end of the assignment, reading the polished drafts, class members were engrossed and often moved by the detailed authenticity and depth of their classmates' writing. They felt the power of such personally committed writing. This experience, and the individual redrafting and writing group work that led up to it, allowed them to realize that no secret formula (known only to teachers and professional writers) exists for writing effectively; student writers could see that they carried the essay "in them" and hard work was required to get it out and onto the paper. Futhermore, as more accomplished writers, they could now begin to understand the process by which professionals write about their experiences, and to have more respect for the results.

But you may be more concerned about Linda, about all the Lindas who came before her and who made themselves vulnerable in such a potentially damaging way. As teachers are we not responsible for the repercussions? To that question I unerringly answer "yes." We have to hold ourselves responsible. Exercises such as this which deal with our students' most intimate and intense memories require us to use care and skill in administering them. Linda's willingness to share her terrible moment was a tacit statement of trust and a plea for it to be returned in kind. She had taken my request seriously and asked me to do the same. While challenging her to enrich and analyze her depiction, I had to keep in mind that this had other implications beyond a writing exercise. The temptation to capitalize upon the high drama of this pedagogical moment has to be tempered by constant vigilance. By remaining sensitive to what Linda was going through as she relived her memory, I could be more certain she would benefit as much as the class from the exercise. In this way, as with all classroom lessons that are basically personal and confrontive in nature, we can ensure that our students will not only be willing to continue with them, but will find them valuable. If we don't manage such exercises well it seems to me that we will be forever doomed with "dummy runs" and essays in which no one is at home. And we will be missing an opportunity for students to come to appreciate literature in a wholly personal way.

Writing and Teaching for Surprise

DONALD M. MURRAY

My students become writers at that moment when they first write what they do not expect to write. They experience the moment of surprise that motivates writers to haul themselves to their writing desks year after year. Writers value the gun that does *not* hit the target at which it is aimed.

Before they experience surprise, students find writing drudgery, something that has to be done after the thinking is over—the dishes that have to be washed after the guests have left. But writing is the banquet itself. As Louise Nevelson said, "My work is a feast for myself."

Writers seek what they do not expect to find. Writers are, like all artists, rationalizers of accident. They find out what they are doing after they have done it.

Students should share in this purposeful unknowing, for writing is not the reporting of what was discovered, but the act of exploration itself. John Galsworthy said, "I sit. I don't intend." E.M. Forster added, "Think before you speak, is criticism's motto; speak before you think is creation's." The evidence from writers goes on and on. Speaking of his play, *The Birthday Party,* Harold Pinter said, "The thinking germinated and bred itself. It proceeded according to its own logic. What did I do? I followed the indications, I kept a sharp eye on the clues I found myself dropping."

When you read what I have written, it may be the agent that causes surprise in you. But that finished text which gave me the satisfaction of completion is far removed from the moment of surprise when I learned what I did not even know I had to learn. Let me try to take you backstage, no, not even backstage, but far beyond that into that almost always private moment when the writer is alone with language and the words escape intention.

> I am sitting with my daybook on my lapdesk, and my notes at the top of the page—notes I had forgotten until I read them now—say, "Lack of faith—read previous text and feel nausea—physical revulsion." I have come to confront a novel I have been working on for years. Drafts have been completed and abandoned, and there is no hope or anticipation of surprise.
>
> I start again the new first chapter that must precede the chapters already written. I write four lines and strike it through, then start again. It goes well enough, but it is a journeyman's job. The writing seems terribly

College English, 46 (January 1984), pp. 1-7. Copyright © 1984 by the National Council of Teachers of English. Reprinted with permission.

expected, and as Robert Frost said, "No surprise for the writer, no surprise for the reader." I slog on knowing that the slog can be changed if ever a surprise occurs.

I write, "He could remember when he first became aware of the sadness. He had come back from a swing through the west coast offices and realized he had the usual post-business trip sadness." I can remember the despair at the triteness of that sentence. Then my pen wrote, " 'Daddy's wearies,' Lucinda told the children"—the sentence isn't finished, but I must interrupt, for that phrase that Lucinda uttered was a small surprise, because I had never heard that expression, and it seemed right, revealing of her and their life. But the sentence went right on, "...and he set up his paints in the backyard to paint the woods. It was May, but he saw no colors."

That was an enormous surprise. I was inside the skull of a man who would, before the chapter was out, murder his children. I had no hint that this is what he saw, but having received that surprise the text became alive to me.

A few weeks later I was directing a session for teachers on writing in public, and so I went to the board to write in public. These fragments I started writing in such workshops are pulling me with a powerful force towards a book I will attempt on my sabbatical. It is a book about World War II, and I don't know whether it is fiction or autobiography or poetry or history, but the continual force of surprise tells me there is a book to be written. I put down the word "boots" on the board, thinking I will write about the Nazi jackboots or my own paratroop boots, and then see that my hand has written below it "bones," and I am digging a foxhole in that field in France when I realized that I was digging in the buried bones of soldiers from World War I. And so I start to write and, again, it is not what I expect to write.

"I am practicing in the side yard and slowly wind up, look over to first base, then turn to the plate and shoot the tennis ball in on Lou Gehrig. Before it hits the garage door I hear the back bedroom cough next door. It coughs with experience, a cough that sounds as if it comes from an empty room. All spring and summer and fall the room coughs while I play; when I try to sleep at night, when I go out to get my bicycle from the garage in the morning dark for my paper route, the room coughs. In winter the window is shut and the storm window went over it, but in the spring the room coughed again."

The man next door, whom I never saw, had been gassed in World War I. That remembered cough, so much louder now that I have experienced war, surprises me. I hope it will surprise and haunt my readers.

Through my daybooks there is a trail of small surprises that led me to give the talk that surprised me enough to draft this article. I had lots of notes about how teachers and students recognize when they were making progress. But the material seemed ordinary to me, when this fragment appeared on the page, "Student breakthrough when achieve surprise." And several days later this almost sentence occurred, "When a student is surprised by what he or she is writing then the student becomes a writer   central act   breakthough" and although I did not know what would be the lead sentence of this article I did know it would be this surprise turned on my lathe and shaped for publication.

I'm tempted to go on, to recover for myself the surprises of poetry, fiction, and nonfiction—even the surprises in a grant proposal—that I see on those pages. But I think that the case may be made that the writer's reason for writing is primarily to read what the writer did not expect to write. The carrot on the stick turns out to be a strawberry or a parsnip or a Granny Smith.

Of course there is false surprise, the vision is a mirage; and there are the new surprises that lead palace coups against old surprises and keep the writing in a continual state of disorder. The experienced writer always has the problem of the excess of surprise and must learn how to decide which mermaid is real. These are problems for experience and craft, but first there must be the possibility of surprise. That is the starting point for the effective writer and the effective teacher, and it seems to me there are six elements that help us achieve surprise.

Expectation

The cart does have to come before the horse. We are much more likely to perceive surprise if we expect to see it. Once we have the experience of surprise then we must remember and build on that moment when language leaves the mind and moves the hand.

The wonderful thing about surprise is that the more you experience surprise the easier it becomes to experience it. Surprise breeds surprise. And you can learn to be patient at your desk waiting for surprise to land.

You can also project surprise onto your students. If you are a writing teacher who writes—who lures and captures surprise—then it becomes easier for you to expect your students to achieve surprise themselves. And once a few students experience surprise in their writing and share it with their peers surprise becomes epidemic in the classroom.

The more you become knowledgeable about surprise through your own writing and teaching experience the more you will learn how to create an environment that will attract and make use of surprise. And your belief that your students can capture surprise on the page will be reinforced.

Habit

I have the habit of writing. My simple tools are always with me: pen and paper. I try to follow the ancients' counsel *nulla dies sine linea,* never a day without a line. A line, however, may not look like a line to a non-writer. It may not be a sentence. It is most likely a phrase or a fragment, a word, a list, a diagram. As a writer I must become used to such literary compost.

My habit involves the use of fragments of time, a moment here and a moment there. I treasure those moments, such as this one, when I can write at a swoop. But those few hours are fertilized by what I accomplish writing for a few minutes or even a few seconds in a parked car, in a meeting, waiting for a class to start, during TV, at a lunch counter. I will be surprised by what I write if I'm in the habit of putting words on paper even if I do not have the time to write.

And, in writing this, I realize my habit includes the stimulation I receive from those with whom I can share my early drafts. These people change by circumstance and, to some degree, by the genre in which I'm writing. But they have two elements in common; they write themselves and can accept the draft as a draft, and they make me want to write when I leave them. These are very special colleagues, these test readers. They can be tough, they can be supportive, they can attack and comfort, often at the same time. They are important because they allow me to stand back from my work and gain distance on it, and because, through their faith that I have something worth saying, they can draw me back to my work.

I must, as a teacher, encourage (force?) my students to develop their own writing habits: to write frequently, at least once a day; to write much more than they will complete or publish (maple syrup is the product of boiling thirty or forty gallons of sap to get one of syrup, and in writing there's a great deal more sap that needs to be boiled down); to read writing that doesn't look like writing but which often contains the essential surprise; to make it possible for the student to share unfinished writing with myself and the other writers in the class in such a way that the habit of writing will be reinforced.

Ease

When Tilly and John Warnock studied one of my daybooks, they were surprised that there was so little evidence of struggle and frustration, that it seemed so easy. I like the martyr pose—writing is so terribly hard for us writers—and was a bit angered at their response. I was surprised at their surprise, and had to look at my daybooks again, and I found they were right.

It takes enormous effort to get to the desk—to shut out the world, to turn off the telephone, to put aside the manuscripts to be read, the letters to be answered, the expense accounts to be filled out, the books and articles to be studied—but I do not write unless the writing comes easily.

I used to force writing, to try to make mashed potatoes pass through a keyhole. But it didn't work. If I am prepared then the writing will flow. If I'm not prepared I'd better return to that reflective state where I may play with language, connecting and disconnecting, listening for voice, fooling around, staring out the window, letting my pen, the blind man's cane, tell me where I'm going.

To free my pen I must develop a special kind of ease. It's ease with intention. It's not retirement or indolence, but a calculated letting go that is essential if you are going to be effective in battle, while giving the speech, after the kick-off of the big game. There has to be a deadline, and there has to be an achieved calm before the deadline. There is nothing easy about this ease; it is an acquired naturalness.

To be ready for surprise you have to have both discipline and freedom, compulsion and forgiveness, awareness and receptivity, energy and passivity, a strong purpose and a disciplined purposelessness.

And I must make such ease an essential part of my students' curriculum. I must allow them space in which to fool around, to have fun, to aim in one direction and hit a target in another. They must learn not to force writing but to let writing build within them so their pens may have the freedom of saying what their brains did not expect them to say.

Recognition

"You can smell the poem before you can see it," says Denise Levertov, and she is right. We must recognize the aura that precedes surprise the same way I recognize the aura that precedes a migraine. It is the sort of thing that can be only learned through experience. I sense that a surprise is on its way, and I make myself quiet, the page blank and on my knee, the pen uncapped and in my hand.

One of the nice things about surprise is that after you've had one or two or three surprises happen then you become a veteran of surprise and will begin to recognize it.

It may be helpful to categorize some of the types of surprise the writer experiences. There is the surprise of perception that I experience when the character in my novel saw no color. There was the surprise of recollection when I heard that terrible cough left over from a previous war. There is the surprise of connection when I related my surprise in writing and my students' surprise to their development as writers.

There is the surprise of resolution when we see the solution to a problem we have been circling in our writing. There is the surprise of celebration when we recreate something—a moment, an event, a person, a scene—and can stand back from it. There is the surprise of implication, the surprise of under-standing, the surprise of caring when we feel more than we expect to feel, and the surprise of pattern when a whole complex of connections click into place on the page. And there are those especially significant surprises: the surprise of authority—I know what others need to know—and the surprise of voice—I can hear myself on the page.

Our students will recognize surprise when we share our surprise at what we are writing, when we allow members of the class to share their writing and their surprises with us, and when we, as teachers, are surprised by what they are writing. They must see the great range of surprise that is possible when writing becomes exploration.

Pounceability

"Art gropes," writes John Gardner. "It stalks like a hunter lost in the woods, listening to itself and to everything around it, unsure of itself, waiting to pounce."

The writer, surprised by what is appearing on the page, must cultivate the craft to take advantage of it. The word, the pattern, the fragment, the sentence appears, and the writer must learn how to follow the clue towards meaning.

Again the tension between freedom and discipline. Most of all, the craft of making use of surprise is the ability to let the writing flow, to develop the potential of the surprise. Peter Drucker calls it the "zero draft." Calvin Trillin calls it the "vomit-all." I like to call it the "discovery draft." Whatever it is named, the writing has to get ahead of the writer.

But not too far ahead. The writer has to have an easy hand on the reins, but the writer can not let the reins go. The craft of the sailor is to make use of the wind, of the painter to make use of the brush, of the cabinetmaker to take advantage of the grain. The writer must learn how—through experience—to develop and exploit the surprise that was only a hint, a revealing snap of a twig, a shadow in the bush before the writer pounced.

The writer will never learn to write, for the craft of writing is never learned, only studied. But the teaching writer can share the continual apprenticeship to craft with the writer's students. And they will be motivated together to practice pounceability, lured on by each new surprise. One of the most exciting things about writing is the fact that surprise is much more than idea. Surprise is experience in seeing the vision of the text come clear. Surprise is felt in the working out of the order, direction, proportion, and pace of the text. Surprise is the reward for the line-by-line crafts of revision and editing—the writing keeps saying what we do not expect to hear.

Acceptance

Surprise, though exciting, may be a discomforting gift. When we are surprised we often do not like what we discover. I am surprised to find I am writing a novel in which the "hero" kills his own children. I do not want to live within his skull, but apparently I must. I do not want to write about World War

II, but my trade is paying attention to what appears on the page, not what I want to appear on the page. I do not want to write another poem that forces me to re-experience the death of my daughter, but the poem stands there before me. I do not want to order the writing process, but as I study the writing process through writing about it I must report the order I perceive.

Those are all surprises of subject matter, but there are other surprises that I must learn to expect. This month I intended to write prose and have found poetry coming out of my pen. Poetry upsets my priorities, ruins the writing schedule, makes havoc of my lists, and has absolutely no sympathy for my dismay. Poetry laughs at a writer who had the arrogance of purpose. This month I write poetry.

And that voice on the page is surely not my voice. In the novel it is a convoluted voice that turns back on itself and questions itself. In the textbook it is a bit too clear. In the poem it does not free itself in the way I intended. I think of all the writers I would like to write like. I hear in the distance my own voice, so much better in my imagination than it ever seems on the page. But I must accept my voice as I accept my size thirteen feet, my mother's heavy step, my father's receding hairline, myself surprised in the mirror after the bath.

If acceptance is hard for the writer, it is harder still for the teacher, for education is geared up for sameness. We want our students to perform to the standards of other students, to study what we plan for them to study, and to learn from it what we or our teachers learned.

Yet our students learn, at least in writing, if they experience difference. The curriculum calls for sameness, and we unleash them into an activity that produces difference.

They do not write how we expect them to write or what we expect them to write. We are surprised by what they say and how they say it, and we are made uncomfortable by our surprise. And we can make them uncomfortable. And if we do the game is lost. We must learn to accept and delight in the difference we find in our students, for surprise is the most significant element in writing. It is the motivating force that makes writers of us and of our students. Surprise is the measure of the importance of writing. We do not write to repeat what others have written, but to discover our own surprises, what we have to say and how we can say it.

I have plans for tomorrow's writing, but if I am lucky my writing will surprise me and destroy my plans. I have plans for my students' writing, but if we are lucky we will be surprised at what they write and how—and all our plans will be abandoned as we pursue surprise.

The Why of Cognition:
Emotion and the Writing Process

ALICE G. BRAND

No number of studies of writer's block or apprehension make up for the lack of serious research on the role of affect in writing (Brand, "Hot"). The profession may concede that emotions motivate. But it also seems to believe that emotions have little to do with actual composing and less to do with revising. In this essay, on the other hand, I show that a realistic and complete psychology of writing must include affective as well as cognitive phenomena.

It is easy to understand our respect for writing as an intellectual enterprise. Written discourse is considered a quintessential representation of thought. And, like thought, it can be identified by levels of sophistication, whether the writing model is based on function, physical science, or psychological distance between writer, audience, and subject. We assess cognitive maturity through such syntactic features as t-unit length and incidence of subordination; or such rhetorical features as elaboration of argument, versatility of diction, and critical thinking.

It is in critical thinking, the capacity to identify, organize, and manipulate relationships systematically, that considerable isomorphism between writing and thought is found. Skilled critical thinkers transcend the printed word and the here and now. They arrange and rearrange. They decide what belongs and what doesn't. They make inferences. They exercise possibilities. They remember. They predict.

> The act of writing demands that concepts, generally global or even imagistic in storage, be forced into linear patterns of writing, patterns organized by the analytical determination of thesis, sub-theses and details.
>
> ...The act of analysis...implements thinking skills: students select parts of their concepts and arrange them logically—side-by-side or embedded within each other. Students write them clearly in sentences and then gather those together in paragraphs. (Goldberg 41)

Thinking also materializes on paper as outlines, branching sequences of specificity, inductive and deductive reasoning, summaries, and so on—all left brain activities. This is right and good, but it stops too soon and leaves out too much.

College Composition and Communication, 38 (December 1987), pp. 436-443. Copyright © 1987 by the National Council of Teachers of English. Reprinted with permission.

Emotion, Memory, Motivation, Values

Philosopher Susanne Langer states that the giving of names to things is the vastest generative idea ever conceived, because from names generalization and concept form—the wellspring of our intellectual life. Cognitive psychologists tell us, however, that words have a way of escaping us too (Clark and Clark 172). The precise repetition of any spoken sentence, for example, is a rarity. Our immediate memory for discourse is limited in capacity and quickly dumps the exact wording of a sentence. Rather, we build an interpretation from verbatim wording, but then get rid of it, leaving only the gist or interpretation. Interpretation means reorganizing and storing ideas (in this case, in linguistic form) in line with our interests and values. This is not new. However, psychologist Lev Vygotsky took this idea a step further. Contrary to Jean Piaget he contended that linguistic thought develops as social speech moves inward. Speech syntax becomes increasingly abbreviated. Articles and adjectives disappear, pronouns drop off, and predicates shrink to verbs—until what remains in our mind is only the single naming word. Fully internalized, that single word carries the most information and comes closest to pure meaning. The thinking we do in pure meaning is saturated with sense. Sense, according to Vygotsky, is the sum of all the psychological events associated with that word. Cognitive processes are surely part of those psychological events, but they are not the whole of them. Pure meaning is endowed with images and connotation. Pure meaning is saturated with affect. But the profession sidesteps this.

Current writing theory also suffers a blind spot when it explains how longterm memory and language interact. The construct of memory is central to cognition. Just as the entire visual field is potentially available to us at any given moment, so too all of memory theoretically is available. But perceiving an entire visual field or retrieving all of memory is humanly impossible. We choose. Psychologists tell us that these choices are not random, but the cognitivists come up short when they try to explain why we choose what we choose, and how. In language, parallels exist at the word level through every conceivable rhetorical mode and discursive form. Writing, too, is an exercise in inclusion and exclusion, a lesson in decision making and choice. It is the basis on which we make those selections that determines cognitive style and writing style. And, as I will trace later, such choices link language to affect.

In any discussion of affect, the construct of motivation should not go unmentioned. A term grounded in psychoanalytic theory, "motivation" has received more lip-service by writing specialists than emotion but equally scant systematic attention. This may be attributed in part to early developmental and cognitive psychologists who blurred emotion and motivation, ranked both considerably below the intellect, and failed to address either beyond their energistic capabilities.

In writing education, motivation is mentioned quickly then crowded out by more cognitive concepts—clearly because the field patterns itself after the harder sciences. It is tucked, for example, into corners of work by James Britton and by Linda Flower and John Hayes ("Cognitive Process," "Images") to be pulled out when other explanations fail. Or motivation and emotion are delicately skirted by referring to intuition, interpretation, or goal-setting. I would like to think that the neglect of motivation and emotion is evidence of our humility in the face of such a complicated wilderness. But I rather think it is a clear-headed disregard of all affective phenomena in the face of evidence to the contrary. For in major psychosocial and human development theories, like those of Erik Erikson and Jean Piaget, affect is repeatedly implicated. I am referring to the emotions of apathy, anxiety, disequilibrium, alienation, despair, and commitment. English educators know that these emotions play a part in language learning (Brand, *Therapy*), but they show little interest beyond that.

Given the link between cognitive maturity and critical thinking, a most recent coupling has occurred between writing and moral maturity. Inspired in part by Piaget and Erikson, the theories of David Krathwohl, Lawrence Kohlberg, and William Perry depict ethical consciousness as developing through age-related stages. As we would expect, these authors contend that the more advanced the stage, the more likely a person will use formal reasoning to reconcile moral discrepancies. And this involvement of critical thinking in the upper reaches of ethical maturity led others to recognize the potential of moral development for assessing rhetorical effectiveness. Andrew Wilkinson's scales, for example, provide not only cognitive and stylistic but also moral and affective measures of writing development. David Winter applies affective criteria to story themes in order to determine how broadly students are schooled. The biases are all too clear. Emotional neutrality is considered morally the most advanced. Winter (32) so much as says that the writing evaluation scale can be used as a test of the ability to remain aloof from one's emotions—apparently the hallmark of the liberally educated.

But aloofness really is impossible. At the risk of oversimplifying, I believe that, if cognitive ability may be measured by moral orientation, then it can be traced to emotion. If we are looking at critical thinking, we are also looking at moral orientation. If we are looking at moral orientation, we are looking at belief systems. If we are looking at belief systems, we are looking at attitude. If we are looking at attitude, we are looking at preference. If we are looking at preference, we are looking at the fundamental polarities of good and bad and are expected to choose the good over the bad. If we are deciding on the goodness or badness of things, we are trading in the affect. We need reminding that the very idea of being both human and impartial is a contradiction in terms. As Michael Polanyi states, into "every act of knowing there enters a passionate contribution of the person knowing what is being known" (viii). We make a commitment. We believe.

Limitations of Cognitive Models of Writing

Over the last two decades, the study of writing has not only emerged as a discipline but has pressed for recognition as a science. The composing process has become synonymous with the intellect which, for all intents and purposes, is synonymous with cognitive psychology. This most recent thrust for a strong, cognitive education can be traced to the 1957 launching of Sputnik, which jolted American education with new demands for intellectual excellence of which writing was a part. Except for the period following the Dartmouth Conference, where a more humanistic perspective for English education was endorsed, the profession has supported an uncompromisingly cognitive perspective.

Led by Linda Flower and John Hayes, the cognitive psychology of writing institutionalized itself quickly (Freedman, Dyson, and Flower; Gregg and Steinberg; Scardamalia and Bereiter), and for good reason. It promised to remedy the aimlessness of the expressive approach and the rigidity of the stage approaches. It promised to reunite writing and thinking. It consolidated the shift from product to process by focussing on more acts of the mind that individuals continuously go through when writing, regardless of the stage their text is in. Using results from think-aloud protocols, the cognitive process model attempts to show how writers bring complex and recursive mental activities to bear on composing.

Despite the respect afforded the cognitive process theory of writing, its methodology, utility, and prematurity have raised questions. Judging by the way many of us find ourselves writing, we know that logic often is not the normal mode of human thought. Peter Elbow's strong voice was not the only one to forward this idea (Hunt). And some critics of protocol-based research point out that, although "thoughts that run through our heads while writing...are diffuse, highly branched, visual as well as verbal" (Cooper and Holzman 290), some protocols appear remarkably disciplined and empty of affective tone. Why? Because "their introspectors notice virtually nothing other than that which is to the point" (290).

Protocols, then, are limited to what people can articulate, and by what they are asked to articulate. Protocol-based research also is limited by the degree to which protocol transcripts are summarized. Presumably, statements subject to reduction or omission are of little or no value—as defined by Flower and Hayes' research goals. But I say that the more telling material probably is just what protocols summarize or overlook. What composition research really needs is an account of how much was lost, in a protocol, through data reduction, where it occurred, and what it was. Such an account would undoubtedly include a lot of grunts and groans. But it would also reveal imagistic and free associative thinking and connotative commentary. This is precisely where differences in cognitive style and personality may be observed. This is where emotions happen. Without that information, can we really say that we have an accurate description of the mental activities that underlie writing?

Then, there is the problem of nomenclature. First, as it stands, the cognitive process model provides no language to deal with emotion. It precludes access to affective phenomena by excluding them from research plans and any corresponding pedagogies. Having no name or place in the paradigm is tantamount to stating that affective phenomena do not exist, even though affect is apparent at virtually every juncture of the çognitive process model: exigencies, plan/write boundaries, goal-setting, process interruptions, conflict in subprocess, cognitive strain, diagnosis, levels of acceptability, and evaluation.

Second, critics argue that the model uses jargon that gives it the respectability of high science but demonstrates little new explanatory power (Petrosky 233). After all, how different is the idea of the "agent" or "executive," cognitive terms, from the "individual" or "person," more common words? How different is "retrieving" from "remembering," "reprocessing" from "revising"? How different is "instantiation" from "developing by example"? What is gained by calling a weak essay an "inadequate representation"? My concern is not only with what the model omits but what it suggests about people. The cognitive notions of Monitors and Operators are not people but incorporeal automatons. Disembodied Editors, not humans, detect flaws. Disembodied Inspectors evaluate performance (Flower et al., "Detection"). These entities have decision-making powers through us, but they are not us. We are circuits. We are transistors, fire alarms, smoke detectors, switching yards, semaphore signals, radar, and PCs. The problem with these metaphors is that they promote a mechanistic view of the human mind. Digital system metaphors are poor if not fearful lies about what happens psychologically when we compose. We may sometimes think of ourselves *as if* we are computers. But computers do not grow. They do not learn with practice or understand what they do. And computers do not feel (Dreyfus; Neisser; Searle).

The cognitive model, then, fails to capture the rich, psychological dynamics of humans in the very act of cognizing. But by far my greatest worry about the cognitive model concerns our students. This approach encourages teachers to apply it directly, "to teach students to behave as the model says people behave" (Cooper and Holzman 286). It suggests that good writers may be distinguished from weak writers by their loyalty to the model (Flower, *Problem;* Glatthorn 5). I think what goes wrong here is that, time after time, students refuse to see the errors of their ways that, we tell them, are certain to make them good writers. It reminds me of expecting my children to hang up their coats—well, because doesn't everybody like a neat house? The model assumes a motivation that does not exist. It assumes a flat, uncomplicated objectivity. How poorly that fits my experience with student writers. Does that mean that I don't teach any strong writers? Of course not. Each of us receives accomplished writing from students who defy all our good words about process and ineffective writing from mindlessly obedient believers. What the cognitive models suggest is not so much that there are different composing styles but that one is better than the other. Nothing could be further from the truth.

Potential of Studies into the Emotions

Cognitive theories of writing study acts of conscious, deliberate, information processing by which writers determine what they want to accomplish and how they want to accomplish it. These are ambitious and admirable objectives. Their authors are not wrong, just incomplete. The distinctive freedom of affect from attentive control, its speed, and the range and depth of language that results suggest something special about its influence on writing.

Future studies should try to make knowledge about affective processes clear and useful to teachers and students. For example, if I may borrow from Murray's questions about internal revision ("Internal" 94-98), students should know what their emotions can and cannot do during writing. They should become familiar with the emotional as well as intellectual cues that tell them they are ready to write, ready to stop, and ready to do a number of things in between. What in fact does happen affectively between having an idea for writing and beginning a first draft? How do students read their own writing and envision lexical choices? How do writers' affective states vary with audience, topic, and time restrictions? These task constraints invariably involve motivation and preference, both affective in origin.

Examining the impact of the emotions on writing may also help us understand why some problems occur during writing and how we can solve them. For example, studying the affective involvement of professionals and people who write when they don't have to might help writing teachers work with students who do not write easily. Such students may be able to improve at a wide range of writing tasks if they can appreciate and recruit certain emotions at critical junctures in the process.

Composition research also should explore the affective and cognitive styles through which their writing occurs. This line of inquiry should help us understand the extent to which certain types of persons are successful in some language activities but not in others; why they exhibit certain writing behaviors but not others; why they produce certain written content but not others. We know that affective traits and personality overlap conceptually and empirically (Plutchik and Kellerman). We are just now recognizing that personality may govern discursive style (Jensen and DiTiberio; Selzer), just as discursive style has an impact on personality (Brand, *Therapy;* Denman). In fact, how personality influences the way writers function is the direction I think composition research is ultimately headed.

Historically, the field of composition looked first at the what of writing, the product. Over the last two decades, it has added the how of writing, the process. It follows that the field look next at the why of writing, affective content and motivation. Understanding the collaboration of emotion and cognition in writing is both fundamental and far-reaching. It is in cognition that ideas make sense. But it is in emotion that this sense finds value. Without such priorities we could not think. The more comprehensive out understanding of the affective and cognitive content of discourse in any form, the more likely it will reflect their true interpenetration.

References

Brand, Alice G. "Hot Cognition: Emotions and Writing Behavior." *Journal of Advanced Composition* 6 (1985): forthcoming. ERIC ED 236 677.

——————— . *Therapy in Writing: A Psycho-educational Enterprise.* Lexington, MA: Heath, 1980.

Britton, James, et al. *The Development of Writing Abilities 11-18.* London: Macmillan Education, 1975.

Clark, Herbert, and Eve Clark. *Psychology and Language.* New York: Harcourt, 1977.

Cooper, Marilyn, and Michael Holzman. "Talking about Protocols." *College Composition and Communication* 34 (1983): 284-93.

Denman, M.E. "Personality Changes Concomitant with Learning Writing." *Research in the Teaching of English* 15 (1981): 170-71.

Dreyfus, Hubert L. *What Computers Can't Do: The Limits of Artificial Intelligence.* New York: Harper, 1979.

Erikson, Erik H. *Identity: Youth and Crisis.* New York: Norton, 1968.

Flower, Linda. *Problem-Solving Strategies for Writing.* 2nd ed. San Diego: Harcourt, 1985.

Flower, Linda, et al. "Detection, Diagnosis, and the Strategies of Revision." *College Composition and Communication* 37 (1986): 16-55.

Flower, Linda, and John R. Hayes. "A Cognitive Process Theory of Writing." *College Composition and Communication* 32 (1981): 365-87.

——————— . "Images, Plans and Prose: The Representation of Meaning in Writing." *Written Communication* 1 (1984): 120-60.

Freedman, Sarah W., Ann H. Dyson, and Linda Flower. "The Center for the Study of Writing: The Mission of the Center." *The Quarterly of the National Writing Project and The Center for the Study of Writing* 8 (1986): 1-5.

Glatthorn, Allan. *Writing in the Schools.* Reston, VA: National Association of Secondary School Principals, 1981.

Goldberg, Marilyn. "Recovering and Discovering Treasures of the Mind." *The Writer's Mind: Writing as a Mode of Thinking.* Ed. J.N. Hays, et al. Urbana, IL: NCTE, 1983. 35-42.

Gregg, Lee W., and Erwin R. Steinberg. *Cognitive Processes in Writing.* Hillsdale, NJ: Lawrence Erlbaum, 1980.

Jensen, George H., and John K. DiTiberio. "Personality and Individual Writing Processes." *College Composition and Communication* 35 (1984): 285-300.

Hunt, Morton. "How the Mind Works." *The New York Times Magazine* 24 Jan. 1982: 29.

Kohlberg, Lawrence. "The Cognitive-Developmental Approach to Moral Education." *Phi Delta Kappan* (1975): 670-77.

Krathwohl, David R., Benjamin S. Bloom, and Bertram B. Masia. *Taxonomy of Educational Objectives: The Classification of Educational Goals. Handbook 2: Affective Domain.* New York: David McKay, 1964.

Langer, Susanne K. *Mind: An Essay on Human Feeling. Vol. 1,* Baltimore: The Johns Hopkins UP, 1967.

Murray, Donald M. "Internal Revision: A Process of Discovery." *Research on Composing: Points of Departure.* Ed. Charles Cooper and Lee Odell. Urbana, IL: NCTE, 1978. 85-103.

——————— . *A Writer Teaches Writing: A Practical Method of Teaching Composition.* Boston: Houghton Mifflin, 1968.

Neisser, Ulric. "The Limits of Cognition." *The Nature of Thought: Essays in Honor of D.O. Hebb.* Ed. Peter W. Jusczyk and Raymond M. Klein. Hillsdale, NJ: Lawrence Erlbaum, 1980. 115-32.

Perry, William Jr. *Forms of Intellectual and Ethical Development in the College Years.* New York: Holt, 1970.

Petrosky, Anthony. Rev. of *Problem-Solving Strategies for Writing.* by Linda Flower. *College Composition and Communication* 34 (1983): 233-35.

Piaget, Jean. *The Language and Thought of the Child.* Trans. Marjorie Warden. London: K. Paul Trench, Trubner; New York: Harcourt, 1926.

Plutchik, Robert, and Henry Kellerman, eds. *Theories of Emotion.* Vol. 1 of *Emotions: Theory, Research and Experience.* New York: Academic Press, 1980.

Polanyi, Michael. *Personal Knowledge: Toward a Post-Critical Philosophy.* Chicago: U of Chicago P, 1958.

Scardamalia, Marlene, and Carl Bereiter. "Assimilative Processes in Composition Planning." *Educational Psychologist* 17 (1982): 165-71.

Searle, John. *Minds, Brains, and Science.* Cambridge, MA: Harvard UP, 1984.

Selzer, Jack. "Exploring Options in Composing." *College Composition and Communication* 35 (1984): 276-84.

Vygotsky, Lev. *Thought and Language.* Ed. and Trans. E. Hanfmann and G. Vakav. New York and Cambridge, MA: John Wiley and MIT Press.

Wilkinson, Andrew, et al. *Assessing Language Development.* Oxford Studies in Education. Oxford, England: Oxford UP, 1980.

Winter, David D., David C. McClelland, and Abigail J. Stewart. *A New Case for the Liberal Arts.* San Franscisco: Jossey-Bass, 1981.

PART FOUR

Style

"Gradually thoughts will suggest themselves with increasing readiness, the words will answer to our call and rhythmical arrangement will follow, till everything will be found fulfilling its proper function as in a well-ordered household."

Quintilian

The subject of style has always been an important part of the composition curriculum. Roughly speaking, style refers to the specific ways a writer expresses ideas—from the smallest detail, like word choice and the articulation of sentences, to more global concerns, like arrangement of ideas, balance, and general "flow." Style is important because it is so obvious. We cannot look into the mind of another person, but observing a writer's style may be the next best thing. Speech "runs away," but writing, like speech frozen in time, is permanent. We can take our time to look at it, analyze it, judge its worth. The focus on style in this book, however, is not so much to judge the writing of others but to improve our own.

The word "style" often evokes a homey image of the craftsman, someone with practical experience, someone who possesses a good eye and hand, who really cares about quality. Whenever I watch a cabinetmaker or a quiltmaker at work, I think of writing and wonder if I am as careful in my craft as they are in theirs. Sometimes what starts out as craft achieves the level of art. In some shining moment when all the parts come together into a coherent whole, then we begin to think of writing as art.

The article which received the largest number of recommendations for this edition is "Grammar, Grammars, and the Teaching of Grammar" by Patrick Hartwell. Scholarly, thought-provoking, and thorough, this article addresses an old but still nagging question among teachers of writing: How much grammar is necessary for learning to write? Hartwell offers convincing evidence "that the grammar question is not open to resolution by experimental research" but is rather a function of deeper assumptions and beliefs held by individual teachers. Our views of teaching, he argues, influence the way we think about grammar. Hartwell's own model of teaching "predicts a rich and complex interaction of learner and environment in mastering literacy, an interaction that has little to do with sequences of skills instruction as such."

Hartwell describes five kinds of grammar, and all the succeeding essays in this section fall into the realm of Grammar 5, that is, grammars of style. All were written with an eye toward helping the young writer become more effective through a deeper understanding of certain technical constraints in the written language. In "The Syntax of Error," Valerie Krishna describes a common flaw in student writing, the weak structural core. Krishna explains how to get the main idea out of some remote spot in the sentence and into the subject slot where it belongs.

One of the most influential essays of this century is Francis Christensen's "A Generative Rhetoric of the Sentence," which was first published in 1963 and has been reprinted numerous times since then. Christensen's view of style is dynamic. He saw the cumulative sentence as the proverbial grain of sand which contains in microcosm a multitude of rhetorical principles. Understanding the principles of the cumulative sentence, he argues, enhances one's understanding of other rhetorical principles and eventually leads to growth in writing ability.

"One of our major tasks as teachers of composition," writes Winston Weathers, "is to identify compositional options and teach students the mastery of the options and the liberating use of them." In his article "Grammars of Style: New Options in Composition," Weathers describes a variety of distinctly new and refreshing forms of writing. Over the years, many of my students have testified that Grammar B is indeed "liberating," and that many of their ideas find their best expression in that mode.

The final essay in this section deals with the structure of the paragraph. Drawing on the work of European linguists, William Vande Kopple shows how the arrangement of new information and old information enhances readability. "Something Old, Something New: Functional Sentence Perspective" provides good guidelines for arranging information in sentences and paragraphs.

Each day, classroom teachers unconsciously act out their theories of teaching style through their practice and behavior. One of the greatest needs of this decade, indeed of the coming century, is an understanding in the profession about the ways our teaching influences not only our students' stylistic growth but their personal growth as well.

Grammar, Grammars, and the Teaching of Grammar

PATRICK HARTWELL

For me the grammar issue was settled at least twenty years ago with the conclusion offered by Richard Braddock, Richard Lloyd-Jones, and Lowell Schoer in 1963.

> In view of the widespread agreement of research studies based upon many types of students and teachers, the conclusion can be stated in strong and unqualified terms: the teaching of formal grammar has a negligible or, because it usually displaces some instruction and practice in composition, even a harmful effect on improvement in writing.[1]

Indeed, I would agree with Janet Emig that the grammar issue is a prime example of "magical thinking": the assumption that students will learn only what we teach and only because we teach.[2]

But the grammar issue, as we will see, is a complicated one. And, perhaps surprisingly, it remains controversial, with the regular appearance of papers defending the teaching of formal grammar or attacking it.[3] Thus Janice Neuleib, writing on "The Relation of Formal Grammar to Composition" in *College Composition and Communication* (23 [1977], 247-50), is tempted "to sputter on paper" at reading the quotation above and Martha Kolln, writing in the same journal three years later ("Closing the Books on Alchemy," *CCC,* 32 [1981], 139-51), labels people like me "alchemists" for our perverse beliefs. Neuleib reviews five experimental studies, most of them concluding that formal grammar instruction has no effect on the quality of students' writing nor on their ability to avoid error. Yet she renders in effect a Scots verdict of "Not proven" and calls for more research on the issue. Similarly, Kolln reviews six experimental studies that arrive at similar conclusions, only one of them overlapping with the studies cited by Neuleib. She calls for more careful definition of the word *grammar*—her definition being "the internalized system that native speakers of a language share" (p. 140)—and she concludes with a stirring call to place grammar instruction at the center of the composition curriculum: "our goal should be to help students understand the system they know unconsciously as native speakers, to teach them the necessary categories and labels that will enable them to think about and talk about their language" (p. 150). Certainly our textbooks and our pedagogies—though they vary widely

College English, 47 (February 1985), pp. 105-127. Copyright © 1985 by the National Council of Teachers of English. Reprinted with permission.

in what they see as "necessary categories and labels"—continue to emphasize mastery of formal grammar, and popular discussions of a presumed literacy crisis are almost unanimous in their call for a renewed emphasis on the teaching of formal grammar, seen as basic for success in writing.[4]

An Instructive Example

It is worth noting at the outset that both sides in this dispute—the grammarians and the anti-grammarians—articulate the issue in the same positivistic terms: what does experimental research tell us about the value of teaching formal grammar? But seventy-five years of experimental research has for all practical purposes told us nothing. The two sides are unable to agree on how to interpret such research. Studies are interpreted in terms of one's prior assumptions about the value of teaching grammar: their results seem not to change those assumptions. Thus the basis of the discussion, a basis shared by Kolln and Neuleib and by Braddock and his colleagues—"what does educational research tell us?"—seems designed to perpetuate, not to resolve, the issue. A single example will be instructive. In 1976 and then at greater length in 1979, W.B. Elley, I.H. Barham, H. Lamb, and M. Wyllie reported on a three-year experiment in New Zealand, comparing the relative effectiveness at the high school level of instruction in transformational grammar, instruction in traditional grammar, and no grammar instruction.[5] They concluded that the formal study of grammar, whether transformational or traditional, improved neither writing quality nor control over surface correctness.

> After two years, no differences were detected in writing performance or language competence; after three years small differences appeared in some minor conventions favoring the TG [transformational grammar] group, but these were more than offset by the less positive attitudes they showed towards their English studies. (p. 18)

Anthony Petrosky, in a review of research ("Grammar Instruction: What We Know," *English Journal,* 66, No. 9 [1977], 86-88), agreed with this conclusion, finding the study to be carefully designed, "representative of the best kind of educational research" (p. 86), its validity "unquestionable" (p. 88). Yet Janice Neuleib in her essay found the same conclusions to be "startling" and questioned whether the findings could be generalized beyond the target population, New Zealand high school students. Martha Kolln, when her attention is drawn to the study ("Reply to Ron Shook," *CCC,* 32 [1981], 139-151), thinks the whole experiment "suspicious." And John Mellon has been willing to use the study to defend the teaching of grammar; the study of Elley and his colleagues, he has argued, shows that teaching grammar does no harm.[6]

It would seem unlikely, therefore, that further experimental research, in and of itself, will resolve the grammar issue. Any experimental design can be nitpicked, any experimental population can be criticized, and any experimental conclusion can be questioned or, more often, ignored. In fact, it may well be that the grammar question is not open to resolution by experimental research, that, as Noam Chomsky has argued in *Reflections on Language* (New York: Pantheon, 1975), criticizing the trivialization of human learning by behavioral psychologists, the issue is simply misdefined.

> There will be "good experiments" only in domains that lie outside the organism's cognitive capacity. For example, there will be no "good experiments" in the study of human learning.
>
> This discipline. . . will, of necessity, avoid those domains in which an organism is specially designed to acquire rich cognitive structures that enter into its life in an intimate fashion. The discipline will be of virtually no intellectual interest, it seems to me, since it is restricting itself in principle to those questions that are guaranteed to tell us little about the nature of organisms. (p. 36)

Asking the Right Questions

As a result, though I will look briefly at the tradition of experimental research, my primary goal in this essay is to articulate the grammar issue in different and, I would hope, more productive terms. Specifically, I want to ask four questions:

1. Why is the grammar issue so important? Why has it been the dominant focus of composition research for the last seventy-five years?
2. What definitions of the word *grammar* are needed to articulate the grammar issue intelligibly?
3. What do findings in cognate disciplines suggest about the value of formal grammar instruction?
4. What is our theory of language, and what does it predict about the value of formal grammar instruction? (This question—"what does our theory of language predict?"—seems a much more powerful question than "what does educational research tell us?")

In exploring these questions I will attempt to be fully explicit about issues, terms, and assumptions. I hope that both proponents and opponents of formal grammar instruction would agree that these are useful as shared points of reference: care in definition, full examination of the evidence, reference to relevant work in cognate disciplines, and explicit analysis of the theoretical bases of the issue.

But even with that gesture of harmony it will be difficult to articulate the issue in a balanced way, one that will be acceptable to both sides. After all, we are dealing with a professional dispute in which one side accuses the other of "magical thinking," and in turn that side responds by charging the other as "alchemists." Thus we might suspect that the grammar issue is itself embedded in larger models of the transmission of literacy, part of quite different assumptions about the teaching of composition.

Those of us who dismiss the teaching of formal grammar have a model of composition instruction that makes the grammar issue "uninteresting" in a scientific sense. Our model predicts a rich and complex interaction of learner and environment in mastering literacy, an interaction that has little to do with sequences of skills instruction as such. Those who defend the teaching of grammar tend to have a model of composition instruction that is rigidly skills-centered and rigidly sequential: the formal teaching of grammar, as the first step in that sequence, is the cornerstone or linchpin. Grammar teaching is thus supremely interesting, naturally a dominant focus for educational research. The controversy over the value of grammar instruction, then, is inseparable from two other inssues: the issues of sequence in the teaching of composition and of the role of the composition teacher. Consider, for example, the force of these two issues in Janice Neuleib's conclusion: after calling for yet more experimental research on the value of teaching grammar, she ends with an absolute (and unsupported) claim about sequences and teacher roles in composition.

> We do know, however, that some things must be taught at different levels. Insistence on adherence to usage norms by composition teachers does improve usage. Students can learn to organize their papers if teachers do not accept papers that are disorganized. Perhaps composition teachers can teach those two abilities before they begin the more difficult tasks of developing syntactic sophistication and a winning style. ("The Relation of Formal Grammar to Composition," p. 250)

(One might want to ask, in passing, whether "usage norms" exist in the monolithic fashion the phrase suggests and whether refusing to accept disorganized papers is our best available pedagogy for teaching arrangement.)[7]

But I want to focus on the notion of sequence that makes the grammar issue so important: first grammar, then usage, then some absolute model or organization, all controlled by the teacher at the center of the learning process, with other matters, those of rhetorical weight—"syntactic sophistication and a winning style"—pushed off to the future. It is not surprising that we call each other names: those of us who question the value of teaching grammar are in fact shaking the whole elaborate edifice of traditional composition instruction.

The Five Meanings of "Grammar"

Given its centrality to a well-established way of teaching composition, I need to go about the business of defining grammar rather carefully, particularly in view of Kolln's criticism of the lack of care in earlier discussions. Therefore I will build upon a seminal discussion of the word *grammar* offered a generation ago, in 1954, by W. Nelson Francis, often excerpted as "The Three Meanings of Grammar."[8] It is worth reprinting at length, if only to re-establish it as a reference point for future discussions.

The first thing we mean by "grammar" is "the set of formal patterns in which the words of a language are arranged in order to convey larger meanings." It is not necessary that we be able to discuss these patterns self-consciously in order to be able to use them. In fact, all speakers of a language above the age of five or six know how to use its complex forms of organization with considerable skill; in this sense of the word—call it "Grammar 1"—they are thoroughly familiar with its grammar.

The second meaning of "grammar"—call it "Grammar 2"—is "the branch of linguistic science which is concerned with the description, analysis, and formulization of formal language patterns." Just as gravity was in full operation before Newton's apple fell, so grammar in the first sense was in full operation before anyone formulated the first rule that began the history of grammar as a study.

The third sense in which people use the word "grammar" is "linguistic etiquette." This we may call "Grammar 3." The word in this sense is often coupled with a derogatory adjective: we say that the expression "he ain't here" is "bad grammar."...

As has already been suggested, much confusion arises from mixing these meanings. One hears a good deal of criticism of teachers of English couched in such terms as "they don't teach grammar any more." Criticism of this sort is based on the wholly unproven assumption that teaching Grammar 2 will improve the student's proficiency in Grammar 1 or improve his manners in Grammar 3. Actually, the form of Grammar 2 which is usually taught is a very inaccurate and misleading analysis of the facts of Grammar 1; and it therefore is of highly questionable value in improving a person's ability to handle the structural patterns of his language. (pp. 300-301)

Francis' Grammar 3 is, of course, not grammar at all, but usage. One would like to assume that Joseph Williams' recent discussion of usage ("The Phenomenology of Error," *CCC,* 32 (1981), 152-168), along with his references, has placed those shibboleths in a proper perspective. But I doubt it, and I suspect that popular discussions of the grammar issue will be as flawed by the intrusion of usage issues as past discussions have been. At any rate I will make only passing reference to Grammar 3—usage—naively assuming that this issue has been discussed elsewhere and that my readers are familiar with those discussions.

We need also to make further discriminations about Francis' Grammar 2, given that the purpose of his 1954 article was to substitute for one form of Grammar 2, that "inaccurate and misleading" form "which is usually taught," another form, that of American structuralist grammar. Here we can make use of a still earlier discussion, one going back to the days when *PMLA* was willing to publish articles on rhetoric and linguistics, to a 1927 article by Charles Carpenter Fries, "The Rules of the Common School Grammars" (42 [1927], 221-237). Fries there distinguished between the scientific tradition of language study (to which we will now delimit Francis' Grammar 2, scientific grammar) and the separate tradition of "the common school grammars," developed unscientifically, largely based on two inadequate principles—appeals to "logical principles," like "two negatives make a positive," and analogy to Latin grammar; thus, Charlton Laird's characterization, "the grammar of Latin, ingeniously warped to suggest English" (*Language in America* [New York: World, 1970], p. 294). There is, of course, a direct link between the "common school grammars" that Fries criticized in 1927 and the grammar-based texts of today, and thus it seems wise, as Karl W. Dykema suggests ("Where Our Grammar Came From," *CE,* 22 (1961), 455-465), to separate Grammar 2, "scientific grammar," from Grammar 4, "school grammar," the latter meaning, quite literally, "the grammars used in the schools."

Further, since Martha Kolln points to the adaptation of Christensen's sentence rhetoric in a recent sentence-combining text as an example of the proper emphasis on "grammar" ("Closing the Books on Alchemy," p. 140), it is worth separating out, as still another meaning of *grammar,* Grammar 5, "stylistic grammar," defined as "grammatical terms used in the interest of teaching prose style." And, since stylistic grammars abound, with widely variant terms and emphases, we might appropriately speak parenthetically of specific forms of Grammar 5—Grammar 5 (Lanham); Grammar 5 (Strunk and White): Grammar 5 (Williams, *Style*); even Grammar 5 (Christensen, as adapted by Daiker, Kerek, and Morenberg).[9]

The Grammar in Our Heads

With these definitions in mind, let us return to Francis' Grammar 1, admirably defined by Kolln as "the internalized system of rules that speakers of a language share" ("Closing the Books on Alchemy," p. 140), or, to put it more simply, the grammar in our heads. Three features of Grammar 1 need to be stressed: first, its special status as an "internalized system of rules." as tacit and unconscious knowledge; second, the abstract, even counterintuitive, nature of these rules, insofar as we are able to approximate them indirectly as Grammar 2 statements; and third, the way in which the form of one's Grammar 1 seems profoundly affected by the acquisition of literacy. This sort of review is designed to firm up our theory of language, so that we can ask what it predicts about the value of teaching formal grammar.

A simple thought experiment will isolate the special status of Grammar 1 knowledge. I have asked members of a number of different groups—from sixth graders to college freshmen to high-school teachers—to give me the rule for ordering adjectives of nationality, age, and number in English. The response is always the same: "We don't know the rule." Yet when I ask these groups to perform an active language task, they show productive control over the rule thay have denied knowing. I ask them to arrange the following words in a natural order:

French   the   young   girls   four

I have never seen a native speaker of English who did not immediately produce the natural order, "the four young French girls." The rule is that in English the order of adjectives is first, number, second, age, and third, nationality. Native speakers can create analogous phrases using the rule—"the seventy-three aged Scandinavian lechers"; and the drive for meaning is so great that they will create contexts to make sense out of violations of the rule, as in foregrounding for emphasis: "I want to talk to the French four young girls." (I immediately envision a large room, perhaps a banquet hall, filled with tables at which are seated groups of four young girls, each group of a different nationality.) So Grammar 1 is eminently usable knowledge—the way we make our life through language—but it is not accessible knowledge; in a profound sense, we do not know that we have it. Thus neurolinguist Z.N. Pylyshyn speaks of Grammar 1 as "autonomous," separate from common-sense reasoning and as "cognitively inpenetrable," not available for direct examination.[10] In philosophy and linguistics, the distinction is made between formal, conscious, "knowing about" knowledge (like Grammar 2 knowledge) and tacit, unconscious, "knowing how" knowledge (like Grammar 1 knowledge). The importance of this distinction for the teaching of composition—it provides a powerful theoretical justification for mistrusting the ability of Grammar 2 (or Grammar 4) knowledge to affect Grammar 1 performance—was pointed out in this journal by Martin Steinmann, Jr., in 1966 ("Rhetorical Research," *CE*, 27 [1966], 278-285).

Further, the more we learn about Grammar 1—and most linguists would agree that we know surprisingly little about it—the more abstract and implicit it seems. . . .

Moreover, . . . the form of the Grammar 1 in the heads of literate adults seems profoundly affected by the acquisition of literacy. Obviously, literate adults have access to different morphological codes: the abstract print -*s* underlying the predicitable /s/ and /z/ plurals, the abstract print -*ed* underlying the spoken past tense markers /t/, as in "walked," /ed/, as in "surrounded," /d/, as in "scored," and the symbol /ɫ/ for no surface realization, as in the relaxed standard pronunciation of "I walked to the store." Literate adults also have access to distinctions preserved only in the code of print (for example, the distinction between "a good sailer" and "a good sailor" that Mark Aranoff points out in "An English Spelling Convention," *Linguistic Inquiry*, 9 [1978], 299-303). More significantly, Irene Moscowitz speculates that the ability of third graders to form abstract nouns on analogy with pairs like *divine::divinity* and *serene::serenity*, where the spoken vowel changes but the spelling preserves meaning, is a factor of knowing how to read. Carol Chomsky finds a three-stage developmental sequence in the grammatical performance of seven-year-olds, related to measures of kind and variety of reading; and Rita S. Brause finds a nine-stage developmental sequence in the ability to understand semantic ambiguity, extending from fourth graders to graduate students.[11] John Mills and Gordon Hemsley find that level of education, and presumably level of literacy, influence judgments of grammaticality, concluding that literacy changes the deep structure of one's internal grammar; Jean Whyte finds that oral language functions develop differently in readers and non-readers; José Morais, Jésus Alegria, and Paul Bertelson find that illiterate adults are unable to add or delete sounds at the beginning of nonsense words, suggesting that awareness of speech as a series of phones is provided by learning to read an alphabetic code. Two experiments—one conducted by Charles A. Ferguson, the other by Mary E. Hamilton and David Barton—find that adults' ability to recognize segmentation in speech is related to degree of literacy, not to amount of schooling or general ability.[12]

It is worth noting that none of these investigators would suggest that the developmental sequences they have uncovered be isolated and taught as discrete skills. They are natural concomitants of literacy, and they seem best characterized not as isolated rules but as developing schemata, broad strategies for approaching written language.

Grammar 2

We can, of course, attempt to approximate the rules of schemata of Grammar 1 by writing fully explicit descriptions that model the competence of a native speaker. Such rules, like the rules for pluralizing nouns or ordering adjectives discussed above, are the goal of the science of linguistics, that is, Grammar 2. There are a number of scientific grammars—an older structuralist model and several versions within a generative-transformational paradigm, not to mention isolated schools like tagmemic grammar, Montague grammar, and the like. In fact, we cannot think of Grammar 2 as a stable entity, for its form changes with each new issue of each linguistics journal, as new "rules of grammar" are proposed and debated. Thus Grammar 2, though of great theoretical interest to the composition teacher, is of little practical use in the classroom, as Constance Weaver has pointed out (*Grammar for Teachers* [Urbana, Ill.: NCTE, 1979], pp. 3-6). Indeed Grammar 2 is a scientific model of Grammar 1, not a description of it, so that questions of psychological reality, while important, are less important than other, more theoretical factors, such as the elegance of formulation or the global power of rules. We might, for example, wish to replace the rule for ordering adjectives of age, number, and nationality cited above with a more general rule—what linguists call a "fuzzy" rule—that adjectives in English are ordered by their abstract quality of "nouniness": adjectives that are very much like nouns, like *French* or *Scandinavian,* come physically closer to nouns than do adjectives that are less "nouny," like *four* or *aged.* But our motivation for accepting the broader rule would be its global power, not its psychological reality.[13]

I try to consider a hostile reader, one committed to the teaching of grammar, and I try to think of ways to hammer in the central point of this distinction, that the rules of Grammar 2 are simply unconnected to productive control over Grammar 1. I can argue from authority: Noam Chomsky has touched on this point whenever he has concerned himself with the implications of linguistics for language teaching, and years ago transformationalist Mark Lester stated unequivocally, "there simply appears to be no correlation between a writer's study of language and his ability to write."[14] I can cite analogies offered by others: Francis Christensen's analogy in an essay originally published in 1962 that formal grammar study would be "to invite a centipede to attend to the sequence of his legs in motion,"[15] or James Britton's analogy, offered informally after a conference presentation, that grammar study would be like forcing starving people to master the use of a knife and fork before allowing them to eat. I can offer analogies of my own, contemplating the wisdom of asking a pool player to master the physics of momentum before taking up a cue or of making a prospective driver get a degree in automotive engineering before engaging the clutch. I consider a hypothetical argument, that if Grammar 2 knowledge affected Grammar 1 performance, then linguists would be our best writers. (I can certify that they are, on the whole, not). Such a position, after all, is only in accord with other domains of science: the formula for catching a fly ball in baseball ("Playing It by Ear," *Scientific American*, 248, No. 4 [1983], 76) is of such complexity that it is beyond my understanding—and, I would suspect, that of many workaday centerfielders. But perhaps I can best hammer in this claim—that Grammar 2 knowledge has no effect on Grammar 1 performance—by offering a demonstration.

The diagram on page 172 is an attempt by Thomas N. Huckin and Leslie Leslie A. Olsen (*English for Science and Technology* [New York: McGraw-Hill, 1983]) to offer, for students of English as a second language, a fully explicit formulation of what is, for native speakers, a trivial rule of the language—the choice of definite article, indefinite article, or no definite article. There are obvious limits to such a formulation, for article choice in English is less a matter of rule than of idiom ("I went to college" versus "I went to a university" versus British "I went to university"), real-world knowledge (using indefinite "I went into a house" instantiates definite "I looked at the ceiling," and indefinite "I visited a university" instantiates definite "I talked with the professors"), and stylistic choice (the last sentence above might alternatively end with "the choice of the definite article, the indefinite article, or no article"). Huckin and Olsen invite non-native speakers to use the rule consciously to justify article choice in technical prose, such as the passage below from P.F. Brandwein (*Matter: An Earth Science* [New York: Harcourt Brace Jovanovich, 1975]). I invite you to spend a couple of minutes doing the same thing, with the understanding that this exercise is a test case: you are using a very explicit rule to justify a fairly straightforward issue of grammatical choice.

Imagine a cannon on top of _____ highest mountain on earth. It is firing _____ cannonballs horizontally. _____ first cannonball fired follows its path. As _____ cannonball moves, _____ gravity pulls it down, and it soon hits _____ ground. Now _____ velocity with which each succeeding cannonball is fired is increased. Thus, _____ cannonball goes farther each time. Cannonball 2 goes farther than _____ cannonball 1 although each is being pulled by _____ gravity toward the earth all _____ time. _____ last cannonball is fired with such tremendous velocity that it goes completely around _____ earth. It returns to _____ mountaintop and continues around the earth again and again. _____ cannonball's inertia causes it to continue in motion indefinitely in _____ orbit around earth. In such a situation, we could consider _____ cannonball to be _____ artificial satellite, just like _____ weather satellites launched by _____ U.S. Weather Service. (p. 209)

Most native speakers of English who have attempted this exercise report a great deal of frustration, a curious sense of working against, rather than with, the rule. The rule, however valuable it may be for non-native speakers, is, for the most part, simply unusable for native speakers of the language.

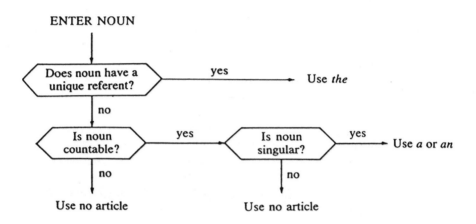

Cognate Areas of Research

We can corroborate this demonstration by turning to research in two cognate areas, studies of the induction of rules of artificial languages and studies of the role of formal rules in second language acquisition. Psychologists have studied the ability of subjects to learn artificial languages, usually constructed of non-sense syllables or letter strings. Such languages can be described by phrase structure rules:

$$S \Rightarrow VX$$
$$X \Rightarrow MX$$

More clearly, they can be presented as flow diagrams:

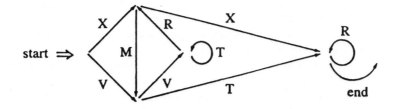

This diagram produces "sentences" like the following:

VVTRXRR.   XMVTTRX.   XXRR.
XMVRMT.   VVTTRMT.   XMTRRR.

The following "sentences" would be "ungrammatical" in this language:

*VMXTT.   *RTXVVT.   *TRVXXVVM.

Arthur S. Reber, in a classic 1967 experiment, demonstrated that mere exposure to grammatical sentences produced tacit learning: subjects who copied several grammatical sentences performed far above chance in judging the grammaticality of other letter strings. Further experiments have shown that providing subjects with formal rules—giving them the flow diagram above, for example—remarkably degrades performance: subjects given the "rules of language" do much less well in acquiring the rules than do subjects not given the rules. Indeed, even telling subjects that they are to induce the rules of an artificial language degrades performance. Such laboratory experiments are admittedly contrived, but they confirm predictions that our theory of language would make about the value of formal rules in language learning.[16]

The thrust of recent research in second language learning similarly works to constrain the value of formal grammar rules. The most explicit statement of the value of formal rules is that of Stephen D. Krashen's monitor model.[17] Krashen divides second language mastery into *acquisition*—tacit, informal mastery, akin to first language acquisition—and *formal learning*—conscious application of Grammar 2 rules, which he calls "monitoring" output. In another essay Krashen uses his model to predict a highly individual use of the monitor and a highly constrained role for formal rules:

> Some adults (and very few children) are able to use conscious rules to increase the grammatical accuracy of their output, and even for these people, very strict conditions need to be met before the conscious grammar can be applied.[18]...

An ingenious experiment by Herbert W. Seliger complicates the issue yet further ("On the Nature and Function of Language Rules in Language Learning," *TESOL Quarterly*, 13 [1979], 359-369). Seliger asked native and non-native speakers of English to orally identify pictures of objects (e.g., "an apple," "a pear," "a book," "an umbrella"), noting whether they used the correct form of the indefinite articles *a* and *an*. He then asked each speaker to state the rule for choosing between *a* and *an*. He found no correlation between the ability to state the rule and the ability to apply it correctly, either with native or non-native speakers. Indeed, three of four adult non-native speakers in his sample produced a correct form of the rule, but they did not apply it in speaking. A strong conclusion from this experiment would be that formal rules of grammar seem to have no value whatsoever. Seliger, however, suggests a more paradoxical interpretation. Rules are of no use, he agrees, but some people think they are, and for these people, assuming that they have internalized the rules, even inadequate rules are of heuristic value, for they allow them to access the internal rules they actually use.

The Incantations of the "Common School Grammars"

Such a paradox may explain the fascination we have as teachers with "rules of grammar" of the Grammar 4 variety, the "rules" of the "common school grammars." Again and again such rules are inadequate to the facts of written language; you will recall that we have known this since Francis' 1927 study. R. Scott Baldwin and James M. Coady, studying how readers respond to punctuation signals ("Psycholinguistic Approaches to a Theory of Punctuation," *Journal of Reading Behavior,* 10 [1978], 363-83), conclude that conventional rules of punctuation are "a complete sham" (p. 375). My own favorite is the Grammar 4 rule for showing possession, always expressed in terms of adding -*'s* or -*s'* to nouns, while our internal grammar, if you think about it, adds possession to noun phrases, albeit under severe stylistic constraints: "the horses of the Queen of England" are "the Queen of England's horses" and "the feathers of the duck over there" and "the duck over there's feathers." Suzette Haden Elgin refers to the "rules" of Grammar 4 as "incantations" (*Never Mind the Trees,* p. 9: see footnote 3).

It may simply be that as hyperliterate adults we are conscious of "using rules" when we are in fact doing something else, something far more complex, accessing tacit heuristics honed by print literacy itself. We can clarify this notion by reaching for an acronym coined by technical writers to explain the readability of complex prose—COIK: "clear only if known." The rules of Grammar 4—no, we can at this point be more honest—the incantations of Grammar 4 are COIK. If you know how to signal possession in the code of print, then the advice to add -*'s* to nouns makes perfect sense, just as the collective noun *monies* is a fine example of changing -*y* to -*i* and adding -es to form the plural. But if you have not grasped, tacitly, the abstract representation of possession in print, such incantations can only be opaque.

Worse yet, the advice given in "the common school grammars" is unconnected with anything remotely resembling literate adult behavior. Consider, as an example, the rule for not writing a sentence fragment as the rule is described in the best-selling college grammar text, John C. Hodges and Mary S.

Whitten's *Harbrace College Handbook,* 9th ed. (New York: Harcourt Brace Jovanovich, 1982). In order to get to the advice, "as a rule, do not write a sentence fragment" (p. 25), the student must master the following learning tasks:

> Recognizing verbs.
> Recognizing subjects and verbs.
> Recognizing all part of speech. (*Harbrace* lists eight.)
> Recognizing phrases and subordinate clauses. (*Harbrace* lists six types of phrases, and it offers incomplete lists of eight relative pronouns and eighteen subordinating conjunctions.)
> Recognizing main clauses and types of sentences.

These learning tasks completed, the student is given the rule above, offered a page of exceptions, and then given the following advice (or is it an incantation?):

> Before handing in a composition,...proofread each word group written as a sentence. Test each one for completeness. First, be sure that it has at least one subject and one predicate. Next, be sure that the word group is not a dependent clause beginning with a subordinating conjunction or a relative clause. (p. 27)

The school grammar approach defines a sentence fragment as a conceptual error—as not showing conscious knowledge of the school grammar definition of *sentence.* It demands heavy emphasis on rote memory, and it asks students to behave in ways patently removed from the behaviors of mature writers. (I have never in my life tested a sentence for completeness, and I am a better writer— and probably a better person—as a consequence.) It may be, of course, that some developing writers, at some points in their development, may benefit from such advice—or, more to the point, may think that they benefit—but, as Thomas Friedman points out in "Teaching Error, Nurturing Confusion" (*CE,* 45 [1983], 390-399), our theory of language tells us that such advice is, at the best, COIK. As the Maine joke has it, about a tourist asking directions from a farmer, "you can't get there from here."

Redefining Error

In the specific case of sentence fragments, Mina P. Shaughnessy (*Errors and Expectations* [New York: Oxford Univeristy Press, 1977]) argues that such errors are not conceptual failures at all, but performance errors—mistakes in punctuation. Muriel Harris' error counts support this view ("Mending the Fragmented Free Modifier," *CCC,* 32 [1981], 175-182). Case studies show example after example of errors that occur *because of* instruction—one thinks, for example, of David Bartholmae's student explaining that he added an -*s* to *children* "because it's a plural" ("The Study of Error," *CCC,* 31 [1980], 262). Surveys, such as that by Muriel Harris ("Contradictory Perceptions of the Rules of Writing,' *CCC,* 30 [1979], 218-220), and our own observations suggest that students consistently misunderstand such Grammar 4 explanations (COIK, you will recall). For example, from Patrick Hartwell and Robert H. Bentley and from Mike Rose, we have two separate anecdotal accounts of students, cited for punctuating a *because*-clause as a sentence, who have decided to avoid using *because.* More generally, Collette A. Daiute's analysis of errors made by college students shows that errors tend to appear at clause boundaries, suggesting short-term memory load and not conceptual deficiency as a cause of error.[19]

Thus, if we think seriously about error and its relationship to the worship of formal grammar study, we need to attempt some massive dislocation of our traditional thinking, to shuck off our hyperliterate perception of the value of formal rules, and to regain the confidence in the tacit power of unconscious knowledge that our theory of language gives us. Most students, reading their writing aloud, will correct in essence all errors of spelling, grammar, and, by intonation, punctuation, but usually without noticing that what they read departs from what they wrote.[20] And Richard H. Haswell ("Minimal Marking," *CE,* 45 [1983], 600-604) notes that his students correct 61.1% of their errors when they are identified with a simple mark in the margin rather than by error type. Such findings suggest that we need to redefine error, to see it not as a cognitive or linguistic problem, a problem of not knowing a "rule of grammar" (whatever that may mean), but rather, following the insight of Robert J. Bracewell ("Writing as a Cognitive Activity," *Visible Language,* 14 [1980], 400-422), as a problem of metacognition and metalinguistic awareness, a matter of accessing knowledges that, to be of any use, learners must have already internalized by means of exposure to the code. (Usage issues—Grammar 3—probably represent a different order of problem. Both Joseph Emonds and Jeffrey Jochnowitz establish that the usage issues we worry most about are linguistically unnatural, departures from the grammar in our heads.)[21]

The notion of metalinguistic awareness seems crucial. The sentence below, created by Douglas R. Hofstadter ("Metamagical Themas," *Scientific American,* 235, No. 1 [1981], 22-32), is offered to clarify that notion; you are invited to examine it for a moment or two before continuing.

Their is four errors in this sentence. Can you find them?

Three errors announce themselves plainly enough, the misspellings of *there* and *sentence* and the use of *is* instead of *are.* (And, just to illustrate the perils of hyperliteracy, let it be noted that, through three years of drafts, I referred to the choice of *is* and *are* as a matter of "subject-verb agreement.") The fourth error resists detection, until one assesses the truth value of the sentence itself—the fourth error is that there are not four errors, only three. Such a sentence (Hofstadter calls it a "self-referencing sentence") asks you to look at it in two ways, simultaneously as statement and as linguistic artifact—in other words, to exercise metalinguistic awareness.

A broad range of cross-cultural studies suggest that metalinguistic awareness is a defining feature of print literacy. Thus Sylvia Scribner and Michael

Cole, working with the triliterate Vai of Liberia (variously literate in English, through schooling; in Arabic, for religious purposes; and in an indigenous Vai script, used for personal affairs), find that metalinguistic awareness, broadly conceived, is the only cognitive skill underlying each of the three literacies. The one statistically significant skill shared by literate Vai was the recognition of word boundaries. Moreover, literate Vai tended to answer "yes" when asked (in Vai), "Can you call the sun the moon and the moon the sun?" while illiterate Vai tended to have grave doubts about such metalinguistic play. And in the United States Henry and Lila R. Gleitman report quite different responses by clerical workers and PhD candidates asked to interpret nonsense compounds like "house-bird glass": clerical workers focused on meaning and plausibility (for example, "a house-bird made of glass"), while PhD canidates focused on syntax (for example, "a very small drinking cup for canaries" or "a glass that protects house-birds").[22] More general research findings suggest a clear relationship between measures of metalinguistic awareness and measures of literacy level.[23] William Labov, speculating on literacy acquisition in inner-city ghettoes, contrasts "stimulus-bound" and "language-bound" individuals, suggesting that the latter seem to master literacy more easily.[24] The analysis here suggests that the causal relationship works the other way, that it is the mastery of written language that increases one's awareness of language as language.

This analysis has two implications. First, it makes the question of socially nonstandard dialects, always implicit in discussions of teaching formal grammar, into a non-issue.[25] Native speakers of English, regardless of dialect, show tacit mastery of the conventions of Standard English, and that mastery seems to transfer into abstract orthographic knowledge through interaction with print.[26] Developing writers show the same patterning of errors, regardless of dialect.[27] Studies of reading and of writing suggest that surface features of spoken dialect are simply irrelevant to mastering print literacy.[28] Print is a complex cultural code—or better yet, a system of codes—and my bet is that, regardless of instruction, one masters those codes from the top down, from pragmatic questions of voice, tone, audience, register, and rhetorical strategy, not from the bottom up, from grammar to usage to fixed forms of organization.

Second, this analysis forces us to posit multiple literacies, used for multiple purposes, rather than a single static literacy, engraved in "rules of grammar." These multiple literacies are evident in cross-cultural studies.[29] They are equally evident when we inquire into the uses of literacy in American communities.[30] Further, given that students, at all levels, show widely variant interactions with print literacy, there would seem to be little to do with grammar—with Grammar 2 or with Grammar 4—that we could isolate as a basis for formal instruction.[31]

Grammar 5: Stylistic Grammar

Similarly, when we turn to Grammar 5, "grammatical terms used in the interest of teaching prose style," so central to Martha Kolln's argument for teaching formal grammar, we find that the grammar issue is simply beside the point. There are two fully-articulated positions about "stylistic grammar," which I will label "romantic" and "classic," following Richard Lloyd-Jones and Richard E. Young.[32] The romantic position is that stylistic grammars, though perhaps useful for teachers, have little place in the teaching of composition, for students must struggle with and through language toward meaning. This position rests on the theory of language ultimately philosophical rather than linguistic (witness, for example, the contempt for linguists in Ann Berthoff's *The Making of Meaning: Metaphors, Models, and Maxims for Writing Teachers* [Montclair, N.J.: Boynton/Cook, 1981]); it is articulated as a theory of style by Donald M. Murray and, on somewhat different grounds (that stylistic grammars encourage overuse of the monitor), by Ian Pringle. The classic position, on the other hand, is that we can find ways to offer developing writers helpful suggestions about prose style, suggestions such as Francis Christensen's emphasis on the cumulative sentence, developed by observing the practice of skilled writers, and Joseph Williams' advice about predication, developed by psycholinguistic studies of comprehension.[33] James A. Berlin's recent survey of composition theory (*CE*, 45 [1982], 765-777) probably understates the gulf between these two positions and the radically different conceptions of language that underlie them, but it does establish that they share an overriding assumption in common: that one learns to control the language of print by manipulating language in meaningful contexts, not by learning about language in isolation, as by the study of formal grammar. Thus even classic theorists, who choose to present a vocabulary of style to students, do so only as a vehicle for encouraging productive control of communicative structures.

We might put the matter in the following terms. Writers need to develop skills at two levels. One, broadly rhetorical, involves communication in meaningful contexts (the strategies, registers, and procedures of discourse across a range of modes, audiences, contexts, and purposes). The other, broadly metalinguistic rather than linguistic, involves active manipulation of language with conscious attention to surface form. This second level may be developed tacitly, as a natural adjunct to developing rhetorical competencies—I take this to be the position of romantic theorists. It may be developed formally, by manipulating language for stylistic effect, and such manipulation may involve, for pedagogical continuity, a vocabulary of style. But it is primarily developed by any kind of language activity that enhances the awareness of language as language.[34] David T. Hakes, summarizing the research on metalinguistic awareness, notes how far we are from understanding this process:

> the optimal conditions for becoming metalinguistically competent involve growing up in a literate environment with adult models who are

themselves metalinguistically competent and who foster the growth of that competence in a variety of ways as yet little understood. ("The Development of Metalinguistic Abilities," p. 205: see footnote 23)

Such a model places language, at all levels, at the center of the curriculum, but not as "necessary categories and labels" (Kolln, "Closing the Books on Alchemy," p. 150), but as literal stuff, verbal clay, to be molded and probed, shaped and reshaped, and, above all, enjoyed.

The Tradition of Experimental Research

Thus, when we turn back to experimental research on the value of formal grammar instruction, we do so with firm predictions given us by our theory of language. Our theory would predict that formal grammar instruction, whether instruction in scientific grammar or instruction in "the common school grammar," would have little to do with control over surface correctness nor with quality of writing. It would predict that any form of active involvement with language would be preferable to instruction in rules or definitions (or incantations). In essence, this is what the research tells us. In 1893, the Committee of Ten (*Report of the Committee of Ten on Secondary School Studies* [Washington, D.C.: U.S. Government Printing Office, 1893]) put grammar at the center of the English curriculum, and its report established the rigidly sequential mode of instruction common for the last century. But the committee explicitly noted that grammar instruction did not aid correctness, arguing instead that it improved the ability to think logically (an agrument developed from the role of the "grammarian" in the classical rhetorical tradition, essentially a teacher of literature—see, for example, the etymology of *grammar* in the *Oxford English Dictionary*).

But Franklin S. Hoyt, in a 1906 experiment, found no relationship between the study of grammar and the ability to think logically; his research led him to conclude what I am constrained to argue more than seventy-five years later, that there is no "relationship between a knowledge of a technical grammar and the ability to use English and to interpret language" ("The Place of Grammar in the Elementary Curriculum," *Teachers College Report, 7* [1906], 483-484). Later studies, through the 1920s, focused on the relationship of knowlege of grammar and ability to recognize error; experiments reported by James Boraas in 1917 and by William Asker in 1923 are typical of those that reported no correlation. In the 1930s, with the development of the functional grammar movement, it was common to compare the study of formal grammar with one form or another of active manipulation of language; experiments by I.O. Ash in 1935 and Ellen Frogner in 1939 are typical of studies showing the superiority of active involvement with language.[35] In a 1959 article, "Grammar in Language Teaching" (*Elementary English,* 36 [1959], 412-421), John J. DeBoer noted the consistency of these findings.

> The impressive fact is...that in all these studies, carried out in places and at times far removed from each other, often by highly experienced and disinterested investigators, the results have been consistently negative so far as the value of grammar in the improvement of language expression is concerned. (p. 417)

In 1960 Ingrid M. Strom, reviewing more than fifty experimental studies, came to a similarly strong and unqualified conclusion:

> direct methods of instruction, focusing on writing activities and the structuring of ideas, are more efficient in teaching sentence structure, usage, punctuation, and other related factors than are such methods as nomenclature drill, diagramming, and rote memorization of grammatical rules.[36]

In 1963, two research reviews appeared, one by Braddock, Lloyd-Jones, and Schoer, cited at the beginning of this paper, and one by Henry C. Meckel, whose conclusions, though more guarded, are in essential agreement.[37] In 1969 J. Stephen Sherwin devoted one-fourth of his *Four Problems in Teaching English: A Critique of Research* (Scranton, Penn.: International Textbook, 1969) to the grammar issue, concluding that "instruction in formal grammar is an ineffective way to help students achieve proficiency in writing" (p. 135). Some early experiments in sentence combining, such as those by Donald R. Bateman and Frank J. Zidonis and by John C. Mellon, showed improvement in measure of syntactic complexity with instruction in transformational grammar keyed to sentence combining practice. But a later study by Frank O'Hare achieved the same gains with no grammar instruction, suggesting to Sandra L. Stotsky and to Richard Van de Veghe that active manipulation of language, not the grammar unit, explained the earlier results.[38] More recent summaries of research—by Elizabeth I. Haynes, Hillary Taylor Holbrook, and Marcia Farr Whiteman—support similar conclusions. Indirect evidence for this position is provided by surveys reported by Betty Bamberg in 1978 and 1981, showing that time spent in grammar instruction in high school is the least important factor, of eight factors examined, in separating regular from remedial writers at the college level.[39]

More generally, Patrick Scott and Bruce Castner, in "Reference Sources for Composition Research: A Practical Survey" (*CE*, 45 [1983], 756-768), note that much current research is not informed by an awareness of the past. Put simply, we are constrained to reinvent the wheel. My concern here has been with a far more serious problem: that too often the wheel we reinvent is square.

It is, after all, a question of power. Janet Emig, developing a consensus from composition research, and Aaron S. Carton and Lawrence V. Castiglione, developing the implications of language theory for education, come to the same conclusion: that the thrust of current research and theory is to take power from the teacher and to give that power to the learner.[40] At no point in the English curriculum is the question of power more blatantly posed than in the issue of formal grammar instruction. It is time that we, as teachers, formulate theories of language and literacy and let those theories guide our teaching, and it is time that we, as researchers, move on to more interesting areas of inquiry.

Notes

[1] *Research in Written Composition* (Urbana, Ill.: National Council of Teachers of English, 1963), pp. 37-38.

[2] "Non-magical Thinking: Presenting Writing Developmentally in Schools," in *Writing: Process, Development and Communication,* Vol. II of *Writing: The Nature, Development and Teaching of Written Communication,* ed. Charles H. Frederiksen and Joseph F. Dominic (Hillsdale, N.J.: Lawrence Erlbaum, 1980), pp. 21-30.

[3] For arguments in favor of formal grammar teaching, see Patrick F. Basset, "Grammar—Can We Afford Not to Teach It?" *NASSP Bulletin,* 64, No. 10 (1980), 55-63; Mary Epes, et al., "The COMP-LAB Project: Assessing the Effectiveness of a Laboratory-Centered Basic Writing Course on the College Level" (Jamaica, N.Y.: York College, CUNY, 1979) ERIC 194 908; June B. Evans, "The Analogous Ounce: The Analgesic for Relief," *English Journal,* 70, No. 2 (1981), 38-39; Sydney Greenbaum, "What Is Grammar and Why Teach It?" (a paper presented at the meeting of the National Council of Teachers of English, Boston, Nov. 1982) ERIC 222 917; Marjorie Smelstor, *A Guide to the Role of Grammar in Teaching Writing* (Madison: University of Wisconsin School of Education, 1978) ERIC 176 323; and A.M. Tibbetts, *Working Papers: A Teacher's Observations on Composition* (Glenview, Ill.: Scott, Foresman, 1982).

For attacks on formal grammar teaching, see Harvey A. Daniels, *Famous Last Words: The American Language Crisis Reconsidered* (Carbondale: Southern Illinois University Press, 1983); Suzette Haden Elgin, *Never Mind the Trees: What the English Teacher Really Needs to Know about Linguistics* (Berkeley: University of California College of Education, Bay Area Writing Project Occasional Paper No. 2, 1980) ERIC 198 536; Mike Rose, "Remedial Writing Courses: A Critique and a Proposal." *College English,* 45 (1983), 109-128; and Ron Shook, "Response to Martha Kolln," *College Composition and Communication,* 34 (1983), 491-495.

[4] See, for example, Clifton Fadiman and James Howard, *Empty Pages: A Search for Writing Competence in School and Society* (Belmont, Cal.: Fearon Pitman, 1979); Edwin Newman, *A Civil Tongue* (Indianapolis, Ind.: Bobbs-Merrill, 1976); and *Strictly Speaking* (New York: Warner Books, 1974); John Simon, *Paradigms Lost* (New York: Clarkson N. Potter, 1980); A.M. Tibbetts and Charlene Tibbetts, *What's Happening to American English?* (New York: Scribner's, 1978); and "Why Johnny Can't Write," *Newsweek,* 8 Dec. 1975, pp. 58-63.

[5] "The Role of Grammar in a Secondary School English Curriculum." *Research in the Teaching of English,* 10 (1976), 5-21; *The Role of Grammar in a Secondary School Curriculum* (Wellington: New Zealand Council of Teachers of English, 1979).

[6] "A Taxonomy of Compositional Competencies," in *Perspectives on Literacy,* ed. Richard Beach and P. David Pearson (Minneapolis: University of Minnesota College of Education, 1979), pp. 247-272.

[7] On usage norms, see Edward Finegan, *Attitudes toward English Usage: The History of a War of Words* (New York: Teachers College Press, 1980), and Jim Quinn, *American Tongue in Cheek: A Populist Guide to Language* (New York: Pantheon, 1980); on arrangement, see Patrick Hartwell, "Teaching Arrangement: A Pedagogy," *CE,* 40 (1979), 548-554.

[8] "Revolution in Grammar," *Quarterly Journal of Speech,* 40 (1954), 229-312.

[9] Richard A. Lanham, *Revising Prose* (New York: Scribner's, 1979); William Strunk and E.B. White, *The Elements of Style,* 3rd ed. (New York: Macmillan, 1979); Joseph Williams, *Style:*

Ten Lessons in Clarity and Grace (Glenview, Ill.: Scott, Foresman, 1981); Francis Christensen, "A Generative Rhetoric of the Sentence," *CCC*, 14 (1963), 155-161; Donald A. Daiker, Andrew Kerek, and Max Morenberg, *The Writer's Options: Combining to Composing*, 2nd ed. (New York: Harper & Row, 1982).

[10] "A Psychological Approach," in *Psychobiology of Language*, ed. M. Studdert-Kennedy (Cambridge, Mass.: MIT Press, 1983), pp. 16-19. See also Noam Chomsky, "Language and Unconscious Knowledge," in *Psychoanalysis and Language: Psychiatry and the Humanities*, Vol. III, ed. Joseph H. Smith (New Haven, Conn.: Yale University Press, 1978), pp. 3-44.

[11] Moscowitz, "On the Status of Vowel Shift in English," in *Cognitive Development and the Acquisition of Language*, ed. T.E. Moore (New York: Academic Press, 1973), pp. 223-60; Chomsky, "Stages in Language Development and Reading Exposure," *Harvard Educational Review*, 42 (1972), 1-33; and Brause, "Developmental Aspects of the Ability to Understand Semantic Ambiguity, with Implications for Teachers," *RTE*, 11 (1977), 39-48.

[12] Mills and Hemsley, "The Effect of Levels of Education on Judgments of Grammatical Acceptability," *Language and Speech*, 19 (1976), 324-342; Whyte, "Levels of Language Competence and Reading Ability: An Exploratory Investigation," *Journal of Research in Reading*, 5 (1982), 123-132; Morais, et al., "Does Awareness of Speech as a Series of Phones Arise Spontaneously?" *Cognition*, 7 (1979), 323-331; Ferguson, *Cognitive Effects of Literacy: Linguistic Awareness in Adult Non-readers* (Washington, D.C.: National Institute of Education Final Report, 1981) ERIC 222 857; Hamilton and Barton, "A Word Is a Word: Metalinguistic Skills in Adults of Varying Literacy Levels" (Stanford, Cal.: Stanford University Department of Linguistics, 1980) ERIC 222 859.

[13] On the question of the psychological reality of Grammar 2 descriptions, see Maria Black and Shulamith Chiat, "Psycholinguistics without 'Psychological Reality'," *Linguistics*, 19 (1981), 37-61; Joan Bresnan, ed., *The Mental Representation of Grammatical Relations* (Cambridge, Mass.: MIT Press, 1982); and Michael H. Long, "Inside the 'Black Box': Methodological Issues in Classroom Research on Language Learning," *Language Learning*, 30 (1980), 1-42.

[14] Chomsky, "The Current Scene in Linguistics," *College English*, 27 (1966), 587-595; and "Linguistic Theory," in *Language Teaching: Broader Contexts*, ed. Robert C. Meade, Jr. (New York: Modern Language Association, 1966), pp. 43-49; Mark Lester, "The Value of Transformational Grammar in Teaching Composition," *CCC*, 16 (1967), 228.

[15] Christensen, "Between Two Worlds," in *Notes toward a New Rhetoric: Nine Essays for Teachers*, rev. ed., ed. Bonniejean Christensen (New York: Harper & Row, 1978), pp. 1-22.

[16] Reber, "Implicit Learning of Artificial Grammars," *Journal of Verbal Learning and Verbal Behavior*, 6 (1967), 855-863; "Implicit Learning of Synthetic Languages: The Role of Instructional Set," *Journal of Experimental Psychology: Human Learning and Memory*, 2 (1976), 889-94; and Reber, Saul M. Kassin, Selma Lewis, and Gary Cantor, "On the Relationship Between Implicit and Explicit Modes in the Learning of a Complex Rule Structure," *Journal of Experimental Psychology: Human Learning and Memory*, 6 (1980), 492-502.

[17] "Individual Variation in the Use of the Monitor," in *Principles of Second Language Learning*, ed. W. Richie (New York: Academic Press, 1978), pp. 175-185.

[18] "Applications of Psycholinguistic Research to the Classroom," in *Practical Applications of Research in Foreign Language Teaching*, ed. D.J. James (Lincolnwood, Ill.: National Textbook, 1983), p. 61.

[19] Hartwell and Bentley, *Some Suggestions for Using* Open to Language (New York: Oxford University Press, 1982), p. 73; Rose, *Writer's Block: The Cognitive Dimension* (Carbondale: Southern Illinois University Press, 1983), p. 99; Daiute, "Psycholinguistic Foundations of the Writing Process," *RTE*, 15 (1981), 5-22.

[20] See Bartholmae, "The Study of Error"; Patrick Hartwell, "The Writing Center and the Paradoxes of Written-Down Speech," in *Writing Centers: Theory and Administration,* ed. Gary Olson (Urbana, Ill.: NCTE, 1984), pp. 48-61; and Sondra Perl, "A Look at Basic Writers in the Process of Composing," in *Basic Writing: A Collection of Essays for Teachers, Researchers, and Administrators* (Urbana, Ill.: NCTE, 1980), pp. 13-32.

[21] Emonds, *Adjacency in Grammar: The Theory of Language-Particular Rules* (New York: Academic, 1983); and Jochnowitz, "Everybody Likes Pizza, Doesn't He or She?" *American Speech,* 57 (1982), 198-203.

[22] Scribner and Cole, *Psychology of Literacy* (Cambridge, Mass.: Harvard University Press, 1981); Gleitman and Gleitman, "Language Use and Language Judgment," in *Individual Differences in Language Ability and Language Behavior,* ed. Charles J. Fillmore, Daniel Kemper, and William S.-Y. Wang (New York: Academic Press, 1979), pp. 103-126.

[23] There are several recent reviews of this developing body of research in psychology and child development: Irene Athey, "Language Development Factors Related to Reading Development," *Journal of Educational Research,* 76 (1983), 197-203; James Flood and Paula Menyuk, "Metalinguistic Development and Reading/Writing Achievement," *Claremont Reading Conference Yearbook,* 46 (1982), 122-132; and the following four essays: David T. Hakes, "The Development of Metalinguistic Abilities: What Develops?," pp. 162-210; Stan A. Kuczaj, II, and Brooke Harbaugh, "What Children Think about the Speaking Capabilities of Other Persons and Things," pp. 211-227; Karen Saywitz and Louise Cherry Wilkinson, "Age-Related Differences in Metalinguistic Awareness," pp. 229-250; and Harriet Salatas Waters and Virginia S. Tinsley, "The Development of Verbal Self-Regulation: Relationships between Language, Cognition, and Behavior," pp. 251-277; all in *Language, Thought, and Culture,* Vol. II of *Language Development,* ed. Stan Kuczaj, Jr. (Hillsdale, N.J.: Lawrence Erlbaum, 1982). See also Joanne R. Nurss, "Research in Review: Linguistic Awareness and Learning to Read," *Young Children,* 35, No. 3 [1980], 57-66.

[24] "Competing Value Systems in Inner City Schools," in *Children In and Out of School: Ethnography and Education,* ed. Perry Gilmore and Allan A. Glatthorn (Washington, D.C.: Center for Applied Linguistics, 1982), pp. 148-171; and "Locating the Frontier between Social and Psychological Factors in Linguistic Structure," in *Individual Differences in Language Ability and Language Behavior,* ed. Fillmore, Kemper, and Wang, pp. 327-340.

[25] See, for example, Thomas Farrell, "IQ and Standard English," *CCC,* 34 (1983), 470-484; and the responses by Karen L. Greenberg and Patrick Hartwell, *CCC,* 35 (December 1984): 455-465.

[26] Jane W. Torrey, "Teaching Standard English to Speakers of Other Dialects," in *Applications of Linguistics: Selected Papers of the Second International Conference of Applied Linguistics,* ed. G.E. Perren and J.L.M. Trim (Cambridge, Mass.: Cambridge University Press, 1971), pp. 423-428; James W. Beers and Edmund H. Henderson, "A Study of the Developing Orthographic Concepts among First Graders," *RTE,* 11 (1977), 133-148.

[27] See the error counts of Samuel A. Kirschner and G. Howard Poteet, "Non-Standard English Usage in the Writing of Black, White, and Hispanic Remedial English Students in an Urban Community College," *RTE,* 7 (1973), 351-355; and Marilyn Sternglass, "Close Similarities in Dialect Features of Black and White College Students in Remedial Composition Classes," *TESOL Quarterly,* 8 (1974), 271-283.

[28] For reading, see the massive study by Kenneth S. Goodman and Yetta M. Goodman, *Reading of American Children Whose Language Is a Stable Rural Dialect of English or a Language other than English* (Washington, D.C.: National Institute of Education Final Report, 1978) ERIC 175 754; and the overview by Rudine Sims, "Dialect and Reading: Toward Redefining the Issues," in *Reader Meets Author/Bridging the Gap: A Psycholinguistic and Sociolinguistic Approach,*

ed. Judith A. Langer and M. Tricia Smith-Burke (Newark, Del.: International Reading Association, 1982), pp. 222-232. For writing, see Patrick Hartwell, "Dialect Interference in Writing: A Critical View," *RTE,* 14 (1980), 101-118; and the anthology edited by Barry M. Kroll and Roberta J. Vann, *Exploring Speaking-Writing Relationships: Connections and Contrasts* (Urbana, Ill.: NCTE, 1981).

[29] See, for example, Eric A. Havelock, *The Literacy Revolution in Greece and Its Cultural Consequences* (Princeton, N.J.: Princeton University Press, 1982); Leslie Milroy on literacy in Dublin, *Language and Social Networks* (Oxford: Basil Blackwell, 1980); Ron Scollon and Suzanne B.K. Scollon on literacy in central Alaska, *Interethnic Communication: An Athabascan Case* (Austin, Tex.: Southwest Educational Development Laboratory Working Papers in Sociolinguistics, No. 59, 1979) ERIC 175 276; and Scribner and Cole on literacy in Liberia, *Psychology of Literacy* (see footnote 22.)

[30] See, for example, the anthology edited by Deborah Tannen, *Spoken and Written Language: Exploring Orality and Literacy* (Norwood, N.J.: Ablex, 1982); and Shirley Brice Heath's continuing work: "Protean Shapes in Literacy Events: Ever-Shifting Oral and Literate Traditions," in *Spoken and Written Language,* pp. 91-117; *Ways with Words: Language, Life and Work in Communities and Classrooms* (New York: Cambridge University Press, 1983); and "What No Bedtime Story Means," *Language in Society,* 11 (1982), 49-76.

[31] For studies at the elementary level, see Dell H. Hymes, et al., eds., *Ethnographic Monitoring of Children's Acquisition of Reading/Language Arts Skills In and Out of the Classroom* (Washington, D.C.: National Institute of Education Final Report, 1981) ERIC 208 096. For studies at the secondary level, see James L. Collins and Michael M. Williamson, "Spoken Language and Semantic Abbreviation in Writing," *RTE,* 15 (1981), 23-36. And for studies at the college level, see Patrick Hartwell and Gene LoPresti, "Sentence Combining as Kid-Watching," in *Sentence Combining: Toward a Rhetorical Perspective,* ed. Donald A. Daiker, Andrew Kerek, and Max Morenberg (Carbondale: Southern Illinois University Press, 1984).

[32] Lloyd-Jones, "Romantic Revels—I Am Not You," *CCC,* 23 (1972), 251-271; and Young, "Concepts of Art and the Teaching of Writing," in *The Rhetorical Tradition and Modern Writing,* ed. James J. Murphy (New York: Modern Language Association, 1982), pp. 130-141.

[33] For the romantic position, see Ann E. Berthoff, "Tolstoy, Vygotsky, and the Making of Meaning," *CCC,* 29 (1978), 249-255; Kenneth Dowst, "The Epistemic Approach," in *Eight Approaches to Teaching Composition,* ed. Timothy Donovan and Ben G. McClellan (Urbana, Ill.: NCTE, 1980), pp. 65-85; Peter Elbow, "The Challenge for Sentence Combining"; and Donald Murray, "Following Language toward Meaning," both in *Sentence Combining: Toward a Rhetorical Perspective* (Carbondale: Southern Illinois University Press, 1984, 107-126); and Ian Pringle, "Why Teach Style? A Review-Essay," *CCC,* 34 (1983), 91-98.

For the classic position, see Christensen's "A Generative Rhetoric of the Sentence"; and Joseph Williams' "Defining Complexity," *CE,* 41 (1979), 595-609; and his *Style: Ten Lessons in Clarity and Grace* (see footnote 9).

[34] Courtney B. Cazden and David K. Dickinson, "Language and Education: Standardization versus Cultural Pluralism," in *Language in the USA,* ed. Charles A. Ferguson and Shirley Brice Heath (New York: Cambridge University Press, 1981), pp. 446-468; and Carol Chomsky, "Developing Facility with Language Structure," in *Discovering Language with Children,* ed. Gay Su Pinnell (Urbana, Ill.: NCTE, 1980), pp. 56-59.

[35] Boraas, "Formal English Grammar and the Practical Mastery of English." Diss. University of Illinois, 1917; Asker, "Does Knowledge of Grammar Function?" *School and Society,* 17 (27 January 1923), 109-111; Ash, "An Experimental Evaluation of the Stylistic Approach in Teaching Composition in the Junior High School," *Journal of Experimental Education,* 4 (1935), 54-62; and Frogner, "A Study of the Relative Efficacy of a Grammatical and a Thought

Approach to the Improvement of Sentence Structure in Grades Nine and Eleven," *School Review,* 47 (1939), 663-675.

[36] "Research on Grammar and Usage and Its Implications for Teaching Writing," *Bulletin of the School of Education,* Indiana University, 36 (1960), pp. 13-14.

[37] Meckel, "Research on Teaching Composition and Literature," in *Handbook of Research on Teaching,* ed. N.L. Gage (Chicago: Rand McNally, 1963), pp. 966-1006.

[38] Bateman and Zidonis, *The Effect of a Study of Transformational Grammar on the Writing of Ninth and Tenth Graders* (Urbana, Ill.: NCTE, 1966); Mellon, *Transformational Sentence Combining: A Method for Enhancing the Development of Fluency in English Composition* (Urbana, Ill.: NCTE, 1969); O'Hare, *Sentence-Combining: Improving Student Writing without Formal Grammar Instruction* (Urbana, Ill.: NCTE, 1971); Stotsky, "Sentence-Combining as a Curricular Activity: Its Effect on Written Language Development," *RTE,* 9 (1975), 30-72; and Van de Veghe, "Research in Written Composition: Fifteen Years of Investigation," ERIC 157 095.

[39] Haynes, "Using Research in Preparing to Teach Writing," *English Journal,* 69, No. 1 (1978), 82-88; Holbrook, "ERIC/RCS Report: Whither (Wither) Grammar," *Language Arts,* 60 (1983), 259-263; Whiteman, "What We Can Learn from Writing Research," *Theory into Practice,* 19 (1980), 150-156; Bamberg, "Composition in the Secondary English Curriculum: Some Current Trends and Directions for the Eighties," *RTE,* 15 (1981), 257-266; and "Composition Instruction Does Make a Difference: A Comparison of the High School Preparation of College Freshmen in Regular and Remedial English Classes," *RTE,* 12 (1978), 47-59.

[40] Emig, "Inquiry Paradigms and Writing," *CCC,* 33 (1982), 64-75; Carton and Castiglione, "Educational Linguistics: Defining the Domain," in *Psycholinguistic Research: Implications and Applications,* ed. Doris Aaronson and Robert W. Rieber (Hillsdale, N.J.: Lawrence Erlbaum, 1979), pp. 497-520.

The Syntax of Error

VALERIE KRISHNA

Perhaps the most vexing problem that teachers of basic writing face is the fact that the most serious errors that appear in student papers are those that we are the least equipped to handle, those that are in fact next to impossible to deal with by traditional methods. Unfortunately, the mistakes that students make are not always those clear-cut and predictable errors that are the most precisely described and categorized in the grammar books—errors of punctuation, spelling, agreement, tense, case, and so on. Important as these details are, they dwindle in significance next to problems of incoherence, illogicality, lack of conventional idiom or clear syntax—amorphous and unpredictable errors involving the structure of the whole sentence that are difficult to pinpoint, define, and analyze. The fact is that the most serious and most intractable mistakes are those that do not fit into neat categories and defy analysis. Here are a few examples.

1. In regard to the Watergate affair and the recent problems that the White House is involved with, it is of concern to all citizens.
2. The use of the pilgrimage was created to make the scene more realistic.
3. His concern for outward appearances is mainly to use it to convey the inner character.
4. Man has invented various types of poisons to kill insects; among the surviving insects, they have all become immune to these poisons.
5. By limiting the open enrollment program won't help to solve the problem.

A teacher who discovers a sentence of this type in the student's paper is hard put to know how to begin to deal with it. It is clear that the student has committed some sort of error. It is also clear that the error is a more serious, more fundamental mistake than the "classical" errors of verb agreement, punctuation, pronoun case, and so on that are systematically set out in the grammar books. A conscientious teacher will recognize the gravity of the problem and will wish to deal with it before moving on to work on conventional errors of detail. However, it is not exactly clear just what the error is that has been committed. The sentence might be labeled "illogical" or "incoherent"; the writer might be said to have "shifted syntax" in mid-sentence. Grammar books caution against illogicality and incoherence, and some of

Journal of Basic Writing, I (Spring 1975), pp. 43-49. Copyright © 1975 by The English Department, City College of New York. Reprinted by permission of the editor.

them even give a name to this type of syntax shift—the "mixed construction"—but most offer little help in correcting any of these problems. They offer little help because gross structural errors of this type are not amenable to correction by the method that is used for errors of detail.

We eradicate errors of detail by concentrating on them. Grammar books isolate, define, categorize, and in general supply us with a great deal of information about them. We know, for example, exactly where an error involving verb agreement is likely to occur (in sentences in which the subject and the verb are separated by a prepositional phrase, the verb comes before the subject, or the subject is a collective noun, and so on). Thus an error such as this is comprehensible, predictable, and amenable to correction. We can anticipate such errors and try to head them off, either by having students do exercises that duplicate the kinds of sentences that we know are likely to give rise to such errors or by training students to be especially alert for verb agreement errors in these kinds of sentences when they proofread.

We have no such guidelines for errors such as the mixed construction and other errors involving problems of structure, coherence, and logic. For one thing, labels like "illogical" and "incoherent" and terms like "mixed construction" are vague: they do not isolate and define an error clearly. For another, there are so many different ways in which a writer can shift syntax in the middle of a sentence or "mix his constructions" that such errors simply cannot be categorized and predicated in precisely the way that errors of verb agreement can. Similarly, no one can possibly anticipate all of the different ways in which a piece of writing might be illogical or incoherent. Errors of verb agrrement can almost be thought of as one error—or several very well understood variations on one error—that is committed over and over again. Every mixed construction, every incoherence, every illogicality seems to be a unique and original creation. Therefore, because grammar books cannot deal with them in the same way they deal with errors of detail, they lack information on structural errors. Hence, the teacher despairs as he feels that such errors are random, unpredictable, and impossible to handle at the same time that he recognizes that they are the most serious problems that can appear in a student's papers.

The impossibility of classifying structural errors per se and of dealing with them in the traditional way forces us into another approach. Rather than concentrating on the errors themselves as finished products and attempting to define them as such, I believe that we can understand and deal with them best by understanding the type of approach to the sentence that stands behind such errors. That is, though I do not believe that structural errors in themselves can be categorized, I do believe that the sentences in which they appear can. Many of these structural errors are not the random aberrations that they seem to be, but instead are the direct outgrowth of what I call a *weak structural core* that is disjoined from the idea that a writer is trying to express. Students who are making structural errors, though they are committing mistakes that are unique and unclassifiable in themselves, are often following a stereotyped formula in constructing sentences in which these mistakes appear. Such writers habitually "back into" their sentences, putting the heart of their idea into prepositional phrases, object noun clauses, adjectives, adverbs, or other ancillary parts of the sentence, wasting the subject and/or the verb position on indefinite, evasive expressions such as *it is, it appears, this seems to be the case*, or on other general, abstract, imprecise words (or omitting the subject or verb entirely), and finally joining the ancillary part of the sentence to the main clause awkwardly and illogically. This habitual wasting of the subject-verb position, along with the frantic struggle to fit a central thought into a peripheral expression and then to fit the expression to the main clause is the source of many, perhaps most, of the structural errors that appear in student papers, and, I believe, contributes to idiomatic, stylistic, and grammatical errors as well. The structural errors that are the most difficult to fit into a neat category and thus the most difficult to deal with are especially likely to occur in sentences that have this feeble structure: an anemic main clause too weak or indefinite to hold up modifiers and a clumsily attached, overburdened prepositional phrase into which the writer has attempted to cram the central idea of his sentence. The way to correct such mistakes, as well as to avoid them, is to strengthen the main clause, to move the central idea into the subject and/or the verb.

This common thread runs through the examples cited above, which seem at first glance idiosyncratic and baffling. Let us look again at the first sentence.

> In regard to the Watergate affair and the recent problems that the White House is involved with, it is of concern to all citizens.

In this sentence, whatever the student wants to put forward as his central idea (and the teacher, of course, cannot be sure what it is) is very far from the core of the sentence—the subject and the verb—which is occupied by the vague expression *it is*. A teacher can help a student to rewrite this sentence by instructing him to move his central idea into the core of the sentence. Generally, if one asks the writer of such a sentence what the subject of the sentence is, he will answer "Watergate affair," "recent problems" (or both), or "White House"; that is, he will name the *logical* subject of the sentence. The teacher can then point out that the logical subject is not in the position of grammatical subject, which is occupied by the uninformative word *it*. The teacher can then explain to the student that the logical subject and the grammatical subject ought to coincide and instruct the student to recompose the sentence, using the logical subject as the grammatical subject. I have found that, when students recompose sentences in this way, structural errors frequently disappear. For example, if the student decides that both "Watergate affair" and "recent problems" are his subject and moves them out of the prepositional phrase and into the position of subject, there is no longer any place for the indefinite *it* (which happens also to be a pronoun without a clear reference), which is messing up the structure of the sentence, and the student will have little difficulty in restructuring the whole sentence since the source of the problem has been removed (though he may run into a verb agreement problem because of the compound subject):

> The Watergate affair and the recent problems that the White House is involved with are [or is, as the case may be!] of concern to all citizens.

If the student is instructed to do the same thing with the verb that he has done with the subject, the sentence improves stylistically:

> The Watergate affair and the recent problems that the White House is involved with concern all citizens.

Similarly, the second sentence cited above is easy for a student to finish, once the student has moved whatever he considers his logical subject into the position of grammatical subject, occupied in the original sentence by the vague word *use*:

> The *pilgrimage* was created to make the scene more realistic.
>
>   or
>
> The *writer* (or *Chaucer*) created the pilgrimage to make the scene more realistic.

The third sentence may be rewritten in several ways, depending again on what the student decides is his logical subject. The important point is that when a word that expresses his idea more precisely is moved into the position of subject, the rest of the sentence follows easily:

> Outward appearances are used to convey inner character.
>
>   or
>
> The author (or a proper name) uses outward appearances to convey inner character.

The fourth and fifth sentences seem at first glance to exemplify errors that are very different: one of faulty pronoun reference and the other a missing verb. However, in both cases, what appears to be the logical subject has been buried in a prepositional phrase and needs to be elevated to the position of grammatical subject:

> Man has invented various types of poisons to kill insects; the surviving insects have all become immune to these poisons.

> Limiting the open enrollment program won't help to solve the problem. problem.

Idiomatic errors, also difficult for teachers to deal with, may also be eliminated when the main clause is strengthened. Many idiomatic errors involve prepositions, and these often appear in sentences in which the writer has similarly put his central thought into a prepositional phrase, rather than into the subject and verb, and then joined this phrase with the wrong preposition to the main clause. The following sentence is an example:

> Everybody in the world tries to make money, but everybody thinks differently in using it.

When I questioned the student who wrote this sentence, she said that she had felt uneasy about the prepositional phrase but didn't know how to go about "fixing it." I asked her what action she wanted to talk about in the second part of the sentence, whether she really wished to say something about *thinking*. She replied that she had actually wanted to say something about *using*, and then went on immediately to *but everybody uses it differently*, automatically eliminating the unidiomatic preposition.

Some conventional grammatical errors, such as dangling participles, can also be corrected by this method, as in the following example:

By paying directly, it is assured that we get better service.

Once a student substitutes a noun that expresses his thought more precisely than the indefinite *it*, the core of the sentence is strengthened, and the dangling participle disappears:

Paying directly assures us better service.

By paying directly we are assured better service.

We cannot help but wonder why students write in this way. Three possibilities suggest themselves to me.

1. It may simply be that students have a habit of attacking sentences in this roundabout way because they have the mistaken notion that simplicity and directness are the mark of the simple-minded and are trying to "dress up" their writing. These introductory circumlocutions may appear impressive to them, and they may be using them to make their writing look profound. If so, this habit may be nothing more than a variation of the pompous, inflated writing affected by writers of all types (with the difference, of course, that basic writing students have a hard time pulling it off without making structural and grammatical errors).

2. Perhaps students write in this way to disguise the fact, from the reader and from themselves, that they are not thinking clearly or that they actually have nothing to say. It could be that, when ideas fail them, they take refuge in this construction simply as a means of filling up the page, hoping that the reader will not notice the difference. (There is a kind of wild logic in this process, because if one has nothing to say, it makes sense for the subject and the verb to be as nearly empty of meaning as possible.) . . .

3. A third possibility is that students write in this way because they find writing painful and words treacherous and are trying to tread as lightly as possible in the world of the written word in order not to make fools of themselves. If this is so, then attacking errors indirectly through sentence structure in the way described here, rather than directly through teaching students everything we know about errors and daily painting a bleaker and bleaker picture of all the possible ways their writing might go wrong, might be even more important than I have so far suggested. Teaching students what *to do*, if it could be worked out as completely and systematically as has our traditional method of teaching them what *not* to do, how to construct a sentence rather than how not to, may be the only kind of craftsmanship that we can present without inhibiting our students so much that we drive them into the very errors that we are trying to teach them to avoid.

A Generative Rhetoric of the Sentence

FRANCIS CHRISTENSEN

If the new grammar is to be brought to bear on composition, it must be brought to bear on the rhetoric of the sentence. We have a workable and teachable, if not a definitive, modern grammar; but we do not have, despite several titles, a modern rhetoric.

In composition courses we do not really teach our captive charges to write better—we merely *expect* them to. And we do not teach them how to write better because we do not know how to teach them to write better. And so we merely go through the motions. Our courses with their tear-out work books and four-pound anthologies are elaborate evasions of the real problem. They permit us to put in our time and do almost anything else we'd rather be doing instead of buckling down to the hard work of making a difference in the student's understanding and manipulation of language.

With hundreds of handbooks and rhetorics to draw from, I have never been able to work out a program for teaching the sentence as I find it in the work of contemporary writers. The chapters on the sentence all adduce the traditional rhetorical classification of sentences as loose, balanced, and periodic. But the term *loose* seems to be taken as a pejorative (it sounds immoral); our students, no Bacons or Johnsons, have little occasion for balanced sentences; and some of our worst perversions of style come from the attempt to teach them to write periodic sentences. The traditional grammatical classification of sentences is equally barren. Its use in teaching composition rests on a semantic confusion, equating complexity of structure with complexity of thought and vica versa. But very simple thoughts may call for very complex grammatical constructions. Any moron can say "I don't know who done it." And some of us might be puzzled to work out the grammar of "All I want is all there is," although any chit can think it and say it and act on it.

The chapters on the sentence all appear to assume that we think naturally in primer sentences, progress naturally to compound sentences, and must be taught to combine the primer sentences into complex sentences—and that complex sentences are the mark of maturity. We need a rhetoric of the sentence that will do more than combine the ideas of primer sentences. We need one that will *generate* ideas.

For the foundation of such a generative or productive rhetoric I take the statement from John Erskine, the originator of the Great Books courses,

College Composition and Communication, 14 (October 1963), pp. 155-161. Copyright © 1963 by the National Council of Teachers of English. Reprinted with permission.

himself a novelist. In an essay "The Craft of Writing" (*Twentieth Century Writing*, Philosophical Library, 1946) he discusses a principle of the writer's craft which, though known he says to all practitioners, he has never seen discussed in print. The principle is this: "When you write, you make a point, not by subtracting as though you sharpened a pencil, but by adding." We have all been told that the formula for good writing is the concrete noun and the active verb. Yet Erskine says, "What you say is found not in the noun but in what you add to qualify the noun. . . . The noun, the verb, and the main clause serve merely as the base on which meaning will rise. . . . The modifier is the essential part of any sentence." The foundation, then, for a generative or productive rhetoric of the sentence is that composition is essentially a process of *addition*.

But speech is linear, moving in time, and writing moves in linear space, which is analogous to time. When you add a modifier, whether to the noun, the verb, or the main clause, you must add it either before the head or after it. If you add it before the head, the direction of modification can be indicated by an arrow pointing forward; if you add it after, by an arrow pointing backward. Thus we have the second principle of a generative rhetoric—the principle of *direction of modification* or *direction of movement*.

Within the clause there is not much scope of operating with this principle. The positions of the various sorts of close, or restrictive, modifiers are generally fixed and the modifiers are often obligatory—"The man who came to dinner remained till midnight." Often the only choice is whether to add modifiers. What I have seen of attempts to bring structural grammar to bear on composition usually boils down to the injunction to "load the patterns." Thus "pattern practice" sets students to accreting sentences like this: "The small boy on the red bicycle who lives with his happy parents on our shady street often coasts down the steep street until he comes to the city park." This will never do. It has no rhythm and hence no life; it is tone-deaf. It is the seed that will burgeon into gobbledegook. One of the hardest things in writing is to keep the noun clusters and verb clusters short.

It is with modifiers added to the clause—that is, with sentence modifiers —that the principle comes into full play. The typical sentence of modern English, the kind we can best spend our efforts trying to teach, is what we may call the *cumulative sentence*. The main clause, which may or may not have a sentence modifier before it, advances the discussion; but the additions move backward, as in this clause, to modify the statement of the main clause or more often to explicate or exemplify it, so that the sentence has a flowing and ebbing movement, advancing to a new position and then pausing to consolidate it, leaping and lingering as the popular ballad does. The first part of the preceding compound sentence has one addition, placed within it; the second part has 4 words in the main clause and 49 in the five additions placed after it.

The cumulative sentence is the opposite of the periodic sentence. It does not represent the idea as conceived, pondered over, reshaped, packaged, and delivered cold. It is dynamic rather than static, representing the mind thinking. The main clause ("the additions move backward" above) exhausts the mere fact of the idea; logically, there is nothing more to say. The additions stay with the same idea, probing its bearings and implications, exemplifying it or seeking an analogy or metaphor for it, or reducing it to details. Thus the mere form of the sentence generates ideas. It serves the needs of both the writer and the reader, the writer by compelling him to examine his thought, the reader by letting him into the writer's thought.

Addition and direction of movement are structural principles. They involve the grammatical character of the sentence. Before going on to other principles, I must say a word about the best grammar as the foundation for rhetoric. I cannot conceive any useful transactions between teacher and students unless they have in common a language for talking about sentences. The best grammar for the present purpose is the grammar that best displays the layers of structure of the English sentence. The best I have found in a textbook is the combination of immediate constituent and transformation grammar in Paul Roberts' *English Sentences*. Traditional grammar, whether over-simple as in the school tradition or over-complex as in the scholarly tradition, does not reveal the language as it operates; it leaves everything, to borrow a phrase from Wordsworth, "in disconnection dead and spiritless." *English Sentences* is oversimplified and it has gaps, but it displays admirably the structures that rhetoric must work with—primarily sentence modifiers, including nonrestrictive relative and subordinate clauses, but, far more important, the array of noun, verb, and adjective clusters. It is paradoxical that Professor Roberts, who has done so much to make the teaching of composition possible, should himself be one of those who think that it cannot be taught. Unlike Ulysses, he does not see any work for Telemachus to work.

Layers of structure, as I have said, is a grammatical concept. To bring in the dimension of meaning, we need a third principle—that of *levels of generality* or *levels of abstraction*. The main or base clause is likely to be stated in general or abstract or plural terms. With the main clause stated, the forward movement of the sentence stops, the writer shifts down to a lower level of generality or abstraction or to singular terms, and goes back over the same ground at this lower level.[1] There is no theoretical limit to the number of structural layers or levels, each[2] at a lower level of generality, any or all of them compounded, that a speaker or writer may use. For a speaker, listen to Lowell Thomas; for a writer, study William Faulkner. To a single independent clause he may append a page of additions, but usually all clear, all grammatical, once we have learned how to read him. Or, if you prefer, study Hemingway, the master of the simple sentence: "George was coming down in the telemark position, kneeling, one leg forward and bent, the other trailing, his sticks hanging like some insect's thin legs, kicking up puffs of snow, and finally the whole kneeling, trailing figure coming around in a beautiful right curve, crouching, the legs shot forward and back, the body leaning out against the swing, the sticks accenting the curve like points of light, all in a wild cloud of snow." Only from the standpoint of school grammar is this a simple sentence.

This brings me to the fourth, and last, principle, that of texture. *Texture* provides a descriptive or evaluative term. If a writer adds to few of his nouns or verbs or main clauses and adds little, the texture may be said to be thin. The style will be plain or bare. The writing of most of our students is thin—even threadbare. But if he adds frequently or much or both, then the texture may be said to be dense or rich. One of the marks of an effective style, especially in narrative, is variety in the texture producing the change in pace. It is not true, as I have seen it asserted, that fast action calls for short sentences; the action is fast in the sentence by Hemingway above. In our classes, we have to work for greater density and variety in texture and greater concreteness and particularity in what is added.

I have been operating at a fairly high level of generality. Now I must downshift and go over the same points with examples. The most graphic way to exhibit the layers of structure is to indent the word groups of a sentence and to number the levels. The first three sentences illustrate the various positions of the added sentence modifiers—initial, medial, and final. The symbols mark the grammatical character of the additions: SC, subordinate clause; RC, relative clause; NC, noun cluster; VC, verb cluster; AC, adjective cluster; A + A, adjective series; Abs, absolute (i.e., a VC with a subject of its own); PP, prepositional phrase. The elements set off as on a lower level are marked as sentence modifiers by junctures or punctuation. The examples have been chosen to illustrate the range of constructions used in the lower levels; after the first few they are arranged by the number of levels. The examples could have been drawn from poetry as well as from prose. Those not attributed are by students.

1

1 He dipped his hands in the bichloride solution and shook them,
   2 a quick shake, (NC)
      3 fingers down, (Abs)
         4 like the fingers of a pianist above the keys. (PP)

Sinclair Lewis

2

   2 Calico-coated, (AC)
   2 small-bodied, (AC)
      3 with delicate legs and pink faces in which their mismatched eyes rolled wild and subdued, (PP)
1 they huddled,
   2 gaudy motionless and alert, (A + A)
   2 wild as deer, (AC)
   2 deadly as rattlesnakes, (AC)
   2 quiet as doves. (AC)

William Faulkner

3

1 The bird's eye, / , remained fixed upon him;
   2 / bright and silly as a sequin (AC)

1 its little bones, / , seemed swooning in his hand,
  2 wrapped . . . in a warm padding of feathers. (VC)
Stella Benson

4

1 The jockeys sat bowed and relaxed,
  2 moving a little at the waist with the movement of their horses. (VC)
Katherine Anne Porter

5

1 The flame sidled up the match,
  2 driving a film of moisture and a thin strip of darker grey before it.
    (VC)

6

1 She came among them behind the man,
  2 gaunt in the gray shapeless garment and the sunbonnet, (AC)
  2 wearing stained canvas gymnasium shoes. (VC)
Faulkner

7

1 The Texan turned to the nearest gatepost and climbed to the top of it,
  2 his alternate thighs thick and bulging in the tight-trousers, (Abs)
  2 the butt of the pistol catching and losing the sun in pearly gleams.
    (Abs)
Faulkner

8

1 He could sail for hours,
  2 searching the blanched grasses below him with his telescopic eyes,
    (VC)
  2 gaining height against the wind, (VC)
  2 descending in mile-long, gently declining swoops when he curved
    and rode back, (VC)
  2 never beating a wing. (VC)
Walter Van Tilburg Clark

9

1 They regarded me silently,
  2 Brother Jack with a smile that went no deeper than his lips, (Abs)
    3 his head cocked to one side, (Abs)
    3 studying me with his penetrating eyes; (VC)
  2 the other blank-faced, (Abs)
    3 looking out of eyes that were meant to reveal nothing and to stir
    profound uncertainty. (VC)
Ralph Ellison

10

1 He stood at the top of the stairs and watched me,
  2 I waiting for him to call me up, (Abs)

  2 he hesitating to come down, (Abs)
    3 his lips nervous with the suggestion of a smile, (Abs)
    3 mine asking whether the smile meant come, or go away. (Abs)

11

1 Joad's lips stretched tight over his long teeth for a moment, and
1 he licked his lips,
  2 like a dog, (PP)
    3 two licks, (NC)
      4 one in each direction from the middle. (NC)

Steinbeck

12

1 We all live in two realities:
  2 one of seeming fixity, (NC)
    3 with institutions, dogmas, rules of punctuation, and routines,
       (PP)
      4 the calendared and clockwise world of all but futile round on
         round; (NC) and
  2 one of whirling and flying electrons, dreams, and possibilities, (NC)
    3 behind the clock. (PP)

Sidney Cox

13

1 It was as though someone, somewhere, had touched a lever and shifted
   gears, and
1 the hospital was set for night running,
  2 smooth and silent, (A + A)
  2 its normal chatter and hum muffled, (Abs)
  2 the only sounds heard in the whitewalled room distant and unreal:
     (Abs)
    3 a low hum of voices from the nurses' desk, (NC)
      4 quickly stifled, (VC)
    3 the soft squish of rubber-soled shoes on the tiled corridor,
       (NC)
    3 starched white cloth rustling against itself, (Abs) and, outside,
    3 the lonesome whine of wind in the country night (NC) and
    3 the Kansas dust beating against the windows. (NC)

14

1 The beach sounds are jazzy,
  2 percussion fixing the mode—(Abs)
    3 the surf cracking and booming in the distance, (Abs)
    3 a little nearer dropped bar-bells clanking, (Abs)
    3 steel gym rings, / , ringing, (Abs)
    /4 flung together, (VC)
    3 palm fronds rustling above me, (Abs)
      4 like steel brushes washing over a snare drum, (PP)
    3 troupes of sandals splatting and shuffling on the sandy cement,
       (Abs)

4   their beat varying, (Abs)
   5   syncopation emerging and disappearing with changing
      paces. (Abs)

15

1   A small Negro girl develops from the sheet of glare-frosted walk,
   2   walking barefooted, (VC)
      3   her bare legs stiking and coiling from the hot cement, (Abs)
         4   her feet curling in, (Abs)
            5   only the outer edges touching. (Abs)

The best starting point for a composition unit based on these four principles is with two-level narrative sentences, first with one second-level addition (sentences 4, 5), then with two or more parallel ones (6, 7, 8). Anyone sitting in his room with his eyes closed could write the main clause of most of the examples; the discipline comes with the additions, provided they are based at first on immediate observation, requiring the student to phrase an exact observation in exact language. This can hardly fail to be exciting to a class: it is life, with the variety and complexity of life; the workbook exercise is death. The situation is ideal also for teaching diction—abstract-concrete, general-specific, literal-metaphorical, denotative-connotative. When the sentences begin to come out right, it is time to examine the additions for their grammatical character. From then on the grammar comes to the aid of the writing and the writing reinforces the grammar. One can soon go on to multi-level narrative sentences (1, 9-11, 15) and then to brief narratives of three to six or seven sentences on actions with a beginning, a middle, and an end that can be observed over and over again—beating eggs, making a cut with a power saw, or following a record changer's cycle or a wave's flow and ebb. (Bring the record changer to class.) Description, by contrast, is static, picturing appearance rather than behavior. The constructions to master are the noun and adjective clusters and the absolute (13,14). Then the descriptive noun cluster must be taught to ride piggy-back on the narrative sentence, so that description and narration are interleaved: "In the morning we went out into a new world, a glistening crystal and white world, each skeleton tree, each leafless bush, even the heavy, drooping power lines sheathed in icy crystal." The next step is to develop the sense for variety in texture and change in pace that all good narrative demands.

. . . The same four principles can be applied to the expository paragraph. But this is a subject for another paper.

I want to anticipate two possible objections. One is that the sentences are long. By freshman English standards they are long, but I could have produced far longer ones from works freshmen are expected to read. Of the sentences by students, most were written as finger exercises in the first few weeks of the course. I try in narrative sentences to push to level after level, not just two or three, but four, five, or six, even more, as far as the students' powers of observation will take them. I want them to become sentence acrobats, to dazzle by their syntactic dexterity. I'd rather have to deal with hyperemia than anemia. I want to add my voice to that of James Coleman (*CCC*, December 1962) deploring our concentration on the plain style.

The other objection is that my examples are mainly descriptive and narrative—and today in freshman English we teach only exposition. I deplore the limitation as much as I deplore our limitation to the plain style. Both are a sign that we have sold our proper heritage for a pot of message. In permitting them, the English department undercuts its own discipline. Even if our goal is only utilitarian prose, we can teach diction and sentence structure far more effectively through a few controlled exercises in description and narration than we can by starting right off with exposition (Theme One, 500 words, precipitates *all* the problems of writing). There is no problem of invention; the student has something to communicate—his immediate sense of impressions, which can stand a bit of exercising. The material is not already verbalized—he has to match language to sense impressions. His acuteness in observation and in choice of words can be judged by fairly objective standards—is the sound of a bottle of milk being set down on a concrete step suggested better by *clink* or *clank* or *clunk*? In the examples, study the diction for its accuracy, rising at times to the truly imaginative. Study the use of metaphor, of comparison. This verbal virtuosity and syntactical ingenuity can be made to carry over into expository writing.

But it is still utilitarian. What I am proposing carries over of itself into the study of literature. It makes the student a better reader of literature. It helps him thread the syntactical mazes of much mature writing, and it gives him insight into that elusive thing we call style. Last year a student told of rereading a book by her favorite author, Willa Cather, and of realizing for the first time *why* she liked reading her: she could understand and appreciate the style. For some students, moreover, such writing makes life more interesting as well as giving them a way to share their interest with others. When they learn how to put concrete details into a sentence, they begin to look at life with more alertness. If it is liberal education we are concerned with, it is just possible that these things are more important than anything we can achieve when we set our sights on the plain style in expository prose.

I want to conclude with a historical note. My thesis in this paragraph is that modern prose like modern poetry has more in common with the seventeenth than with the eighteenth century and that we fail largely because we are operating from an eighteenth century base. The shift from the complex to the cumulative sentence is more profound than it seems. It goes deep in grammar, requiring a shift from the subordinate clause (the staple of our trade) to the cluster and the absolute (so little understood as to go almost unnoticed in our textbooks). And I have only lately come to see that this shift has historical implications. The cumulative sentence is the modern form of the loose sentence that characterized the anti-Ciceronian movement in the seventeenth century. This movement, according to Morris W. Croll,[3] began with Montaigne and Bacon and continued with such men as Donne, Browne, Taylor, Pascal. To Montaigne, its art was the art of being natural; to Pascal, its eloquence was the eloquence that mocks formal eloquence;

to Bacon, it presented knowledge so that it could be examined, not so that it must be accepted.

But the Senecan amble was banished from England when "the direct sensuous apprehension of thought" (T. S. Eliot's words) gave way to Cartesian reason or intellect. The consequences of this shift in sensibility are well summarized by Croll:

> To this mode of thought we are to trace almost all the features of modern literary education and criticism, or at least of what we should have called modern a generation ago: the study of the precise meaning of words; the reference to dictionaries as literary authorities; the study of the sentence as a logical unit alone; the careful circumscription of its limits and the gradual reduction of its length; . . . [4] the attempt to reduce grammar to an exact science; the idea that forms of speech are always either correct or incorrect; the complete subjection of the laws of motion and expression in style to the laws of logic and standardization—in short, the triumph, during two centuries, of grammatical over rhetorical ideas.

Here is a seven-point scale any teacher of composition can use to take stock. He can find whether he is based in the eighteenth century or in the twentieth and whether he is consistent—completely either an ancient or a modern—or is just a crazy mixed-up kid.

Notes

[1] Cf. Leo Rockas "Abstract and Concrete Sentences," *CCC*, May 1963. Rockas describes sentences as abstract or concrete, the abstract implying the concrete and vice versa. Readers and writers, he says, must have the knack of apprehending the concrete in the abstract and the abstract in the concrete. This is true and valuable. I am saying that within a single sentence the writer may present more than one level of generality, translating the abstract into the more concrete in added levels.

[2] This statement is not quite tenable. Each helps to make the idea of the base clause more concrete or specific, but each is not more concrete or specific than the one immediately above it.

[3] "The Baroque Style in Prose," *Studies in English Philology; A Miscellany in Honor of Frederick Klaeber* (1929), reprinted in *Style, Rhetoric and Rhythm: Essays by Morris W. Croll* (1966) and A. M. Witherspoon and F. J. Warnke, *Seventeenth-Century Prose and Poetry*, 2nd ed. (1963). I have borrowed from Croll in my description of the cumulative sentence.

[4] The omitted item concerns punctuation and is not relevant here. In using this scale, note "what we should have called modern a generation ago" and remember that Croll was writing in 1929.

Grammars of Style:
New Options in Composition

WINSTON WEATHERS

One of our major tasks as teachers of composition is to identify compositional options and teach students the mastery of the options and the liberating use of them. We must identify options in all areas—in vocabulary, usage, sentence forms, dictional levels, paragraph types, ways of organizing materials into whole compositions: options in all that we mean by style. Without options, there can be no rhetoric for there can be no adjustment to the diversity of communication occasions that confront us in our various lives.

To identify options we must not only know about those already established in the language but we must also be alert to emerging ones, and in some cases we must even participate in creating options that do not yet exist but which would be beneficial if they did. We must never suppose that the options in front of us represent the complete and final range of possibilities and that now we can relax: that because we have options enough to avoid rigidity and totalitarianism that we have thus fulfilled our obligations to do all we can to free the human mind and the communication issuing from it.

Most of us do, of course, make options available to our students. Most of us have long shucked off the prescriptions and strictures of an earlier day that gave us "no choice" in how to write but insisted only upon the "one good way." Most of us who teach writing attempt to provide our students with a repertoire of writing styles—from the plain to the elegant, from the tough to the sweet, from the colloquial to the formal, from the simple to the complex—in order that our students may make more refined stylistic decisions in consideration of subject matter, audience, occasion, and so forth. Many of us have argued for many years now that our task is to reveal to our students a full range of styles and to provide our students with a rationale for making appropriate selections from that range.

Yet even in our acceptance and inculcation of pluralism and diversity, we stay—if we stop and think about it—within the safe confines of a general "grammar of style," a grammar within which our options are related one to another, all basically kin, none of which takes us outside a certain approved and established area.

By "grammar of style" I mean the "set of conventions governing the

The essay here is an abridged version of the one under the same title appearing in *Freshman English News*, 4 (Winter 1976), pp. 1-4, 12-18. Copyright © 1976 by Winston Weathers. Reprinted by permission of the author and publisher. The full, text-length treatment of Grammar B appears in Winston Weathers, *An Alternate Style: Options in Composition* (Montclair, NJ: Boynton/Cook Publishers, 1980).

construction of a whole composition; the criteria by which a writer selects the stylistic materials, method of organization and development, compositional pattern and structure he is to use in preparing any particular composition." This "grammar" defines and establishes the boundaries in which a composition must take place and defines the communication goals to which a composition is committed.

Any number of such "grammars" may theoretically exist and be available to a writer at any one time. Yet on a practical level, in today's classroom we keep all our stylistic options within the confines of one grammar only—a grammar that has no particular name (we can call it the "traditional" grammar of style/ or maybe even call it Grammar A) but has the characteristics of continuity, order, reasonable progression and sequence, consistency, unity, etc. We are all familiar with these characteristics for they are promoted in nearly every freshman English textbook and taught by nearly every English teacher.

Our assumption—regardless of liberality so far as diversity of styles is concerned—is that every composition must be well-organized and unified, must demonstrate logic, must contain well-developed paragraphs; that its structure will manifest a beginning, middle, and end; that the composition will reveal identifiable types of order; that so far as the composition deals with time it will reveal a general diachronicity; etc. Our teaching and texts will be concerned, almost without exception, with "subject and thesis," "classification and order," "beginning and ending," "expansion," "continuity," "emphasis," and the like. All remains, in other words, within a particular grammar of style that leads to compositions that "make sense": it is a grammar that cannot tolerate a mixed metaphor because a mixed metaphor is not "reasonable," and cannot tolerate a mixture of the impersonal third-person "one" and the impersonal "you" because that would be "inconsistent" and contrary to "unity."

We allow options "within reason." We allow options, but only those that fit within a particular box. In our charity, we allow our students to write in one style or another—

> Arriving in London in the spring of 1960, when crocuses were first blooming in Regency Park, I went directly to the Mount Royal Hotel (the hostelry that many an American tourist knows very well, located as it is on Oxford Street, near the Marble Arch and Hyde Park and conveniently located near everything the American tourist wants to see) where I registered for a room and indicated my intention to stay for seven or eight weeks at least.

> I arrived in London in the spring of 1960. Crocuses were blooming in Regency Park. I went directly to the Mount Royal Hotel. It's located on Oxford Street, near Marble Arch and Hyde Park, and it's convenient to a lot of things the American tourist wants to see. I checked in at the hotel and told the clerk I was going to stay in London seven or eight weeks at least.

but both must do just about the same thing. You can try to write like Henry James or you can try to write like Ernest Hemingway, but you must not forget that both James and Hemingway, quite different in their literary styles, wrote within the same "grammar of style"; neither of them went beyond the parameters that Grammar A provides.

It is as though we told a card-player that his deck of fifty-two cards (equal let's say to the "things we can do with language, our stylistic materials") is good only for playing the game of bridge. As good teachers, we explain the rules of bridge and at the same time point out to the student/player his options within bridge: he can play the Culbertson system or the Goren system or the Jacoby system. And indeed he can play his bridge hands even contrary to best advice if he himself so decides, though tradition and good sense usually suggest that he draw trumps early in the hand and play second hand low. We teach him to play bridge, to practice a certain freedom within it (he can conceivably play "high style" or "low style" or "middle style") but there is no way under the sun that he can, in playing bridge, meld a pinochle or "shoot the moon."

Not that anyone really argues that while playing bridge one should not play bridge. But our fault is that we teach students to play bridge only and to have access only to the options that bridge provides. We teach only one "grammar" and we only provide square/rectangular boxes. We don't teach students other games with other options. And in our teaching, when someone does "meld a pinochle" at the bridge table, all we know to do is to mark it in red ink and say "wrong," without ever suggesting to the student that if he wants to meld pinochle he might like to know about *another game* where it would be very "right."

We identify our favored "grammar of style," our favored game and box, as the "good" grammar of style, and we identify what it produces as "good writing." And anything that looms upon the horizon as a distinctly different possibility we generally attack as "bad writing," or identify as "creative writing which we don't teach in this class" or ignore altogether, claiming it is a possibility that only rare persons (like James Joyce or Gertrude Stein) could do anything with and that ordinary mortals should scrupulously avoid.

Yet there it is. The beast sniffing outside the door. And ultimately we must deal with it.

It is, of course, *another* grammar of style, another set of conventions and criteria, another way of writing that offers yet more options and offers us yet further possibilities for rhetorical adaptations and adjustments. It is not just another "style"—way out on the periphery of our concerns—but is an altogether different "grammar" of style, an alternate grammar, Grammar B, with characteristics of variegation, synchronicity, discontinuity, ambiguity, and the like. It is an alternate grammar, no longer an experiment, but a mature grammar used by competent writers and offering students of writing a well tested "set of options" that, added to the traditional grammar of style, will give give them a much more flexible voice, a much greater communication capacity, a much greater opportunity to put into effective language all the things they have to say.

And be assured: Grammar B in no way threatens Grammar A. It uses the same stylistic "deck of fifty-two cards" and embraces the same English language with which we are familiar. Acknowledging its existence and discovering how it works and including it in our writing expertise, we simply become better teachers of writing, making a better contribution to the intellectual and emotional lives of our students.

The writer who wishes to practice the alternate grammar—for whatever reasons—will want to master a number of stylistic maneuvers and conventions from which he may select, just as he does in the traditional grammar, the particular devices/schemes/techniques that seem useful in a particular communication/rhetorical situation and that he can combine into the "style" appropriate, as he so judges, to the composition he is writing. The following presentation of such maneuvers/conventions/devices is not complete, of course, but is representative of the sort of writing practices found in the alternate grammar and does provide a writer with a basic and beginning set of "things to do":

The *Crot*. A crot (crots, plural) is an obsolete word meaning "bit" or "fragment." The term was given new life by Tom Wolfe in his "Introduction" to a collection of *Esquire* magazine fiction, *The Secret Life of Our Times*, edited by Gordon Lish (New York: Doubleday, 1973). A basic element in the alternate grammar of style, and comparable somewhat to the "stanza" in poetry, the crot may range in length from one sentence to twenty or thirty sentences. It is fundamentally an autonomous unit, characterized by the absence of any transitional devices that might relate it to the preceding or subsequent crots and because of this independent and discrete nature of crots, they create a general effect of metastasis—using that term from classical rhetoric to label, as Fritz Senn recently suggested in the *James Joyce Quarterly* (Summer, 1975), any "rapid transition from one point of view to another." In its most intense form, the crot is characterized by a certain abruptness in its termination: "As each crot breaks off," Tom Wolfe says, "it tends to make one's mind search for some point that must have just been made—*presque vu!*—almost seen! In the hands of a writer who really understands the device, it will have you making crazy leaps of logic, leaps you never dreamed of before."

The provenance of the crot may well be in the writer's "note" itself—in the research note, in the sentence or two one jots down to record a moment or an idea or to describe a person or place. The crot is essentially the "note" left free of verbal ties with other surrounding notes.

Very brief crots have the quality of an aphorism or proverb, while longer crots may have the quality of descriptive or narrative passages found in the traditional grammar of style. The crots, of whatever kind, may be presented in nearly random sequence or in sequences that finally suggest circularity. Rarely is any stronger sense of order (such as would be characteristic of traditional grammar) imposed upon them—though the absence of traditional order is far more pronounced when the grammar is used in fiction and poetry. The general idea of unrelatedness present in crot writing suggests correspondence—for those who seek it—with the fragmentation and even egalitarianism of contemporary experience, wherein the events, personalities, places of life have no particular superior or inferior status to dictate priorities of presentation.

Nearly always crots are separated one from the other by white space, and at times each crot is given a number or, upon rare occasion, a title. That little spectrum—white space only, white space plus a numbering, white space plus a titling—provides a writer with a way of indicating an increase in separation, discreteness, isolation. Occasionally, but rarely, crots are not separated one from the other typographically but the reader is left to discover the "separation" while he seems to be reading a linear, continuous text; jamming crots against each other becomes a fourth option in presentation, one that provides a greater sense of surprise (or perhaps bewilderment) for the reader.

The effect of writing in crots is intensified, of course, as the number increases. Since each crot is not unlike a "snapshot" or a color slide, the overall composition, using crots, is similar to a "slide" show, especially if the slides have not been arranged into any neat and tidy sequence. "My Trip to New Orleans" written in traditional grammar will have some sort of orderly quality to it: the trip will be presented chronologically, spatially, or what have you. But "My Trip to New Orleans," written in the alternate grammar, will depend, not upon the order in which the "slides" appear, but upon the sharp, exceptional quality of each crot or "slide" and upon the "crazy leaps of logic" that Wolfe mentioned, with the reader jolted from one snapshot to the next, frequently surprised to be given an "aerial view of New Orleans as the plane begins its descent to the airport" and immediately after that "a close-up of an antique candelabrum used in a Louisiana antebellum mansion and now on sale in a New Orleans antique store" followed by "a broad shot of Canal Street" followed by a picture of "Marge and Myrtle getting into the taxicab at the airport to come into the city."

Crots at their best will not be all that banal of course in content, but will have some sharp, arresting, or provocative quality to them. Even if they are unable to stand alone as mini-compositions (sometimes they actually are capable of that) and gain their full effect in association with others, each one should have a certain integrity and interestingness about it. Crots may be written in any dictional style deemed appropriate to the communication occasion, with a single dictional style prevailing, usually, throughout an entire composition. On rare occasions, dictional level may shift from one crot to another, but usually the level of diction is a constant.

Crots are akin, obviously, to a more general kind of "block" writing—the kind of writing found, for instance, in E. M. Forster's *Two Cheers for Democracy* and in Katherine Anne Porter's essay "Audubon's Happy Land." In such block writing, the authors have strung together short, fairly discrete units of composition to make whole compositions. Likewise, a series of crots is not unlike a collection of aphorisms—say those of Eric Hoffer who, in a book like *The Passionate State of Mind and Other Aphorisms*, has brought together brief compositional units, some a sentence long, some several paragraphs long, each quite distinct from the other, yet grouped into a whole composition on the basis of a certain attitude and view of life common to them all. These compositions of "blocks" or "aphorisms" are so much in the spirit of crot writing that they may be considered a part of its development out of a traditional grammar of style into the alternate grammar. The writing of Forster, Porter, and Hoffer—in fiction *and* nonfiction—gives evidence of the usefulness of something other than the ordered, linear procedure of traditional grammar even to writers who would not be identified as especially experimental or stylistically daring.

The *Labyrinthine Sentence* and the *Sentence Fragment.* Though the alternate grammar of style uses the ordinary range of sentence types, it makes use also, and more frequently, of two radical sentence types: the labyrinthine sentence and the sentence fragment. And it tolerates a certain mixture of sentence types that would not be found in the traditional grammar of style. The alternate grammar tolerates great leaps from the long, labyrinthine sentence to the short fragmentary sentence, creating a sharp, startling effect at times. Yet it is not committed entirely to the startling juxtaposing: often enough a composition in the alternate style will be wholly labyrinthine or wholly fragmentary. Or at times, a most ordinary traditional sentence "style" will prevail. Usually, if traditional sentence types are to be mixed with the more radical forms, the mix will involve only traditional types and sentence fragments. Rarely do the traditional sentences and labyrinthine sentences mix successfully.

The labyrinthine sentence is a long complex sentence, with a certain "endless" quality to it, full of convolutions, marked by appositives, parentheses, digressions. A parody through exaggeration of the highly structured Johnsonian sentence of the eighteenth century, the labyrinthine has immediate ancestry in the long, radical sentences of twentieth-century fiction—such as the famous Molly Bloom one-sentence soliloquy that ends Joyce's *Ulysses*. The current master of the labyrinthine sentence is John Barth—but there are numerous other practitioners: one interesting (and perhaps unlikely) example that comes to mind is the opening sentence of *Rousseau and Revolution* by Will and Ariel Durant.

This long, almost picaresque sentence—through which an author rides picaro like—works for many writers as a correspondence to the complexity, confusion, even sheer talkativeness of modern society. When a writer talks about Walt Whitman this way—

> Walt Whitman, born on Paumanok (that is: Long Island), saw in that island's shape (understandably, when you look at the map) the fish that, in the context of Western-Christian iconography, equals Christ equals rebirth equals, especially for Whitman, messianic connotations and (given Whitman's translation of biological events and conditions into transcendental mythological patterns) therefore portend for "I, Walt Whitman" (to be born later, again, with the writing of *Leaves of*

Grass) a divine dimension and a capacity for illuminating the masses who, though they never read him, remained always his projected audience, and revealing, to the enslaved (more than "the slaves," of course; all of us at one time or another) a certain kind of liberation, freedom, escape from the prison.

—he is suggesting, via style, the entangling environment in which the masses and the enslaved live and are living and from which Whitman sought to rescue them.

In contrast with this kind of labyrinthine sentence but often its companion (a la Quixote and Panza), the sentence fragment—frequently a single word or a very short phrase of only two or three words—suggests a far greater awareness of separation and fragmentation: not entanglement but isolation. It is also a highly emphatic kind of sentence and, in conjunction with other sentence types, creates a variegated, more sharply pointed kind of reading line. Gertrude Stein was a great pioneer in the use of the single word/word phrase/sentence fragment unit: as Robert Bartlett Haas says in an introductory note to Stein's essay on "Grant or Rutherford B. Hayes": "During the late 1920's and early 1930's, Gertrude Stein seems to have been dealing with . . . what the sentence was . . . as seen from the standpoint of an American syntax. Another concern was the description of events by protraying movement so intense as to be a thing in itself, not a thing in relation to something else.

" 'Grant or Rutherford B. Hayes' attempts to do this by replacing the noun and the adjective and emphasizing the more active parts of speech. Here a driving pulse is created by syncopating the sentence. The thrust comes from a concentrated use of verb and verb phrases." (Gertrude Stein, *How Writing is Written*, ed. R. B. Haas; Los Angeles: Black Sparrow Press, 1974, p. 12).

Only a few words from Stein's essay are needed to indicate her method: Grant or Rutherford B. Hayes.

Jump. Once for all. With the praising of. Once for all.

As a chance. To win.

Once for all. With a. Chance. To win.

The farther reach of sentence types in the alternate grammar of style provides the writer with a much greater number of options. He can write the crots of the alternate grammar (a) in the traditional sentence types, (b) in the labyrinthine sentence, (c) in sentence fragments, or (d) in combinations of (i.) traditional sentences and sentence fragments or (ii.) labyrinthine sentences and sentence fragments.

The *List*. To create a list, a writer presents a series of items, usually removed from sentence structure or at least very independent of such structure. Usually a list contains a minimum of five items, the items being related in subject matter but presented in list form to avoid indicating any other relationship among the items than that they are *all there at once*, that they are parts of the whole. Presenting a list of items is comparable to presenting a "still life" of objects without indication of foreground or background, without any indication of relative importance, without any suggestion at all of cause-effect, this-before-that, rank, or the like. Obviously the items on the list must be presented one first, one second, one third—but the sequence is generally arbitrary and meaningless.

Adapted from the plethora series found in traditional grammar of style, and antedated by "catalogues" such as appear in Whitman's poetry, the list stands in stark simplicity—a list of objects, observations, or what have you—to give a quick representation of a character, a situation, a place by the simple device of selecting items to represent the subject under discussion. Donald Barthelme, a frequent user of lists, can range—as he does in a short story, "City Life,"—from a list dealing with television viewing ("On 7 there's 'Johnny Allegro' with George Raft and Nina Foch. On 9 'Johnny Angel' with George Raft and Claire Trevor," all the way through a total of eight variations to the final "On 31 is 'Johnny Trouble' with Stuart Whitman and Ethel Barrymore") to a "list" description of a wedding with such items as "Elsa and Jacques bombarded with flowers" to "The minister raises his hand" to such a simple item as "Champagne."

Though lists may be presented in a straight reading line, they are usually presented in columnar form, the items arranged typographically one beneath the other just as one writes a grocery list.

One of the attractions of the list to the contemporary writer is that—disregarding the fact that bias may have entered into the selection of the items in the first place—the list is basically a presentation of items without commentary, seeming to say, "Consider these items without any help from the writer. The writer is keeping his mouth shut. He is simply giving you the data, the evidence, the facts, the object. You, the reader, must add them up and evaluate them." Or there is the suggestion that there are no "values" at all that can be imposed upon the list, that reality stands before us neutral, amoral, and that if we do impose values upon a list it is an arbitrary act upon our part.

Whereas in the traditional grammar of style, one might write—
Whitman grew up as a boy on Long Island, absorbing all the images of sea and sky and shore, all the images of the pastoral world that were always to be a part of his poetry even as he later celebrated the urban glories of Manhattan.

—in the alternate grammar one might well write—
Whitman grew up as a boy on Long Island.
   Sea.
   Gulls.
   Sky.
   Shore.
   Stones.
   Roses.
   Salt air.

Tides.
Farms.
Dusty Roads.
Mockingbirds.
Horses.
Summer Clouds.

Later: Brooklyn. Later: Manhattan. But always: Sea. Stones. Cattle. Birds. Lilacs. Even as the metropolis paved its way toward mercantile grandeur and urban glory.

The difference between the two is not a matter of "quality," but is a matter of differing effects, differing reader involvement, differing authorial voice. One is no more creative than the other; one is no more fictional than the other.

Double-Voice. Even in nonfiction, as in fiction, a writer speaks with a "voice"—if not always the same voice in all his writing, certainly a given voice in a given composition. Indeed, the creation of "voice" is one of the tasks of "style," and the traditional grammar of style has always been used for that purpose among others. In the alternate grammar, however, voice is not always considered a singular characteristic, but often enough a plural characteristic—not a surprising consideration in an age of stereophonics and multi-media dispositions in general.

Writers use double-voice many times when they feel that they could say this *or* that about a subject; when they feel that two attitudes toward a subject are equally valid; when they wish to suggest that there are two sides to the story (whatever the story may be); when they wish to distinguish between their roles as (a) provider of information and data, and (b) commentator upon information and data; or when they wish to effect a style "corresponding" to ambiguous realities.

The double-voice may be presented in straight-line form—

Whitman was born on Long Island in 1819. Are island children marked for a certain sense of individuality, or separation? He was the Whitman's second child. Do "second" children make a greater struggle for identity than the oldest or the youngest? Whitman moved with his parents to Brooklyn when he was four years old. Have children, by the age of four, absorbed most of their primary images, established their essential attitudes and feelings toward life regardless where they move?

Straight-line presentation of double voice is what John Barth uses, for instance, in "Lost in the Funhouse": one example occurs in the opening paragraph of the story:

For Ambrose it is *a place of fear and confusion.* He has come to the seashore with his family for the holiday, *the occasion of their visit is Indepence Day, the most important secular holiday of the United States of America.* A single straight underline is the manuscript mark for italics *which in turn* is the printed equivalent to. . . .

The shift of voice that comes with the words "A single straight underline" provides Barth with a way of writing both as story-teller and as "observer" of the story-teller.

Obviously, one effective way for writers to present double-voice is to present parallel passages in column form, simply running two tracks of composition down the page, side by side. John Cage does this often enough, notably in his essay "Erik Satie," in *Silence* (Wesleyan University Press, 1961; M.T.T. Press, 1966). In this essay, Cage alternates two voices, one indicated by italics to the left of the page, the other by roman type to the right of the page. In another essay, "Where Are We Going? And What Are We Doing?" Cage sets up double-voice, at times even triple-voice, by writing this way—

The candles at the Candlelight Concert are
One New Year's Eve I had too
electric. It was found dangerous
many invitations. I decided to
for them to be wax. It has not yet

and so forth.

By far, though, the standard way of presenting double-voice is simply to present the columns without any further complications:

Whitman was born in 1819 on Long Island. When he was four, his parents moved to Brooklyn where Whiman grew up and went to school. All his youth he spent, one place or another, in town or in country, betwixt East River and the Atlantic Ocean.	We are born by accident in a certain location, yet the location impinges upon our soul and psyche, and we absorb the shapes and sounds and sights peculiar to that location and our view of reality is constructed from this primary, childhood material.

And obviously, two *lists* can run parallel to each other—doing all that lists themselves do and at the same time creating the double voice:

Sea	Atlantic/Womb & Tomb/Such Mystery
Gulls	Arcs of whiteness/plaintive screams
Sky	Endless/one should not stare into space too long a time
Shore	Boundaries/the line between
Stones	Foundation & Crushing Force
Roses	Perfume & Thorn
Salt Air	Wake me up! Sting against my face!
Tides	Of blood
Farms	Pastoral themes/dirty labor in barns
Country Roads	Delicate tracks/muddy ruts
Mockingbirds	Music & Irony
Horses	I stare into their eyes & wonder about the universe.

Summer Clouds   Like every child, I Walt Whitman,
                  lie & stare into their magic
                  shapes, their shifting forms,
                  and see men and beasts.

(Double-voice embraces, actually, what might be called double-percep-
tion or double-thought, and it is sometimes difficult to distinguish between a
dual vision and a dual sound. Many times the writer, in juxtaposing two
statements, gives less attention to distinguishing his "voices" and concen-
trates upon the fact that he is seeing two scenes at once or is approaching a
subject from two different angles at once.)

Repetitions/Repetends/Refrains. Repetitions play a more important
part in the alternate grammar than they do in the traditional; repetitions are
used to achieve a kind of momentum in composition when traditional continuity has been suppressed, eliminated, or handled with such subtlety that it
scarcely seems present at all. The repetitions come in all forms: simple *repetitions* of individual words; phrases and sentences used as *refrains*; words,
phrases, or sentences used as *repetends.* The repetitions are mostly devoted
to binding and holding together, creating even at times a certain rhythm that
carries a reader through disjointed sentences and passages. Perhaps the concern with repetitions in the alternative grammar is compensatory for a pervasive acceptance of fragmentation and discontinuity.

In the recent volume, *Style and Text* (ed. Hakan Ringbom, issued by
the Abo Akademie, Finiand), Irma Ranavaara notes, in her essay on Virginia
Woolf's style, that Woolf makes great use of repetition, a use that ranges
through all parts of speech. Some examples given by Professor Ranavaara are
these, taken from Woolf's last novel, *Between the Acts*:

She had come into the stable yard where the dogs were chained; where
the buckets stood; where the great pear tree spread its ladder of
branches against the wall.
what a cackle, what a raggle, what a yaffle—as they call the wood-
pecker, the laughing bird that flits from tree to tree.

Faster, faster, faster, it whizzed, whirred, buzzed.

The cook's hands cut, cut, cut.

Woolf was concerned in all her writing, of course, with answering the
question, "How can we combine the old words in new orders so they survive,
so that they create beauty, so that they tell the truth?" And she foraged into
the alternate grammar of style, trying this and trying that, with repetiton
being one of the stylistic devices she used heavily to escape the very economy of the traditional grammar and all the implications of that economy.

Woolf's repetitions, though of high incidence, are essentially limited to
an easily achieved epizeuxis. Gertrude Stein, in such an essay as "American
Food and American Houses" (1938), uses a slightly more subtle kind of
repetition and in ways more typical of the alternate grammar. Stein writes
such sentences as "salads fruit salads have immensely taken their place,"

with the "salad" repetition being quite different from ordinary epizeuxis. Likewise, her repetition of the word "pancake" in this sentence—

> Then there used to be so many kinds of pancakes, every kind of pancake, that too has disappeared the pancake has pretty well disappeared and I imagine that there are lots of little Americans who have never even heard of them never even heard of the word pancakes. (Haas, ed., Gertrude Stein, *op. cit.*)

The efforts of a Stein or a Woolf are simply preludes to the full use of repetition that we find in full-blown examples of the alternate grammar. When we come to Tom Wolfe's essay "Las Vegas!!! (What?) Las Vegas (Can't Hear you! Too Noisy!) Las Vegas!!!" we find him opening with a tremendously exaggerated super-epizeuxis, repeating the word "hernia" thirty times in a row; then—after a slight interruption for the phrase "eight is the point, the point is eight"—repeating the word "hernia" another seven times, pausing for the phrase "hard eight," then finishing out the opening paragraph with another sixteen "hernia" 's.

Wolfe's repetition in this case suggests movement and energy, and probably most repetitions, when presented in tightly concentrated form this way, are "corresponding" to a certain "throb of life." Sometimes, though, repetitions are less concentrated, more scattered—as in this passage from John Dos Passos' *U.S.A.*—

> Thomas Edison at eighty-two worked sixteen hours a day; he never worried about mathematics or the social system or generalized philosophical concepts; in collaboration with Henry Ford and Harvey Firestone who never worried about mathematics or the social system or generalized philosophical concepts;
>
> he worked sixteen hours a day trying to find a substitute for rubber; whenever he read about anything he tried it out; whenever he got a hunch he went to the laboratory and tried it out.

In such repetition the correspondence is probably more with the idea of inevitable recurrence of experience, the "sameness" and "inevitability" of reality, a recognition that in reality there are both stabilizing "things we count on" and boring things that never go away. Different writers will find different values in the repetition, some writers using it sparingly but some writers creating, with it, a great sense of saturation and density. Once again, the writer has options.

Given such stylistic maneuvers and devices as these (there are many more, of course—including the many that are shared with traditional grammar and including more exceptional devices absolutely beyond the pale of traditional grammar, e.g. the non sequitur and the mixed metaphor) the contemporary writer can mix and match as his own compositional inclinations and rhetorical commitments determine. He may, in his use of such maneuvers and devices, achieve, as he often does, two stylistic effects quite characteristic of compositions in the alternate grammar. They are the effects of (a) synchronicity and (b) collage-montage.

Synchronicity. In the traditional grammar of style all "time" considerations are diachronic or chronological. Even the devices of "foreshadowing" and "flashback" are still part of a diachronic conceptualization. In the alternate grammar, however, there is an acceptance of "all things present in the present moment" with many of the devices already mentioned implying this effect: double-voice implies a certain simultaneity in reality: two things going on at once. Repetitions/repetends/refrains also imply recurrence: certain material occurs in the composition; one reads it and passes on, assuming *those words* to be in the "past" of the composition; but no—we meet the material again; it was not a prisoner of the "past" but is present now, the same as it was, transcending a past/present/future sequence.

If the desire of the writer is to suggest synchronicity, he can indeed make use of double-voice and repetition. He can make use of the double-column list. He can make use of the labyrinthine sentence, especially when it emphasizes circularity (borrowing epanalepsis from the traditional grammar and making heavy, exaggerated use of it).

Much use is made also of the present tense to achieve synchronicity since the present tense can equal both the real present and the historical present; without moving from one verb to another, synchronicity can be created —as in such a passage as this—

Whitman is crossing East River on the Brooklyn Ferry. A woman is giving birth on a farm on Long Island on the thirty-first of May. He observes the reflections in the water. Whitman is dying in Camden. Peter Doyle conducts the trolley through the broad streets of Washington and the old man stares out the window, stares at the American people. The woman calls her second child Walter. And crossing on the ferry with him are all types of people, all the diverse faces, all the diverse parts of the American whole. So he walks through Camden. So he walks through Washington, D.C. He climbs up on the trolley and visits with Peter Doyle. He shortens his name to Walt. He tells his mother he is going to cross on the ferry, make his way to Manhattan, he has things to say. Thus Whitman is born on Paunmanok, 1819. Thus he is dying, carefully, in the spring of 1892. He is making a kind of journey through the flow of people and across the broad river.

(Note: In synchronicity, use is often made of transitional and relating words—such as "so," "therefore," "thus," "then"—in a kind of "binding of time," parodying the traditional grammar of syle wherein transition/relationship is accepted and expected. The resulting non-sequiturs are a by-product, yet become an important characteristic of the alternate grammar, since the non-sequiturs cut through old logical patterns and question the validity of old connections.)

Synchronicity is often achieved simply through the scrambling of sentences or paragraphs or crots, scrambling them out of ordinary time sequences, so that one keeps encountering them again and again in a certain time period. For instance, if one had crots dealing with (a) one's arrival in

New Orleans, (b) one's visit to the French Quarter, (c) in particular one's dining at Antoine's, and (d) one's departure from New Orleans, synchronicity would be achieved by scrambling the crots to present now one from group b, now one from group c, now one from group a, now one from group b, now one from group d, now one from group c, now one from group d, etc. Even if the individual crots use appropriate verb tenses (past tense primarily, with some past perfect) still the effect of the scrambling would be synchronic—all events indistinguishable within one large time frame.

Synchronicity is, of course, a stylistic effect used to support a writer's concern with the "here and now," the contemporary. Synchronicity also allows the writer to concentrate upon the immediate moment and yet include matter from the past without having to compromise the discussion of the present. If, in the opinion of a writer, the only reality is what stands in front of him here and now, then his knowledge of the past is best presented in present terms. With appreciative nods toward such a history theorist as R. G. Collingwood, the writer conceives his very "knowledge of the past" as a current knowledge: knowledge *in* the present *of* the past is a synchronous situation. All in all, synchronicity provides stylistic correspondence to the "timelessness of events."

Collage/Montage. Another frequent effect of the alternate grammar is collage/montage in which diverse elements are patched together to make the whole composition. Easily achieved with crots and the other stylistic devices so far identified, collage/montage reacts against the "categorizing" of traditional grammar and insists on packaging together into a heterogenous community all those matters that in traditional grammar would be grouped into homogenous units. Quite compatible with and similar to synchronicity, the collage/montage effect (which in traditional grammar would be considered random, hodge-podge, patchwork) is a stylistic effort at synthesis, distinguishable from traditional grammar's effort, nearly always, at analysis.

In extreme form, collage/montage can mean something as radical as William Burroughs's famous cut-up method, whereby texts written in traditional grammar are arbitrarily cut up, horizontally and vertically, and converted into near-unintelligible scraps of text. The scraps are then shuffled (or folded in) and joined randomly. Sometimes Burroughs carries his cut-up method so far as to cut up individual sentences into fragments, then paste the fragments back into new sentences. He does this for instance in *A Distant Hand Lifted*, wherein a typical sequence reads: " . . . remember/my/ messages between remote posts of/exploded star/fold in/distant sky/example agent K9 types out a/distant hand lifted. . . . " Burroughs says this collage "method can approximate walky talky immediacy."

Less radical, and more useable, are methods of collage that use larger and more intelligible units of composition, each unit—like the crot—communicative within itself, simply being joined in the collage to other communication units, perhaps from different periods, perhaps dealing with different subject matter, perhaps even containing different sentence/dictional style, texture, tone. Collage at its best actually countermands much of the discontinuity and fragmentation of the alternate style by revealing, by the time a composition ends, a synthesis and a wholeness that might not have been suspected at any station along the way.

As the compositional units to be "synthesized" become larger, more substantial, and more complete within themselves, we come to the sense of montage—a presentation in sequence, side by side, of compositional units less fragmental, yet fairly disparate so far as form or content are concerned. Frequently the disparate units are actually examples of various established compositional forms—e.g. poem, aphorism, letter, description, narration, anecdote, interview, questionnaire, etc. William Blake achieved such a montage effect in the prefaces to the various chapters of *Jerusalem*: In the preface to the first chapter, for instance, he presents (a) a prose apologia for the writing of *Jerusalem*, (b) a verse apologia and address to readers, (c) a verse quatrain, (d) a brief prose theological essay, (e) a thirty-five line poem in a rough kind of iambic pentameter, (f) a three-stanza hymn-like poem made up of four-lined stanzas in generally rhymed tetrameters.

In current montage effects, writers create multi-genre compositions, using as Dylan Thomas does, for instance, in his essay "Reminiscences of Childhood," a sequence of (a) description, (b) an original poem, (c) more prose description containing (d) passages of dialogue, and ending with (e) an aphoristic-like statement, "The memories of childhood have no order, and no end."

This kind of multi-genre montage effect in the alternate grammar replaces, somewhat, the more traditional method of citation and quotation, though quotations themselves—in isolated forms—are often used in montage.

The use of various genres within the prose nonfiction composition— (e.g. the "mimeographed schedule" in Terry Southern's "Twirling at Ole Miss"; the dramatic "scene" complete with dialogue, along with song lyrics and individual "testimonial" statements by Frank Sinatra's family in Gay Talese's "Frank Sinatra Has a Cold"; tape transcripts of earth-to-moon conversations in Norman Mailer's *Of a Fire on the Moon*)—is valued by contemprorary writers because it suggests that there is little difference between genres, between fiction/nonfiction in the verbal response to reality, that the category lines separating "literary forms" in the traditional areas do not really make sense if we begin to perceive reality and the verbal response to that reality in new and different ways. Hence: Norman Mailer's *The Armies of the Night*: History as a Novel, The Novel as History; Truman Capote's nonfiction novel *In Cold Blood*.

Something Old, Something New:
Functional Sentence Perspective

WILLIAM J. VANDE KOPPLE

Functional Sentence Perspective (FSP) is a theory that predicts how units of information should be distributed in a sentence and how sentences of information should be related in a discourse.[1] The theory originated in Europe in the work of Weil (1878). In this century his work inspired Mathesius, who with several other linguists, many of whom are associated with the Prague linguistic circle, further developed the principles of FSP, primarily by analyzing the interworking syntax with semantics in German, Russian, and Czech. In America, linguists such as Chomsky (1965), Fillmore (1970), Chafe (1970), and Lakoff (1971) have tried to account for FSP distinctions and constraints in various components of an adequate grammar. Others, including Gundell (1974), Keenan and Schieffelin (1976), and Kuno (1978) have used the theory to explain such linguistic phenomena as gapping, forward and backward pronominalization, and left and right dislocation sentence patterns. And several rhetoricians, such as Strunk and White (1962), Tichy (1966), McCrimmon (1967), Macrorie (1968), Elsbree and Bracher (1972), and Williams (1970) have written about principles for cohesion and emphasis that are consistent with FSP.

In brief, for Functional Sentence Perspectivists a sentence conveys its message most effectively if its two major parts, the topic and comment, perform specific semantic and communicative tasks. In English, the topic usually includes the grammatical subject and its adjuncts. The comment usually includes the verb and objects or carries primary sentence stress.

For each part theorists posit slightly different but often corresponding communicative functions. They claim that the topic should express either the theme of the sentence, the elements with the least communicative dynamism (a measure of how much an element contributes to the development of a communication), the least important information, or the old information. They assert that the comment should express either information about the theme, the elements with the most communicative dynamism, the most important information, or the new information.

However, most assign the topic the role of expressing the old information in a sentence, that which is either stated in, recoverable from, or relatively more accessible in the prior context. And most assign the comment

Research in the Teaching of English, 17 (February 1983), pp. 85-99. Copyright © 1983 by the National Council of Teachers of English. Reprinted with permission.

the role of expressing the new information, that which is not expressed in, is difficult to derive from, or is relatively less accessible in the prior context. Although these specific functions sometimes correspond to the others that are posited for the topic and comment, they do not correspond in every case. This does not mean that the other functions are insignificant. It does mean that many scholars believe that the distinction between old and new information is the principal one underlying the topic/comment articulation (see Chafe, 1970) and that a more objective decision can probably be made about what is old and new information than about what information the other communicative functions would subsume.

My primary question in research was whether an English discourse that is consistent with FSP as detailed above has cognitive advantages over one with the same content but that is contradictory to FSP. Weil has claimed that the movement from topic to comment "reveals the movement of the mind itself" (cited by Firbas, 1974, p. 12). If this is true, a discourse consistent with FSP should be more readable and memorable than one contradictory to FSP. But we have all probably encountered writers who consistently place new information early in their sentences. Is this style due to carelessness or impatience to express new information? Or could this order actually be easier for us to process?

Clearly, we need to test FSP. But what should the tests be like?

First, they should use connected discourses as materials. After all, almost every time we encounter writing, we process connected discourse, not nonsense syllables, individual words, isolated sentences, or pairs of sentences. And in order to decide what is old and new information in a sentence, we must know what information precedes the sentence in discourse.

Second, the discourses should be entirely natural. No one should question whether they could occur in normal language situations. They should be clear, natural, even "well-written."

Third, the discourse should vary only along the old-new dimension. The sentences of one discourse should express the old and new information in accord with FSP; sentences in the variant should reverse the positions of old and new information.

Although some semanticists might disagree, I believe that such discourses have the same truth values; thus truth value should not be a relevant variable. For some evidence, I refer to Sachs's finding that "two sentences can have different forms but express the same meaning" (1967, p. 438). And it is probable that even if there were slight differences in truth values, very few people reading normally would notice them.

These comments do not apply to discourses composed of different orderings of the same simple statements or sentences. For even if we vary the order of sentences in a passage carefully, we probably affect the logical connections within the passage as well as its overall semantic structure. However, researchers might claim that some of these differences are not cognitively significant. Yet discourse consisting of sentences that can be moved around freely must at least verge on the unnatural or rare.

Is such research reported in the scholarly journals? The studies that come closest to meeting our needs are de Beaugrande's (1979), Clements' (1979), and Rothkopf's (1962). Yet these fail to provide the specific help we need for one or more reasons.

De Beaugrande's passages were composed of different orders of the same sentences. And he varied the position of sentences and paragraphs, not just bits of information within sentences, without an explicit principle. Clements also composed passages by varying the order of the same sentences without a detailed principle. Furthermore, he assumed that the FSP principle for distributing information in a sentence is justified in itself and applies to the distribution of information in an entire discourse. Finally, Rothkopf's passages also were composed of the same sentences in different orders, his experimental sentences "are probably not a representative sample of the population of instructional sentences" (p. 673), and he did not vary the location of the same bit of information according to FSP.

Therefore, the applicability of FSP to continuous natural discourse remains unproved. To begin testing it, I performed three readability and three retention experiments on paragraphs that I wrote by following or contradicting the FSP principles that Daneš presents (1974, p. 118). In general, each sentence of a rule-governed form expresses old information in its topic and new information in its comment. In each sentence of a variant, the positions of old and new bits of information are reversed.

More specifically, the rule-governed forms are topically linked. Their topics are identical or closely related through pronoun substitution, synonym substitution, specification, additional characterization, slight qualification, or enumeration of set members. For an example, consider paragraph 1 (with main topics italicized):

Currently *the Marathon* is the best waxless ski for recreational cross-country skiing. Its weight is a mere two pounds. Yet *its two-inch width* allows the skier to break a trail through even the heaviest snow. *Its most unique characteristic* is the fishscale design for its bottom. *The Marathon* is almost as effective as most waxable skis. In fact, *it* is even better than some waxable skis when the snow is very wet. *The Marathon* can be used with most conventional bindings. However, *it* works best with the Suomi double-lock. Finally, *the Marathon* is available in six different colors.

In the variation of paragraph 1, most of the topics are only remotely related. Consider paragraph 2 (with main topics italicized):

Currently *the best waxless ski for recreational cross-country skiing* is the Marathon. *A mere two pounds* is its weight. Yet *the skier* can break a trail through even the heaviest snow with its two-inch width. *The fishscale design for its bottom* is its most unique characteristic. *Most waxable skis* are only slightly more effective than the Marathon. In fact, *some waxable skis* are not as good as it when the snow is very wet. *Most conventional bindings* can be used with the Marathon. However, *the*

Suomi double-lock works best with it. Finally, *six different colors* are available for the Marathon.

However, paragraph 2 contains exactly as many topics and the same propositional information as paragraph 1. And I examined both of these paragraphs, as well as all experimental paragraphs, to ensure that they were identical or very similar in numbers of words, clauses, sentences, nominalizations, reversible and non-reversible passives, as well as in introductory conjunctions, adverbs, and prepositional phrases. I also established that the corresponding sentences in each paragraph were about the same length and contained many of the same words and full verbs.

After this was established, a colleague who was familiar with FSP underlined the topics in the paragraphs. In all cases her judgments agreed with mine. To ensure that no words or sentences in the paragraphs were markedly awkward, I asked several colleagues to evaluate them. Usually nine read a rule-governed paragraph and nine others read its variant, commenting on any words or sentences that they considered awkward. If one evaluator objected to a word or sentence, I changed it to what he suggested. Therefore, one of a pair of paragraphs should not have had an advantage in experiments because it contained fewer inappropriate words or awkward sentences than the other. Finally, I selected and distributed all subjects at random.

Descriptions of the three readability and three retention experiments follow:

Readability Experiment 1:

Subjective Judgments of Readability with Subjects Alerted Before a Single Reading

Materials used were the topically linked paragraph 3a and its variant, 3b. (3a and 3b are slightly altered versions of paragraphs 1 and 2, printed above. Copies of these and all other experimental paragraphs and materials are available upon request.) Subjects were 72 high-school sophomores and 59 high-school seniors. I told them that they would read two paragraphs identical in subject matter but different in form, that after reading them once they should indicate on the separate answer sheet whether one paragraph was easier to read or whether they could detect no significant difference in readability between them, and finally, that they should try to justify their decision in writing. Then I gave them a copy of 3a and 3b, which I had prepared almost identically. I decided which subjects read one paragraph before the other by flipping a coin and correcting for equal numbers at the end.

Eighty-six of the 131 total subjects chose paragraph 3a, twenty-seven chose paragraph 3b, and eighteen saw no difference between the two. Testing the hypothesis that the probability of subjects favoring 3a is less than one-half by using the normal approximation to the binomial distribution leads to a z for these figures of 3.58, significant at the .0002 level. These and additional data appear in Table 1.

TABLE 1

Subjective Judgments of Readability with
Subjects Alerted Before a Single Reading

	3a	3b	no difference	z	p
total subjects	86	27	18	3.58	.0002
sophomores	50	16	6	3.30	.0005
seniors	36	11	12	1.69	.05

Readability Experiment 2:
Subjective Judgments of Readability with Subjects Alerted After a
Single Reading

Again I used paragraphs 3a and 3b. My subjects were 73 different high-school
sophomores and 67 different high-school seniors. I proceeded as I did in the
first experiment except that I waited until immediately after the students
had read the paragraphs once to inform them that they should judge readability. If a significant number of students favored 3a, we would have
stronger evidence of its greater readability than that from the first experiment because of the advantages of 3a must have persisted in memory.

Of the 140 total subjects, 87 indicated that 3a was easier to read than
3b, 38 decided that 3b was easier than 3a, and 15 felt that there was no difference between the two. The z for the number preferring 3a is 2.87, significant at the .002 level. These and additional data appear in Table 2.

TABLE 2

Subjective Judgments of Readability with
Subjects Alerted After a Single Reading

	3a	3b	no difference	z	p
total subjects	87	38	15	2.87	.002
sophomores	45	20	8	1.99	.02
seniors	42	18	7	2.08	.02

Readability Experiment 3:
Subjective Judgments of Readability After Many Readings

Materials were the topically linked paragraph 5a and its variant, 5b. I designed this experiment to compensate for the possibility that one reading of
paired paragraphs might not have allowed subjects to make the most careful
judgments of readability. My subjects were 118 high-school sophomores and
66 high-school seniors, all of whom had also participated in one of the first
two experiments. I gave them a sheet on which 5a and 5b appeared. One-half
of the subjects saw 5a above 5b; the other half saw 5b on top. I told them to
read the paragraphs as often as they wished within eight minutes. After eight
minutes, they had to indicate on the bottom of the sheet whether one paragraph was easier to read, or whether they could detect no significant difference in their readability. Also, they were supposed to comment on their

decision. They all finished this task easily.

Most students favored 5a over 5b. 121 of the 184 total subjects preferred 5a over 5b, 41 preferred 5b over 5a, and 22 said they perceived no difference between the two. The z for these figures, that is, the normal approximation to the distribution of those who preferred 5a is 4.28, significant at less than the .0001 level. These and other data appear in Table 3.

TABLE 3

Subjective Judgments of Readability After Many Readings

	5a	5b	no difference	z	p
total subjects	121	41	22	4.28	<.0001
sophomores	74	31	13	2.76	.006
seniors	47	10	9	3.45	.0006

Retention Experiment 1:
The Double-distractor Recognition Test

I used the topically linked paragraph 11a and its variant, 11b. My subjects were 74 high-school sophomores. I first gave them all a three-page practice booklet. The first page, the instructions, informed them that on a signal they should flip to the second page and read the practice paragraph printed there carefully but only once. For the practice paragraph, I adapted a paragraph from the *Encyclopaedia Britannica* so that one-half of the sentences could provide a target from their topic and the other half could provide a target from their comment. However, I did not alternate sentences with topic targets with those with comment targets since trying that seemed to make the paragraph awkward. In this way, I tried to avoid predisposing subjects to look for targets in only certain parts of sentences. After the subjects read the paragraph, they were to flip to the third page, on which were randomly ordered numbers, words, and short phrases. Ten of these were in the practice paragraph; twenty were distractors. The subjects were to circle the targets and avoid the distractors.

I allowed them ample time for the practice test. When they were finished, we corrected it together, tabulating scores by subtracting the sum of distractors circled and targets omitted from the number of targets circled. Other scoring methods are possible. For example, one can simply count the number of targets circled. But Klare et al. (1957) demonstrated that the method I used is good to compensate for guessing and to measure what subjects retain.

Immediately after the practice, I gave the students another three-page booklet. All students saw identical first pages (instructions) and third pages (10 targets and 20 distractors in random order). However, 37 of them saw 11a on their second page, while 37 saw 11b. All of them proceeded as they had on the practice sheet.

Each of the 10 targets expressed new information that was contained in a comment in 11a and in a topic in 11b. Two colleagues helped me select the two distractors for each target. I asked them to work individually, looking for items which were likely to be confused with targets because they were associated with them, sounded like them, or meant something similar to them. If both of them suggested the same distractor, I automatically accepted it. When they suggested different ones, I chose the one I thought could more easily be confused with the target. And occasionally I used a distractor which neither had suggested but which occurred to me because of their suggestions.

The 34 subjects who had read the topically linked paragraph 11a performed somewhat better than did the thirty-four who had read 11b. Those who had read 11a had an average score of 7.16 on the recognition task, and those who had read 11b had an average score of 6.54. Using a *t*-test on these data produced a *t* of 1.01, which is significant between the .15 and .2 levels.

Retention Experiment 2:

The Short-answer Test

Materials were the topically linked paragraph 9a and its variant 9b. Seventy-four high-school sophomores participated. I first gave them a three-page practice booklet. The first page informed them that on a signal they should flip to the second page, read the practice paragraph (adapted from the *Encyclopaedia Britannica* so that one-half of the sentences could provide an answer from their topic and one-half could provide an answer from their comment) found there once, and then flip to the third page and provide short answers to the 10 randomly ordered questions printed there. All the answers appeared in the practice paragraph.

I gave them as much time as they needed. When they had answered the questions, we corrected the tests together, subtracting the number of incorrect answers from the number correct. To be scored as correct, answers had to appear exactly as they had in the paragraph.

Then we moved to the actual test. I gave each subject another three-page booklet. All saw identical first pages (instructions) and third pages (randomly ordered questions). However, 37 found 9a on their second page, while 37 found 9b. All proceeded as they had on the practice test.

I wrote the 10 questions myself, avoiding any words found in only one of the two paragraphs. The answers were numbers, words, or short phrases, each of which expressed new information and appeared in a comment in 9a and in a topic in 9b.

Those who had read the topically linked paragraph 9a answered significantly more questions correctly than did those who had read 9b. The former averaged 7.03 correct answers; the latter averaged 5.62 correct responses. A *t*-test applied to these data produced a *t* of 2.8, significant between the .0005 and the .005 levels.

Retention Experiment 3:

The Immediate Recall Test

I used the topically linked paragraph 3a and its variant, 3b. Seventy-two high-school sophomores took this test. Again I first gave them a three-page practice booklet. From instructions on the first page they learned that on a signal they were to flip to the second page and read the paragraph (from *Time*) printed there once, and then immediately flip over to the blank third page and write a recall protocol for the paragraph. I gave them as much time as they needed, and then I simply collected the booklets.

Immediately after the practice test, I gave them another three-page booklet. All saw identical first pages (instructions) and blank third pages. But 36 found 3a on their second page, while 36 found 3b. They proceeded exactly as they had in the practice test.

In scoring the protocols, I followed the guidelines of King (1960). That is, in each protocol I counted the number of function words, content words, and three-word sequences. (ABCDE contains the following three-element sequences: ABC, BCD, CDE.) I accepted misspelled words only if they were unambiguous.

Students who had read 3b recalled an average of 4.66 function words, while those who had read 3a recalled an average of only 4.57 function words. However, those who had read the topically linked 3a excelled in the other two categories. They recalled an average of 22.72 content words, and those who had read 3b recalled an average of 19.81 content words. Also, readers of 3a recalled an average of 11.19 three-word sequences, as contrasted to the average of 8.28 recalled by the readers of 3b. These data as well as the results of the *t*-test are in Table 4.

TABLE 4

The Immediate Recall Test

	mean function words	*t/p*	mean content words	*t/p*	mean 3-word sequences	*t/p*
paragraph 3a	4.566		22.722	1.399/ .1<*p*<.15	11.194	1.918/ .025<*p*<.05
paragraph 3b	4.661	insignificant	19.806		8.278	

We will have to wait for additional tests using both older and younger subjects on these and other paragraph forms before we can come to a definite conclusion about the validity of FSP, but, taken together, these six experiments provide strong evidence for the theory.

A very probable explanation why linked forms were superior to their variants is that they probably facilitated Haviland and Clark's (1974) proposed given-new strategy of comprehension. According to Haviland and Clark, when we read a sentence, we first divide it into its given (what we already know) and new information. We view the given as a pointer to a matching antecedent in memory and search for it. If we cannot find an antecedent, we either construct one with an inferential bridge, view all the information as new and begin a new and separate memory structure, or try to reanalyze what is given and new in the sentence. Thus a sentence will be easy to comprehend if the given information is clearly marked and obviously matches an antecedent in memory. A sentence will be difficult if the given information is not clearly marked, does not match an antecedent in memory, or demands an inference for identification.

Now consider how subjects probably process a topically linked form. Since they see the paragraph in no special context, they should view all information in the first sentence as new. When they reach the second sentence, however, they probably try to relate it to information in the first. That should be easy since the given information is either identical or closely related to information in the first and since the given appears early in the sentence. While reading only the beginning of the second sentence, therefore, subjects can already know what antecedent to look for and can feel confident that the rest of the sentence probably expresses new information. Moreover, since the bits of given information are identical or related and are expressed in topics throughout the paragraph, subjects can reinforce the old information in memory. And after a number of sentences, perhaps they can even predict that the next sentence will have the identical old information in its topic. This would help them since it would decrease time they need to process the old and increase the amount of attention they can give to the new.

Contrasting how subjects probably process a variant provides a good explanation why such forms did not test out as well. Again, subjects probably regard all information in the first sentence as new. When they begin to read the second sentence, they immediately encounter more new information. They then must decide whether to begin a new memory structure or to continue into the sentence before deciding that it expresses no given information. They decide to continue reading, which leads them to given information. They then can search for the antecedent in the first. But before adding the new information to it, they might have to re-scan the first part of the second sentence to refresh their memory about what was new. They probably repeat this process in the subsequent sentences, although after a certain number of sentences they might begin expecting the given to be expressed in the comment. Such mental hesitations and shifts in direction must take time and probably prevent subjects from reinforcing the old and new information in memory to the extent possible in a linked paragraph. Therefore, I hypothesize that the topically linked forms were more readable and memorable in experiments than their variants because they facilitated the given-new strategy of comprehension while the variants frustrated this strategy to some degree.

The best empirical evidence that subjects actually added new information to an anchor of old information emerged from the protocols in the immediate recall test on paragraph 3b. Many of the 36 subjects who read and recalled 3b actually rearranged the information in its sentences, writing protocols that resembled the topically linked 3a. That is, they often took the identical old information expressed in the comments of 3b and topic-alized it. Doing this gave them a common reference point near the begin-ning of each sentence. For example, one student's protocol for 3b, printed with its mechanical errors, reads as follows:

> Currently the best wax-less ski is the Marathon. It is only four pounds in weight. Yet, it can go thru heavy snow with its mere 3 inch width. It is good for both kick and glide. The Marathon can be used in wet snow where other waxed skis aren't as good. It can take any kind of binding but the Adidas binding is the best. Last of all, the Marathon comes in 4 colors.

To determine the extent of this tendency, I first counted how many grammatical sentences after the opener were in the 36 protocols. I omitted the first since it usually appeared exactly as in 3b. Then I counted the num-ber of these which expressed the old information not in their comment but in their topic. Sixty of the 101 grammatical sentences did. Twenty-five of the 36 subjects switched the old and new information around in at least one sen-tence. Thus the tendency in protocols to topicalize identical or related old information was strong indeed. It shows that subjects were very dependent on identical reference points when storing information from 3b.

As I noted earlier, I believe that experimental evidence for FSP has important implications for discourse analysts. That the experiments justified FSP for English might surprise some of them. Some have assumed that the rigid control that syntax exercises over word order in English severely re-stricts the operation of FSP principles. Indeed, Mathesius characterizes Eng-lish as "so little susceptible to the requirements of FSP as to frequently disre-gard them altogether" (cited in Firbas, 1974, p. 17). It would follow from this claim that English writers and speakers are not very sensitive to or signi-ficantly affected by the position of old and new information in sentences. However, the tests reported here provide evidence that when syntax allows us to express old information in the topic and new information in the com-ment, we definitely should. Accordingly, discourse analysts should try to dis-cover how we can systematically relate the morpho-phonological and syn-tactic structures of English to topic and comment (see van Dijk, 1977, p. 115).

Evidence for FSP also has important implications for teachers of writ-ing. We should teach both the principles of FSP and the ways in which our students can reconcile them with English syntax. Doing this would be bene-ficial in several ways.

First, we would be teaching principles that are founded in experiments, with implications about how we process and store information. Some of the principles we inculcate now are not justified by empirical evidence.

Second, once our students learn and work with the principles of FSP, their discourses should become more readable and memorable.

Third, our students should develop a more thoughtful approach to their writing processes. Many of them seem to record and leave information as they think of it. And many, perhaps because of impatience, customarily express bits of new information in sentence topics. If they knew the principles of F SP, they could learn to identify old and new bits of information and position them according to the theory.

Fourth, their discourses should also become more cohesive. After all, students trained in the principles of F SP should become highly skilled at identifying and relating appropriate bits of old and new information in discourses. And this skill should be helpful in recognizing, interpreting, and using many of the devices of cohesion that researchers such as Williams (1970), Fowler (1977), van Dijk (1972, 1977), and perhaps most notably, Halliday (1968, 1970) and Halliday and Hasan (1976) have investigated and described recently. If we examine Halliday's (1977) most recent summary of his and Hasan's work on cohesion, we shall see that many of the devices of cohesion he describes are based on connections between bits of old information in the sentences of discourse. Many of the devices are anaphoric; they depend on our recognizing that older, more derivable information is being referred to, substituted for, or repeated.

For example, consider the elements that Halliday says function by reference. These elements include the personals (*she*), the demonstratives (*this*), and the comparatives (*earlier*). All of these are "interpretable only by reference to something other than themselves" (1977, p. 188). The "something other" is frequently information that is expressed earlier in the text. And Halliday notes that when we connect personals, demonstratives, and comparatives to older information, cohesion is established between the two points in a text (1977, p. 189).

Similar comments apply to the linguistic devices Halliday says function by substitution. These "function as alternatives to the repetition of a particular item and hence cohere with the passage in which the item occurs" (1977, p. 189). For example, in the text "Last week I called on my neighbor. Having done so, I feel quite cheerful," *Having done so* substitutes for the first sentence. We must relate *Having done so* to the older information in order for the text to cohere and make sense.

Finally, another way that we can create cohesion in a text is by reiteration or collocation. Halliday calls this lexical cohesion. For example, in texts we often repeat the same word, substitute a synonym for a word, or replace a word with one that is closely associated with it or has a more general meaning than it. In doing so, we again link elements to older information.

Students who have worked with the principles of F SP should be especially adept at recognizing and interpreting such cohesive devices. Perhaps they will become more sensitive to the possibilities for cohesion in their own discourses and more apt to use cohesive devices. And they should also be able to add insights to the work on cohesion. For on the basis of the empirical evidence we have, they would know that in order to facilitate processing of texts, they should express elements that are linked to older information in sentence topics whenever possible and whenever there is no good reason not to. If students had an anaphoric element in each sentence and expressed each element in a sentence topic, their discourses would be quite similar to the topically linked paragaphs I used in experiments. I believe we can consider such forms cohesive not only because they contain many devices of cohesion but also because they relate information in accord with F SP, thereby probably facilitating processing.

Are there other forms of discourse which we might consider cohesive on these same grounds? Daneš (1974) shows that there are at least two others, both of which we should examine with our students when we work on cohesion. In one, which we can for convenience call rhetorically linked, the topic of each sentence except the first repeats or is closely related to information in the comment of the preceding sentence. In other words, the information in the comment of each sentence carries over to the topic of the next sentence. This pattern produces a chain of old and new information throughout the discourse. One of Daneš's short examples of this form is the following: "The first of the antibiotics was discovered by Sir Alexander Fleming in 1928. He was busy at the time investigating a certain species of germ which is responsible for boils and other troubles" (p. 118).

In the other form, the topic of the first sentence introduces a general subject or hypertheme, and the topics of subsequent sentences express subthemes that are derivable from the hypertheme. Often, given the hypertheme, the subthemes are predictable. Daneš says that this form of discourse has derived topics. His English example is as follows:

New Jersey is flat along the coast and southern portion; the northwestern region is mountainous. The coastal climate is mild, but there is considerable cold in the mountain areas during the winter months. Summers are fairly hot. The leading industrial production includes chemicals, processed foods, coal, petroleum, metals and electrical equipment. The most important cities are Newark, Jersey City, Paterson, Trenton, Camden. Vacation districts include Asbury Park, Lakewood, Cape May, and others. (p. 120)

Daneš notes that the choice and sequence of the derived topics will be controlled primarily by various extralinguistic constraints.

Of course, we must stress with our students that it is rare to find a discourse that conforms perfectly to any of these patterns. Daneš himself points out that some discourses are made up of combinations of these patterns, and that others omit parts of the sequence or disrupt the sequence by insertions. And obviously there are many discourses with structures that we have not been able to describe adequately yet. But helping our composition student identify such patterns in discourse should both reinforce the principles of F SP and alert them to possibilities for cohesion in texts, cohesion dependent on what seems to be proper information flow.

In addition to the benefits discussed above, teaching composition students the principles of F SP and exploring their relationships to other aspects of texts might lead to some significant insights about discourse and the writing process in the future. It is possible, for example, that if we examine the progression of topics in a text, we might be able to develop an explicit method to determine what topic of discourse (see van Dijk, 1977) is entailed by the sentence topics. It is also possible that if we examine how the comments of a discourse relate to each other, we might be able to formulate a method to describe how certain kinds of discourses are generated. And we might even be able to relate paragraphing practices in English to amounts of and relationships between new information.

I conclude by noting that several important questions related to F SP remain to be answered. For example, in how many different ways can new information relate to old? How can we determine what the topic and comment of initial sentences in discourse are? To answer that, how much will we have to know about the situation in which a discourse occurs? Does such a posited function as transition have cognitive reality? Do complex sentences have a topic-comment structure that we can describe? Do certain kinds of writing differ in the amounts of new information they contain? When do we develop the ability to relate new information to old, or when does this ability show itself? Finally, do people of similar educational and cultural backgrounds develop similar cognitive hierarchies, schemata, or sets of old and new information?

Notes

[1] The author wishes to thank Janel Mueller and Joseph M. Williams for advice.

References

Chafe, Wallace. *Meaning and the Structure of Language*. Chicago: The University of Chicago Press, 1970.

Chomsky, Noam. *Aspects of the Theory of Syntax*. Cambridge, MA: MIT Press, 1965.

Clements, Paul. "The Effects of Staging on Recall from Prose." In Roy O. Freedle (Ed.), *Advances in Discourse Processes*. Vol. II. Norwood: Ablex, 1979, pp. 287-330.

Daneš, František. "Functional Sentence Perspective and the Organization of the Text." In Daneš (Ed.), *Papers on Functional Sentence Perspective*. The Hague: Mouton, 1974, pp. 106-128.

De Beaugrande, Robert. "Psychology and Composition." *College Composition and Communication*, 1979, *30*, 50-57.

Elsbree, Langdon, & Bracher, F. *Heath's College Handbook of Composition*. Eighth ed. Lexington, MA: D.C. Heath, 1972.

Fillmore, Charles J. "Types of Lexical Information." In Kiefer (Ed.), *Studies in Syntax and Semantics*. Dordrecht: D. Reidel, 1970. Pp. 109-137.

Firbas, Jan. "Some Aspects of the Czechoslovak Approach to Problems of Functional Sentence Perspective." In Daneš (Ed.), *Papers on Functional Sentence Perspective*. The Hague: Mouton, 1974. Pp. 11-37.

Fowler, Roger. "Cohesive, Progressive, and Localizing Aspects of Text Structures." In van Dijk and Petöfi (Eds.), *Grammars and Descriptions*. New York: Walter de Gruyter, 1977. Pp. 64-84.

Gundell, J. *The Role of Topic and Comment in Linguistic Theory.* Doctoral dissertation, University of Texas, 1974.

Halliday, M. A. K. "Notes on Transitivity and Theme in English, Part 2." *Journal of Linguistics, 1968, 3,* 199-244.

Halliday, M. A. K. "Language Structure and Language Function." In Lyons (Ed.), *New Horizons in Linguistics.* Harmondsworth: Penguin Books, 1970. Pp. 140-165.

Halliday, M. A. K. "Text as Semantic Choice in Social Contexts." In van Dijk and Petöfi (Eds.), *Grammars and Descriptions.* New York: Walter de Gruyter, 1977. Pp. 176-225.

Halliday, M. A. K., & Hasan, R. *Cohesion in English.* London: Longman, 1976.

Haviland, Susan E. & Clark, H. H. "What's New? Acquiring New Information as a Process in Comprehension." *Journal of Verbal Learning and Verbal Behavior, 1974, 13,* 512-521.

Keenan, E. O., & Schieffelin, B. B. *Foregrounding Referents: A Reconsideration of Left Dislocation in Discourse.* Mimeographed paper, 1976.

King, David J. "On the Accuracy of Written Recall: A Scaling and Factor Analytic Study." *The Psychological Record, 1960, 10,* 113-122.

Klare, George R. , *et al.* "The Relationship of Style Difficulty, Practice, and Ability to Efficiency of Reading and to Retention." *Journal of Applied Psychology, 1957, 41,* 222-226.

Kuno, Susumu. "Generative Discourse Analysis in America." In Wolfgang U. Dressler (Ed.), *Current Trends in Textlinguistics.* New York: Walter de Gruyter, 1978. Pp. 275-294.

Lakoff, George. "On Generative Semantics." In Steinberg and Jakobovits (Eds.), *Semantics. An Interdisciplinary Reader in Philosophy, Linguistics and Psychology.* Cambridge: Cambridge University Press, 1971. Pp. 232-296.

Macrorie, Ken. *Writing to Be Read.* New York: Hayden Book Co., 1968.

McCrimmon, James M. *Writing with a Purpose* (Fourth ed.). Boston: Houghton Mifflin, 1967.

Rothkopf, Ernst Z. "Learning from Written Sentences: Effects of Order of Presentation on Retention." *Psychological Reports, 1962, 10,* 667-674.

Sachs, Jacqueline S. "Recognition Memory for Syntactic and Semantic Aspects of Connected Discourse." *Perception and Psychophysics, 1967, 2,* 437-442.

Strunk, William Jr., & White, E. B. *The Elements of Style.* New York: Macmillan, 1962.

Tichy, Henrietta J. *Effective Writing for Engineers, Managers, Scientists.* New York: Wiley & Sons, 1966.

Van Dijk, T. A. *Some Aspects of Text Grammars.* The Hague: Mouton, 1972.

Van Dijk, T. A. *Text and Context Explorations in the Semantics and Pragmatics of Discourse.* London: Longman, 1977.

Weil, Henri. *The Order of Words in the Ancient Languages Compared with That of the Modern Languages.* Trans. C. W. Super. Boston, 1878.

Williams, Joseph M. *The New English.* New York: The Free Press, 1970.

PART FIVE

New Perspectives, New Horizons

"Within the new paradigm, old terms, concepts, and experiments fall into new relationships one with the other."

Thomas S. Kuhn

During the past thirty years, the teaching of writing has experienced phenomenal growth and change. The energy driving this change is still at work—now, however, among a new generation of teachers. An example: in 1989 the National Council of Teachers of English created the Whole Language Assembly, a move which gives credence to the process movement in the teaching of writing and holds promise for influencing scores of English teachers nationwide. Another example: almost every issue of *College English* includes an article on the theoretical basis of teaching writing, which, to be understood, requires extensive background reading in a collateral field, sometimes from a European perspective. There are two forces at work in the teaching of writing which seem contradictory but in reality are mutually supportive and beneficial. The first of these is a stablizing force which attempts to apply and make permanent the theories recently articulated. The second is the force of discovery and creation which thrives on the frontiers of new knowledge. Each force complements the other and contributes in its own way to the health and vitality of the profession. The presence of both signifies an active and growing discipline.

In considering new perspectives in the teaching of writing, one is struck first of all with the enormous amount of material available. In some instances, a single essay here will be representative of others on the same topic which have appeared in the journals, all of which may refer to some common source outside the discipline. This section, then, should not be considered a comprehensive survey but rather a sample of promising new directions in the teaching of writing.

The lead essay in this section is Stephen M. North's "The Idea of a Writing Center." North shows how the work of the writing center has been misunderstood, especially within the English department itself, but his argument could extend to the writing classroom as well. The writing center, North

229

writes, "represents the marriage of what are arguably the two most powerful contemporary perspectives on teaching writing: first, that writing is most usefully viewed as a process; and second, that writing curricula need to be student-centered." The idea that it is "writers, and not necessarily their texts [which] get changed" deserves thoughtful consideration.

In "Closing My Eyes as I Speak: An Argument for Ignoring Audience," Peter Elbow not only provides the reader with a view of the rich complexity in the idea of audience—from real audiences to "unconscious or tacit audiences"— but illustrates how paradox and ambiguity are ever present in the teaching of writing. Things are not always what they seem to be; the shortest distance between two points is not always a straight line. The modes of thinking Elbow suggests are fertile ground for powerful, engaged writing.

"I was raised in a working-class home in Philadelphia, but it was only when I went away to college that I heard the term *working class* used or began to think of myself as part of it." Thus Joseph Harris introduces the idea of community and its significance in the teaching of writing. Drawing on the work of David Bartholomae and Patricia Bizzell, Harris argues that we are "always *simultaneously* a part of several discourses, several communities." Moving from one community to another is not easy; it sometimes creates strains or crises with one's identity structure. Nevertheless, the idea of community is a powerful influence in our writing and our lives.

The shifting role of privileged positions in discourse is described by Linda Brodkey in "On the Subjects of Class and Gender in 'The Literacy Letters'." Brodkey's study involved a series of letters between teachers enrolled in a graduate seminar and students in an Adult Basic Education class. The author was familiar with Basic Writing, but she writes, "Nothing I had read or remembered from my own teaching prepared me for occasional moments of linguistic as well as discursive awkwardness from the teachers." Brodkey concludes that the unconscious privileged positions permeating "the dialect of educational discourse" are often destructive and debilitating.

The influence of gender is further explored in Elizabeth Flynn's essay, "Composing as a Woman." Flynn suggests that the composing processes of men and women may be different and offers examples of student writing to prove her point. "We ought not to assume that males and females use language in identical ways or represent the world in a similar fashion," she writes. An exploration of the differences in the modes of thinking and ways of composing promises to be a fruitful area for research.

The next essay addresses a continuing problem which composition teachers face—evaluation. Peter Elbow and Pat Belanoff argue that the portfolio is a more effective means of evaluation than the proficiency exam. The portfolio includes a wide variety of writing done over an extended period of time, whereas the proficiency exam is much more limited in scope. The kind of evaluation described in "Portfolios as a Substitute for Proficiency Examinations" can be adapted for use in many educational settings and holds promise for improving a difficult aspect of the profession.

The reader will be surprised at how many ideas running through this book come together in the concluding essay, Ann E. Berthoff's "Paulo Freire's Liberation Pedagogy," which was originally delivered as a General Session address at the NCTE Convention in Baltimore in November, 1989. The only real learning is learning that transforms, both the individual and the world. A pedagogy of liberation champions creativity; it argues for self-determination, freedom, and individual responsibility. The reader senses in this essay something larger than the local scene. Here is a pedagogy worthy of the drive for individual political freedom reverberating around the world. Perhaps there is no better or more beautiful way to announce the coming of a new century than in the word "liberation."

The Idea of a Writing Center

STEPHEN M. NORTH

This is an essay that began out of frustration. Despite the reference to writing centers in the title, it is not addressed to a writing center audience but to what is, for my purposes, just the opposite: those not involved with writing centers. Do not exclude yourself from this group just because you know that writing centers (or labs or clinics or places or however you think of them) exist; "involved" here means having directed such a place, having worked there for a minimum of 100 hours, or, at the very least, having talked about writing of your own there for five or more hours. The source of my frustration? Ignorance: the members of my profession, my colleagues, people I might see at MLA or CCCC or read in the pages of *College English,* do not understand what I do. They do not understand what does happen, what can happen, in a writing center.

Let me be clear here. Misunderstanding is something one expects—and almost gets used to—in the writing center business. The new faculty member in our writing-across-the-curriculum program, for example, who sends his students to get their papers "cleared up" in the Writing Center before they hand them in; the occasional student who tosses her paper on our reception desk, announcing that she'll "pick it up in an hour"; even the well-intentioned administrators who are so happy that we deal with "skills" or "fundamentals" or, to use the word that seems to subsume all others, "grammar" (or usually "GRAMMAR")—these are fairly predictable. But from people in English departments, people well trained in the complex relationship between writer and text, so painfully aware, if only from the composing of dissertations and theses, how lonely and difficult writing can be, I expect more. And I am generally disappointed.

What makes the situation particularly frustrating is that so many such people will vehemently claim that they do, *really,* understand the idea of a writing center. The non-English faculty, the students, the administrators—they may not understand what a writing center is or does, but they have no investment in their ignorance, and can often be educated. But in English departments this second layer of ignorance, this false sense of knowing, makes it doubly hard to get a message through. Indeed, even as you read now, you may be dismissing my argument as the ritual plaint of a "remedial" teacher begging for respectability, the product of a kind of professional paranoia. But while I might admit that there are elements of such a plaint involved—no one likes not

College English, 46 (September 1984), pp. 433-446. Copyright © 1984 by the National Council of Teachers of English. Reprinted with permission.

to be understood—there is a good deal more at stake. For in coming to terms with this ignorance, I have discovered that it is only a symptom of a much deeper, more serious problem. As a profession I think we are holding on tightly to attitudes and beliefs about the teaching and learning of writing that we thought we had left behind. In fact, my central contention—in the first half of this essay, anyway—is that the failure or inability of the bulk of the English teaching profession, including even those most ardent spokespersons of the so-called "revolution" in the teaching of writing, to perceive the idea of a writing center suggests that, for all our noise and bother about composition, we have fundamentally changed very little.

Let me begin by citing a couple of typical manifestations of this ignorance from close to home. Our writing center has been open for seven years. During that time we have changed our philosophy a little bit as a result of lessons learned from experience, but for the most part we have always been open to anybody in the university community, worked with writers at any time during the composing of a given piece of writing, and dealt with whole pieces of discourse, and not exercises on what might be construed as "subskills" (spelling, punctuation, etc.) outside of the context of the writer's work.

We have delivered the message about what we do to the university generally, and the English department in particular, in a number of ways: letters, flyers, posters, class presentations, information booths, and so on. And, as long as there has been a writing committee, advisory to the director of the writing program, we have sent at least one representative. So it is all the more surprising, and disheartening, that the text for our writing program flyer, composed and approved by that committee, should read as follows:

> The University houses the Center for Writing, founded in 1978 to sponsor the interdisciplinary study of writing. Among its projects are a series of summer institutes for area teachers of writing, a resource center for writers and teachers of writing, *and a tutorial facility for those with special problems in composition.* (My emphasis)

I don't know, quite frankly, how that copy got past me. What are these "special problems"? What would constitute a regular problem, and why wouldn't we talk to the owner of one? Is this hint of pathology, in some mysterious way, a good marketing ploy?

But that's only the beginning. Let me cite another, in many ways more common and painful instance. As a member, recently, of a doctoral examination committee, I conducted an oral in composition theory and practice. One of the candidate's areas of concentration was writing centers, so as part of the exam I gave her a piece of student writing and asked her to play tutor to my student. The session went well enough, but afterward, as we evaluated the entire exam, one of my fellow examiners—a longtime colleague and friend—said that, while the candidate handled the tutoring nicely, he was surprised that the student who had written the paper would have bothered with the Writing Center in the first place. He would not recommend a student to the Center, he said, "unless there were something like twenty-five errors per page."

People make similar remarks all the time, stopping me or members of my staff in the halls, or calling us into offices, to discuss—in hushed tones, frequently—their current "impossible" or difficult students. There was a time, I will confess, when I let my frustration get the better of me. I would be more or less combative, confrontational, challenging the instructor's often well-intentioned but not very useful "diagnosis." We no longer bother with such confrontations; they never worked very well, and they risk undermining the genuine compassion our teachers have for the students they single out. Nevertheless, their behavior makes it clear that for them, a writing center is to illiteracy what a cross between Lourdes and a hospice would be to serious illness: one goes there hoping for miracles, but ready to face the inevitable. In their minds, clearly, writers fall into three fairly distinct groups: the talented, the average, and the others; and the Writing Center's only logical *raison d'etre* must be to handle those others—those, as the flyer proclaims, with "special problems."

Mine is not, of course, the only English department in which such misconceptions are rife. One comes away from any large meeting of writing center people laden with similar horror stories. And in at least one case, a member of such a department—Malcolm Hayward of the Indiana University of Pennsylvania—decided formally to explore and document his faculty's perceptions of the center, and to compare them with the views the center's staff held.[1] His aim, in a two-part survey of both groups, was to determine, first, which goals each group deemed most important in the teaching of writing; and, second, what role they thought the writing center ought to play in that teaching, which goals it ought to concern itself with.

Happily, the writing faculty and the center staff agreed on what the primary goals in teaching writing should be (in the terms offered by Hayward's questionnaire): the development of general patterns of thinking and writing. Unhappily, the two groups disagreed rather sharply about the reasons for referring students to the center. For faculty members the two primary criteria were grammar and punctuation. Tutors, on the other hand, ranked organization "as by far the single most important factor for referral," followed rather distantly by paragraphing, grammar, and style. In short, Hayward's survey reveals the same kind of misunderstanding on his campus that I find so frustrating on my own: the idea that a writing center can only be some sort of skills center, a fix-it shop.

Now if this were just a matter of local misunderstanding, if Hayward and I could straighten it out with a few workshops or lectures, maybe I wouldn't need to write this essay for a public forum. But that is not the case. For whatever reasons, writing centers have gotten mostly this kind of press, have been represented—or misrepresented—more often as fix-it shops than in any other way, and in some fairly influential places. Consider, for example, this passage from Barbara E. Fassler Walvoord's *Helping Students Write Well: A Guide for Teachers in All Disciplines* (New York: Modern Language Association, 1981).

What makes it particularly odd, at least in terms of my argument, is that Professor Walvoord's book, in many other ways, offers to faculty the kind of perspective on writing (writing as a complex process, writing as a way of learning) that I might offer myself. Yet here she is on writing centers:

> If you are very short of time, if you think you are not skilled enough to deal with mechanical problems, or if you have a number of students with serious difficulties, you may wish to let the skills center carry the ball for mechanics and spend your time on other kinds of writing and learning problems. (p. 63)

Don't be misled by Professor Walvoord's use of the "skills center" label; in her index the entry for "Writing centers" reads "See skills centers"—precisely the kind of interchangeable terminology I find so abhorrent. On the other hand, to do Professor Walvoord justice, she does recommend that teachers become "at least generally aware of how your skills center works with students, what it's basic philosophy is, and what goals it sets for the students in your class," but it seems to me that she has already restricted the possible scope of such a philosophy pretty severely: "deal with mechanical problems"? "carry the ball for mechanics"?

Still, as puzzling and troubling as it is to see Professor Walvoord publishing misinformation about writing centers, it is even more painful, downright maddening, to read one's own professional obituary; to find, in the pages of a reputable professional journal, that what you do has been judged a failure, written off. Maxine Hairston's "The Winds of Change: Thomas Kuhn and the Revolution in the Teaching of Writing" (*College Composition and Communication*, 33 [1982], 76-88) is an attempt to apply the notion of a "paradigm shift" to the field of composition teaching. In the course of doing so, Professor Hairston catalogues, under the subheading "Signs of Change," what she calls "ad hoc" remedies to the writing "crisis":

> Following the pattern that Kuhn describes in his book, our first response to crisis has been to improvise ad hoc measures to try to patch the cracks and keep the system running. Among the first responses were the writing labs that sprang up about ten years ago to give first aid to students who seemed unable to function within the traditional paradigm. Those labs are still with us, but they're still only giving first aid and treating symptoms. They have not solved the problem. (p. 82)

What first struck me about this assessment—what probably strikes most people in the writing center business—is the mistaken history, the notion that writing labs "sprang up about ten years ago." The fact is, writing "labs," as Professor Hairston chooses to call them, have been around in one form or another since at least the 1930s when Carrie Stanley was already working with writers at the University of Iowa. Moreover, this limited conception of what such places can do—the fix-it shop image—has been around far longer than ten years, too. Robert Moore, in a 1950 *College English* article, "The Writing Clinic and the Writing Laboratory" (7 [1950], 388-393), writes that "writing clinics and writing laboratories are becoming increasingly popular among American universities and colleges as remedial agencies for removing students' deficiencies in composition" (p. 388).

Still, you might think that I ought to be happier with Professor Hairston's position than with, say, Professor Walvoord's. And to some extent I am: even if she mistakenly assumes that the skill and drill model represents all writing centers equally well, she at least recognizes its essential futility. Nevertheless—and this is what bothers me most about her position—her dismissal fails to lay the blame for these worst versions of writing centers on the right heads. According to her "sprang up" historical sketch, these places simply appeared—like so many mushrooms?—to do battle with illiteracy. "They" are still with "us," but "they" haven't solved the problem. What is missing here is a doer, an agent, a creator—someone to take responsibility. The implication is that "they" done it—"they" being, apparently, the places themselves.

But that won't wash. "They," to borrow from Walt Kelly, is *us:* members of English departments, teachers of writing. Consider, as evidence, the pattern of writing center origins as revealed in back issues of *The Writing Lab Newsletter:* the castoff, windowless classroom (or in some cases literally, closet), the battered desks, the old textbooks, a phone (maybe), no budget, and, almost inevitably, a director with limited status—an untenured or non-tenure track faculty member, a teaching assistant, an undergraduate, a "paraprofessional," etc. Now who do you suppose has determined what is to happen in that center? Not the director, surely; not the staff, if there is one. The mandate is clearly from the sponsoring body, usually an English department. And lest you think that things are better where space and money are not such serious problems, I urge you to visit a center where a good bit of what is usually grant money has been spent in the first year or two of the center's operation. Almost always, the money will have been used on materials: drills, texts, machines, tapes, carrels, headphones—the works. And then the director, hired on "soft" money, without political clout, is locked into an approach because she or he has to justify the expense by using the materials.

Clearly, then, where there is or has been misplaced emphasis on so-called basics or drill, where centers have been prohibited from dealing with the writing that students do for their classes—where, in short, writing centers have been of the kind that Professor Hairston is quite correctly prepared to write off—it is because the agency that created the center in the first place, too often an English department, has made it so. The grammar and drill center, the fix-it shop, the first aid station—these are neither the vestiges of some paradigm left behind nor pedagogical aberrations that have been overlooked in the confusion of the "revolution" in the teaching of writing, but that will soon enough be set on the right path, or done away with. They are, instead, the vital and authentic reflection of a way of thinking about writing and the teaching of writing that is alive and well and living in English departments everywhere.

* * *

But if my claims are correct—if this is not what writing centers are or, if it is what they are, it is not what they should be—then what are, and what *should* they be? What *is* the idea of a writing center? By way of answer, let me return briefly to the family of metaphors by which my sources have characterized their idea of a writing center: Robert Moore's "removing students' deficiencies," Hairston's "first aid" and "treating symptoms," my colleague's "twenty-five errors per page," Hayward's punctuation and grammar referrers, and Walvoord's "carrying the ball for mechanics" (where, at least, writing centers are athletic and not surgical). All these imply essentially the same thing: that writing centers define their province in terms of a given curriculum, taking over those portions of it that "regular" teachers are willing to cede or, presumably, unable to handle. Over the past six years or so I have visited more than fifty centers, and read descriptions of hundreds of others, and I can assure you that there are indeed centers of this kind, centers that can trace their conceptual lineage back at least as far as Moore. But the "new" writing center has a somewhat shorter history. It is the result of a documentable resurgence, a renaissance if you will, that began in the early 1970s. In fact, the flurry of activity that caught Professor Hairston's attention, and which she mistook for the beginnings of the "old" center, marked instead the genesis of a center which defined its province in a radically different way. Though I have some serious reservations about Hairston's use of Kuhn's paradigm model to describe what happens in composition teaching, I will for the moment put things in her terms: the new writing center, far from marking the end of an era, is the embodiment, the epitome, of a new one. It represents the marriage of what are arguably the two most powerful contemporary perspectives on teaching writing: first, that writing is most usefully viewed as a process; and second, that writing curricula need to be student-centered. This new writing center, then, defines its province not in terms of some curriculum, but in terms of the writers it serves.

To say that writing centers are based on a view of writing as a process is, original good intentions notwithstanding, not to say very much anymore. The slogan—and I daresay that is what it has become—has been devalued, losing most of its impact and explanatory power. Let me use it, then, to make the one distinction of which it still seems capable: in a writing center the object is to make sure that writers, and not necessarily their texts, are what get changed by instruction. In axiom form it goes like this: Our job is to produce better writers, not better writing. Any given project—a class assignment, a law school application letter, an encyclopedia entry, a dissertation proposal—is for the writer the prime, often the exclusive concern. That particular text, its success or failure, is what brings them to talk to us in the first place. In the center, though, we look beyond or through that particular project, that particular text, and see it as an occasion for addressing *our* primary concern, the process by which it is produced.

At this point, however, the writing-as-a-process slogan tends to lose its usefulness. That "process," after all, has been characterized as everything from the reception of divine inspriation to a set of nearly algorithmic rules for producing the five paragraph theme. In between are the more widely accepted and, for the moment, more respectable descriptions derived from composing aloud protocols, interviews, videotaping, and so on. None of those, in any case, represent the composing process we seek in a writing center. The version we want can only be found, in as yet unarticulated form, in the writer we are working with. I think probably the best way to describe a writing center tutor's relationship to composing is to say that a tutor is a holist devoted to a participant-observer methodology. This may seem, at first glance, too passive —or, perhaps, too glamorous, legitimate, or trendy—a role in which to cast tutors. But consider this passage from Paul Diesing's *Patterns of Discovery in the Social Sciences* (Hawthorne, N.Y.: Aldine, 1971):

> Holism is not, in the participant-observer method, an a priori belief that everything is related to everything else. It is rather the methodological necessity of pushing on to new aspects and new kinds of evidence in order to make sense of what one has already observed and to test the validity of one's interpretations. A belief in the organic unity of living systems may also be present, but this belief by itself would not be sufficient to force a continual expansion of one's observations. It is rather one's inability to develop an intelligible and validated partial model that drives one on. (p. 167)

How does this definition relate to tutors and composing? Think of the writer writing as a kind of host setting. What we want to do in a writing center is fit into—observe and participate in—this ordinarily solo ritual of writing. To do this, we need to do what any participant-observer must do: see what happens during this "ritual," try to make sense of it, observe some more, revise our model, and so on indefinitely, all the time behaving in a way the host finds acceptable. For validation and correction of our model, we quite naturally rely on the writer, who is, in turn, a willing collaborator in—and, usually, beneficiary of—the entire process. This process precludes, obviously, a reliance on or a clinging to any predetermined models of "the" composing process, except as crude topographical guides to what the "territory" of composing processes might look like. The only composing process that matters in a writing center is "a" composing process, and it "belongs" to, is acted out by, only one given writer.

It follows quite naturally, then, that any curriculum—any plan of action the tutor follows—is going to be student-centered in the strictest sense of that term. That is, it will not derive from a generalized model of composing, or be based on where the student ought to be because she is a freshman or sophomore, but will begin from where the student is, and move where the student moves—an approach possible only if, as James Moffett suggests in *Teaching the Universe of Discourse* (Boston: Houghton Mifflin, 1968), the teacher (or tutor in this case) "shifts his gaze from the subject to the learner, for the subject is in the learner" (p. 67). The result is what might be called a pedagogy of direct intervention. Whereas in the "old" center instruction tends to take place after or apart from writing, and tends to focus on the correction of textual problems, in the "new" center the teaching takes place as much as possible during writing, during the activity being learned, and tends to focus on the activity itself.

I do not want to push the participant-observer analogy too far. Tutors are not, finally, researchers: they must measure their success not in terms of the constantly changing model they create, but in terms of changes in the writer. Rather than being fearful of disturbing the "ritual" of composing, they observe it and are charged to change it: to interfere, to get in the way, to participate in ways that will leave the "ritual" itself forever altered. The whole enterprise seems to me most natural. Nearly everyone who writes likes—and needs—to talk about his or her writing, preferably to someone who will really listen, who knows how to listen, and knows how to talk about writing too. Maybe in a perfect world, all writers would have their own ready auditor—a teacher, a classmate, a roommate, an editor—who would not only listen but draw them out, ask them questions they would not think to ask themselves. A writing center is an institutional response to this need. Clearly writing centers can never hope to satisfy this need themselves; on my campus alone, the student-to-tutor ratio would be about a thousand to one. Writing centers are simply one manifestation—polished and highly visible—of a dialogue about writing that is central to higher education.

* * *

As is clear from my citations in the first half of this essay, however, what seems perfectly natural to me is not so natural for everyone else. One part of the difficulty, it seems to me now, is not theoretical at all, but practical, a question of coordination or division of labor. It usually comes in the form of a question like this: "If I'm doing process-centered teaching in my class, why do I need a writing center? How can I use it?" For a long time I tried to soft-pedal my answers to this question. For instance, in my dissertation ("Writing Centers: A Sourcebook," Diss. SUNY at Albany, 1978) I talked about complementing or intensifying classroom instruction. Or, again, in our center we tried using, early on, what is a fairly common device among writing centers, a referral form; at one point it even had a sort of diagnostic taxonomy, a checklist, by which teachers could communicate to us their concerns about the writers they sent us.

But I have come with experience to take a harder, less conciliatory position. The answer to the question in all cases is that teachers, as teachers, do not need, and cannot use, a writing center: only writers need it, only writers can use it. You cannot parcel out some portion of a given student for us to deal with ("You take care of editing, I'll deal with invention"). Nor should you require that all of your students drop by with an early draft of a research paper to get a reading from a fresh audience. You should not scrawl, at the bottom of a failing paper, "Go to the Writing Center." Even those of you who, out of genuine concern, bring students to a writing center, almost by the hand, to make sure they know that we won't hurt them—even you are essentially out of line. Occasionally we manage to convert such writers from people who have to see us to people who want to, but most often they either come as if for a kind of detention, or they drift away. (It would be nice if in writing, as in so many things, people would do what we tell them because it's good for them, but they don't. If and when *they* are ready, we will be here.)

In short, we are not here to serve, supplement, back up, complement, reinforce, or otherwise be defined by any external curriculum. We are here to talk to writers. If they happen to come from your classes, you might take it as a compliment to your assignments, in that your writers are engaged in them enough to want to talk about their work. On the other hand, we do a fair amount of trade in people working on ambiguous or poorly designed assignments, and far too much work with writers whose writing has received caustic, hostile, or otherwise unconstructive commentary.

I suppose this declaration of independence sounds more like a declaration of war, and that is obviously not what I intend, especially since the primary casualites would be the students and writers we all aim to serve. And I see no reason that writing centers and classroom teachers cannot cooperate as well as coexist. For example, the first rule in our Writing Center is that we are professionals at what we do. While that does, as I have argued, give us the freedom of self-definition, it also carries with it a responsibility to respect our fellow professionals. Hence we never play student-advocates in teacher-student relationships. The guidelines are very clear. In all instances the student must understand that we support the teacher's position completely. (Or, to put it in less loaded terms—for we are not teacher advocates either—the instructor is simply part of the rhetorical context in which the writer is trying to operate. We cannot change that context: all we can do is help the writer learn how to operate in it and other contexts like it.) In practice, this rule means that we never evaluate or second-guess any teacher's syllabus, assignments, comments, or grades. If students are unclear about any of those, we send them back to the teacher to get clear. Even in those instances I mentioned above—where writers come in confused by what seem to be poorly designed assignments, or crushed by what appear to be unwarrantedly hostile comments—we pass no judgment, at least as far as the student is concerned. We simply try, every way we can, to help the writer make constructive sense of the situation.

In return, of course, we expect equal professional courtesy. We need, first of all, instructors' trust that our work with writers-in-progress on academic assignments is not plagiarism, any more than a conference with the teacher would be—that, to put it the way I most often hear it, we will not write students' papers for them. Second, instructors must grant us the same respect we grant them—that is, they must neither evaluate nor second-guess our work with writers. We are, of course, most willing to talk about that work. But we do not take kindly to the perverse kind of thinking represented in remarks like,

"Well, I had a student hand in a paper that he took to the writing center, and it was *still* full of errors." The axiom, if you will recall, is that we aim to make better writers, not necessarily—or immediately—better texts.

Finally, we can always use classroom teachers' cooperation in helping us explain to students what we do. As a first step, of course, I am asking that they revise their thinking about what a writing center can do. Beyond that, in our center we find it best to go directly to the students ourselves. That is, rather than sending out a memo or announcement for the teachers to read to their classes, we simply send our staff, upon invitation, into classes to talk with students or, better yet, to do live tutorials. The standard presentation, a ten-minute affair, gives students a person, a name, and a face to remember the Center by. The live tutorials take longer, but we think they are worth it. We ask the instructor to help us find a writer willing to have a draft (or a set of notes or even just the assignment) reproduced for the whole class. Then the Writing Center person does, with the participation of the entire class, what we do in the Center: talk about writing with the writer. In our experience the instructors learn as much about the Center from these sessions as the students.

* * *

To argue that writing centers are not here to serve writing class curricula is not to say, however, that they are here to replace them. In our center, anyway, nearly every member of the full-time staff is or has been a classroom teacher of writing. Even our undergraduate tutors work part of their time in an introductory writing course. We all recognize and value the power of classroom teaching, and we take pride in ourselves as professionals in that setting too. But working in both situations makes us acutely aware of crucial differences between talking about writing in the context of a class, and talking about it in the context of the Center. When we hold student conferences in our classes, we are the teacher, in the writers' minds especially, the assigner and evaluator of the writing in question. And for the most part we are pretty busy people, with conference appointments scheduled on the half hour, and a line forming outside the office. For efficiency the papers-in-progress are in some assigned form—an outline, a first draft, a statement of purpose with bibliography and note cards; and while the conference may lead to further composing, there is rarely the time or the atmosphere for composing to happen during the conference itself. Last but not least, the conference is likely to be a command performance, our idea, not the writer's.

When we are writing center tutors, all of that changes. First of all, conferences are the writer's idea; he or she seeks us out. While we have an appointment book that offers half hour appointment slots, our typical session is fifty minutes, and we average between three and four per writer; we can afford to give a writer plenty of time. The work-in-progress is in whatever form the writer has managed to put it in, which may make tutoring less efficient, but which clearly makes it more student-centered, allowing us to begin where the writers are, not where we told them to be. This also means that in most cases the writers come prepared, even anxious to get on with their work, to begin or to keep on composing. Whereas going to keep a conference with a teacher is, almost by definition, a kind of goal or deadline—a stopping place— going to talk in the writing center is a means of getting started, or a way to keep going. And finally—in a way subsuming all the rest—we are not the teacher. We did not assign the writing, and we will not grade it. However little that distinction might mean in our behaviors, it seems to mean plenty to the writers.

What these differences boil down to, in general pedagogical terms, are timing and motivation. The fact is, not everyone's interest in writing, their need or desire to write or learn to write, coincides with the fifteen or thirty weeks they spend in writing courses—especially when, as is currently the case at so many institutions, those weeks are required. When writing does become important, a writing center can be there in a way that our regular classes cannot. Charles Cooper, in an unpublished paper called "What College Writers Need to Know" (1979), put it this way:

> The first thing college writers need to know is that they can improve as writers and the second is that they will never reach a point where they cannot improve further. One writing course, two courses, three courses may not be enough. If they're on a campus which takes writing seriously, they will be able to find the courses they need to feel reasonably confident they can fulfill the requests which will be made of them in their academic work. . . . Throughout their college years they should also be able to find on a drop-in, no-fee basis expert tutorial help with any writing problem they encounter in a paper. (p. 1)

A writing center's advantage in motivation is a function of the same phenomenon. Writers come looking for us because, more often than not, they are genuinely, deeply engaged with their material, anxious to wrestle it into the best form they can: they are motivated to write. If we agree that the biggest obstacle to overcome in teaching anything, writing included, is getting learners to decide that they want to learn, then what a writing center does is cash in on motivation that the writer provides. This teaching at the conjunction of timing and motivation is most strikingly evident when we work with writers doing "real world" tasks: application essays for law, medical, and graduate schools, newspaper and magazine articles, or poems and stories. Law school application writers are suddenly willing—sometimes overwhelmingly so—to concern themselves with audience, purpose, and persona, and to revise over and over again. But we see the same excitement in writers working on literature or history or philosophy papers, or preparing dissertation proposals, or getting ready to tackle comprehensive exams. Their primary concern is with their material, with some existential context where new ideas must merge with old, and suddenly writing is a vehicle, a means to an end, and not an end in itself. These opportunities to talk with excited writers at the height of their engagement with their work are the lifeblood of a writing center.

The essence of the writing center method, then, is this talking. If we conceive of writing as a relatively rhythmic and repeatable kind of behavior, then for a writer to improve, that behavior, that rhythm, has to change—preferably, though not necessarily, under the writer's control. Such changes can be fostered, of course, by work outside of the act of composing itself—hence the success of the classical discipline of imitation, or more recent ones like sentence combining or the tagmemic heuristic, all of which, with practice, "merge" with and affect composing. And, indeed, depending on the writer, none of these tactics would be ruled out in a writing center. By and large, however, we find that the best breaker of old rhythms, the best creator of new ones, is our style of live intervention, our talk in all its forms.

The kind of writing does not substantially change the approach. We always want the writer to tell us about the rhetorical context—what the purpose of the writing is, who its audience is, how the writer hopes to present herself. We want to know about other constraints—deadlines, earlier experiences with the same audience or genre, research completed or not completed, and so on. In other ways, though, the variations on the kind of talk are endless. We can question, praise, cajole, criticize, acknowledge, badger, plead—even cry. We can read: silently, aloud, together, separately. We can play with options. We can both write—as, for example, in response to sample essay exam questions—and compare opening strategies. We can poke around in resources—comparing, perhaps, the manuscript conventions of the Modern Language Association with those of the American Psychological Association. We can ask writers to compose aloud while we listen, or we can compose aloud, and the writer can watch and listen.

In this essay, however, I will say no more about the nature of this talk. One reason is that most of what can be said, for the moment, has been said in print already. There is, for example, my own "Training Tutors to Talk About Writing" (*CCC,* 33 [1982], 434-441), or Muriel Harris' "Modeling: A Process Method of Teaching" (*College English,* 45, [1983], 74-84). And there are several other sources, including a couple of essay collections, that provide some insights into the hows and whys of tutorial talk.[2]

A second reason, though, seems to me more substantive, and symptomatic of the kinds of misunderstanding I have tried to dispel here. We don't know very much, in other than a practitioner's anecdotal way, about the dynamics of the tutorial. The same can be said, of course, with regard to talk about writing in any setting—the classroom, the peer group, the workshop, the teacher-student conference, and so on. But while ignorance of the nature of talk in those settings does not threaten their existence, it may do precisely that in writing centers. That is, given the idea of the writing center I have set forth here, talk is everything. If the writing center is ever to prove its worth in other than quantitative terms—numbers of students seen, for example, or hours of tutorials provided—it will have to do so by describing this talk: what characterizes it, what effects it has, how it can be enhanced.

Unfortunately, the same "proofreading-shop-in-the-basement" mentality that undermines the pedagogical efforts of the writing center hampers research as well. So far, most of the people hired to run such places have neither the time, the training, nor the status to undertake any serious research. Moreover, the few of us lucky enough to even consider the possibility of research have found that there are other difficulties. One is that writing center work is often not considered fundable—that is, relevant to a wide enough audience—even though there are about a thousand such facilities in the country, a figure which suggests that there must be at least ten or fifteen thousand tutorials every school day, and even though research into any kind of talk about writing is relevant for the widest possible audience. Second, we have discovered that focusing our scholarly efforts on writing centers may be a professional liability. Even if we can publish our work (and that is by no means easy), there is no guarantee that it will be viewed favorably by tenure and promotion review committees. Composition itself is suspect enough; writing centers, a kind of obscure backwater, seem no place for a scholar.

These conditions may be changing. Manuscripts for *The Writing Center Journal*, for example, suggest that writing center folk generally are becoming more research-oriented; there were sessions scheduled at this year's meetings of the MLA and NCTE on research in or relevant to writing centers. In an even more tangible signal of change, the State University of New York has made funds available for our Albany center to develop an appropriate case study methodology for writing center tutorials. Whether this trend continues or not, my point remains the same. Writing centers, like any other portion of a college writing curriculum, need time and space for appropriate research and reflection if they are to more clearly understand what they do, and figure out how to do it better. The great danger is that the very misapprehensions that put them in basements to begin with may conspire to keep them there.

* * *

It is possible that I have presented here, at least by implication, too dismal a portrait of the current state of writing centers. One could, as a matter of fact, mount a pretty strong argument that things have never been better. There are, for example, several regional writing center associations that have annual meetings, and the number of such associations increases every year. Both *The Writing Lab Newsletter* and *The Writing Center Journal*, the two publications in the field, have solid circulations. This year at NCTE, for the first time, writing center people met as a recognized National Assembly, a major step up from their previous Special Interest Session status.

And on individual campuses all over the country, writing centers have begun to expand their institutional roles. So, for instance, some centers have established resource libraries for writing teachers. They sponsor readings or reading series by poets and fiction writers, and annual festivals to celebrate writing of all kinds. They serve as clearinghouses for information on where to publish, on writing programs, competitions, scholarships, and so on; and they sponsor such competitions themselves, even putting out their own publications.

They design and conduct workshops for groups with special needs—essay exam takers, for example, or job application writers. They are involved with, or have even taken over entirely, the task of training new teaching assistants. They have played central roles in the creation of writing-across-the-curriculum programs. And centers have extended themselves beyond their own institutions, sending tutors to other schools (often high schools), or helping other institutions set up their own facilities. In some cases, they have made themselves available to the wider community, often opening a "Grammar Hotline" or "Grammarphone"—a service so popular at one institution, in fact, that a major publishing company provided funding to keep it open over the summer.

Finally, writing centers have gotten into the business of offering academic credit. As a starting point they have trained their tutors in formal courses or, in some instances, "paid" their tutors in credits rather than money. They have set up independent study arrangements to sponsor both academic and non-academic writing experiences. They have offered credit-bearing courses of their own; in our center, for example, we are piloting an introductory writing course that uses Writing Center staff members as small group leaders.

I would very much like to say that all this activity is a sure sign that the idea of a writing center is here to stay, that the widespread misunderstandings I described in this essay, especially those held so strongly in English departments, are dissolving. But in good conscience I cannot. Consider the activities we are talking about. Some of them, of course, are either completely or mostly public relations: a way of making people aware that a writing center exists, and that (grammar hotlines aside) it deals in more than usage and punctuation. Others—like the resource library, the clearinghouse, or the training of new teaching assistants—are more substantive, and may well belong in a writing center, but most of them end up there in the first place because nobody else wants to do them. As for the credit generating, that is simply pragmatic. The bottom line in academic budget making is calculated in student credit hours; when budgets are tight, as they will be for the foreseeable future, facilities that generate no credits are the first to be cut. Writing centers—even really good writing centers—have proved no exception.

None of these efforts to promote writing centers suggest that there is any changed understanding of the idea of a writing center. Indeed, it is as though what writing centers do that really matters—talking to writers—were not enough. That being the case, enterprising directors stake out as large a claim as they can in more visible or acceptable territory. All of these efforts—and, I assure you, my center does its share—have about them an air of shrewdness, or desperation, the trace of a survival instinct at work. I am not such a purist as to suggest that these things are all bad. At the very least they can be good for staff morale. Beyond that I think they may eventually help make writing centers the centers of consciousness about writing on campuses, a kind of physical locus for the ideas and ideals of college or university or high school commitment to writing—a status to which they might well aspire and which, judging by results on a few campuses already, they can achieve.

But not this way, not via the back door, not—like some marginal ballplayer—by doing whatever it takes to stay on the team. If writing centers are going to finally be accepted, surely they must be accepted on their own terms, as places whose primary responsibility, whose only reason for being, is to talk to writers. That is their heritage, and it stretches back farther than the last 1960s or the early 1970s, or to Iowa in the 1930s—back, in fact, to Athens, where in a busy marketplace a tutor called Socrates set up the same kind of shop: open to all comers, no fees charged, offering, on whatever subject a visitor might propose, a continuous dialectic that is, finally, its own end.

Notes

1 "Assessing Attitudes Toward the Writing Center," *The Writing Center Journal,* 3, No. 2 (1983), 1-11.

2 See, for example, *Tutoring Writing: A Sourcebook for Writing Labs,* ed. Muriel Harris (Glenview, Ill.: Scott-Foresman, 1982); and *New Directions for College Learning Assistance: Improving Writing Skills,* ed. Phyllis Brooks and Thom Hawkins (San Francisco: Jossey-Bass, 1981).

Closing My Eyes as I Speak:
An Argument for Ignoring Audience

PETER ELBOW

Very often people don't listen to you when you speak to them. It's only when you talk to yourself that they prick up their ears.

John Ashbery

When I am talking to a person or a group and struggling to find words or thoughts, I often find myself involuntarily closing my eyes as I speak. I realize now that this behavior is an instinctive attempt to blot out awareness of audience when I need all my concentration for just trying to figure out or express what I want to say. Because the audience is so imperiously *present* in a speaking situation, my instinct reacts with this active attempt to avoid audience awareness. This behavior—in a sense impolite or anti-social—is not so uncommon. Even when we write, alone in a room to an absent audience, there are occasions when we are struggling to figure something out and need to push aside awareness of those absent readers. As Donald Murray puts it, "My sense of audience is so strong that I have to suppress my conscious awareness of audience to hear what the text demands" (Berkenkotter and Murray 171). In recognition of how pervasive the role of audience is in writing, I write to celebrate the benefits of ignoring audience.[1]

It will be clear that my argument for writing without audience awareness is not meant to undermine the many good reasons for writing *with* audience awareness some of the time. (For example, that we are liable to neglect audience because we write in solitude; that young people often need more practice in taking into account points of view different from their own; and that students often have an impoverished sense of writing as communication because they have only written in a school setting to teachers.) Indeed I would claim some part in these arguments for audience awareness—which now seem to be getting out of hand.

I start with a limited claim: even though ignoring audience will usually lead to weak writing at first—to what Linda Flower calls "writer-based prose," this weak writing can help us in the end to better writing than we would have written if we'd kept readers in mind from the start. Then I will make a more

College English, 49 (January 1987), pp. 50-69. Copyright © 1987 by the National Council of Teachers of English. Reprinted with permission.

ambitious claim: writer-based prose is sometimes better than reader-based prose. Finally I will explore some of the theory underlying these issues of audience.

A Limited Claim

It's not that writers should never think about their audience. It's a question of when. An audience is a field of force. The closer we come—the more we think about these readers—the stronger the pull they exert on the contents of our minds. The practical question, then, is always whether a particular audience functions as a helpful field of force or one that confuses or inhibits us.

Some audiences, for example, are *inviting* or *enabling*. When we think about them as we write, we think of more and better things to say—and what we think somehow arrives more coherently structured than usual. It's like talking to the perfect listener: we feel smart and come up with ideas we didn't know we had. Such audiences are helpful to keep in mind right from the start.

Other audiences, however, are powerfully *inhibiting*—so much so, in certain cases, that awareness of them as we write blocks writing altogether. There are certain people who always make us feel dumb when we try to speak to them: we can't find words or thoughts. As soon as we get out of their presence, all the things we wanted to say pop back into our minds. Here is a student telling what happens when she tries to follow the traditional advice about audience.

> You know _____ [author of a text] tells us to pay attention to the audience that will be reading our papers, and I gave that a try. I ended up without putting a word on paper until I decided the hell with _____ ; I'm going to write to who I damn well want to; otherwise I can hardly write at all.

Admittedly, there are some occasions when we benefit from keeping a threatening audience in mind from the start. We've been putting off writing that letter to that person who intimidates us. When we finally sit down and write *to* them—walk right up to them, as it were, and look them in the eye—we may manage to stand up to the threat and grasp the nettle and thereby find just what we need to write.

Most commonly, however, the effect of audience awareness is somewhere between the two extremes: the awareness disturbs or disrupts our writing and thinking without completely blocking it. For example, when we have to write to someone we find intimidating (and of course students often perceive teachers as intimidating), we often start thinking wholly defensively. As we write down each thought or sentence, our mind fills with thoughts of how the intended reader will criticize or object to it. So we try to qualify or soften what we've just written—or write out some answer to a possible objection. Our writing becomes tangled. Sometimes we get so tied in knots that we cannot even figure out what we *think*. We may not realize how often audience awareness has this effect on our students when we don't see the writing processes behind their papers: we just see texts that are either tangled or empty.

Another example. When we have to write to readers with whom we have an awkward relationship, we often start beating around the bush and feeling shy or scared, or start to write in a stilted, overly careful style or voice. (Think about the cute, too-clever style of many memos we get in our departmental mailboxes—the awkward self-consciousness academics experience when writing to other academics.) When students are asked to write to readers they have not met or cannot imagine, such as "the general reader" or "the educated public," they often find nothing to say except cliches they know *they* don't even quite believe.

When we realize that an audience is somehow confusing or inhibiting us, the solution is fairly obvious. We can ignore that audience altogether during the *early* stages of writing and direct our words only to ourselves or to no one in particular—or even to the "wrong" audience, that is, to an *inviting* audience of trusted friends or allies. This strategy often dissipates the confusion; the clenched, defensive discourse starts to run clear. Putting audience out of mind is of course a traditional practice: serious writers have long used private journals for early explorations of feeling, thinking, or language. But many writing teachers seem to think that students can get along without the private writing serious writers find so crucial—or even that students will *benefit* from keeping their audience in mind for the whole time. Things often don't work out that way.

After we have figured out our thinking in copious exploratory or draft writing—perhaps finding the right voice or stance as well—*then* we can follow the traditional rhetorical advice: think about readers and revise carefully to adjust our words and thoughts to our intended audience. For a particular audience it may even turn out that we need to *disguise* our point of view. But it's hard to disguise something while engaged in trying to figure it out. As writers, then, we need to learn when to think about audience and when to put readers out of mind.

Many people are too quick to see Flower's "writer-based prose" as an analysis of what's wrong with this type of writing and miss the substantial degree to which she was celebrating a natural, and indeed developmentally enabling, response to cognitive overload. What she doesn't say, however, despite her emphasis on planning and conscious control in the writing process, is that we can *teach* students to notice when audience awareness is getting in their way—and when this happens, consciously to put aside the needs of readers for a while. She seems to assume that when an overload occurs, the writer-based gear will, as it were, automatically kick into action to relieve it. In truth, of course, writers often persist in using a malfunctioning *reader*-based gear despite the overload—thereby mangling their language or thinking. Though Flower likes to rap the knuckles of people who suggest a "correct" or "natural" order for steps in the writing process, she implies such an order here:

when attention to audience causes an overload, start out by ignoring them while you attend to your thinking; after you work out your thinking, turn your attention to audience.

Thus if we ignore audience while writing on a topic about which we are not expert or about which our thinking is still evolving, we are likely to produce exploratory writing that is unclear to anyone else—perhaps even inconsistent or a complete mess. Yet by doing this exploratory "swamp work" in conditions of safety, we can often coax our thinking through a process of new discovery and development. In this way we can end up with something better than we could have produced if we'd tried to write to our audience all along. In short, ignoring audience can lead to worse drafts but better revisions. (Because we are professional and adults, we often write in the role of expert: we may know what we think without new exploratory writing; we may even be able to speak confidently to critical readers. But students seldom experience this confident professional stance in their writing. And think how much richer *our* writing would be if we defined ourselves as *in*expert and allowed ourselves private writing for new explorations of those views we are allegedly sure of.)

Notice then that two pieties of composition theory are often in conflict:

1. Think about audience as you write (this stemming from the classical rhetorical tradition).

2. Use writing for *making new meaning,* not just transmitting old meanings already worked out (this stemming from the newer epistemic tradition I associate with Ann Berthoff's classic explorations).

It's often difficult to work out new meaning while thinking about readers.

A More Ambitious Claim

I go further now and argue that ignoring audience can lead to better writing—immediately. In effect, writer-based prose can be *better* than reader-based prose. This might seem a more controversial claim, but is there a teacher who has not had the experience of struggling and struggling to no avail to help a student untangle his writing, only to discover that the student's casual journal writing or freewriting is untangled and strong? Sometimes freewriting is stronger than the essays we get only because it is expressive, narrative, or descriptive writing and the student was not constrained by a topic. But teachers who collect drafts with completed assignments often see passages of free-writing that are strikingly stronger *even* when they are expository and constrained by the assigned topic. In some of these passages we can sense that the strength derives from the student's unawareness of readers.

It's not just unskilled, tangled writers, though, who sometimes write better by forgetting about readers. Many competent and even professional writers produce mediocre pieces *because* they are thinking too much about how their readers will receive their words. They are acting too much like a salesman trained to look the customer in the eye and to think at all times about the characteristics of the "target audience." There is something too staged or planned or self-aware about such writing. We see this quality in much second-rate newspaper or magazine or business writing: "good-student writing" in the awful sense of the term. Writing produced this way reminds us of the ineffective actor whose consciousness of self distracts us: he makes us too aware of his own awareness of us. When we read such prose, we wish the writer would stop thinking about us—would stop trying to "adjust" or "fit" what he is saying to our frame of reference. "Damn it, put all your attention on what you are saying," we want to say, "and forget about us and how we are reacting."

When we examine really good student or professional writing, we can often see that its goodness comes from the writer's having gotten sufficiently wrapped up in her meaning and her language as to forget all about audience needs: the writer manages to "break through." The Earl of Shaftesbury talked about writers needing to escape their audience in order to find their own ideas (Cooper 1:109; see also Griffin). It is characteristic of much truly good writing to be, as it were, on fire with its meaning. Consciousness of readers is burned away; involvement in subject determines all. Such writing is analogous to the performance of the actor who has managed to stop attracting attention to her awareness of the audience watching her.

The arresting power in some writing by small children comes from their obliviousness to audience. As readers, we are somehow sucked into a more-than-usual connection with the meaning itself because of the child's gift for more-than-usual concentration on what she is saying. In short, we can feel some pieces of children's writing as being very writer-based. Yet it's precisely that quality which makes it powerful for us as readers. After all, why should we settle for a writer's entering our point of view, if we can have the more powerful experience of being sucked out of our point of view and into her world? This is just the experience that children are peculiarly capable of giving because they are so expert at total absorption in their world as they are writing. It's not just a matter of whether the writer "decenters," but of whether the writer has a sufficiently strong focus of attention to make the *reader* decenter. This quality of concentration is what D.H. Lawrence so admires in Melville:

> [Melville] was a real American in that he always felt his audience in front of him. But when he ceases to be American, when he forgets all audience, and gives us his sheer apprehension of the world, then he is wonderful, his book [*Moby-Dick*] commands a stillness in the soul, an awe. (158)

What most readers value in really excellent writing is not prose that is right for readers but prose that is right for thinking, right for language, or right for the subject being written about. If, in addition, it is clear and well suited to readers, we appreciate that. Indeed we feel insulted if the writer did not somehow try to make the writing *available* to us before delivering it. But if it succeeds at being really true to language and thinking and "things," we are willing to put up with much difficulty as readers:

[G]ood writing is not always or necessarily an adaptation to communal norms (in the Fish/Bruffee sense) but may be an attempt to construct (and instruct) a reader capable of reading the text in question. The literary history of the "difficult" work—from Mallarmé to Pound, Zukofsky, Olson, etc.—seems to say that much of what we value in writing we've had to learn to value by learning how to read it. (Trimbur)

The effect of audience awareness on *voice* is particularly striking—if paradoxical. Even though we often develop our voice by finally "speaking up" to an audience or "speaking out" to others, and even though much dead student writing comes from students' not really treating their writing as a communication with real readers, nevertheless, the opposite effect is also common: we often do not really develop a strong, authentic voice in our writing till we find important occasions for *ignoring* audience—saying, in effect, "To hell with whether they like it or not. I've got to say this the way *I* want to say it." Admittedly, the voice that emerges when we ignore audience is sometimes odd or idiosyncratic in some way, but usually it is stronger. Indeed, teachers sometimes complain that student writing is "writer-based" when the problem is simply the idiosyncracy—and sometimes in fact the *power*—of the voice. They would value this odd but resonant voice if they found it in a published writer (see "Real Voice," Elbow, *Writing with Power*). Usually we cannot *trust* a voice unless it is unaware of us and our needs and speaks out in its own terms (see the Ashbery epigraph). To celebrate writer-based prose is to risk the charge of *romanticism:* just warbling one's woodnotes wild. But my position also contains the austere *classic* view that we must nevertheless *revise* with conscious awareness of audience in order to figure out which pieces of writer-based prose are good as they are—and how to discard or revise the rest.

To point out that writer-based prose can be *better* for readers than reader-based prose is to reveal problems in these two terms. Does *writer-based* mean:

(1) That the text doesn't work for readers because it is too much oriented to the writer's point of view?

(2) Or that the writer was not thinking about readers as she wrote, although the text *may* work for readers?

Does *reader-based* mean:

(3) That the text works for readers—meets their needs?

(4) Or that the writer was attending to readers as she wrote although her text may *not* work for readers?

In order to do justice to the reality and complexity of what actually happens in both writers and readers, I was going to suggest four terms for the four conditions listed above, but I gradually realized that things are even too complex for that. We really need to ask about what's going on in three dimensions—in the *writer,* in the *reader,* and in the *text*—and realize that the answers can occur in virtually any combination:

— Was the *writer* thinking about readers or oblivious to them?

— Is the *text* oriented toward the writer's frame of reference or point of view, or oriented toward that of readers? (A writer may be thinking about readers and still write a text that is largely oriented towards her own frame of reference.)

— Are the readers' needs being met? (The text may meet the needs of readers whether the writer was thinking about them or not, and whether the text is oriented toward them or not.)

Two Models of Cognitive Development

Some of the current emphasis on audience awareness probably derives from a model of cognitive development that needs to be questioned. According to this model, if you keep your readers in mind as you write, you are operating at a higher level of psychological development than if you ignore readers. Directing words to readers is "more mature" than directing them to no one in particular or to yourself. Flower relates writer-based prose to the inability to "decenter" which is characteristic of Piaget's early stages of development, and she relates reader-based prose to later more mature stages of development.

On the one hand, of course this view must be right. Children do decenter as they develop. As they mature they get better at suiting their discourse to the needs of listeners, particularly to listeners very different from themselves. Especially, they get better at doing so *consciously*—thinking *awarely* about how things appear to people with different viewpoints. Thus, much unskilled writing is unclear or awkward *because* the writer was doing what it is so easy to do—unthinkingly taking her own frame of reference for granted and not attending to the needs of readers who might have a different frame of reference. And, of course, this failure is more common in younger, immature, "egocentric" students (and also more common in writing than in speaking since we have no audience present when we write).

But on the other hand, we need the contrary model that affirms what is also obvious once we reflect on it, namely that the ability to *turn off* audience awareness—especially when it confuses thinking or blocks discourse—is also a "higher" skill. I am talking about an ability to use language in "the desert island mode," an ability that tends to require learning, growth, and psychological development. Children, and even adults who have not learned the art of quiet, thoughtful, inner reflection, are often unable to get much cognitive action going in their heads unless there are other people present to have action *with*. They are dependent on live audience and the social dimension to get their discourse rolling or to get their thinking off the ground.

For in contrast to a roughly Piagetian model of cognitive development that says we start out as private, egocentric little monads and grow up to be public and social, it is important to invoke the opposite model that derives variously from Vygotsky, Bakhtin, and Meade. According to this model, we *start out* social and plugged into others and only gradually, through learning and development, come to "unplug" to any significant degree so as to function in a more private, individual and differentiated fashion: "Development in thinking is not from the individual to the socialized, but from the social to the individual" (Vygotsky 20). The important general principle in this model is that we tend to *develop* our important cognitive capacities by means of social interaction with others, and having done so we gradually learn to perform them alone. We fold the "simple" back-and-forth of dialogue into the "complexity" (literally, "foldedness") of individual, private reflection.

Where the Piagetian (individual psychology) model calls our attention to the obvious need to learn to enter into viewpoints other than our own, the Vygotskian (social psychology) model calls our attention to the equally important need to learn to produce good thinking and discourse *while alone.* A rich and enfolded mental life is something that people achieve only gradually through growth, learning, and practice. We tend to associate this achievement with the fruits of higher education.

Thus, we see plenty of students who lack this skill, who have nothing to say when asked to freewrite or to write a journal. They can dutifully "reply" to a question or a topic, but they cannot seem to *initiate* or *sustain* a train of thought on their own. Because so many adolescent students have this difficulty, many teachers chime in: "Adolescents have nothing to write about. They are too young. They haven't had significant experience." In truth, adolescents don't lack experience or material, no matter how "sheltered" their lives. What they lack is practice and help. Desert island discourse is a learned cognitive process. It's a mistake to think of private writing (journal writing and freewriting) as merely "easy"—merely a relief from trying to write right. It's also hard. Some exercises and strategies that help are Ira Progoff's "Intensive Journal" process, Sondra Perl's "Composing Guidelines," or Elbow's "Loop Writing" and "Open Ended Writing" processes (*Writing with Power* 50-77).

The Piagetian and Vygotskian developmental models (language-begins-as-private vs. language-begins-as-social) give us two different lenses through which to look at a common weakness in student writing, a certain kind of "thin" writing where the thought is insufficiently developed or where the language doesn't really explain what the writing implies or gestures toward. Using the Piagetian model, as Flower does, one can specify the problem as a weakness in audience orientation. Perhaps the writer has immaturely taken too much for granted and unthinkingly assumed that her limited explanations carry as much meaning for readers as they do for herself. The cure or treatment is for the writer to think more about readers.

Through the Vygotskian lens, however, the problem and the "immaturity" look altogether different. Yes, the writing isn't particularly clear or satisfying for readers, but this alternative diagnosis suggests a failure of the private desert island dimension: the writer's explanation is too thin because she didn't work out her train of thought fully enough *for herself.* The suggested cure or treatment is *not* to think more about readers but to think more for herself, to practice exploratory writing in order to learn to engage in that reflective discourse so central to mastery of the writing process. How can she engage readers more till she has engaged herself more?

The current emphasis on audience awareness may be particularly strong now for being fueled by *both* psychological models. From one side, the Piagetians say, in effect, "The egocentric little critters, we've got to *socialize* 'em! Ergo, make them think about audience when they write!" From the other side, the Vygotskians say, in effect, "No wonder they're having trouble writing. They've been bamboozled by the Piagetian heresy. They think they're solitary individuals with private selves when really they're just congeries of voices that derive from their discourse community. Ergo, let's intensify the social context —use peer groups and publication: make them think about audience when they write! (And while we're at it, let's hook them up with a better class of discourse community.)" To advocate ignoring audience is to risk getting caught in the crossfire from two opposed camps.

Two Models of Discourse: Discourse as Communication and Discourse as Poesis or Play

We cannot talk about writing without at least implying a psychological or developmental model. But we'd better make sure it's a complex, paradoxical, or spiral model. Better yet, we should be deft enough to use two contrary models or lenses. (Bruner pictures the developmental process as a complex movement in an upward reiterative spiral—not a simple movement in one direction.)

According to one model, it is characteristic of the youngest children to direct their discourse to an audience. They learn discourse *because* they have an audience; without an audience they remain mute, like "the wild child." Language is social from the start. But we need the other model to show us what is also true, namely that it is characteristic of the youngest children to use language in a *non-social* way. They use language not only because people talk to them but also because they have such a strong propensity to play and to build— often in a *non*-social or non-audience-oriented fashion. Thus, although one paradigm for discourse is social communication, another is private exploration or solitary play. Babies and toddlers tend to babble in an exploratory and reflective way—to themselves and not to an audience—often even with no one else near. This archetypally private use of discourse is strikingly illustrated when we see a pair of toddlers in "parallel play" alongside each other—each busily talking but not at all trying to communicate with the other.

Therefore, when we choose paradigms for discourse, we should think not only about children using language to communicate, but also about children building sandcastles or drawing pictures. Though children characteristically show their castles or pictures to others, they just as characteristically trample or crumple them before anyone else can see them. Of course, sculptures and pictures are different from words. Yet discourse implies more media than words; and even if you restrict discourse to words, one of our most mature uses

of language is for building verbal pictures and structures for their own sake—
not just for communicating with others.

Consider this same kind of behavior at the other end of the life cycle:
Brahms staggering from his deathbed to his study to rip up a dozen or more
completed but unpublished and unheard string quartets that dissatisfied him.
How was he relating to audience here—worrying too much about audience or
not giving a damn? It's not easy to say. Consider Glenn Gould deciding to
renounce performances before an audience. He used his private studio to
produce recorded performances for an audience, but to produce ones that
satisfied *himself,*he clearly needed to suppress audience awareness. Consider
the more extreme example of Kerouac typing page after page—burning each as
soon as he completed it. The language behavior of humans is slippery. Surely
we are well advised to avoid positions that say it is "always X" or "essentially
Y."

James Britton makes a powerful argument that the "making" or poesis
function of language grows out of the expressive function. Expressive language
is often for the sake of communication with an audience, but just as often it is
only for the sake of the speaker—working something out for herself (66-67,
74ff). Note also that "writing to learn," which writing-across-the-curriculum
programs are discovering to be so important, tends to be writing for the self or
even for no one at all rather than for an outside reader. You throw away the
writing, often unread, and keep the mental changes it has engendered.

I hope this emphasis on the complexity of the developmental process—
the limits of our models and of our understanding of it—will serve as a rebuke
to the tendency to label students as being at a lower stage of cognitive
development just because they don't yet write well. (Occasionally they *do* write
well—in a way—but not in the way that the labeler finds appropriate.)
Obviously the psychologistic labeling impulse started out charitably. Shaughnessy was fighting those who called basic writers *stupid* by saying they weren't
dumb, just at an earlier developmental stage. Flower was arguing that writer-
based prose is a natural response to a cognitive overload and indeed developmentally enabling. But this kind of talk can be dangerous since it labels students
as literally "retarded" and makes teachers and administrators start to think of
them as such. Instead of calling poor writers *either* dumb or slow (two forms of
blaming the victim), why not simply call them poor writers? If years of
schooling haven't yet made them good writers, perhaps they haven't gotten the
kind of teaching and support they need. Poor students are often deprived of the
very thing they need most to write well (which is given to good students): lots
of extended and adventuresome writing for self and for audience. Poor students
are often asked to write *only* answers to fill-in exercises.

As children get older, the developmental story remains complex or spiral.
Though the first model makes us notice that babies start out with a natural gift
for using language in a social and communicative fashion, the second model
makes us notice that children and adolescents must continually learn to relate
their discourse better to an audience—must struggle to decenter better. And

though the second model makes us notice that babies also start out with a natural gift for using language in a *private,* exploratory and playful way, the first model makes us notice that children and adolescents must continually learn to master this solitary, desert island, poesis mode better. Thus, we mustn't think of language only as communication—nor allow communication to claim dominance either as the earliest or as the most "mature" form of discourse. It's true that language is inherently communicative (and without communication we don't develop language), yet language is just as inherently the stringing together of exploratory discourse for the self—or for the creation of objects (play, poesis, making) for their own sake.

In considering this important poesis function of language, we need not discount (as Berkenkotter does) the striking testimony of so many witnesses who think and care most about language: professional poets, writers, and philosophers. Many of them maintain that their most serious work is *making,* not *communicating,* and that their commitment is to language, reality, logic, experience, not to readers. Only in their willingness to cut loose from the demands or needs of readers, they insist, can they do their best work. Here is William Stafford on this matter:

> I don't want to overstate this...but...my impulse is to say I don't think of an audience at all. When I'm writing, the satisfactions in the process of writing are my satisfactions in dealing with the language, in being surprised by phrasings that occur to me, in finding that this miraculous kind of convergent focus begins to happen. That's my satisfaction, and to think about an audience would be a distraction. I try to keep from thinking about an audience. (Cicotello 176)

And Chomsky:

> I can be using language in the strictest sense with no intention of communicating....As a graduate student, I spent two years writing a lengthy manuscript, assuming throughout that it would never be published or read by anyone. I meant everything I wrote, including nothing as to what anyone would [understand], in fact taking it for granted that there would be no audience....[C]ommunication is only one function of language, and by no means an essential one. (Qtd. in Feldman 5-6.)

It's interesting to see how poets come together with philosophers on this point—and even with mathematicians. All are emphasizing the "poetic" function of language in its literal sense—"poesis" as "making." They describe their writing process as more like "getting something right" or even "solving a problem" for its own sake than as communicating with readers or addressing an audience. The task is not to satisfy readers but to satisfy the rules of the system: "[T]he writer is not thinking of a reader at all; he makes it 'clear' as a contract with *language*" (Goodman, 164).

Shall we conclude, then, that solving an equation or working out a piece of symbolic logic is at the opposite end of the spectrum from communicating with readers or addressing an audience? No. To draw that conclusion would be to fall again into a one-sided position. Sometimes people write mathematics *for* an audience, sometimes not. The central point in this essay is that we cannot answer audience questions in an *a priori* fashion based on the "nature" of discourse or of language or of cognition—only in terms of the different *uses* or *purposes* to which humans put discourse, language, or cognition on different occasions. If most people have a restricted repertoire of uses for writing—if most people use writing only to send messages to readers, that's no argument for constricting the *definition* of writing. It's an argument for helping people expand their repertoire of uses.

The value of learning to ignore audience while writing, then, is the value of learning to cultivate the private dimension: the value of writing in order to make meaning to oneself, not just to others. This involves learning to free oneself (to some extent, anyway) from the enormous power exerted by society and others, to unhook oneself from external prompts and social stimuli. We've grown accustomed to theorists and writing teachers puritanically stressing the *problem* of writing: the tendency to neglect the needs of readers because we usually write in solitude. But let's also celebrate this same feature of writing as one of its glories: writing *invites* disengagement too, the inward turn of mind, and the dialogue with self. Though writing is deeply social and though we usually help things by enhancing its social dimension, writing is also the mode of discourse best suited to helping us develop the reflective and private dimension of our mental lives.

"But Wait a Minute, ALL Discourse is Social"

Some readers who see *all* discourse as social will object to my opposition between public and private writing (the "trap of oppositional thinking") and insist that *there is no such thing as private discourse*. What looks like private, solitary mental work, they would say, is really social. Even on the desert island I am in a crowd.

> [B]y ignoring audience in the conventional sense, we return to it in another sense. What I get from Vygotsky and Bakhtin is the notion that audience is not really out there at all but is in fact "always already" (to use that poststructuralist mannerism...) inside, interiorized in the conflicting languages of others—parents, former teachers, peers, prospective readers, whomever—that writers have to negotiate to write, and that we do negotiate when we write whether we're aware of it or not. The audience we've got to satisfy in order to feel good about our writing is as much in the past as in the present or future. But we experience it (it's so internalized) as *ourselves*. (Trimbur)

(Ken Bruffee likes to quote from Frost: "'Men work together,.../Whether they work together or apart'" ["The Tuft of Flowers"]). Or—putting it slightly differently—when I engage in what seems like private non-audience-directed writing, I am really engaged in communication with the "audience of self." For the self is multiple, not single, and discourse to self is communication from one entity to another. As Feldman argues, "The self functions as audience in much the same way that others do" (290).

Suppose I accept this theory that all discourse is really social—including what I've been calling "private writing" or writing I don't intend to show to any reader. Suppose I agree that all language is essentially communication directed toward an audience—whether some past internalized voice or (what may be the same thing) some aspect of the self. What would this theory say to my interest in "private writing"?

The theory would seem to destroy my main argument. It would tell me that there's no such thing as "private writing": it's impossible *not* to address audience; there are no vacations from audience. But the theory might try to console me by saying not to worry, because we don't *need* vacations from audience. Addressing audience is as easy, natural, and unaware as breathing— and we've been at it since the cradle. Even young, unskilled writers are already expert at addressing audiences.

But if we look closely we can see that, in fact, this theory doesn't touch my central practical argument. For even if all discourse is naturally addressed to *some* audience, it's not naturally addressed to the *right* audience—the living readers we are actually trying to reach. Indeed the pervasiveness of past audiences in our heads is one more reason for the difficulty of reaching present audiences with our texts. Thus, even if I concede the theoretical point, there still remains an enormous practical and phenomenological difference between writing "public" words for others to read and writing "private" words for no one to read.

Even if "private writing" is "deep down" social, the fact remains that, as we engage in it, we don't have to worry about whether it works on readers or even makes sense. We can refrain from doing all the things that audience-awareness advocates advise us to do ("keeping our audience in mind as we write" and trying to "decenter"). Therefore this social-discourse theory doesn't undermine the benefits of "private writing" and thus provides no support at all for the traditional rhetorical advice that we should "always try to think about (intended) audience as we write."

In fact, this social-discourse theory reinforces two subsidiary arguments I have been making. First, even if there is no getting away from *some* audience, we can get relief from an inhibiting audience by writing to a more inviting one. Second, audience problems don't come only from *actual* audiences but also from phantom "audiences in the head" (Elbow, *Writing with Power* 186ff). Once we learn how to be more aware of the effects of both external and internal readers and how to direct our words elsewhere, we can get out of the shadow even of a troublesome phantom reader.

And even if all our discourse is *directed to* or *shaped by* past audiences or voices, it doesn't follow that our discourse is *well directed to* or *successfully shaped for* those audiences or voices. Small children *direct* much talk to others, but that doesn't mean they always *suit* their talk to others. They often fail. When adults discover that a piece of their writing has been "heavily shaped" by some audience, this is bad news as much as good: often the writing is crippled by defensive moves that try to fend off criticism from this reader.

As teachers, particularly, we need to distinguish and emphasize "private writing" in order to teach it, to teach that crucial cognitive capacity to engage in extended and productive thinking that doesn't depend on audience prompts or social stimuli. It's sad to see so many students who can reply to live voices but cannot engage in productive dialogue with voices in their heads. Such students often lose interest in an issue that had intrigued them—just because they don't find other people who are interested in talking about it and haven't learned to talk reflectively to *themselves* about it.

For these reasons, then, I believe my main argument holds force even if I accept the theory that all discourse is social. But, perhaps more tentatively, I resist this theory. I don't know all the data from developmental linguistics, but I cannot help suspecting that babies engage in *some* private poesis—or "play-language"—some private babbling in addition to social babbling. Of course Vygotsky must be right when he points to so much social language in children, but can we really trust him when he denies *all* private or nonsocial language (which Piaget and Chomsky see)? I am always suspicious when someone argues for the total nonexistence of a certain kind of behavior or event. Such an argument is almost invariably an act of definitional aggrandizement, not empirical searching. To say that *all* language is social is to flop over into the opposite onesidedness that we need Vygotsky's model to save us from.

And even if all language is *originally* social, Vygotsky himself emphasizes how "inner speech" becomes more individuated and private as the child matures. "[E]gocentric speech is relatively accessible in three-year-olds but quite inscrutable in seven-year-olds: the older the child, the more thoroughly has his thought become inner speech" (Emerson 254; see also Vygotsky 134). "The inner speech of the adult represents his 'thinking for himself' rather than social adaptation. . . . Out of context, it would be incomprehensible to others because it omits to mention what is obvious to the 'speaker'" (Vygotsky 18).

I also resist the theory that all private writing is really communication with the *"audience of self."* ("When we represent the objects of our thought in language, we intend to make use of these representations at a later time. . . . [T]he speaker-self must have audience directed intentions toward a listener-self" [Feldman 289].) Of course, private language often *is* a communication with the audience of self:

— When we make a shopping list. (It's obvious when we can't decipher that third item that we're confronting *failed* communication with the self.)

— When we make a rough draft for ourselves but not for others' eyes. Here we are seeking to clarify our thinking with the leverage that comes from standing outside and reading our own utterance as audience—experiencing our discourse as receiver instead of as sender.

— When we experience ourselves as slightly split. Sometimes we experience ourselves as witness to ourselves and hear our own words from the outside—sometimes with great detachment, as on some occasions of pressure or stress.

But there are other times when private language is *not* communication with audience of self:

— Freewriting to no one: for the *sake* of self but not *to* the self. The goal is not to communicate but to follow a train of thinking or feeling to see where it leads. In doing this kind of freewriting (and many people have not learned it), you don't particularly plan to come back and read what you've written. You just write along and the written product falls away to be ignored, while only the "real product"—any new perceptions, thoughts, or feelings produced in the mind by the freewriting—is saved and looked at again. (It's not that you don't experience your words *at all* but you experience them only as speaker, sender, or emitter—not as receiver or audience. To say that's the same as being audience is denying the very distinction between "speaker" and "audience.")

As this kind of freewriting actually works, it often *leads* to writing we look at. That is, we freewrite along to no one, following discourse in hopes of getting somewhere, and then at a certain point we often sense that we have *gotten* somewhere: we can tell (but not because we stop and read) that what we are now writing seems new or intriguing or important. At this point we may stop writing; or we may keep on writing, but in a new audience-relationship, realizing that we *will* come back to this passage and read it as audience. Or we may take a new sheet (symbolizing the new audience-relationship) and try to write out for ourselves what's interesting.

— Writing as exorcism is a more extreme example of private writing *not* for the audience of self. Some people have learned to write in order to get rid of thoughts or feelings. By freewriting what's obsessively going round and round in our head we can finally let it go and move on.

I am suggesting that some people (and especially poets and freewriters) engage in a kind of discourse that Feldman, defending what she calls a "communication-intention" view, has never learned and thus has a hard time imagining and understanding. Instead of always using language in an audience-directed fashion for the sake of communication, these writers unleash language for its own sake and let *it* function a bit on its own, without much *intention* and without much need for *communication*, to see where it leads—and thereby end up with some intentions and potential communications they didn't have before.

It's hard to turn off the audience-of-self in writing—and thus hard to imagine writing to no one (just as it's hard to turn off the audience of *outside* readers when writing an audience-directed piece). Consider "invisible writing" as an intriguing technique that helps you become less of an audience-of-self for your writing. Invisible writing prevents you from seeing what you have written: you write on a computer with the screen turned down, or you write with a spent ball-point pen on paper with carbon paper and another sheet underneath. Invisible writing tends to get people not only to write faster than they normally do, but often better (see Blau). I mean to be tentative about this slippery issue of whether we can really stop being audience to our own discourse, but I cannot help drawing the following conclusion: just as in freewriting, suppressing the *other* as audience tends to enhance quantity and sometimes even quality of writing; so in invisible writing, suppressing the *self* as audience tends to enhance quantity and sometimes even quality.

Contraries in Teaching

So what does all this mean for teaching? It means that we are stuck with two contrary tasks. On the one hand, we need to help our students enhance the social dimension of writing: to learn to be *more* aware of audience, to decenter better and learn to fit their discourse better to the needs of readers. Yet it is every bit as important to help them learn the private dimension of writing: to learn to be *less* aware of audience, to put audience needs aside, to use discourse in the desert island mode. And if we are trying to advance contraries, we must be prepared for paradoxes.

For instance, if we emphasize the social dimension in our teaching (for example, by getting students to write to each other, to read and comment on each others' writing in pairs and groups, and by staging public discussions and even debates on the topics they are to write about), we will obviously help the social, public, communicative dimension of writing—help students experience writing not just as jumping through hoops for a grade but rather as taking part in the life of a community of discourse. But "social discourse" can also help private writing by getting students sufficiently involved or invested in an issue so that they finally want to carry on producing discourse alone and in private—and for themselves.

Correlatively, if we emphasize the private dimension in our teaching (for example, by using lots of private exploratory writing, freewriting, and journal writing and by helping students realize that of course they may need practice with this "easy" mode of discourse before they can use it fruitfully), we will obviously help students learn to write better reflectively for themselves without the need for others to interact with. Yet this private discourse can also help public, social writing—help students finally feel full enough of their *own* thoughts to have some genuine desire to *tell* them to others. Students often feel they "don't have anything to say" until they finally succeed in engaging themselves in private desert island writing for themselves alone.

Another paradox: whether we want to teach greater audience awareness or the ability to ignore audience, we must help students learn not only to "try harder" but also to "just relax." That is, sometimes students fail to produce reader-based prose because they don't *try* hard enough to think about audience needs. But sometimes the problem is cured if they just relax and write *to* people—as though in a letter or in talking to a trusted adult. By unclenching, they effortlessly call on social dicourse skills of immense sophistication. Sometimes, indeed, the problem is cured if the student simply writes in a more social *setting*—in a classroom where it is habitual to share lots of writing. Similarly, sometimes students can't produce sustained private discourse because they don't try hard enough to keep the pen moving and forget about readers. They must persist and doggedly push aside those feelings of, "My head is empty, I have run out of anything to say." But sometimes what they need to learn through all that persistence is how to relax and let go—to unclench.

As teachers, we need to think about what it means to *be an audience* rather than just be a teacher, critic, assessor, or editor. If our only response is to tell students what's weak, and how to improve it (diagnosis, assessment, and advice), we actually *undermine* their sense of writing as a social act. We reinforce their sense that writing means doing school exercises, producing for authorities what they already know—*not* actually trying to say things to readers. To help students experience us as *audience* rather than as assessment machines, it helps to respond by "replying" (as in a letter) rather than always "giving feedback."

Paradoxically enough, one of the best ways teachers can help students learn to turn off audience awareness and write in the desert island mode—to turn off the babble of outside voices in the head and listen better to quiet inner voices—is to be a special kind of private audience to them, to be a reader who nurtures by trusting and believing in the writer. Britton has drawn attention to the importance of teacher as "trusted adult" for school children (67-68). No one can be good at private, reflective writing without some *confidence and trust in self*. A nurturing reader can give a writer a kind of permission to forget about other readers or to be one's own reader. I have benefitted from this special kind of audience and have seen it prove useful to others. When I had a teacher who believed in me, who was interested in me and interested in what I had to say, I wrote well. When I had a teacher who thought I was naive, dumb, silly, and in need of being "straightened out," I wrote badly and sometimes couldn't write at all. Here is an interestingly paradoxical instance of the social-to-private principle from Vygotsky and Meade: we learn to listen better and more trustingly to *ourselves* through interaction with trusting *others*.

Look for a moment at lyric poets as paradigm writers (instead of seeing them as aberrant), and see how they heighten *both* the public and private dimensions of writing. Bakhtin says that lyric poetry implies "the absolute certainty of the listener's sympathy" (113). I think it's more helpful to say that lyric poets learn to create more than usual privacy in which to write *for themselves*—and then they turn around and let *others overhear*. Notice how poets tend to argue for the importance of no-audience writing, yet they are especially gifted at being public about what they produce in private. Poets are revealers—sometimes even grandstanders or showoffs. Poets illustrate the need for opposite or paradoxical or double audience skills: on the one hand, the ability to be private and solitary and tune out others—to write only for oneself and not give a damn about readers, yet on the other hand, the ability to be more than usually interested in audience and even to be a ham.

If writers really need these two audience skills, notice how bad most conventional schooling is on both counts. Schools offer virtually no privacy for writing: everything students write is collected and read by a teacher, a situation so ingrained students will tend to complain if you don't collect and read every word they write. Yet on the other hand, schools characteristically offer little or no social dimension for writing. It is *only* the teacher who reads, and students seldom feel that in giving their writing to a teacher they are actually communicating something they really want to say to a real person. Notice how often they are happy to turn in to teachers something perfunctory and fake that they would be embarrassed to show to classmates. Often they feel shocked and insulted if we want to distribute to classmates the assigned writing they hand in to us. (I think of Richard Wright's realization that the naked white prostitutes didn't bother to cover themselves when he brought them coffee as a black bellboy because they didn't really think of him as a man or even a person.) Thus, the conventional school setting for writing tends to be the least private and the least public—when what students need, like all of us, is practice in writing that is the most private and also the most public.

Practical Guidelines about Audience

The theoretical relationships between discourse and audience are complex and paradoxical, but the practical morals are simple:

(1) Seek ways to heighten both the *public* and *private* dimensions of writing. (For activities, see the previous section.)

(2) When working on important audience-directed writing, we must try to emphasize audience awareness *sometimes*. A useful rule of thumb is to start by putting the readers in mind and carry on as long as things go well. If difficulties arise, try putting readers out of mind and write either to no audience, to self, or to an inviting audience. Finally, always *revise* with readers in mind. (Here's another occasion when orthodox advice about writing is wrong—but turns out right if applied to revising.)

(3) Seek ways to heighten awareness of one's writing process (through process writing and discussion) to get better at taking control and deciding when to keep readers in mind and when to ignore them. Learn to discriminate factors like these:

(a) The writing task. Is this piece of writing *really* for an audience? More often than we realize, it is not. It is a draft that only we will see, though the final version will be for an audience; or exploratory writing for figuring something out; or some kind of personal private writing meant only for ourselves.

(b) Actual readers. When we put them in mind, are we helped or hindered?

(c) One's own temperament. Am I the sort of person who tends to think of what to say and how to say it when I keep readers in mind? Or someone (as I am) who needs long stretches of forgetting all about readers?

(d) Has some powerful "audience-in-the-head" tricked me into talking to it when I'm really trying to talk to someone else—distorting new business into old business? (I may be an inviting teacher-audience to my students, but they may not be able to pick up a pen without falling under the spell of a former, intimidating teacher.)

(e) Is *double audience* getting in the way? When I write a memo or report, I probably have to suit it not only to my "target audience" but also to some colleagues or supervisor. When I write something for publication, it must be right for readers, but it won't be published unless it is also right for the editors—and if it's a book it won't be much read unless it's right for reviewers. Children's stories won't be bought unless they are right for editors and reviewers *and* parents. We often tell students to write to a particular "real-life" audience—or to peers in the class—but of course they are also writing for us as graders. (This problem is more common as more teachers get interested in audience and suggest "second" audiences.)

(f) Is *teacher-audience* getting in the way of my students' writing? As teachers we must often read in an odd fashion: in stacks of 25 or 50 pieces all on the same topic; on topics we know better than the writer; not for pleasure or learning but to grade or find problems (see Elbow, *Writing with Power* 216-36).

To list all these audience pitfalls is to show again the need for thinking about audience needs—yet also the need for vacations from readers to think in peace.

References

Bakhtin, Mikhail. "Discourse in Life and Discourse in Poetry." Appendix. *Freudianism: A Marxist Critique,* By V.N. Volosinov. Trans. I.R. Titunik. Ed. Neal H. Bruss. New York: Academic, 1976. (Holquist's attribution of this work to Bakhtin is generally accepted.)

Berkenkotter, Carol, and Donald Murray. "Decisions and Revisions: The Planning Strategies of a Publishing Writer and the Response of Being a Rat—or Being Protocoled." *College Compsition and Communication* 34 (1983): 156-72.

Blau, Sheridan. "Invisible Writing." *College Composition and Communication* 34 (1983): 297-312.

Booth, Wayne. *The Rhetoric of Fiction.* Chicago: U of Chicago P, 1961.

Britton, James. *The Development of Writing Abilities,* 11-18. Urbana: NCTE, 1977.

Bruffee, Kenneth A. "Liberal Education and the Social Justification of Belief." *Liberal Education* 68 (1982): 95-114.

Bruner, Jerome. *Beyond the Information Given: Studies in the Psychology of Knowing.* Ed. Jeremy Anglin. New York: Norton, 1973.

——————. *On Knowing: Essays for the Left Hand.* Expanded ed. Cambridge: Harvard UP, 1979.

Chomsky, Noam. *Reflections on Language.* New York: Random, 1975.

Cicotello, David M. "The Art of Writing: An Interview with William Stafford." *College Composition and Communication* 34 (1983): 173-77.

Clarke, Jennifer, and Peter Elbow. "Desert Island Discourse: On the Benefits of Ignoring Audience." *The Journal Book.* Ed. Toby Fulwiler. Montclair, NJ: Boynton, 1987.

Cooper, Anthony Ashley, 3rd Earl of Shaftesbury. *Characteristics of Men, Manners, Opinions, Times, Etc.* Ed. John M. Robertson. 2 vols. Gloucester, MA: Smith, 1963.

Ede, Lisa, and Andrea Lunsford. "Audience Addressed/Audience Invoked: The Role of Audience in Composition Theory and Pedagogy." *College Composition and Communication* 35 (1984): 140-54.

Elbow, Peter. *Writing with Power.* New York: Oxford UP, 1981.

——————— . *Writing Without Teachers.* New York: Oxford UP, 1973.

Emerson, Caryl. "The Outer Word and Inner Speech: Bakhtin, Vygotsky, and the Internalization of Language." *Critical Inquiry* 10 (1983): 245-64.

Feldman, Carol Fleisher. "Two Functions of Language." *Harvard Education Review* 47 (1977): 282-93.

Flower, Linda. "Writer-Based Prose: A Cognitive Basis for Problems in Writing," *College English* 41 (1979): 19-37.

Goodman, Paul. *Speaking and Language: Defense of Poetry.* New York: Random, 1972.

Griffin, Susan. "The Internal Voices of Invention: Shaftesbury's Soliloquy." Unpublished. 1986.

Lawrence, D.H. *Studies in Classic American Literature.* Garden City: Doubleday, 1951.

Ong, Walter. "The Writer's Audience Is Always a Fiction." *PMLA* 90 (1975): 9-21.

Park, Douglas B. "The Meanings of 'Audience.'" *College English* 44 (1982): 247-57.

Perl, Sondra. "Guidelines for Composing." Appendix A. *Through Teachers' Eyes: Portraits of Writing Teachers at Work.* By Sondra Perl and Nancy Wilson. Portsmouth, NH: Heinemann, 1986.

Progoff, Ira. *At a Journal Workshop.* New York: Dialogue, 1975.

Shaughnessy, Mina. *Errors and Expectations: A Guide for the Teacher of Basic Writing.* New York: Oxford UP, 1977.

Trimbur, John. Letter to the author. September 1985.

——————— . "Beyond Cognition: Voices in Inner Speech." *Rhetoric Review,* Spring, 1987.

Vygotsky, L.S. *Thought and Language,* Trans. and ed. E. Hanfmann and G. Vakar. 1934. Cambridge: MIT P, 1962.

Walzer, Arthur E. "Articles from the 'California Divorce Project': A Case Study of the Concept of Audience." *College Composition and Communication* 36 (1985): 150-59.

Wright, Richard. *Black Boy.* New York: Harper, 1945.

I benefited from much help from audiences in writing various drafts of this piece. I am grateful to Jennifer Clarke, with whom I wrote a collaborative piece containing a case study on this subject. I am also grateful for extensive feedback from Pat Belanoff, Paul Connolly, Sheryl Fontaine, John Trimbur, and members of the Martha's Vineyard Summer Writing Seminar.

The Idea of Community in the Study of Writing

JOSEPH HARRIS

If you stand, today, in Between Towns Road, you can see either way; west to the spires and towers of the cathedral and colleges; east to the yards and sheds of the motor works. You see different worlds, but there is no frontier between them; there is only the movement and traffic of a single city.

Raymond Williams
Second Generation (9)

In *The Country and the City,* Raymond Williams writes of how, after a boyhood in a Welsh village, he came to the city, to Cambridge, only then to hear "from townsmen, academics, an influential version of what country life, country literature, really meant: a prepared and persuasive cultural history" (6). This odd double movement, this irony, in which one only begins to understand the place one has come from through the act of leaving it, proved to be one of the shaping forces of Williams's career—so that, some 35 years after having first gone down to Cambridge, he was still to ask himself: "Where do I stand...in another country or in this valuing city?" (6).

A similar irony, I think, describes my own relations to the university. I was raised in a working-class home in Philadelphia, but it was only when I went away to college that I heard the term *working class* used or began to think of myself as part of it. Of course, by then I no longer was quite part of it, or at least no longer wholly or simply part of it, but I had also been at college long enough to realize that my relations to it were similarly ambiguous—that here too was a community whose values and interests I could in part share but to some degree would always feel separate from.

This sense of difference, of overlap, of tense plurality, of being at once part of several communities and yet never wholly a member of one, has accompanied nearly all the work and study I have done at the university. So when, in the past few years, a number of teachers and theorists of writing began to talk about the idea of *community* as somehow central to our work, I

College Composition and Communication, 40 (February 1989), pp. 11-22. Copyright © 1989 by the National Council of Teachers of English. Reprinted with permission.

was drawn to what was said. Since my aim here is to argue for a more critical look at a term that, as Williams has pointed out, "seems never to be used unfavorably" (*Keywords* 66), I want to begin by stating my admiration for the theorists—in particular, David Bartholomae and Patricia Bizzell—whose work I will discuss. They have helped us, I think, to ask some needed questions about writing and how we might go about teaching it.[1]

Perhaps the most important work of these theorists has centered on the demystifying of the concept of *intention*. That is, rather than viewing the intentions of a writer as private and ineffable, wholly individual, they have helped us to see that it is only through being part of some ongoing discourse that we can, as individual writers, have things like points to make and purposes to achieve. As Bartholomae argues: "It is the discourse with its projects and agendas that determines what writers can and will do" (139). We write not as isolated individuals but as members of communities whose beliefs, concerns, and practices both instigate and constrain, at least in part, the sorts of things we can say. Our aims and intentions in writing are thus not merely personal, idiosyncratic, but reflective of the communities to which we belong.

But while this concern with the power of social forces in writing is much needed in a field that has long focused narrowly on the composing processes of individual writers, some problems in how we have imagined those forces are now becoming clear. First, recent theories have tended to invoke the idea of community in ways at once sweeping and vague: positing discursive utopias that direct and determine the writings of their members, yet failing to state the operating rules or boundaries of these communities. One result of this has been a view of "normal discourse" in the university that is oddly lacking in conflict or change. Recent social views of writing have also often presented university discourse as almost wholly foreign to many of our students, raising questions not only about their chances of ever learning to use such an alien tongue, but of why they should want to do so in the first place. And, finally, such views have tended to polarize our talk about writing: One seems asked to defend either the power of the discourse community or the imagination of the individual writer.

Williams and the Problem of Community

In trying to work towards a more useful sense of *community*, I will take both my method and theme from Raymond Williams in his *Keywords: A Vocabulary of Culture and Society*. Williams's approach in this vocabulary reverses that of the dictionary-writer. For rather than trying to define and fix the meanings of the words he discusses, to clear up the many ambiguities involved with them, Williams instead attempts to sketch "a history and complexity of meanings" (15), to show how and why the meanings of certain words—*art, criticism, culture, history, literature,* and the like—are still being contested. Certainly *community*, at once so vague and suggestive, is such a word too, and I will begin, then, with what Williams has to say about it:

Community can be the warmly persuasive word to describe an existing set of relationships, or the warmly persuasive word to describe an alternative set of relationships. What is most important, perhaps, is that unlike all other terms of social organization (*state, nation, society,* etc.) it seems never to be used unfavourably, and never to be given any positive opposing or distinguishing term. (66)

There seem to me two warnings here. The first is that, since it has no "positive opposing" term, *community* can soon become an empty and sentimental word. And it is easy enough to point to such uses in the study of writing, particularly in the many recent calls to transform the classroom into "a community of interested readers," to recast academic disciplines as "communities of knowledgeable peers," or to translate standards of correctness into "the expectations of the academic community." In such cases, *community* tends to mean little more than a nicer, friendlier, fuzzier version of what came before.

But I think Williams is also hinting at the extraordinary rhetorical power one can gain through speaking of community. It is a concept both seductive and powerful, one that offers us a view of shared purpose and effort and that also makes a claim on us that is hard to resist. For like the pronoun *we, community* can be used in such a way that it invokes what it seems merely to describe. The writer says to his reader: "We are part of a certain community; they are not"— and, if the reader accepts, the statement is true. And, usually, the gambit of community, once offered, is almost impossible to decline—since what is invoked is a community of those in power, of those who know the accepted ways of writing and interpreting texts. Look, for instance, at how David Bartholomae begins his remarkable essay on "Inventing the University":

Every time a student sits down to write for us, he has to invent the university for the occasion—invent the university, that is, or a branch of it, like history or anthropology or economics or English. The student has to learn *to speak our language, to speak as we do,* to try on the peculiar ways of knowing, selecting, evaluating, reporting, concluding, and arguing that define *the discourse of our community.* (134, my emphases)

Note here how the view of discourse at the university shifts subtly from the dynamic to the fixed—from something that a writer must continually reinvent to something that has already been invented, a language that "we" have access to but that many of our students do not. The university becomes "our community," its various and competing discourses become "our language," and the possibility of a kind of discursive free-for-all is quickly rephrased in more familiar terms of us and them, insiders and outsiders.

This tension runs throughout Bartholomae's essay. On one hand, the university is pictured as the site of many discourses, and successful writers are seen as those who are able to work both within and against them, who can find a place for themselves on the margins or borders of a number of discourses. On the other, the university is also seen as a cluster of separate communities, disciplines, in which writers must locate themselves through taking on "the commonplaces, set phrases, rituals and gestures, habits of mind, tricks of persuasion, obligatory conclusions and necessary connections that determine 'what might be said'" (146). Learning to write, then, gets defined both as the forming of an aggressive and critical stance towards a number of discourses, and as a more simple entry into the discourse of a single community.

Community thus becomes for Bartholomae a kind of stabilizing term, used to give a sense of shared purpose and effort to our dealings with the various discourses that make up the university. The question, though, of just who this "we" is that speaks "our language" is never resolved.[2] And so while Bartholomae often refers to the "various branches" of the university, he ends up claiming to speak only of "university discourse in its most generalized form" (147). Similarly, most of the "communities" to which other current theorists refer exist at a vague remove from actual experience: The University, The Profession, The Discipline, The Academic Discourse Community. They are all quite literally utopias—nowheres, meta-communities—tied to no particular time or place, and thus oddly free of many of the tensions, discontinuities, and conflicts in the sorts of talk and writing that go on everyday in the classrooms and departments of an actual university. For all the scrutiny it has drawn, the idea of community thus still remains little more than a notion—hypothetical and suggestive, powerful yet ill-defined.[3]

Part of this vagueness stems from the ways that the notion of "discourse community" has come into the study of writing—drawing on one hand from the literary-philosophical idea of "interpretive community," and on the other from the sociolinguistic concept of "speech community," but without fully taking into account the differences between the two. "Interpretive community," as used by Stanley Fish and others, is a term in a theoretical debate; it refers not so much to specific physical groupings of people as to a kind of loose dispersed network of individuals who share certain habits of mind. "Speech community," however, is usually meant to describe an actual group of speakers living in a particular place and time.[4] Thus while "interpretive community" can usually be taken to describe something like a worldview, discipline, or profession, "speech community" is generally used to refer more specifically to groupings like neighborhood, settlements, or classrooms.

What "discourse community" means is far less clear. In the work of some theorists, the sense of community as an active lived experience seems to drop out almost altogether, to be replaced by a shadowy network of citations and references. Linda Brodkey, for instance, argues that:

> To the extent that the academic community is a community, it is a
> literate community, manifested not so much at conferences as in
> bibliographies and libraries, a community whose members know
> one another better as writers than speakers. (12)

And James Porter takes this notion a step further, identifying "discourse community" with the *intertextuality* of Foucault—an argument that parallels in interesting ways E.D. Hirsch's claim, in *Cultural Literacy,* that a literate community can be defined through the clusters of allusions and references that its members share. In such views, *community* becomes little more than a metaphor, a shorthand label for a hermetic weave of texts and citations.

Most theorists who use the term, however, seem to want to keep something of the tangible and specific reference of "speech community"—to suggest, that is, that there really are "academic discourse communities" out there somewhere, real groupings of writers and readers, that we can help "initiate" our students into. But since these communities are not of speakers, but of writers and readers who are dispersed in time and space, and who rarely, if ever, meet one another in person, they invariably take on something of the ghostly and pervasive quality of "interpretive communities" as well.

There have been some recent attempts to solve this problem. John Swales, for instance, has defined "discourse commuity" so that the common space shared by its members is replaced by a discursive "forum," and their one-to-one interaction is reduced to a system "providing information and feedback." A forum is not a community, though, so Swales also stipulates that there must be some common "goal" towards which the group is working (2-3). A similar stress on a shared or collaborative project runs through most other attempts to define "discourse community."[5] Thus while *community* loses its rooting in a particular place, it gains a new sense of direction and movement. Abstracted as they are from almost all other kinds of social and material relations, only an affinity of beliefs and purposes, consensus, is left to hold such communities together. The sort of group invoked is a free and voluntary gathering of individuals with shared goals and interests—of persons who have not so much been forced together as have chosen to associate with one another. So while the members of an "academic discourse community" may not meet each other very often, they are presumed to think much like one another (and thus also much *unlike* many of the people they deal with everyday: students, neighbors, co-workers in other disciplines, and so on). In the place of physical nearness we are given like-mindedness. We fall back, that is, on precisely the sort of "warmly persuasive" and sentimental view of community that Williams warns against.

Insiders and Outsiders

One result of this has been, in recent work on the teaching of writing, the pitting of a "common" discourse against a more specialized or "privileged" one. For instance, Bartholomae argues that:

> The movement towards a more specialized discourse begins...
> both when a student can define a position of privilege, a position
> that sets him against a "common" discourse, and when he or she
> can work self-consciously, critically, against not only the "common"
> code but his or her own. (156)

The troubles of many student writers, Bartholomae suggests, begin with their inability to imagine such a position of privilege, to define their views against some "common" way of talking about their subject. Instead, they simply repeat in their writing "what everybody knows" or what their professor has told them in her lectures. The result, of course, is that they are penalized for "having nothing really to say."

The task of the student is thus imagined as one of crossing the border from one community of discourse to another, of taking on a new sort of language. Again, the power of this metaphor seems to me undeniable. First, it offers us a way of talking about why many of our students fail to think and write as we would like them to *without* having to suggest that they are somehow slow or inept because they do not. Instead, one can argue that the problem is less one of intelligence than socialization, that such students are simply unused to the peculiar demands of academic discourse. Second, such a view reminds us (as Patricia Bizzell has often argued) that one's role as a teacher is not merely to inform but to persuade, that we ask our students to acquire not only certain skills and data, but to try on new forms of thinking and talking about the world as well. The problem is, once having posited two separate communities with strikingly different ways of making sense of the world, it then becomes difficult to explain how or why one moves from one group to the other. If to enter the academic community a student must "learn to speak our language," become accustomed and reconciled to our ways of doing things with words, then how exactly is she to do this?

Bizzell seems to picture the task as one of assimilation, of conversion almost. One sets aside one's former ways to become a member of the new community. As she writes:

> Mastery of academic discourse must begin with socialization to the community's ways, in the same way that one enters any cultural group. One must first "go native." ("Foundationalism" 53)

And one result of this socialization, Bizzell argues, may "mean being completely alienated from some other, socially disenfranchised discourses" (43). The convert must be born again.

Bartholomae uses the language of paradox to describe what must be accomplished:

> To speak with authority [our students] have to speak not only in another's voice but through another's code; and they not only have to do this, they have to speak in the voice and through the codes of those of us with power and wisdom; and they not only have to do this, they have to do it before they know what they are doing, before they have a project to participate in, and before, at least in the terms of our disciplines, they have anything to say. (156)

And so here, too, the learning of a new discourse seems to rest, at least in part, on a kind of mystical leap of mind. Somehow the student must "invent the university," appropriate a way of speaking and writing belonging to others.

Writing as Repositioning

The emphasis of Bartholomae's pedagogy, though, seems to differ in slight but important ways from his theory. In *Facts, Artifacts and Counterfacts,* a text for a course in basic writing, Bartholomae and Anthony Petrosky describe a class that begins by having students write on what they already think and feel about a certain subject (e.g., adolescence or work), and then tries to get them to redefine that thinking through a seminar-like process of reading and dialogue. The course thus appears to build on the overlap between the students' "common" discourses and the "academic" ones of their teachers, as they are asked to work "within and against" both their own languages and those of the texts they are reading (8). The move, then, is not simply from one discourse to another but towards a "hesitant and tenuous relationship" to both (41).

Such a pedagogy helps remind us that the borders of most discourses are hazily marked and often travelled, and that the communities they define are thus often indistinct and overlapping. As Williams again has suggested, one does not step cleanly and wholly from one community to another, but is caught instead in an always changing mix of dominant, residual, and emerging discourses (*Marxism* 121-27, see also Nicholas Coles on "Raymond Williams: Writing Across Borders"). Rather than framing our work in terms of helping students move from one community of discourse into another, then, it might prove more useful (and accurate) to view our task as adding to or complicating their uses of language.

I am not proposing such addition as a neutral or value-free pedagogy. Rather, I would expect and hope for a kind of useful dissonance as students are confronted with ways of talking about the world with which they are not yet wholly familiar. What I am arguing against, though, is the notion that our students should necessarily be working towards the mastery of some particular, well-defined sort of discourse. It seems to me that they might better be encouraged towards a kind of polyphony—an awareness of and pleasure in the various competing discourses that make up their own.

To illustrate what such an awareness might involve, let me turn briefly to some student writings. The first comes from a paper on *Hunger of Memory,* in which Richard Rodriguez describes how, as a Spanish-speaking child growing up in California, he was confronted in school by the need to master the "public language" of his English-speaking teachers and classmates. In her response, Sylvia, a young black woman from Philadelphia, explains that her situation is perhaps more complex, since she is aware of having at least two "private languages": a Southern-inflected speech which she uses with her parents and older relatives, and the "street talk" which she shares with her friends and neighbors. Sylvia concludes her essay as follows:

> My third and last language is one that Rodriguez referred to as "public language." Like Rodriguez, I too am having trouble accepting and using "public language." Specifically, I am referring to Standard English which is defined in some English texts as:

"The speaking and writing of cultivated people...the
variety of spoken and written language which enjoys
cultural prestige, and which is the medium of education,
journalism, and literature. Competence in its use is
necessary for advancement in many occupations."

Presently, I should say that "public language" is *becoming* my
language as I am not yet comfortable in speaking it and even less
comfortable in writing it. According to my mother anyone who
speaks in "proper English" is "putting on airs."
In conclusion, I understand the relevance and importance of
learning to use "public language," but, like Rodriquez, I am also
afraid of losing my "private identity"—that part of me that my
parents, my relatives, and my friends know and understand.
However, on the other hand, within me, there is an intense desire to
grow and become a part of the "public world"—a world that exists
outside of the secure and private world of my parents, relatives, and
friends. If I want to belong, I must learn the "public language" too.

The second passage is written by Ron, a white factory worker in central
Pennsylvania, and a part-time student. It closes an end-of-the-term reflection
on his work in the writing course he was taking.

As I look back over my writings for this course I see a growing
acceptance of the freedom to write as I please, which is allowing me
to almost enjoy writing (I can't believe it). So I tried this approach
in another class I am taking. In that class we need to write
summations of articles each week. The first paper that I handed in,
where I used more feeling in my writing, came back with a ($\checkmark$-) and
the comment, "Stick to the material." My view is, if they open the
pen I will run as far as I can, but I won't break out because I have
this bad habit, it's called eating.

What I admire in both passages is the writer's unwillingness to reduce his
or her options to a simple either/or choice. Sylvia freely admits her desire to
learn the language of the public world. Her "I understand...but" suggests,
however, that she is not willing to loosen completely her ties to family and
neighborhood in order to do so. And Ron is willing to run with the more free
style of writing he has discovered, "if they open the pen." Both seem aware,
that is, of being implicated in not one but a number of discourses, a number of
communities, whose beliefs and practices conflict as well as align. And it is the
tension between those discourses—none repudiated or chosen wholly—that
gives their texts such interest.

There has been much debate in recent years over whether we need, above
all, to respect our students' "right to their own language," or to teach them the
ways and forms of "academic discourse." Both sides of this argument, in the

end, rest their cases on the same suspect generalization: that we and our students belong to different and fairly distinct communities of discourse, that we have "our" "academic" discourse and they have "their own" "common" (?!) ones. The choice is one between opposing fictions. The "languages" that our students bring to us cannot but have been shaped, at least in part, by their experiences in school, and thus must, in some ways, already be "academic." Similarly, our teaching will and should always be affected by a host of beliefs and values that we hold regardless of our roles as academics. What we see in the classroom, then, are not two coherent and competing discourses but many overlapping and conflicting ones. Our students are no more wholly "outside" the discourse of the university than we are wholly "within" it. We are all at once both insiders and outsiders. The fear (or hope) of either camp that our students will be "converted" from "their" language to "ours" is both overstated and misleading. The task facing our students, as Min-zhan Lu has argued, is not to leave one community in order to enter another, but to *reposition* themselves in relation to several continuous and conflicting discourses. Similarly, our goals as teachers need not be to initiate our students into the values and practices of some new community, but to offer them the chance to reflect critically on those discourses—of home, school, work, the media, and the like—to which they already belong.

Community without Consensus

"Alongside each utterance...off-stage voices can be heard," writes Barthes (21). We do not write simply as individuals, but we do not write simply as members of a community either. The point is, to borrow a turn of argument from Stanley Fish, that one does not *first* decide to act as a member of one community rather than some other, and *then* attempt to conform to its (rather than some other's) set of beliefs and practices. Rather, one is always *simultaneously* a part of several discourses, several communities, is always already committed to a number of conflicting beliefs and practices.[6] As Mary Louise Pratt has pointed out: "People and groups are constituted not by single unified belief systems, but by competing self-contradictory ones" (228). One does not necessarily stop being a feminist, for instance, in order to write literary criticism (although one discourse may try to repress or usurp the other). And, as the example of Williams shows, one does not necessarily give up the loyalties of a working-class youth in order to become a university student (although some strain will no doubt be felt).

In *The Country and the City,* Williams notes an "escalator effect" in which each new generation of English writers points to a lost age of harmony and organic community that thrived just before their own, only of course to have the era in which they were living similarly romanticized by the writers who come after them (9-12). Rather than doing much the same, romanticizing academic discourse as occurring in a kind of single cohesive community, I would urge, instead, that we think of it as taking place in something more like a city.

That is, instead of presenting academic discourse as coherent and well-defined, we might be better off viewing it as polyglot, as a sort of space in which competing beliefs and practices intersect with and confront one another. One does not need consensus to have community. Matters of accident, necessity, and convenience hold groups together as well. Social theories of reading and writing have helped to deconstruct the myth of the autonomous essential self. There seems little reason now to grant a similar sort of organic unity to the idea of community.

The metaphor of the city would also allow us to view a certain amount of change and struggle within a community not as threats to its coherence but as normal activity. The members of many classrooms and academic departments, not to mention disciplines, often seem to share few enough beliefs or practices with one another. Yet these communities exert a very real influence on the discourses of their members. We need to find a way to talk about their workings without first assuming a consensus that may not be there. As Bizzell has recently come to argue:

> Healthy discourse communities, like healthy human beings, are also masses of contradictions....We should accustom ourselves to dealing with contradictions, instead of seeking a theory that appears to abrogate them. ("What" 18-19)

I would urge an even more specific and material view of community: one that, like a city, allows for both consensus and conflict, and that holds room for ourselves, our disciplinary colleagues, our university coworkers, *and* our students. In short, I think we need to look more closely at the discourses of communities that are more than communities of discourse alone. While I don't mean to discount the effects of belonging to a discipline, I think that we dangerously abstract and idealize the workings of "academic discourse" by taking the kinds of rarified talk and writing that go on at conferences and in journals as the norm, and viewing many of the other sorts of talk and writing that occur at the university as deviations from or approximations of that standard. It may prove more useful to center our study, instead, on the everyday struggles and mishaps of the talk in our classrooms and departments, with their mixings of sometimes conflicting and sometimes conjoining beliefs and purposes.

Indeed, I would suggest that we reserve our uses of *community* to describe the workings of such specific and local groups. We have other words— *discourse, language, voice, ideology, hegemony*—to chart the perhaps less immediate (though still powerful) effects of broader social forces on our talk and writing. None of them is, surely, without its own echoes of meaning, both suggestive and troublesome. But none, I believe, carries with it the sense of like-mindedness and warmth that make community at once such an appealing *and* limiting concept. As teachers and theorists of writing, we need a vocabulary that will allow us to talk about certain forces as social rather than communal, as involving power but not always consent. Such talk could give us a fuller picture of the lived experience of teaching, learning, and writing in a university today.

Notes

[1] This essay began as part of a 1988 CCCC panel on "Raymond Williams and the Teaching of Composition." My thanks go to my colleagues on that panel, Nicholas Coles and Min-zhan Lu, for their help in conceiving and carrying through this project, as well as to David Bartholomae and Patricia Bizzell for their useful readings of many versions of this text.

[2] One might argue that there never really is a "we" for whom the language of the university (or a particular discipline) is fully invented and accessible. Greg Myers, for instance, has shown how two biologists—presumably well-trained scholars long initiated into the practices of their discipline—had to reshape their writings extensively to make them fit in with "what might be said" in the journals of their own field. Like our students, we too must re-invent the university whenever we sit down to write.

[3] A growing number of theorists have begun to call this vagueness of community into question. See, for instance: Bazerman on "Some Difficulties in Characterizing Social Phenomena in Writing," Bizzell on "What Is a Discourse Community?" Herzberg on "The Politics of Discourse Communities," and Swales on "Approaching the Concept of Discourse Community."

[4] See, for instance, Dell Hymes in *Foundations in Sociolinguistics:* "For our purposes it appears most useful to reserve the notion of community for a local unit, characterized for its members by common locality and primary interaction, and to admit exceptions cautiously" (51).

[5] See, for instance, Bizzell on the need for "emphasizing the crucial function of a collective project in unifying the group" ("What" 1), and Bruffee on the notion that "to learn is to work collaboratively...among a community of knowledgeable peers" (646).

[6] Bruce Robbins makes much the same case in "Professionalism and Politics: Toward Productively Divided Loyalties," as does John Schilb in "When Bricolage Becomes Theory: The Hazards of Ignoring Ideology." Fish too seems recently to be moving towards this position, arguing that an interpretive community is an "engine of change" fueled by the interaction and conflict of the various beliefs and practices that make it up. As he puts it: "Beliefs are not all held at the same level or operative at the same time. Beliefs, if I may use a metaphor, are nested, and on occasion they may affect and even alter one another and so the entire system or network they comprise" ("Change" 429).

References

Barthes, Roland. *S/Z*. Trans. Richard Miller. New York: Hill, 1974.

Bartholomae, David. "Inventing the University." *When a Writer Can't Write*. Ed. Mike Rose. New York, Guilford, 1985. 134-65.

Bartholomae, David, and Anthony Petrosky. *Facts, Artifacts and Counterfacts: Theory and Method for a Reading and Writing Course*. Upper Montclair, NJ: Boynton/Cook, 1986.

Bazerman, Charles. "Some Difficulties in Characterizing Social Phenomena in Writing." Conference on College Composition and Communication. Atlanta, March 1987.

Bizzell, Patricia. "Foundationalism and Anti-Foundationalism in Composition Studies." *Pre/Text* 7 (Spring/Summer 1986): 37-57.

——————— . "What Is a Discourse Community?" Penn State Conference on Rhetoric and Composition. University Park, July 1987.

Brodkey, Linda. *Academic Writing as Social Practice*. Philadelphia: Temple UP, 1987.

Bruffee, Kenneth A. "Collaborative Learning and the 'Conversation of Mankind.'" *College English* 46 (November 1984): 635-52.

Coles, Nicholas. "Raymond Williams: Writing Across Borders." Conference on College Composition and Communication. St. Louis, March 1988.

Fish, Stanley. *Is There a Text in This Class?* Cambridge: Harvard UP, 1980.

———————— . "Change." *South Atlanic Quarterly* 86 (Fall 1987): 423-44.

Herzberg, Bruce. "The Politics of Discourse Communities." Conference on College Composition and Communication. New Orleans, March 1986.

Hirsch, E.D., Jr. *Cultural Literacy: What Every American Needs to Know.* Boston: Houghton, 1987.

Hymes, Dell. *Foundations in Sociolinguistics: An Ethnographic Approach.* Philadelphia: U of Pennsylvania P, 1974.

Lu, Min-zhan. "Teaching the Conventions of Academic Discourse: Structures of Feeling." Conference on College Composition and Communication. St. Louis, March 1988.

Myers, Greg. "The Social Construction of Two Biologists' Proposals." *Written Communication* 2 (July 1985): 219-45.

Porter, James. "Intertextuality and the Discourse Community." *Rhetoric Review* 5 (Fall 1986): 34-47.

Pratt, Mary Louise. "Interpretive Strategies/Strategic Interpretations: On Anglo-American Reader Response Criticism." *Boundary 2* 11.1-2 (Fall/Winter 1982-83): 201-31.

Robbins, Bruce. "Professionalism and Politics: Toward Productively Divided Loyalties." *Profession* 85: 1-9.

Rodriguez, Richard. *Hunger of Memory.* Boston: Godine, 1981.

Schilb, John. "When Bricolage Becomes Theory: The Hazards of Ignoring Ideology." Midwest Modern Language Association. Chicago, November 1986.

Swales, John. "Approaching the Concept of Discourse Community." Conference on College Composition and Communication. Atlanta, March 1987.

Williams, Raymond. *Second Generation.* New York: Horizon, 1964.

———————— . *The Country and the City.* New York: Oxford UP, 1973.

———————— . *Keywords: A Vocabulary of Culture and Society.* New York: Oxford UP, 1976.

———————— . *Marxism and Literature.* New York: Oxford UP, 1977.

On the Subjects of Class and Gender in "The Literacy Letters"

LINDA BRODKEY

In "The Discourse on Language," Michel Foucault dramatizes the desire to be "on the other side of discourse, without having to stand outside it, pondering its particular, fearsome, and even devilish features" (215) in this whimsical colloquy between the individual and the institution.

> Inclination speaks out: "I don't want to have to enter this risky world of discourse; I want nothing to do with it insofar as it is descisive and final; I would like to feel it all around me, calm and transparent, profound, infinitely open, with others responding to my expectations, and truth emerging, one by one. All I want is to allow myself to be borne along, within it, and by it, a happy wreck." Institutions reply: "But you have nothing to fear from launching out; we're here to show you discourse is within the established order of things, that we've waited a long time for its arrival, that a place has been set aside for it—a place that both honours and disarms it; and if it should have a certain power, then it is we, and we alone, who give it that power." (215-16)

What Foucault and other poststructuralists have been arguing the last fifteen or twenty years is considerably easier to state than act on: we are at once constituted and unified as subjects in language and discourse. The discursive subject is of particular interest to those of us who teach writing because language and discourse are understood to be complicit in the representation of self and others, rather than the neutral or arbitrary tools of thought and expression that they are in other modern theories, not to mention handbooks and rhetorics. Among other things, this means that since writers cannot avoid constructing a social and political reality in their texts, as teachers we need to learn how to "read" the various relationships between writer, reader, and reality that language and discourse supposedly produce.

New theories of textuality are inevitably new theories of reading. And in the field of writing, those who teach basic writers and welcome new ways to read their texts are perhaps the most likely to recognize the possibilities of discursive subjectivity. The poststructural David Bartholomae of "Inventing the University," for example, writes less confidently but more astutely of what

College English, 51 (February, 1989), pp. 125-141. Copyright © 1989 by the National Council of Teachers of English. Reprinted with permission.

student errors may signify than the Bartholomae of "The Study of Error," published some years earlier at the height of the field's enthusiasm for empirical research and error analysis. For the startling power of a discourse to confer authority, name errors, and rank order student texts speaks more readily to the experience of reading basic writing than promises of improved reliability or validity in the empirical study of errors. While empiricality is far from moot, it makes little difference if one is right if one is not talking about that which most concerns writing and the teaching of writing. Or, as Sharon Crowley has put it, "the quality of the power that is associated with writing varies with the degree of author-ity granted by a culture to its texts" (96). In this society the authority that teachers are empowered to grant to or withhold from student texts derives from the theory of textuality governing their reading.

The question then is how to read what students write. And at issue is the unquestioned power of a pedagogical authority that insists that teachers concentrate on form at the expense of content.

> I'm siting at home now when I have more time to write to you I enjoyed rending your letters. I under stand reading them one word I had a little trouble with the word virginia but know about me well that is hard but I will try.

The errors in spelling and punctuation in this passage are serious, but not nearly as egregious, I suspect, as the tradition that warrants reducing a text to its errors. Remember the anger you feel when someone corrects your pronunciation or grammar while you are in the throes of an argument, and you can recover the traces of the betrayal students must experience when a writing assignment promises them seemingly unlimited possibilities for expression, and the response or evaluation notes only their limitations. The errors are there, and the passage is hard to read. Yet to see only the errors strikes me as an unwarranted refusal to cede even the possibility of discursive subjectivity and authority to the woman who wrote this passage, barring of course that of basic writer which an error analysis would without question grant her.

Changing the Subject

This is an essay about the ways discourses construct our teaching. In postmodern theories of subjectivity:

1) all subjects are the joint creations of language and discourse;
2) all subjects produced are ideological;
3) all subject positions are vulnerable to the extent that individuals do not or will not identify themselves as the subjects (i.e., the effects) of a discourse.

Those who occupy the best subject positions a discourse has to offer would have a vested interest in maintaining the illusion of speaking rather than being spoken by discourse. Postmodern rhetoric would begin by assuming that all discourses warrant variable subject positions ranging from mostly satisfying to mostly unsatisfying for those individuals named by them. Each institutionalized discourse privileges some people and not others by generating uneven and unequal subject positions as various as sterotypes and agents. Hence, it is at least plausible to expect most, though not all, of those individuals whose subjectivity is the most positively produced by a discourse to defend its discursive practices against change. And it is equally plausible to expect some, though again not all, of those individuals whose subjectivity is the most negatively produced to resist its discursive practices. Feminists, for example, regularly resist discursive practices that represent female subjectivity solely in terms of reproductive biology. Of course, neither verbal resistance nor other material forms of protest to such reduced subject positions are universal among women.

Discursive resistance requires opportunities for resistance. Altering an institutionalized discourse probably requires an unremitting negative critique of its ideology, a critique that is most often carried out in the academy by attempting to replace a particular theory (e.g., of science or art or education or law) with another. Recently, theoretical battles have proliferated to such an extent that a cover term, *critical theory,* has come to refer to a variety of ideological critiques of theory, research, and practice across the academy: critical legal studies, critical practice, critical anthropology, critical pedagogy, and so on.

Discursive resistance, however, need not be conducted in such abstract terms as we have recently witnessed in the academy. The more usual practice would be for those individuals who are ambivalent or threatened by their subject positions in a given discourse to interrupt the very notion of the unified self—the traditional Cartesian notion that the self is a transcendent and absolute entity rather than a creation of language and ideology—in their spoken and written texts. Such interruptions are likely to take one of two forms: reversing the negative and positive subject positions in a given discourse—as Carol Gilligan does in her feminist revision of the research on the development of moral reasoning among adolescent girls; or re-presenting a stereotype as an agent in a discourse the least committed to the preservation of the stereotype—as Toni Morrison does when representing Afro-American women and men as the agents rather than the victims of events in her novels.

Studies of these and other interruptive practices, rhetorics of resistance in which individuals shift subject positions from one discourse to another or within a discourse in their speaking and writing, would constitute empirical inquiry into the postmodern speculation that language and discourse are material to the construction of reality, not simply by-products reflecting or reproducing a set of non-discursive, material social structures and political formations. Knowledge of multiple subject positions makes possible both the practical and the theoretical critiques that interrupt the assumption of unchanging, irreversible, and asymmetrical social and political relations between the privileged and unprivileged subjects represented in a particular discourse (see Williams, esp. 75-141).

What is needed is research that addresses what Stuart Hall has recently called "a theory of articulation," which he describes as "a way of understanding how ideological elements come, under certain conditions, to cohere together within a discourse, and a way of asking how they do or do not become articulated, at specific junctures, to certain political subjects" (53). Since articulation separates intentions from effects, or production from reception, Hall has reinserted the possibility of human agency into poststructural theory. More specifically, articulation distinguishes between the desire to be unified in a discourse and what happens in practice, namely, what individuals do in and with the unified subject positions offered them by such recognizable institutional discourses as, say, science, art, education, law, and religion or ethics.

"The Literacy Letters"

What I mean by research on the rhetorics of discursive practice and attendant practices of resistance is amply illustrated in a curriculum project I have referred to elsewhere as "the Literacy Letters" (see Brodkey). The letters were generated in the discourse of education, since they were initiated by six white middle-class teachers (four women and two men) taking my graduate course on teaching basic writing and sustained by six white working-class women enrolled in an Adult Basic Education (ABE) class. The woman who was teaching the ABE class and taking my course hoped that corresponding would provide the students in her class with what she called an authentic reason to write—on the order of a pen-pal experience for adults. The experienced English teachers from my class, most of whom had not taught basic writing, set out to learn more about the reading and writing concerns of their adult correspondents. As for me, I welcomed the chance to study correspondence itself, which seemed to me a remarkable opportunity to examine both the production and reception of self and other in the writing and reading of personal letters.

Permission to photocopy the letters as data for research was granted by all correspondents before the first exchange. For the two months that they wrote, the correspondents agreed not to meet or talk on the phone. The data, then, are the letters written by the six pairs who wrote regularly: one pair exchanged letters eight times; one pair seven times; two pairs six times; and two pairs five times.

When the teachers first reported that they found the letters stressful, I attributed their anxiety to the fact that I would be reading and evaluating their letters as well as those written by the students in the ABE class. But their uneasiness persisted despite repeated assurances that I couldn't look at or read the letters until the semester's end, a standard procedure meant to protect the educational rights of those who agree to participate in classroom research. After reading and thinking about the letter, however, I am no longer so inclined to assume that my presence as such was as threatening or instrusive as I first thought, though doubtless it contributed some to their anxiety.

Learning to Read "The Literacy Letters"

Research on basic writers as well as my own experience teaching amply prepared me for the ungainly prose produced by the women in the ABE class (e.g., Bartholomae, Perl, Shaughnessy). But nothing I had read or remembered from my own teaching prepared me for occasional moments of linguistic as well as discursive awkwardness from the teachers. I am not referring to the necessary clumsiness with which the teachers sought their footing before they knew anything about their correspondents, but to intermittent improprieties that occurred once several letters had been exchanged. In fact, I found these occasional lapses so perplexing that it's fair to say that the teachers' unexpected errors, rather than the students' expected ones, led me to think about the literacy letters in terms of the poststructural discursive practices of reproduction and resistance. Only discourse, more specifically the power of a discourse over even its fluent writers, I decided, could begin to explain the errors of these otherwise literate individuals.

That educational discourse grants teachers authority over the organization of language in the classroom, which includes such commonplace privileges as allocating turns, setting topics, and asking questions, is clear from sociolinguistic studies of classroom language interaction (e.g., Stubbs). Many teachers, including those in this study, attempt to relinquish their control by staging opportunities for students to take the privileged subject position of teacher in, say, group discussions or collaborative assignments that grant them, at least temporarily, a measure of control over educational discursive practice. Attempts to transform classroom discussions into conversations between peers are thwarted to the extent that teachers fail to realize that their interpersonal relationships with students, as well as their institutional ones, are constituted by educational discourse. While the power of a discourse is not absolute, neither is it vulnerable to change by individuals who ignore its power, only by those who interrupt or resist or challenge the seemingly immutable reality of unified subjectivity. In much the same way that you don't resist racism by denying that racism exists, but by confronting it in yourself and others, teachers cannot divest themselves of those vestiges of authority that strike them as unproductive by ignoring the institutional arrangements that unequally empower teachers and students.

At the outset, the teachers in this study attempted to mitigate the power of educational discourse over themselves and their correspondents by "playing" student. Their letters are replete with the desire to represent themselves as students of writing pedagogy and their correspondents as their teachers. The longest running correspondence, for instance, was initiated by a teacher who wrote: "I think that some of the things you could tell me might help me to understand what I can do better when I try to help my students learn to improve thier (sic) writing." Since none of the students made suggestions about either curriculum or instruction, roles were not reversed. But making the requests seems to have mooted the possibility of the teachers practicing the most authoritarian "dialect" of educational discourse in their correspondence.

To wit, no teacher reduced personal correspondence to spelling or grammar lessons; nor, for that matter, did any of the students from the ABE class ask to be taught or corrected.

Bear in mind that the writers of the literacy letters are not held by the usual arrangements between teachers and students. But theirs is what might be called an extracurricular relationship, arranged by the authorized teacher. While the teachers assiduously avoided lessons and hence avoided even the possibility of displacing the classroom teacher's authority, there are nevertheless times in the letters when it certainly looks as if by ignoring rather than contesting the authority of educational discourse, they retained control over such discursive privileges as determining what is and what is not an appropriate topic. The teachers exercise their authority infrequently, but decisively, whenever one of their correspondents interrupts, however incidentally, the educational discursive practice that treats class as irrelevant to the subjectivity of teachers and students. Telegraphed by linguistic and/or discursive lapses, the refusal that signals the teachers' unspoken commitment to a classless discourse provokes additional and more pronounced discursive resistance from the ABE writers.

Personal Narratives in "Literacy Letters"

Discursive hegemony on the part of the teachers is most obvious and discursive resistance on the part of the students is most dramatic during storytelling episodes. Personal correspondence evokes personal narratives. The teachers tell a variety of stories in which they represent themselves as busy professionals trying to resolve conflicts among work, family, and school. Social research on storytelling suggests that in exchange for being granted the time it takes to tell a story, the teller is expected to make it worth the listener's while by raising for evaluation or contemplation that which is problematic or unusual about the narrative conflict and its resolution (see Labov, Pratt). That the teachers tell stories representing themselves as guilty about their inability to find enough time is not surprising, since their busy lives have been made all the more complicated by recently adding course work to schedules already over-burdened by responsibilities at work and home. Nor are the responses to their stress stories unexpected, for the women from the Adult Basic Education class console and commiserate with the teachers in much the way that research suggests interlocutors ordinarily do. The teachers, however, occasionally respond in extraordinary ways when their correspondents reciprocate with stories about their lives.

The ABE students do not tell narratives about not having the time to fulfill their obligations to the three spheres of work, school, and family. Nor are their stories about internal conflicts like guilt. Instead, they write most frequently about external threats to the well-being of themselves and their families or their neighbors. While work and education often figure in their stories, they are important only insofar as they materially affect their lives: a family is besieged by the threat of layoffs; lack of educational credentials means the low paychecks and the moonlighting that robs families of time with the overworked wage earner.

Clearly teachers and students alike told class-based narratives. Yet the teachers' markedly inept responses to their correspondents' narratives suggest that the hegemony of educational discourse warrants teachers not only to represent themselves as subjects unified by the internal conflicts like guilt that preoccupy professionals, but to disclaim narratives that represent a subject alternatively unified in its conflicts with an external material reality. This refusal to acknowledge the content of their correspondents' narratives, most explicable as a professional class narcissism that sees itself everywhere it looks, alienates the ABE writers from educational discourse and, more importantly, from the teachers it ostensibly authorizes.

Don and Dora

The seven-letter exchange between the teacher and student I'll call Don and Dora is disarming. Frequency alone suggests that both teacher and student found corresponding satisfying. For some weeks they wrote about movies, food, and their families, all topics introduced by Don who represented himself in his initial letter as a complex subject, specifically, as a young man beset by personal failings his correspondent would find amusing:

> I won't tell you how long I like to stay in bed in the morning—though I do stay up very late at night (watching old movies)—but let's just say that it's past 11 AM. Oh well, we all have to have at least one vice. Unfortunately, I have more than one. One of my others is Chinese food. There's a Chinese food cart parked right outside the window of the library where I work, so every afternoon I dash out when the line slacks off...I usually try to get some vegetable dishes, even though I most always end up getting the most highly caloric item on the menu.

His comedic self-presentation is amplified by this final request: "Please let me know what you're doing: do you like Chinese food (and if so, what kind?), do you like old movies (and if so, which ones?), do you think I'm too weird to write back to? I'll look forward to your responses, comments, complaints, etc." In her response letter, Dora picks up the topics of movies and food. "I to enjoy the old movies and (love Chinese food)," she writes, but then goes on to conclude about them both, "so [I] guess that make two of us that are (weird)." Notice that while she responds to his question, "do you think I'm too weird to write back to?" writing back is itself material evidence that Dora doesn't find Don's tastes *too* weird. Dora is, as she puts it, "looking forward to writing back this is my first letter I ever wrote."

Over the next few weeks, their letters follow this pattern. Don writes extended and humorous anecdotes that portray him as a man at odds with himself at work, school, and home, and Dora offers consolation by letting him know how amusing she and the other women in her class find his stories: "Rachel [her teacher] ask me to read your letter to the class we all though that your grandmother and father was funning about the candy." After dutifully playing audience for some weeks, however, Dora dramatically reverses the pattern when she not only asserts herself as a narrator, but as the narrator of tragic rather than comedic events, in this letter which in its entirety reads as follows:

> I don't have must to siad this week a good frineds husband was kill satday at 3:15 the man who kill him is a good man he would give you the shirt off of his back it is really self-defense but anyway I see police academy three it was funny but not is good as the first two

Dora's narrative limns as stark a reality as any represented in the literacy letters. However, the abrupt shift from herself as a narrator who reflects on the aftermath of violence to herself as the student who answers a teacher's questions—"but anyway I see police academy three it was funny but not is good as the first two"—is, for me, one of those moments when the power of discourse seems the most absolute.

It's not implausible to imagine that in telling a narrative Dora is trying out the more positive subject position afforded narrators by the discourse of art, and that Don has held throughout their correspondence. But art is only a respite, it seems, for Dora shifts quickly from narrator back to student. Yet in that brief moment when she inserts herself as the narrator, Dora takes on the more complex subjectivity afforded by the discourse of art to narrators. Though short, the story she tells is one in which the narrator's sympathies are clearly divided between the survivors—the friend and the murderer—a narrative position that Dora grounds in the extenuating circumstances of moral character (a good man "would give you the shirt off of his back") and law ("it is really self-defense"). Her narrative point of view considers not the grisly fact of murder and not even what motivated the murder, but the notion that murder is a consequence of circumstances rather than character.

Narrative strikes me as a potentially effective mode of resistance, for the rules governing storytelling more or less require Don to respond to the content of Dora's narrative. Since Dora attentuated the full interruptive force of the discourse of art on educational discourse, however, by interjecting the comment about the movie, she effectively lost her hold on the rhetorical practice in which the narrative critiques a teacher's exclusive right to initiate topics. The abrupt shift from narrator back to audience returns, or offers to return, teacher and student alike to the already established subject positions of teacher/narrator and student/audience.

Even if Dora's interjection is understood as hesitation, Don might have assisted her by simply responding to the content of her story. He might have asked about motive or even asked why she says nothing about the victim. But Don's response suggests only that he is nonplussed:

> I'm sorry to hear about the problem that you wrote about last week. It's always hard to know what to say when the situation is as unusual as that one. I hope that everything is getting a little better, at least for you trying to know what to say and do in that situation.

Several issues about the fragility of the unity that even the most privileged subjects are able to achieve in language and discourse come immediately to mind. Most obvious, perhaps, is the syntactic lapse in the final sentence ("I hope that everything is getting a little better, at least for *you* trying to know what to say and do in that situation"). Less obvious, though equally to the point, is the way that Don's linguistic facility, under the circumstances, only amplifies the discursive inadequacy of this passage as a response to the content of her narrative.

Bearing in mind that she has just told a story in which the "problem" is the aftermath of murder—her friend's husband is dead and the good man who killed him presumably faces prison—the assertion that this is a matter of manners—"It's always hard to know what to say when the situation is as unusual as that one"—is not simply inappropriate. It constitutes a discursive retreat that threatens to reconstitute Don and Dora in the most profoundly alienated subject relationship of all—self and other—and to give over their more or less satisfying discursive relationship as narrator and audience. Even the demonstrative adjective, *that,* underscores the distance Don places between himself and the world in which he resides and the other and the world in which she resides. The contrast between this awkward first paragraph and the plans to visit his grandmother on Mother's Day that complete his letter effectively reiterates the terms of their continued correspondence.

In her next letter, Dora again responds to the content of Don's letter, "I am glad to hear that you are going to see your grandmother." And though she makes no further mention in this or any letter of the murder, she writes "I hope you get more energy about work," which remark is followed by:

> I wouldn't want to see you living in Kensington with the rest of us bums. ha ha

It certainly looks as if she has acknowledged the threat of othering by noting that his self-proclaimed and amply documented laziness throughout their correspondence would, in the eyes of many, make him one of the others—"the rest of us bums"—whose subjectivity he's denying. That her class antagonism increases after the next letter, in which he narrates in the usual humorous detail his visit with his grandmother, is evident in the fact that for first time she makes no reference to his anecdote and ends a brief account of her own Mother's Day with, "I got call back to work today. I am very nervous about it. it like started a new job." In his next letter, in which he makes no mention of her job, Don follows yet another extended narrative about a day at the beach with "Keep cool and write soon!" But this time Dora ignores both the narrative and the imperatives and does not write again.

Don's response is characteristic of the kind of discursive uneasiness that arises whenever one of the students interrupts the educational practice that deems such working-class concerns as neighborhood violence irrelevant. And while this is admittedly one of the more dramatic examples, it suggests the extent to which unacknowledged tension over the control of subject positions contributes to rather than alleviates class antagonism, for we see that the teacher's desire to be preserved as the unified subject of an educational discursive practice that transcends class overrides the student's desire to narrate herself as a subject unified in relation to the violence that visited her working-class neighborhood.

Rita and Esther

The second example comes from the six-letter exchange between an experienced secondary English teacher I'll call Rita and the most fluent and prolific writer from the ABE class, a student I'll call Esther. The set itself is unusual, since these are the only correspondents whose letters are often of similar length. From the outset, it's easy to see that Esther is not only actively resisting playing "student" but sometimes even tries to play "teacher." In response to Rita's initial letter, for instance, Esther first compliments her—"My classmates and I read your wonderful letter"—but then faults her for what she neglected to mention: "you never stated your age or your country in the letter. And also where your Grandmother's home was." And unlike the other ABE writers, in her first and subsequent letters, Esther asks for information that Rita has neither offered nor alluded to:

> What is it like where you live and what are the shopping areas like. How is the transportation and the Climate there. What kind of food do you like to eat. You didn't say if you were married, or if you have children. Please write back and let me know.

Though this is admittedly an insight considerably improved by hindsight, the class antagonism that erupts later can probably be traced to Rita's ambivalance about their relationship, for she seems unable either to accept Esther's assumption that they are peers or to assert herself as a teacher. Rita's reluctance to declare herself as either a teacher or a peer may explain her refusal to do more than name the suburb she lives in or the nearby mall in answer to questions like "What is it like where you live and what are the shopping areas like." In short, Rita replies but does not answer Esther's questions.

In a letter near the end of their correspondence, following yet one more futile effort to establish what Rita's life is like—"Do you live near a beach or the shore? Are you going anywhere special this Summer?"—Esther writes this explanation in response to Rita's comment that she sounded "a little discouraged" in her last letter:

> I'm going to have to look for another house because, the Restate is Selling the house unless somebody invests in it and want me to stay his or her

tennant. That is why I was a little discourage because I didn't have a chance to save any money. I'll still answer your letters. Thank you for writing back.

This is a remarkable passage if only because it is one of the few times in the literacy letters when anyone mentions money by name. There are plenty of coded references to money: vacations taken or not taken, the buying of gifts, the cost of public transportation and food. But this particular statement is about money, about the simple economic fact that changing housing requires capital. And given what Esther has written, Rita's response strikes me as a perverse misreading:

It is difficult to save money. Do you have any idea where you will move? What kind of home are you planning to buy? Interest rates are low now.

The peculiarity arises in the increasing unconnectedness of Rita's sentences to Esther's assertions. The first sentence is a response to Esther's assertion that she hasn't "had a chance to save any money." And the second sentence relates to Esther's claim that she will probably have to move. But in light of what Esther wrote, the assumption that Esther is planning to buy a house or that interest rates are of any consequence to her is, to say the least, surprising. That the question confounds Esther is evident in her next letter, which begins with a passing reference to Rita's sister, whose illness Rita mentioned in her last letter, followed by a brief but pointed attempt to correct the misunderstanding:

I'm very sorry to hear about your sister. I hope she gets better. About the house. The only way I could buy a house is by hitting a number in the Lotto.

As lessons in elementary economics go this is about as clear as any I know. Yet Rita's response to this assertion is, on the face of it, even more bizarre than her statement that "Interest rates are low now." To wit, she ignores Esther's topic, which is housing, and reintroduces gambling, Lotto, as a topic they might discuss:

Do you play Lotto frequently? I never think that I can ever win one of those lotteries. Did you ever know anyone who won? Some people play faithfully.

This is a near perfect example of cross-talk, for two conversations are now in play—one about housing and another about gambling. And were this a conversation between peers, Rita would be charged with illicitly changing the topic, since it is she who played the conversational gambit in which Esther's instructive hyperbole—"the only way I could buy a house is if I win the Lotto"—is taken at its face value, and Lotto, which is not the topic but the comment, is transformed into the topic, now in the form of questions about gambling. It's a familiar teacher's gambit for controlling what does and does not count as knowledge, a remnant, perhaps, of the institutionalized silencing that Michelle Fine suggests "more intimately informs low-income, public schooling than relatively privileged situations" (158).

The salient fact here is that educational discourse empowers teachers to determine what is worthwhile in a student's contributions, presumably even if that judgment has little or no linguistic basis and even if a teacher-student relationship is not entirely warranted. Remember that Esther has been representing herself as an adult whose financial status is precarious and that she has gone to some pains not to occupy the student position that Rita has finally assigned her. It is in Esther's final letter, in which she makes one last attempt to establish subjective parity between herself and Rita, that we see the devastating pedagogical consequences of preserving this particular privilege of educational discursive practice.

> I don't play the Lotto everday except on my birthday when it July 11 (7/11). I'm really messing up this letter. I'm going to an award dinner on May 30th at 7 p.m. And when I get a lucky number. I don't know anyone that ever won. Thank you for your nice letter. Bye for now.

Esther wrote better letters at the beginning than at the end of the semester. The disintegration of syntax in this her last letter ("when it" for "which is") augurs the disappearance of the working-class adult subject she has been representing and the articulation of the Adult Basic Writer, a subject unified by its errors, its sentence fragments ("And when I get a lucky number") and its rhetorical disjunctures (the sentences and phrases whose meanings are recoverable only by association). That Esther sees the failure as her own, "I'm really messing up this letter," echoes Foucault's assertion that it is the power of discourse to create the illusion that "it is we, and we alone, who give it that power." Finally overwhelmed by educational discourse, the adult subject retreats into silence.

Ellen and Pat

The eight-letter exchange between the student and teacher I'll call Pat and Ellen is by many standards, including my own, the most successful not simply because they wrote the most often, but because Pat's letters grew longer and her errors fewer over the two months she corresponded with Ellen. While she shares the other teacher's aversion to class, Ellen differs considerably from them in her initial and repeated representation of herself as unified in relation to family: "I have been married for 21 years," "[I am] the mother of two teenagers," "I'm a very family-centered person." Ellen's representation for her familial self is often completed or articulated by Pat, when, for example, she writes "I'm all so marry for 22 1/2 year. I have 4 kids." The self unified in relation to family is reminiscent of that represented in many of the working-class narratives, except that the self articulated in their letters is decidely female.

That gender is a crucial dimension of their subjectivity first becomes apparent when Ellen responds to Pat's physical description of herself with this measured assertion of indentification: "It sounds as though you and I look somewhat alike." In this instance, it is Ellen who articulates or completes a representation of self initiated by Pat and hence Ellen who identifies herself as the embodied female subject represented in Pat's physical description. This particular articulation stands out because it is the only corporeal representation of self in the letters and because it is also the only self-representation offered by one of the students with which a teacher identifies or articulates. To be sure, Ellen's articulation is tenuous, qualified immediately by "somewhat," and later by assertions such as "I'm trying to lose some weight before the summer season comes so I won't be so embarrassed in my bathing suit" that suggest the middle-class woman's all too familiar and uneasy relationship to her body.

In the course of their reciprocal articulation, and the co-construction of themselves as gendered subjects, Pat and Ellen tell and respond to stories that narrate their shared concerns as mothers. And it is as mother-women that they ignore the class differences that overwhelm the correspondents in the other two example. Their mutual concern for their children's education, for instance, overrides material differences between their children's actual access to education. Ellen writes that she and her husband will be traveling to Williamsburg to bring their daughter home from college for the summer: "So far, each year that we've gone we've had to move her in the rain. It would be nice to be able to keep dry for once during all of the trips back and forth to the car." Pat advises Ellen to "think positive," attending not to the fact that Ellen's daughter attends a private college while her son goes to a local community college, but to the prediction that it will probably rain. In what appears to be yet another attempt to lift Ellen's spirits, Pat then recalls that she, her husband, and three children took a trip to Williamsburg eight years earlier, about which she has only this to say: "Williamsburg is a beautiful place."

Toward the end of their correspondence, Ellen and Pat recount their Mother's Days. Ellen's story is short:

> I hope you had an enjoyable Mother's Day. Did your family treat you to dinner? B [Ellen's daughter] cooked the meal and we had a combination Mother's Day and birthday celebration. My husband was one of those Mother's Day presents when he was born so every eighth year his birthday and Mother's Day fall on the same weekend so it was quite a festive time with lots going on.

Pat responds with an elaborate narrative, at least four times longer than any letter she has written, in the course of which she introduces class concerns that unify her identity as the mother and hence differentiate her experience as a mother from Ellen's. In other words, Pat's narrative interrupts their mutually constructed gender identity with a representation of herself as a subject unified in relation to Mother's Day that differs considerably from the self represented in Ellen's narrative.

In the first of five episodes, Pat establishes mood, explaining that on the Thursday evening before Mother's Day, after finally succeeding in bathing and putting the younger children to bed, she found herself "down hartit" and worrying about how hard her husband works at his two jobs and how his not being at home much means that she feels "like a mom and a dad." She follows this orientation to her state of mind with a second espisode in which her two older children ask what she wants for Mother's Day. She reports telling her son that "a card will do" but confiding to her daughter that "what I want you can't afford-it." Pressed by the daughter to tell, she admits to wanting "a ciling fane for my dinning room." Pat indicates that a ceiling fan is out of the question by writing "she laugh and so did I laugh." The third episode, which opens with an account of the complicated childcare arrangements made in order for her son to take her window shopping for ceiling fans that Friday evening, includes: a brief description of the shopping spree ("there are lots of fanes to look at but I like this one fane a lots"); a scene in which the son surprises her by giving her the money to buy the fan; and an account of what happens when they return home where the children are waiting ("They all where happy for mom but not as thrill as I was inside of me"). On Saturday, the fourth episode begins with a gift of flowers from her son and his "girl friend" and concludes with dinner with the younger children at McDonald's, where a young woman at the counter tells Pat that her son "is an inspriation to the young people here" who "miss he but there is hope for the future." (In the previous letter Pat has explained that her son worked at McDonald's for a year and a half while attending a local community college, but had since taken a job at a hospital where, after three promotions, he was making 10% more than he had as manager of the night shift at McDonald's.) She concludes the fourth episode with "I was so proud of him. Went I was told this." The fifth and final episode begins on Mother's Day morning with her husband making breakfast, after which she receives a box of candy from the smaller children, a card containing ten dollars from all the children, two "shorts sets" from her grandson, and yet another box of candy from the son's "girl friend." Reflecting on events in the conclusion of her letter, Pat writes: "I was surprize it was a beautiful motherday weekend. I feel like I writing a book so I am lifeing now."

The demonstrations of familial affection in Pat's narrative apparently resolve her internal conflict (discouragement). In a family where money is scarce—the husband works two jobs, the son holds a full-time job while attending community college, and the daughter is employed—the members shower the mother with cash and commodities. Rather than confine their celebration of the mother to service—cooking for her or dining out—the family extends it to include both the material tokens—the flowers, the fan, the clothes, and the candy—and the thrill of consumption—the material event of shopping and paying for the fan. The ritual acts of consumption and service that dramatize the mother's value in this working-class family temporarily align all its members with the economy. In other words, the economic realities that are continually threatening its unity are replaced by a four-day fantasy in which the family compensates the mother for her emotional and physical labor.

Middle-class families do not ordinarily celebrate motherhood with consumption rituals. What Ellen has described is the familiar middle-class service ritual in which the mother is released from the specific task of cooking, a symbol of the domestic responsibilities that threaten to alienate those mothers who also work outside the home from their families. In response to Pat's narrative, Ellen writes, "I enjoyed hearing about all your very nice Mother's Day surprises. It sounds as though you have a very loving and considerate family. They must really appreciate how hard you work and all of the many things you do for them." Ellen's is a gracious comment that fully acknowledges their shared understanding of mothers' work and once again articulates Pat's representation of her own and, by extension, Ellen's subjectivity as contingent on class. It's not just that their families understand the mother differently. I suspect that the working-class celebration of the mother would strike Ellen as too much and that the middle-class celebration would strike Pat as too little. Differences in their material circumstances separate them as mothers (neither Ellen nor her middle-class family need ritual relief from economic hardships), and Ellen's comment fails to acknowledge that Pat's class-based narrative places them in distinct rather than the same subject positions as women.

Ellen concludes her letter with a suggestion that draws Pat's attention to what is not said. "Since this is the last week of your classes you can wrtie (sic) me at my home address if you think that you will have the time and would like to continue writing. I know that I would enjoy hearing from you." Pat understands the absence of any expressed desire to write as well as read her letters to mean that Ellen has lost the enthusiasm for writing she expressed in earlier correspondence: "At first I was nervours about writing to someone I didn't know, but now I enjoy writing them and look forward to your letter each week." By invoking the institutional auspices under which they have been corresponding—"this is the last week of your classes"—Ellen effectively shifts from the discourse of art in which they have both been representing and articulating their subjectivity as mothers in personal narratives to the educational discourse in which Pat would presumably be a student writing for a teacher.

Pat interrupts the shift in discourse and subject positions that Ellen has suggested when she writes: "I would like to know, if you would still wiriting me, or not if not it has been nice writing to you. I don't know if it help you are not, I know it has help me a lot. Thank you very must." Pat offers yet another version of their educational relationship in which she and Ellen would continue to learn from one another by corresponding, but she makes it clear, I think, that the decision to write as well as read is Ellen's. And Ellen chooses not to write back.

Conclusion

Since the late 1970s, that is, since the publication of Pierre Bourdieu and Jean-Claude Passerson's *Reproduction in Education, Society and Culture,* many teachers and parents, and some administrators and social theorists and social scientitsts, have been concerned about the extent to which schools not only tolerate but legitimate the very forms of classism, racism, and sexism that American education is publicly charged with eliminating. I mention this by way of pointing out that law provides educational opportunity for those it designates as the subjects of social and economic discrimination. Indeed, it is the state that provides a good deal of the funding for the Adult Basic Education program that the working-class students in the study were attending. Yet the data remind us that law does not protect these students from the dialect of educational discourse in which a teacher's control over discursive practice is contingent on the ideology that classroom language transcends class, race, and gender.

The teachers in this study are not ogres—far from it. They are energetic and inventive practitioners committed to universal education. In their writing, however, that commitment manifests itself in an approach to teaching and learning that many educators share in this country, a view that insists that the classroom is a separate world of its own, in which teachers and students relate to one another undistracted by the classism, racism, and sexism that rage outside the classroom. Discursive hegemony of teachers over students is usually posed and justified in developmental terms—as cognitive deficits, emotional or intellectual immaturity, ignorance, and most recently, cultural illiteracy—any one of which would legitimate asymmetrical relationships between its knowing subjects, teachers, and its unknowing subjects, students. To the credit of the teachers who participated in this study, none took the usual recourse of justifying their discursive control by focusing on errors in spelling, grammar, and mechanics that are indubitably there and that make reading the literacy letters as difficult as reading Lacan, Derrida, Foucault, or Althusser. Yet the teachers frenetically protected educational discourse from class, and in their respective refusals to admit class concerns into the letters, they first distanced and then alienated themselves from their correspondents.

While educational discourse defends its privileged subjects against resistance, against the violence that Dora narrates, against Esther's lesson in economics, and even against Pat's much celebrated mother, the linguistic and rhetorical uneasiness with which these attempts to articulate working-class subjectivity were met suggests that the class-free discourse that seems immutable in theory is, in practice, a source of some ambivalence for the teachers in this study. What is immediately challenged by the narratives is the rhetorical practice in which the privileges of one subject—to tell stories or decide what the topic is—materially diminish the rights of other subjects. What is ultimately challenged is the ideology that class, and by extension race and gender differences, are present in American society but absent from American classrooms. If that's true, it is only true because the representation by students of those concerns inside educational discourse goes unarticulated by teachers.

To teach is to authorize the subjects of educational discourse. We have all been faced with the choice that Pat gave Ellen. To say no to writing is to say no to differences that matter to those students who live on the margins of an educational discourse that insists that they articulate themselves as the subjects teachers represent, or not at all. To say yes to writing is to say yes to those alternative subjectivities that Dora, Esther, and Pat represent in their writing and that are left unchallenged when unarticulated by Don, Rita, and Ellen. In this instance, teachers and students alike lose the opportunity to question the extent to which class figures in any individual's rendering of a unified self. Resistance inside educational discourse is then a practice in cooperative articulation on the part of the students and teachers who actively seek to construct and understand the differences as well as similarities between their respective subject positions.

Notes

The author wishes to thank the students in her class and Rachel Martin and the students in her Adult Basic Education class for generously contributing their letters to this study. She also gratefully acknowledges those whose advice she sought during the drafting of this essay: Mark Clark, Michelle Fine, Ellen Garvey, Henry Giroux, Diane Masar, Ellen Pollak, and Jan Radway.

References

Bartholomae, David. "Inventing the University." *When a Writer Can't Write*. Ed. Mike Rose. New York: Guilford, 1985. 134-65.

—————— . "The Study of Error." *College Composition and Communication* 31 (1980): 253-69.

Bourdieu, Pierre, and Jean-Claude Passeron. *Reproduction in English Society and Culture*. Beverly Hills: Sage, 1977.

Brodkey, Linda. "Tropics of Literacy." *Journal of Education* 168 (1986): 47-54.

Crowley, Sharon. "writing and Writing." *Writing and Reading Differently: Deconstruction and the Teaching of Composition and Literature*. Ed. Douglas Atkins and Michael L. Johnson. Lawrence: UP of Kansas, 1985. 93-100.

Fine, Michelle. "Silencing in the Public Schools." *Language Arts* 64 (1987): 157-74.

Foucault, Michel. "The Discourse on Language." *The Archeology of Knowledge*. New York: Harper & Row, 1976. 215-37.

Hall, Stuart. "On Postmodernism and Articulation: An Interview with Stuart Hall." Ed. Larry Grossberg. *Journal of Communication Inquiry* 10 (1986): 45-60.

Labov, William. *Language in the Inner City: Studies in the Black English Vernacular*. Philadelphia: U of Pennsylvania P, 1972.

Perl, Sondra. "The Composing Processes of Unskilled College Writers." *Research in the Teaching of English* 13 (1997): 317-36.

Pratt, Mary Louise. *Toward a Speech Act Theory of Literary Discourse*. Bloomington: Indiana UP, 1977.

Shaughnessy, Mina. *Errors and Expectations: A Guide for the Teacher of Basic Writing*. New York: Oxford UP, 1977.

Stubbs, Michael. *Language, Schools and Classrooms*. London: Methuen, 1976.

Williams, Raymond. *Marxism and Literature*. New York: Oxford UP, 1977.

Composing as a Woman

ELIZABETH A. FLYNN

> It is not easy to think like a woman in a man's world, in the world of
> the professions; yet the capacity to do that is a strength which we can try
> to help our students develop. To think like a woman in a man's world
> means thinking critically, refusing to accept the givens, making
> connections between facts and ideas which men have left unconnected. It
> means remembering that every mind resides in a body; remaining
> accountable to the female bodies in which we live; constantly retesting
> given hypotheses against lived experience. It means a constant critique of
> language, for as Wittgenstein (no feminist) observed, "The limits of my
> language are the limits of my world." And it means that most difficult
> thing of all: listening and watching in art and literature, in the social
> sciences, in all the descriptions we are given of the world, for the silences,
> the absences, the nameless, the unspoken, the encoded—for there we will
> find the true knowledge of women. And in breaking those silences,
> naming ourselves, uncovering the hidden, making ourselves present, we
> begin to define a reality which resonates to us, which affirms our being,
> which allows the woman teacher and the woman student alike to take
> ourselves, and each other, seriously: meaning, to begin taking charge of
> our lives.

> —Adrienne Rich, "Taking Women Students Seriously"

The emerging field of composition studies could be described as a
feminization of our previous conceptions of how writers write and how writing
should be taught.[1] In exploring the nature of the writing process, composition
specialists expose the limitations of previous product-oriented approaches by
demystifying the product and in so doing empowering developing writers and
readers. Rather than enshrining the text in its final form, they demonstrate
that the works produced by established authors are often the result of an
extended, frequently enormously frustrating process and that creativity is an
activity that results from experience and hard work rather than a mysterious
gift reserved for a select few. In a sense, composition specialists replace the
figure of the authoritative father with an image of a nurturing mother.

College Composition and Communication, 39 (December 1988), pp. 423-435. Copyright ©
1988 by the National Council of Teachers of English. Reprinted with permission.

Powerfully present in the work of composition researchers and theorists is the ideal of a committed teacher concerned about the growth and maturity of her students who provides feedback on ungraded drafts, reads journals, and attempts to tease out meaning from the seeming incoherence of student language. The field's foremothers come to mind—Janet Emig, Mina Shaughnessy, Ann Berthoff, Win Horner, Maxine Hairston, Shirley Heath, Nancy Martin, Linda Flower, Andrea Lunsford, Sondra Perl, Nancy Sommers, Marion Crowhurst, Lisa Ede. I'll admit the term foremother seems inappropriate, as some of these women are still in their thirties and forties—we are speaking here of a very young field. Still, invoking their names suggests that we are also dealing with a field that, from the beginning, has welcomed contributions from women—indeed, has been shaped by women.

The work of male composition researchers and theorists has also contributed significantly to the process of feminization described above. James Britton, for instance, reverses traditional hierarchies by privileging private expression over public transaction, process over product. In arguing that writing for the self is the matrix out of which all forms of writing develop, he valorizes an activity and a mode of expression that have previously been undervalued or invisible, much as feminist literary critics have argued that women's letters and diaries are legitimate literary forms and should be studied and taught alongside more traditional genres. His work has had an enormous impact on the way writing is taught on the elementary and high school levels and in the university, not only in English courses but throughout the curriculum. Writing-Across-the-Curriculum Programs aim to transform pedagogical practices in all disciplines, even those where patriarchal attitudes toward authority are most deeply rooted.

Feminist Studies and Composition Studies

Feminist inquiry and composition studies have much in common. After all, feminist researchers and scholars and composition specialists are usually in the same department and sometimes teach the same courses. Not surprisingly, there have been wonderful moments when feminists have expressed their commitment to the teaching of writing. Florence Howe's essay, "Identity and Expression: A Writing Course for Women," for example, published in *College English* in 1971, describes her use of journals in a writing course designed to empower women. Adrienne Rich's essay, "'When We Dead Awaken': Writing as Re-Vision," politicizes and expands our conception of revision, emphasizing that taking another look at the texts we have generated necessitates revising our cultural assumptions as well.

There have also been wonderful moments when composition specialists have recognized that the marginality of the field of composition studies is linked in important ways to the political marginality of its constituents, many of whom are women who teach part-time. Maxine Hairston, in "Breaking Our Bonds and Reaffirming Our Connections," a slightly revised version of her

Chair's address at the 1985 convention of the Conference on College Composition and Communication, draws an analogy between the plight of composition specialists and the plight of many women. For both, their worst problems begin at home and hence are immediate and daily. Both, too, often have complex psychological bonds to the people who frequently are their adversaries (273).

For the most part, though, the fields of feminist studies and composition studies have not engaged each other in a serious or systematic way. The major journals in the field of composition studies do not often include articles addressing feminist issues, and panels on feminism are infrequent at the Conference on College Composition and Communication.[2] As a result, the parallels between feminist studies and composition studies have not been delineated, and the feminist critique that has enriched such diverse fields as linguistics, reading, literary criticism, psychology, sociology, anthropology, religion, and science has had little impact on our models of the composing process or on our understanding of how written language abilities are acquired. We have not examined our research methods or research samples to see if they are androcentric. Nor have we attempted to determine just what it means to compose as a woman.

Feminist research and theory emphasize that males and females differ in their developmental processes and in their interactions with others. They emphasize, as well, that these differences are a result of an imbalance in the social order, of the dominance of men over women. They argue that men have chronicled our historical narratives and defined our fields of inquiry. Women's perspectives have been suppressed, silenced, marginalized, written out of what counts as authoritative knowledge. Difference is erased in a desire to universalize. Men become the standard against which women are judged.

A feminist approach to composition studies would focus on questions of difference and dominance in written language. Do males and females compose differently? Do they acquire language in different ways? Do research methods and research samples in composition studies reflect a male bias? I do not intend to tackle all of these issues. My approach here is a relatively modest one. I will survey recent feminist research on gender differences in social and psychological development, and I will show how this research and theory may be used in examining student writing, thus suggesting directions that a feminist investigation of composition might take.

Gender Differences in Social and Psychological Development

Especially relevant to a feminist consideration of student writing are Nancy Chodorow's *The Reproduction of Mothering*, Carol Gilligan's *In a Different Voice*, and Mary Belenky, Blythe Clinchy, Nancy Goldberger, and Jill Tarule's *Women's Ways of Knowing*. All three books suggest that women and men have different conceptions of self and different modes of interaction with others as a result of their different experiences, especially their early relationship with their primary parent, their mother.

Chodorow's book, published in 1978, is an important examination of what she calls the "psychoanalysis and the sociology of gender," which in turn influenced Gilligan's *In a Different Voice* and Belenky et al.'s *Women's Ways of Knowing.* Chodorow tells us in her preface that her book originated when a feminist group she was affiliated with "wondered what it meant that women parented women." She argues that girls and boys develop different relational capacities and senses of self as a result of growing up in a family in which women mother. Because all children identify first with their mother, a girl's gender and gender role identification processes are continuous with her earliest identifications whereas a boy's are not. The boy gives up, in addition to his oedipal and preoedipal attachment to his mother, his primary identification with her. The more general identification processes for both males and females also follow this pattern. Chodorow says,

> Girl's identification processes, then, are more continuously embedded in and mediated by their ongoing relationship with their mother. They develop through and stress particularistic and affective relationships to others. A boy's identification processes are not likely to be so embedded in or mediated by a real affective relation to his father. At the same time, he tends to deny identification with and relationship to his mother and reject what he takes to be the feminine world; masculinity is defined as much negatively as positively. Masculine identification processes stress differentiation from others, the denial of affective relation, and categorical universalistic components of the masculine role. Feminine identification processes are relational, whereas masculine identification processes tend to deny relationship. (176)

Carol Gilligan's *In a Different Voice,* published in 1982, builds on Chodorow's findings, focusing especially, though, on differences in the ways in which males and females speak about moral problems. According to Gilligan, women tend to define morality in terms of conflicting responsibilities rather than competing rights, requiring for their resolution a mode of thinking that is contextual and narrative rather than formal and abstract (19). Men, in contrast, equate morality and fairness and tie moral development to the understanding of rights and rules (19). Gilligan uses the metaphors of the web and the ladder to illustrate these distinctions. The web suggests interconnectedness as well as entrapment; the ladder suggests an achievement-orientation as well as in-dividualistic and hierarchical thinking. Gilligan's study aims to correct the inadequacies of Lawrence Kohlberg's delineation of the stages of moral development. Kohlberg's study included only male subjects, and his categories reflect his decidedly male orientation. For him, the highest stages of moral development derive from a reflective understanding of human rights (19).

Belenky, Clinchy, Goldberger, and Tarule, in *Women's Ways of Knowing,* acknowledge their debt to Gilligan, though their main concern is intellectual rather than moral development. Like Gilligan, they recognize that male experience has served as the model in defining processes of intellecutal maturation. The mental processes that are involved in considering the abstract and the impersonal have been labeled "thinking" and are attributed primarily to men, while those that deal with the personal and interpersonal fall under the rubric of "emotions" and are largely relegated to women. The particular study they chose to examine and revise is William Perry's *Forms of Intellectual and Ethical Development in the College Years* (1970). While Perry did include some women subjects in his study, only the interviews with men were used in illustrating and validating his scheme of intellectual and ethical development. When Perry assessed women's development on the basis of the categories he developed, the women were found to conform to the patterns he had observed in the male data. Thus, his work reveals what women have in common with men but was poorly designed to uncover those themes that might be more prominent among women. *Women's Ways of Knowing* focuses on "what else women might have to say about the development of their minds and on alternative routes that are sketchy or missing in Perry's version" (9).

Belenky et al. examined the transcripts of interviews with 135 women from a variety of backgrounds and of different ages and generated categories that are suited for describing the stages of women's intellectual development. They found that the quest for self and voice plays a central role in transformations of women's ways of knowing. Silent women have little awareness of their intellectual capacities. They live—selfless and voiceless—at the behest of those around them. External authorities know the truth and are all-powerful. At the positions of received knowledge and procedural knowledge, other voices and external truths prevail. Sense of self is embedded either in external definitions and roles or in identifications with institutions, disciplines, and methods. A sense of authority arises primarily through identification with the power of a group and its agreed-upon ways for knowing. Women at this stage of development have no sense of an authentic or unique voice, little awareness of a centered self. At the position of subjective knowledge, women turn away from others and any external authority. They have not yet acquired a public voice or public authority, though. Finally, women at the phase of constructed knowledge begin an effort to reclaim the self by attempting to integrate knowledge they feel intuitively with knowledge they have learned from others.

Student Writing

If women and men differ in their relational capacities and in their moral and intellectual development, we would expect to find manifestations of these differences in the student papers we encounter in our first-year composition courses. The student essays I will describe here are narrative descriptions of learning experiences produced in the first of a two-course sequence required of first-year students at Michigan Tech. I've selected the four because they invite commentary from the perspective of the material discussed above. The narratives of the female students are stories of interaction, of connection, or of frustrated connection. The narratives of the male students are stories of achievement, of separation, or of frustrated achievement.

Kim's essay describes a dreamlike experience in which she and her high school girlfriends connected with each other and with nature as a result of a balloon ride they decided to take one summer Sunday afternoon as a way of relieving boredom. From the start, Kim emphasizes communion and tranquility: "It was one of those Sunday afternoons when the sun shines brightly and a soft warm breeze blows gently. A perfect day for a long drive on a country road with my favorite friends." This mood is intensified as they ascend in the balloon: "Higher and higher we went, until the view was overpowering. What once was a warm breeze turned quickly into a cool crisp wind. A feeling of freedom and serenity overtook us as we drifted along slowly." The group felt as if they were "just suspended there on a string, with time non-existent." The experience made them contemplative, and as they drove quietly home, "each one of us collected our thoughts, and to this day we still reminisce about that Sunday afternoon." The experience solidified relationships and led to the formation of a close bond that was renewed every time the day was recollected.

The essay suggests what Chodorow calls relational identification processes. The members of the group are described as being in harmony with themselves and with the environment. There is no reference to competition or discord. The narrative also suggests a variation on what Belenky et al. call "connected knowing," a form of procedural knowledge that makes possible the most desirable form of knowing, constructed knowledge. Connected knowing is rooted in empathy for others and is intensely personal. Women who are connected knowers are able to detach themselves from the relationships and institutions to which they have been subordinated and begin to trust their own intuitions. The women in the narrative were connected doers rather than connected knowers. They went off on their own, left their families and teachers behind (it was summer vacation, after all), and gave themselves over to a powerful shared experience. The adventure was, for the most part, a silent one but did lead to satisfying talk.

Kathy also describes an adventure away from home, but hers was far less satisfying, no doubt because it involved considerably more risk. In her narrative she makes the point that "foreign countries can be frightening" by focusing on a situation in which she and three classmates, two females and a male, found themselves at a train station in Germany separated from the others because they had gotten off to get some refreshments and the train had left without them. She says,

> This left the four of us stranded in an unfamiliar station. Ed was the only person in our group that could speak German fluently, but he still didn't know what to do. Sue got hysterical and Laura tried to calm her down. I stood there stunned. We didn't know what to do.

What they did was turn to Ed, whom Kathy describes as "the smartest one in our group." He told them to get on a train that was on the same track as the original. Kathy realized, though, after talking to some passengers, that they were on the wrong train and urged her classmates to get off. She says,

> I almost panicked. When I convinced the other three we were on the wrong train we opened the doors. As we were getting off, one of the conductors started yelling at us in German. It didn't bother me too much because I couldn't understand what he was saying. One thing about trains in Europe is that they are always on schedule. I think we delayed that train about a minute or two.

In deciding which train to board after getting off the wrong one, they deferred to Ed's judgment once again, but this time they got on the right train. Kathy concludes, "When we got off the train everyone was waiting. It turned out we arrived thirty minutes later than our original train. I was very relieved to see everyone. It was a very frightening experience and I will never forget it."

In focusing on her fears of separation, Kathy reveals her strong need for connection, for affiliation. Her story, like Kim's, emphasizes the importance of relationships, though in a different way. She reveals that she had a strong need to feel part of a group and no desire to rebel, to prove her independence, to differentiate herself from others. This conception of self was a liability as well as a strength in the sense that she became overly dependent on the male authority figure in the group, whom she saw as smarter and more competent than herself. In Belenky et al.'s terms, Kathy acted as if other voices and external truths were more powerful than her own. She did finally speak and act, though, taking it on herself to find out if they were on the right train and ushering the others off when she discovered they were not. She was clearly moving toward the development of an authentic voice and a way of knowing that integrates intuition with authoritative knowledge. After all, she was the real hero of the incident.

The men's narratives stress individuation rather than connection. They are stories of individual achievement or frustrated achievement and conclude by emphasizing separation rather than integration or reintegration into a community. Jim wrote about his "Final Flight," the last cross-country flight required for his pilot's license. That day, everything seemed to go wrong. First, his flight plan had a mistake in it that took 1½ hours to correct. As a result, he left his hometown 2 hours behind schedule. Then the weather deteriorated, forcing him to fly as low as a person can safely fly, with the result that visibility was very poor. He landed safely at his first destination but flew past the second because he was enjoying the view too much. He says,

> Then I was off again south bound for Benton Harbor. On the way south along the coast of Lake Michigan the scenery was a beautiful sight. This relieved some of the pressures and made me look forward to the rest of the flight. It was really nice to see the ice flows break away from the shore. While enjoying the view of a power plant on the shore of Lake Michigan I discovered I had flown past the airport.

He finally landed and took off again, but shortly thereafter had to confront darkness, a result of his being behind schedule. He says,

> The sky turned totally black by the time I was half-way home. This meant flying in the dark which I had only done once before. Flying in the dark was also illegal for me to do at this time. One thing that made flying at night nice was that you could see lights that were over ninety miles away.

Jim does not emphasize his fear, despite the fact that his situation was more threatening than the one Kathy described, and his reference to his enjoyment of the scenery suggests that his anxiety was not paralyzing or debilitating. At times, his solitary flight was clearly as satisfying as Kim's communal one. When he focuses on the difficulties he encountered, he speaks only of his "problems" and "worries" and concludes that the day turned out to be "long and trying." He sums up his experience as follows: "That day I will long remember for both its significance in my goal in getting my pilot's license and all the problems or worries that it caused me during the long and problem-ridden flight." He emerges the somewhat shaken hero of his adventure; he has achieved his goal in the face of adversity. Significantly, he celebrates his return home by having a bite to eat at McDonald's by himself. His adventure does not end with a union or reunion with others.

Jim's story invites interpretation in the context of Chodorow's claims about male interactional patterns. Chodorow says that the male, in order to feel himself adequately masculine, must distinguish and differentiate himself from others. Jim's adventure was an entirely solitary one. It was also goal-directed— he wanted to obtain his pilot's license and, presumably, prove his competence to himself and others. His narrative calls into question, though, easy equations of abstract reasoning and impersonality with male modes of learning since Jim was clearly as capable as Kim of experiencing moments of exultation, of communion with nature.

Joe's narrative of achievment is actually a story of frustrated achievement, of conflicting attitudes toward an ethic of hard work and sacrifice to achieve a goal. When he was in high school, his father drove him twenty miles to swim practice and twenty miles home every Tuesday through Friday night between October and March so he could practice for the swim team. He hated this routine and hated the Saturday morning swim meets even more but continued because he thought his parents, especially his father, wanted him to. He says, "I guess it was all for them, the cold workouts, the evening practices, the weekend meets. I had to keep going for them even though I hated it." Once he realized he was going through his agony for his parents rather than for himself, though, he decided to quit and was surprised to find that his parents supported him. Ultimately, though, he regretted his decision. He says,

> As it turns out now, I wish I had stuck with it. I really had a chance to go somewhere with my talent. I see kids my age who stuck with something for a long time and I envy them for their determination. I wish I had met

up to the challenge of sticking with my swimming, because I could have been very good if I would have had their determination.

Joe is motivated to pursue swimming because he thinks his father will be disappointed if he gives it up. His father's presumed hold on him is clearly tenuous, however, because once Joe realizes that he is doing it for him rather than for himself, he quits. Finally, though, it is his gender role identification, his socialization into a male role and a male value system, that allows him to look back on his decision with regret. In college, he has become a competitor, an achiever. He now sees value in the long and painful practices, in a single-minded determination to succeed. The narrative reminds us of Chodorow's point that masculine identification is predominantly a gender role identification rather than identification with a particular parent.

I am hardly claiming that the four narratives are neat illustrations of the feminist positions discussed above. For one thing, those positions are rich in contradiciton and complexity and defy easy illustration. For another, the narratives themselves are as often characterized by inconsistency and contradiction as by a univocality of theme and tone. Kathy is at once dependent and assertive; Joe can't quite decide if he should have been rebellious or disciplined. Nor am I claiming that what I have found here are characteristic patterns of male and female student writing. I would need a considerably larger and more representative sample to make such a claim hold. I might note, though, that I had little difficulty identifying essays that revealed patterns of difference among the twenty-four papers I had to choose from, and I could easily have selected others. Sharon, for instance, described her class trip to Chicago, focusing especially on the relationship she and her classmates were able to establish with her advisor. Diane described "An Unwanted Job" that she seemed unable to quit despite unpleasant working conditions. Mike, like Diane, was dissatisfied with his job, but he expressed his dissatisfaction and was fired. The frightening experience Russ described resulted from his failed attempt to give his car a tune-up; the radiator hose burst, and he found himself in the hospital recovering from third-degree burns. These are stories of relatedness or entanglement; of separation or frustrated achievement.

The description of the student essays is not meant to demonstrate the validity of feminist scholarship but to suggest, instead, that questions raised by feminist researchers and theorists do have a bearing on composition studies and should be pursued. We ought not assume that males and females use language in identical ways or represent the world in a similar fashion. And if their writing strategies and patterns of representation do differ, then ignoring those differences almost certainly means a suppression of women's separate ways of thinking and writing. Our models of the composing process are quite possibly better suited to describing men's ways of composing than to describing women's.[3]

Pedagogical Strategies

The classroom provides an opportunity for exploring questions about gender differences in language use. Students, I have found, are avid inquirers into their own language processes. An approach I have had success with is to make the question of gender difference in behavior and language use the subject to be investigated in class. In one honors section of first-year English, for instance, course reading included selections from Mary Anne Ferguson's *Images of Women in Literature,* Gilligan's *In a Different Voice,* Alice Walker's *Meridian,* and James Joyce's *A Portrait of the Artist as a Young Man.* Students were also required to keep a reading journal and to submit two formal papers. The first was a description of people they know in order to arrive at generalizations about gender differences in behavior, the second a comparison of some aspect of the Walker and Joyce novels in the light of our class discussions.

During class meetings we shared journal entries, discussed the assigned literature, and self-consciously explored our own reading, writing, and speaking behaviors. In one session, for instance, we shared retellings of Irwin Shaw's "The Girls in Their Summer Dresses," an especially appropriate story since it describes the interaction of a husband and wife as they attempt to deal with the husband's apparently chronic habit of girl-watching. Most of the women were sympathetic to the female protagonist, and several males clearly identified strongly with the male protagonist.

The students reacted favorably to the course. They found Gilligan's book to be challenging, and they enjoyed the heated class discussions. The final journal entry of one of the strongest students in the class, Dorothy, suggests the nature of her development over the ten-week period:

> As this is sort of the wrap-up of what I've learned or how I feel about the class, I'll try to relate this entry to my first one on gender differences.
>
> I'm not so sure that men and women are so similar anymore, as I said in the first entry. The reactions in class especially make me think this. The men were so hostile toward Gilligan's book! I took no offense at it, but then again I'm not a man. I must've even overlooked the parts where she offended the men!
>
> Another thing really bothered me. One day after class, I heard two of the men talking in the hall about how you just have to be really careful about what you say in HU 101H about women, etc. *Why* do they have to be careful? What did these two *really* want to say? That was pretty disturbing.
>
> However, I do still believe that MTU (or most any college acutally) does bring out more similarities than differences. But the differences are still there—I know that.

Dorothy has begun to suspect that males and females read differently, and she has begun to suspect that they talk among themselves differently than they do in mixed company. The reading, writing, and discussing in the course have clearly alerted her to the possibility that gender affects the way in which readers, writers, and speakers use language.

This approach works especially well with honors students. I use somewhat different reading and writing assignments with non-honors students. In one class, for instance, I replaced the Gilligan book with an essay by Dale Spender on conversational patterns in high school classrooms. Students wrote a paper defending or refuting the Spender piece on the basis of their experiences in their own high schools. I have also devised ways of addressing feminist issues in composition courses in which the focus is not explicitly on gender differences. In a course designed to introduce students to fundamentals of research, for instance, students read Marge Piercy's *Woman on the Edge of Time* and did research on questions stimulated by it. They then shared their findings with the entire class in oral presentations. The approach led to wonderful papers on and discussions of the treatment of women in mental institutions, discrimination against minority women, and the ways in which technology can liberate women from oppressive roles.

I return now to my title and to the epigraph that introduces my essay. First, what does it mean to "compose as a woman"? Although the title invokes Jonathan Culler's "Reading as a Woman," a chapter in *On Deconstruction,* I do not mean to suggest by it that I am committed fully to Culler's deconstructive position. Culler maintains that "to read as a woman is to avoid reading as a man, to identify the specific defenses and distortions of male readings and provide correctives" (54). He concludes,

> For a woman to read as a woman is not to repeat an identity or an experience that is given but to play a role she constructs with reference to her identity as a woman, which is also a construct, so that the series can continue: a woman reading as a woman reading as a woman. The noncoincidence reveals an interval, a division within woman or within any reading subject and the "experience" of that subject. (64)

Culler is certainly correct that women often read as men and that they have to be encouraged to defend against this form of alienation. The strategy he suggests is almost entirely reactive, though. To read as a woman is to avoid reading as a man, to be alerted to the pitfalls of men's ways of reading.[4] Rich, too, warns of the dangers of immasculation,[5] of identifying against oneself and learning to think like a man, and she, too, emphasizes the importance of critical activity on the part of the woman student—refusing to accept the givens of our culture, making connections between facts and ideas which men have left unconnected. She is well aware that thinking as a woman involves active construction, the recreation of one's identity. But she also sees value in recovering women's lived experience. In fact, she suggests that women maintain a critical posture in order to get in touch with that experience—to name it, to uncover that which is hidden, to make present that which has been absent. Her approach is active rather than reactive. Women's experience is not entirely a distorted version of male reality, it is not entirely elusive, and it is worthy of recuperation. We must alert our women students to the dangers of immasculation and provide them with a critical perspective. But we must also encourage them to become self-consciously aware of what their experience in the world has been and how this experience is related to the politics of gender. Then we must encourage our women students to write from the power of that experience.

Notes

[1] I received invaluable feedback on drafts of this essay from Carol Berkenkotter, Art Young, Marilyn Cooper, John Willinsky, Diane Shoos, John Flynn, Richard Gebhardt, and three anonyomous *CCC* reviewers.

[2] The 1988 Conference on College Composition and Communication was a notable exception. It had a record number of panels on feminist or gender-related issues and a number of sessions devoted to political concerns. I should add, too, that an exception to the generalization that feminist studies and composition studies have not confronted each other is Cynthia Caywood and Gillian Overing's very useful anthology, *Teaching Writing: Pedagogy, Gender, and Equity.* In their introduction to the book, Caywood and Overing note the striking parallels between writing theory and feminist theory. They conclude, "[T]he process model, insofar as it facilitates and legitimizes the fullest expression of the individual voice, is compatible with the feminist re-visioning of hierarchy, if not essential to it" (xiv). Pamela Annas, in her essay, "Silences: Feminist Language Research and the Teaching of Writing," describes a course she teaches at the University of Massachusetts at Boston, entitled "Writing as Women." In the course, she focuses on the question of silence—"what kinds of silence there are; the voices inside you that tell you to be quiet, the voices outside you that drown you out or politely dismiss what you say or do not understand you, the silence inside you that avoids saying anything important even to yourself, internal and external forms of censorship, and the stress that it produces" (3-4). Carol A. Stanger in "The Sexual Politics of the One-to-One Tutorial Approach and Collaborative Learning" argues that the one-to-one tutorial is essentially hierarchical and hence a male mode of teaching whereas collaborative learning is female and relational rather than hierarchical. She uses Gilligan's images of the ladder and the web to illustrate her point. Elisabeth Daeumer and Sandra Runzo suggest that the teaching of writing is comparable to the activity of mothering in that it is a form of "women's work." Mothers socialize young children to insure that they become acceptable citizens, and teachers' work, like the work of mothers, is usually devalued (45-46).

[3] It should be clear by now that my optimistic claim at the outset of the essay that the field of composition studies has feminized our conception of written communication needs qualification. I have already mentioned that the field has developed, for the most part, independent of feminist studies and as a result has not explored written communication in the context of women's special needs and problems. Also, feminist inquiry is beginning to reveal that work in cognate fields that have influenced the development of composition studies is androcentric. For an exploration of the androcentrism of theories of the reading process see Patrocinio P. Schweickart, "Reading Ourselves: Toward a Feminist Theory of Reading."

[4] Elaine Showalter, in "Reading as a Woman: Jonathan Culler and the Deconstruction of Feminist Criticism," argues that "Culler's deconstructionist priorities lead him to overstate the essentialist dilemma of defining the *woman* reader, when in most cases what is intended and implied is a *feminist* reader" (126).

⁵Judith Fetterley first used the term *immasculation* in "The Resisting Reader: A Feminist Approach to American Fiction" (Bloomington: Indiana University Press, 1977). In speaking of canonical male texts, she says, "In such fiction, the female reader is co-opted into participation in an experience from which she is explicitly excluded; she is asked to identify with a selfhood that defines itself in opposition to her; she is required to identify against herself." (p. xii)

References

Annas, Pamela J. "Silences: Feminist Language Research and the Teaching of Writing." *Teaching Writing: Pedagogy, Gender, and Equity*. Ed. Cynthia L. Caywood and Gillian R. Overing. Albany: State U of New York P, 1987. 3-17.

Belenky, Mary Field, et al. *Women's Ways of Knowing: The Development of Self, Voice and Mind*. New York: Basic Books, 1986.

Britton, James, et al. *The Development of Writing Abilities (11-18)*. London: Macmillan Education, 1975.

Caywood, Cynthia L., and Gillian R. Overing. Introduction. *Teaching Writing: Pedagogy, Gender, and Equity*. Ed. Cynthia L. Caywood and Gillian R. Overing. Albany: State U of New York P, 1987. xi-xvi.

Chodorow, Nancy. *The Reproduction of Mothering: Psychoanalysis and the Sociology of Gender*. Berkeley: U of California P, 1978.

Culler, Jonathan. *On Deconstruction: Theory and Criticism after Structuralism*. Ithaca: Cornell UP, 1982.

Daeumer, Elisabeth, and Sandra Runzo. "Transforming the Composition Classroom." *Teaching Writing: Pedagogy, Gender, and Equity*. Ed. Cynthia L. Caywood and Gillian R. Overing. Albany: State U of New York P, 1987. 45-62.

Gilligan, Carol. *In a Different Voice: Psychological Theory and Women's Development*. Cambridge: Harvard UP, 1982.

Hairston, Maxine. "Breaking Our Bonds and Reaffirming Our Connections." *College Composition and Communication* 36 (October 1985): 272-82.

Howe, Florence. "Identity and Expression: A Writing Course for Women." *College English* 32 (May 1971): 863-71. Rpt. in Howe, *Myths of Coeducation: Selected Essays, 1964-1983*. Bloomington: Indiana UP, 1984. 28-37.

Kohlberg, Lawrence. "Moral Stages and Moralization: The Cognitive-Developmental Approach." *Moral Development and Behavior*. Ed. T. Lickona. New York: Holt, 1976. 31-53.

Perry, William G. *Forms of Intellectual and Ethical Development in the College Years*. New York: Holt, Rinehart & Winston, 1970.

Rich, Adrienne. "Taking Women Students Seriously." *On Lies, Secrets, and Silence: Selected Prose, 1966-1978*. New York: Norton, 1979. 237-45.

———. "'When We Dead Awaken': Writing as Re-Vision." *On Lies, Secrets, and Silence: Selected Prose, 1966-1978*. New York: Norton, 1979. 33-49.

Schweickart, Patrocinio P. "Reading Ourselves: Toward a Feminist Theory of Reading." *Gender and Reading: Essays on Readers, Texts and Contexts*. Ed. Elizabeth A. Flynn and Patrocinio P. Schweickart. Baltimore: Johns Hopkins UP, 1986. 31-62.

Showalter, Elaine. "Reading as a Woman: Jonathan Culler and the Deconstruction of Feminist Criticism." *Men and Feminism*. Ed. Alice Jardine and Paul Smith. New York: Methuen, 1987. 123-27.

Stanger, Carol A. "The Sexual Politics of the One-to-One Tutorial Approach and Collaborative Learning." *Teaching Writing: Pedagogy, Gender, and Equity*. Ed. Cynthia L. Caywood and Gillian R. Overing. Albany: State U of New York P, 1987. 31-44.

Portfolios as a Substitute for Proficiency Examinations

PETER ELBOW and PAT BELANOFF

We were troubled by the proficiency examination we found at Stony Brook. We believe proficiency examinations undermine good teaching by sending the wrong message about the writing process: that proficient writing means having a serious topic sprung on you (with no chance for reading, reflection, or discussion) and writing one draft (with no chance for sharing or feedback or revising). Besides, an exam can't give a valid picture of a student's proficiency in writing: we need at least two or three samples of her writing—in two or three genres at two or three sittings.[1]

After four semesters of small scale experimentation, and in coordination with a new University writing requirement, we gave up the proficiency exam and made portfolios official in the 40-plus sections of our required Writing 101 course. The new requirement says that every student must get a C or higher in 101 or else take it again. The portfolio system says that no student can *get* that C unless her portfolio has been judged worth a C not only by her teacher but also by at least one other teacher who does not know her.

A portfolio system might take different forms. Here is how our version works at the moment. Every 101 student must now develop—out of all the writing done during the semester—a portfolio of three revised papers: (a) a narrative, descriptive, or expressive piece; (b) an essay of any sort (so long as it is in the discourse of the academic community—i.e., not a personal, digressive *essai* as by Montaigne); (c) an analysis of a prose text. With each of these papers students must submit a brief informal cover sheet which explores their writing process in that paper and acknowledges any help they have received. The portfolio must also contain a fourth piece: an in-class essay done without benefit of feedback.

Every 101 teacher is a member of a portfolio group. Experienced teachers create their own small groups. New teachers are in a large group—constituted by the Teaching Practicum that all new teachers take.

At mid-semester *all* teachers meet to discuss sample papers and agree on some verdicts: a "calibration" session. Then teachers meet in their smaller groups and distribute their students' mid-semester "dry run" papers to each other for readings. (We've learned that students need an outside reading of one or two of their portfolio essays at mid-semester—in order to get used to the

College Composition and Communication, 37 (October 1986), pp. 336-339. Copyright ©
1986 by the National Council of Teachers of English. Reprinted with permission.

system and be warned of the standards.) The judgment is a simple binary Yes or No—worth a C or not. Readers make no comments on the papers (except for light checkmarks at unambiguous mistakes in mechanics—especially if a paper fails for that reason). A brief comment by the reader who is not the student's teacher is paper-clipped only to failing papers—usually only a few sentences. It is not the reader's job to diagnose or teach—only to judge. It is the teacher's job to interpret these comments to the student when that is necessary. (We're trying to keep the portfolio system from being much of an extra burden on teachers. Strong portfolios can be read quickly—sometimes just skimmed.)

If the teacher agrees with the verdict, the process is finished—and this is what happens with most papers. But if the teacher disagrees, she can ask for a second reading from another reader. If that second reading is the same, the teacher may feel that she should change her view and go along with those two outside readers; but she is free to seek a third reading to validate her original perception. However, the stakes are not high at midsemester; a failure doesn't count. Teachers tend to prefer stern verdicts at midsemester to keep students from being lulled into false security.

This collaborative evaluating process is repeated at the end of the semester—but with full portfolios: a calibration meeting for all teachers on sample portfolios; small groups for first, second, and occasionally third readings; yes/no judgments on whole portfolios (not separate verdicts on each paper): no comments except on failed portfolios. This time, of course, the gun is loaded: it's the end of the semester and a student who fails her portfolio must repeat the course. However, if the two readers agree that the failure stems from *only one* paper, the student may revise that paper and resubmit the portfolio.

By giving students more time and more chance for help, and by letting them choose their best writing, the system is a way to ask for *better* writing and push *more* students to provide it. Sometimes 50% of the mid-semester "dry run" papers fail, but at semester's end fewer than 10% of the portfolios fail—and that goes down to less than 5% after some are rewritten.

This may sound like trying to raise standards and passing rates at the same time, but evaluation by portfolio gets away from the traditional norm-referenced model of evaluation which has given us most of our gut-level assumptions about testing. The goal in traditional evaluation is to rank or differentiate students into as many different "grades" as possible; it is a tradition of "measuring" minds; the ideal end product is population distributed along a bell-shaped curve (as in IQ or SAT SCORES). The portfolio process uses a very different model of evaluation—criterion-referenced or mastery-based or competence-based—which assumes that the ideal end product is a population of students who have *all* finally passed because they have all been given enough time and help to do what we ask of them.[2]

The portfolio system makes some teachers feel a bit uncomfortable—especially the first time they use it. But it helps teachers too, and has a number of other benefits. Most important, it encourages good teaching and a sound writing process. A proficiency exam rewards playing it safe and plastic, five-paragraph essays; portfolio papers won't pass with a required C unless they show some genuine thought and investment. The portfolio encourages revising, peer feedback, and collaboration among students. (As for cheating: teachers do not submit a portfolio unless they are confident it is the student's own work; students may not change topics at the last minute in revising papers.)

The portfolio system throws the teacher somewhat into the role of *coach* or *editor* because the crucial decision as to whether the student is eligible to get a C (or must repeat the course) depends on someone other than the teacher. The teacher becomes someone who can *help* the student overcome an obstacle posed by a third party and is thus less likely to be seen by students as merely "the enemy." Thus, the portfolio system leads teachers to make comments like this:

> I like this piece. It works for me. But I think some of my pleasure comes from knowing how hard you've worked and how much progress you've made. It helps me to have read some of your earlier drafts and gotten to know you and your concerns. I fear your piece won't work so well for a reader who is a stranger to you.

In effect this sets up the "good cop/bad-cop" game ("I'd like to give you a break but my buddy is a mean son of a bitch"). But the portfolio also sets up the "cop-handcuffed-to-the-prisoner" game: an insecure teacher is liable to feel her student's failure as a reflection on her—and may even be tempted to give *too* much help. Most teachers have gotten burnt once: "I'm sorry, but I seem to have misled you. Your portfolio didn't pass." (Even after going back for third and fourth readings.) Thus teachers learn to say, "I think this is good work, I like it, I would give it at least a C. But we'll have to see what portfolio readers think."

We like what this does to the use of grades in a writing course. Teachers retain *almost* complete power over grades. (They can give any grade to an individual paper; they can give any course grade to students who pass the portfolio; they can give any grade below a C to students who do not pass it.) But the portfolio system anchors that crucial "C" line to negotiation by the community. And the system makes teachers less likely to put grades on weekly papers, more likely to concentrate all their energies on useful comments. Students often ignore comments when there is a grade; teachers often write better comments when not having to justify a grade.

The portfolio system encourages collaboration among teachers. When teachers work in isolation they often drift into believing that they use standards made in heaven—that they *know* what A and F mean. (It's painful to give grades when you experience the full sense of indeterminacy involved.) Yet of course there is enormous inconsistency among the grades of isolated teachers, so *students* often drift in the opposite direction—into complete skepticism or even cynicism about the possibility of evaluation or even judgment at all. They often feel that *all* evaluations or judgments are nothing but accidents of teacher's personalities. Such students think that getting good grades is nothing but psyching out idiosyncracies—figuring out what particular teachers "like" or "want."

Our profession lacks any firm, theoretical, discipline-wide, basis for deciding the right interpretation or evaluation of a text. The only way to bring a bit of trustworthiness to grading is to get teachers negotiating together in a community to make some collaborative judgments. That the portfolio promotes collaboration and works against isolation may be, in the end, its main advantage.

These collaborative discussions of sample papers are interesting. One faction may give powerful arguments for failing the sample paper; someone even says, "How can anyone who considers himself a literate professional possibly give this paper a C?" But another group gives strong arguments in its favor, and the blurter discovers that the defenders of the paper are not just the flakey wimps he suspected but also include a colleague he respects as more perceptive and learned than himself.

Hurtful words are sometimes spoken, e.g., "It's not the paper that flunks, it's the assignment!" Yet over the semesters we have come to treasure these difficult moments. As one of us said just the other day when the heat was rising in the room: "We're sorry you are having a hard time, but *we're* having a ball!" It's a relief for us to see all this disparity of judgment out on the floor *as interaction between people*—as heads butting against other heads. Normally, the disparity is locked inside solitary heads, visible only to students who compare notes and to administrators looking at different teachers' grade sheets. When a newcomer complains, "Why do you encourage all this chaos and disagreement?" it's fun to be able to reply, "We're not making it, we're just getting it out from under the rug."

On most samples there is a decisive majority or even consensus. But when teachers remain divided, it's important for us to intervene, get a quick vote to show where the numbers lie (sometimes the discussion can fool you), and say, "Fine. We're split. Here's a picture of where our community disagrees; here is a paper that will pass in some groups and fail in others; nevertheless this picture can give you some guidance when you go off to make your individual verdicts. We're gradually giving each other a sense of our standards as a community." For even though it is the *disagreement* that is most obvious at such moments, *we,* from where we sit, see such discussions producing much more *agreement* in grading and community standards than we used to have when all teachers graded alone.[3]

Notes

[1] Charles Cooper, *The Nature and Measurement of Competency in English* (Urbana, IL: National Council of Teachers of English, 1981).

[2] See D.C. McClelland, "Testing for Competence Rather Than for 'Intelligence,'" *American Psychologist* 28 (January, 1973), 1-14. Also Gerald Grant and Wendy Kohli, "Contributing to Learning by Assessing Student Performance," in *On Competence,* ed. Gerald Grant and Associates (San Francisco: Jossey-Bass, 1979), pp. 138-59. Also Peter Elbow on the effects of competence-based curricula on teachers: "Trying to Teach While Thinking About the End," in *Embracing Contraries* (New York: Oxford University Press, 1986).

[3] We have written two essays which describe the system more fully: (1) "Using Portfolios to Judge Writing Proficiency at SUNY Stony Brook," in *New Methods in College Writing Programs,* ed. Paul Connolly and Teresa Vilardi (New York: Modern Language Association, 1986); (2) "Using Portfolios to Increase Collaboration and Community in a Writing Program," *WPA: Journal of Writing Program Administration.* 9 (Spring, 1986). For an interesting account of another use of portfolios for grading (but not as a substitute for proficiency examinations), see Christopher Burnham's "Portfolio Evaluation: Room to Breathe and Grow" in *Training the Teacher of College Composition,* ed. Charles Bridges (Urbana, IL: National Council of Teachers of English, 1986).

Paulo Freire's Liberation Pedagogy

ANN E. BERTHOFF

[When Paulo Freire was unable to speak at the Sunday General Session of
the NCTE meeting in Baltimore in November, 1989, Ann E. Berthoff
was asked to substitute. With a few passages omitted, the following is the
text of her address.]

Paulo Freire is difficult to read because he is both a Christian and a
Marxist—and those lexicons are sometimes at odds with one another. His
theory, as I will try to show, is extremely important to us and so is his
remarkable practice. Freire was able to alphabetize illiterate peasants of Brazil
in forty hours. He invented or reclaimed a method as old as Comenius: he
taught the recognition of sounds and letter shapes simultaneously with
meanings of some importance. But that is not why his slide projectors were
destroyed, his primers burned—with the help of the C.I.A. It was not the fact
that he taught literacy which sent him into exile; it was that his method
transformed his learners so that they found a voice, which in this context does
not mean a psychological event of self-realization but a revolutionary move
away from "the culture of silence" towards naming and transforming the world.
The agency of this transformation is what Freire calls *conscientization,* and it is
my hope that in what follows I can make that idea accessible.

Let me begin by reading you what I wrote to introduce Paulo Freire on the
occasion of his visit to Boston in 1985. He spoke at the Kennedy Library, our
neighbor at the Harbor Campus of the University of Massachusetts. The
auditorium was jam-packed and there were at least a hundred admirers
standing in the great lobby. Here's what I said in introducing him to these
masses:

> Paulo Freire recently came to my rescue, as he has done so frequently in
> the past. I was trying to think of a way to explain his particular
> importance to English teachers, what it is about his attitudes that is so
> inspiriting. He reminds me of Montessori, Tolstoy, Danilo Dolci, and,
> most of all, Jane Addams, but though he certainly belongs with these
> great teachers, that classification didn't give me my definition of what's
> special about Freire. But then, in reading *The Politics of Education,* I
> found what I needed. Paulo tells us that in trying "to apprehend
> subjectivity and objectivity in their dialectical relationship"—of under-

Language Arts, 67 (April 1990), pp. 362-369. Copyright © by the National Council of
Teachers of English. Reprinted with permission.

standing, that is to say, both the promise and the limitations of conscientization, in trying to focus his efforts, he has turned himself, as he says, into "a tramp of the obvious, becoming the tramp of demystifying conscientization." "In playing the part of this vagrant," he goes on, "I have also been learning how important the obvious becomes as the object of our critical reflection."

Paulo Freire teaches us to look—and to look again—at our theory and practice and at the method which we can derive from the dialectic of their relationship. Nothing in the field of literacy theory is more important than looking and looking again at the role of an awareness of awareness, of thinking about thinking, of interpreting our interpretations. It's those circularities which make positivists dizzy. They make those whom Freire calls mechanists very impatient with the "pedagogy of the oppressed."

One of the things I love best about Paulo Freire is that he is restless but not impatient. That's the way it is with tramps! They love their leisure and, like Socrates, the first of that ilk, they enjoy speculative and critical dialogue in pastoral settings—but they are also constantly on the move.

Paulo Freire's ideas are powerful because they are presented theoretically and practically. The theory is there and it is based on sound conceptions of language and learning which are just now coming into their own. Freire has the audacity to believe that teachers must be learners, that they learn from students in dialogue. His practice is imaginative, inventive, and thoroughly pragmatic—which does not mean "hard-headed" or "cost-conscious" but "willing and able to bring theory to the test." He helps us think about ends and means, about the mysteries of despair and hope. And he encourages us not to defer change until some propitious moment, not to waste our substance on getting people ready for change, ready to learn, ready for education, but, rather, to recognize that "the readiness is all." He reminds me of A.J. Muste, the pacifist who so annoyed Reinhold Niebuhr. Muste used to say: "There is no way to peace; peace is the way." I think Paulo is saying to us: "There is no way to transformation; transformation is the way." That is not mumbo jumbo; it is not a paradox which should be resolved; it is a dialectic to be enacted.

* * *

I will focus on this statement from *The Pedagogy of the Oppressed:* *Dialogue is the encounter between men, mediated by the world, to name the world.* I offer a close reading.

Dialogue for Freire is an *encounter,* a close encounter, a social encounter. Dialogue is not just conversation; it is dialectic and reflective. Marxists worry about the distinction between dialectic and dialogue, but they are interdependent in the way that process and product are. Freire calls his classroom a "culture circle"; for him to speak of "collaborative learning" would be redundant: there is no other kind. Learning is necessarily collaborative. (But that is not the same as saying that collaboration is necessarily learning or that it is necessarily socially and politically significant, a point I take from Beth Daniells.)

Dialogue is the encounter *between men*. American feminists have seen to it that Freire now speaks not of *man* but of *men and women,* but it creates a muddle here, since we can't say that dialogue is an encounter between *men and women.* And we must remind ourselves that when Freire and his translators speak of dialogue as an "encounter between *human beings,"* it is slightly redundant, because an encounter between *non*-human beings would not be a dialogue. There is nothing dialogic about the encounter of one animal with another, nothing dialogic about a person and his or her pet. (Virtual conversation, yes, but not dialogue.) The most absorbing chapter in *The Pedagogy of the Oppressed* is, I think, a discussion of the difference between the beasts who live in an eternal Now, as Susanne Langer puts it, and Man, who lives in history.

The encounter which is dialogue is *mediated by the world:* Paulo Freire's pedagogy at every point recognizes that there is no direct access to reality. All that we know, we know by means of a mediating representation. Man does not live simply by instinct: his world is built of meanings. And meanings are our means of making further meaning. Just as all learning is necessarily collaborative, so all knowledge is necessarily mediated by our experience of the world, which for Freire is always an experience formed and represented by language. It is odd, perhaps, to recommend one Marxist to illuminate another, but Vygotsky and Freire see eye-to-eye on the nature of language as in dialectic with thought and entailing activity. Freire speaks of "thought-language" and means by it exactly what Vygotsky means by "verbal thought." Freire never dichotomizes language and thought, nor does he set them in antithesis to action. Action and reflection are both entailed in naming the world.

Freire demonstrates that experience must be re-cognized, represented, and interpreted if it is to have pedagogical value. The philosophical source of Freire's conception of experience is existentialism, but it is consonant with John Dewey's ideas and with Louise Rosenblatt's theories of reading. (Indeed, Paulo Freire's "reading the world, reading the word" could serve as a subtitle of *Literature as Exploration.*) One reason that Paulo Freire is so important for the Third World is that they have not had their John Dewey: there is a scarcity of models for a progressive education. My experience of the Third World is very limited, but I did discover in Kenya that the favored educational models were colonial—an example of what psychologists mean when they speak of "internalizing" the oppressor. You get your knuckles rapped if you don't greet your teacher with exactly the right formula.

Paulo Freire's pedagogy of the oppressed offers a revolutionary model for the Third World because it provides a method which does not depend on knowledge that has been "deposited" (in Freire's best-known metaphor of education as banking); rather, it is a method by which learners call upon their capacities as creatures who live in history; they reclaim their powers as language animals, the species-specific power to name the world—to read the world, to write the world. These are all acts of mind: naming, reading, writing are, of course, actual linguistic operations, but they are simultaneously metaphors for interpretation.

The first activity of those in the culture circles is to name the world of their village. They collect the names which represent what is important in their lives. These are the "generative words": they are represented in visual form, they are discussed and renamed. Freire's "generative words" are like Sylvia Ashton-Warner's "key vocabulary," and when she writes that they are "the captions of the dynamic life itself," we can hear the resonance with Freire, if we remember that for Ashton-Warner, no Marxist she, language is a social product.*

The generative words are represented in pictures which are called "situations"; they would more properly be called "situational contexts." Freire carefully differentiates *code* and *codification*—the signal and the message—and invites the as yet unlettered learners to name this part of the world. A hunter is depicted in one of these situations. He is shooting a bird with a bow and arrow. His loin cloth is made of feathers and he wears a feather headdress. And there are feathers on his arrow, of course—like meanings used to make other meanings. In the background, a woman is cooking a fowl in a pot. The leader of the culture circle names the man who is hunting as a *culture-maker:* he transforms what he hunts, making culture from it. The peasants are then shown a picture of a cat—a very mean cat—ready to pounce on a mouse. Is the cat a hunter? "No," says an old man, "he does not make culture. He is only a pursuer."

Nobody has to teach anybody to do that—how to recognize a difference in a sameness; nobody has to teach you how to re-name. Children learn language by re-naming the world metaphorically. What we do teach—what we provide occasions for learners to discover—is *that* they are so doing, *that* they can recognize and re-present and re-name; *that* they can name the world. If you have read Shirley Brice Heath's *Ways with Words,* you will remember that "doin' ethnography" calls upon exactly such capacities, viz., the skill and judgment which enables all human beings to see examples as representative, to recognize general ideas in concrete, palpable form, in perceived objects and events, in remembered or envisaged scenes. The act of collecting details about how an uncle plants his beans emerges from dialogue and leads to reflection on what you think you've found out. The discovery is of more than how to plant beans: it is an enactment of one's powers of naming the world, the discovery *that* one

---

*I would like to note parenthetically that Freire's method deploys a sophisticated understanding of linguistic analysis. The *generative* words are so called not only because they generate questions but because from an analysis of their phonetic structure can be generated other words, by means of "the card of discovery." This procedure is explained in *Education for Critical Consciousness* in a section which I have reprinted in *The Making of Meaning.*

knows. Knowing *that* you know is what Freire means by conscientization. It is the process by which one becomes the subject of what one learns, a subject with a purpose which can be represented, assessed, modified, directed, changed. Conscientization means discovering yourself as a subject, but it is not *self-consciousness*; it is "consciousness of consciousness, intent upon the world."

"To exist humanly," Freire writes, "is to name the world, to change it. Once named, the world in its turn reappears to the namers as a problem and requires of them a new naming." Thus it is that Freire's learners are not problem-solvers but problem-posers. In their re-naming, they are "problematizing their existential situations." In an example I have often cited (described in "The Adult Literary Process as Cultural Action for Freedom," reprinted in *Literacy*), the peasants respond to a bowl of dirty water. One woman, recalling that it was her task as a child to fetch water from a stream some distance away, tells how one day she reached the stream only to find out that it had run dry and that it was full of locusts. She weeps as she remembers. (There is a lot in common here with the Speak Grievance sessions in the early days of *fan-shen*, the process of transformation in the Chinese revolution: it was necessary for the peasants to come to grips with their history in order to differentiate it from their destiny.) In her story of the dry stream, the peasant has spoken a true word: she has transformed the bowl of water to an emblem of a condition which is not the unavoidable drying up of the stream—if indeed that *was* natural and not a preventable ecological disaster. There might be no way to get rid of locusts, *but why don't we have a pump? That* is a revolutionary question! When people learn that their misery and suffering is not necessary, that it is not God's will or the inevitable pattern of Nature, their liberation has begun. Naming the world, speaking a true word, thus becomes the model, the type, for cultural action for freedom.

The capacity to differentiate social conditions which are politically determined from natural necessity is developed from a deep resource, namely the power of recognition and the power of representation. Freire's accounts are filled with moments of recognition. These epiphanies do not come from heaven, dawning on the solitary, alienated consciousness: they are dialogic. In one story, the learners of the culture circle are studying a picture of a harbor with little boats drawn up on the shore, the rim of the bay lined with houses. One of them gets up and goes to the window and looks out; then he comes back and looks again at the picture and exclaims: "It is our village! Monte Mario is like this and we didn't know it!"

The distinction between history and nature figures prominently in Marxist theory, of course, but Marxists do not always understand that the capacity to make that distinction is linguistic in origin and character and operation. The capacity to differentiate the conditions of our lives which we are free to change from those we are not—our mortality and, generally speaking, our gender—this capacity is made possible by the imagination, "the prime agent of all human perception" (Coleridge) and by the heuristic generative power of language. The human capacity to know *that* we know is exercised in the acitivity Freire calls *conscientization,* and conscientization is essential to the pedagogy of knowing, which is how Freire characterizes education. I was once chided by a Marxist who said, "Why do you persist in talking about what you call 'the pedagogy of knowing' instead of Freire's 'pedagogy of the oppressed'?" I skewered him with the information that "the pedagogy of knowing" is Freire's language, Freire's idea, that the pedagogy of knowing and the pedagogy of the oppressed are one and the same!

To take up Paulo Freire's slogans without his philosophy of language will be to misapprehend his philosophy of history. Propounding the pedagogy of the oppressed without its philosophical moorings will be no different than settling for that *alimentary* education which Sartre made fun of: "Here eat this! It's good for you!" What we teachers of English need to know about Paulo Freire's philosophy of language can be represented by what he said to us at UMass on another occasion:

> Systematic education cannot be understood as the lever of transformation. The act of learning to read and write has to start from a very comprehensive understanding of the act of reading the world, something which human beings do before reading the words. Even historically, human beings first changed the world, secondly proclaimed the world, and then wrote the words. These are moments of history. Human beings did not start naming A! F! N! They started freeing the hand, grasping the world.

Dialogue is the encounter between men, mediated by the world, to name the world.

There isn't one of those terms which is not familiar to us, not just in a lexical sense but conceptually. But familiarity breeds comtempt—or at least boredom. What we must do is to become tramps of the obvious. We must look and look again at what we think we are doing when we substitute discussion for lecturing, assign what we think of as relevant topics, turn our students loose in the community to do oral histories, when we think about mediation. Whatever we might do to adapt Paulo Freire's theory and practice to our own courses and curricula will be unsettling: he speaks of an "unquiet pedagogy," and that's what we tramps will have. We can orient ourselves by developing "the opposite case," identifying examples of what we do *not* want our pedagogy to be. For Paulo Freire, the opposite case is E.D. Hirsch, Jr. His *Philosophy of Composition* exemplifies very well what Freire means by the mechanist approach, and *Cultural Literacy* represents, better than any book I can think of except *The Closing of the American Mind,* what Paulo Freire means by the banking concept of education. (I don't generally mention names in my polemics, but I do when they are best sellers.)

When we come to consider Paulo Freire's relevance to our own classrooms, we will encounter the criticism that he is so contextualized, his pedagogy so complexly related to one or another society, that it cannot be generalized; some have even claimed that he has no theory! Others have dismissed him as a utopian, a dreamer merely. These criticisms are, in my opinion, entirely expectable from positivists who have never understood the dialectic of theory and practice and wouldn't recognize method if it bit them. Freire's local knowledge is always simultaneously of Man and of the men and women he engages in dialogic action. I have elsewhere claimed that that is a hermeneutic insight. To see each person as representative of humanity is, I believe, centrally important if we are to assure that interpretation is at the heart of all learning. If we read Freire alongside Schleiermacher, the father of a general hermeneutics (a theory of interpretation)—if we read the Protestant minister and the Catholic revolutionary together, the dialogue ensuing will be very lively. Both are teachers who see teaching literacy as a hermeneutic enterprise, a means of realizing the vision of a humane society.

I believe that the best way to grasp this dimension of Freire's pedagogy is to recognize the role he has played in Liberation Theology, the church movement in Latin America which has had so profound an effect on the political fortunes of those countries. For the nuns and priests who have taken it as their mission to engage in the struggle for the liberation of their parishioners, Paulo Freire's pedagogy has been the model. And the murder of the six Jesuits in San Salvador reminds us that this is not an "academic" undertaking.

Freire speaks of three churches: the conservative, altar-oriented church as represented by the current pope, who, you will remember, ordered all clerics to cease and desist from social and political action (including my congressman, Father Drinan); the liberal church—good-hearted, right-minded, but offering only upgraded, more technologically efficient versions of the old ways; and then there is the prophetic church—risking and trusting in order to transform. Paulo talking about the prophetic church reminds me of Pietro Spina in Silone's *Bread and Wine,* the revolutionary hiding from the Fascists in an obscure village, disguised as a priest. Pietro Spina declares that Jesus, were he here today, would be working in the countryside to organize soviets— communes. The prophetic church proclaims and enacts the doctrine of the brotherhood of man; it recognizes that man is a spirit; it invites each person to recognize that he or she is representative of humanity. That is what it means to become a *subject,* as Paulo says. It is subjectivity which is realized in a social context and made possible by reason of our species-specific powers of language.

Liberation pedagogy offers a comparable program. For teachers, it means liberation from tired isolation. (At Rutgers a couple of weeks ago, I heard a teacher remark that one reason teachers burn out is that they are burning alone). Liberation pedagogy could free us from fashion and fads—the foolish rush to whatever the educationist-publishing complex is beating drums about. Liberation pedagogy can defend us against the hostile demands made on us by a public duped into thinking that "a nation at risk" can be saved by screaming ACCOUNTABILITY! or NATIONAL CURRICULUM! Last Spring I visited one of my favorite revolutionaries, Pat D'Arcy, who is English Supervisor for Wiltshire. We attended an all-day conference of elementary school teachers meeting to analyze and to respond constructively to the demands made by Mrs. Thatcher's oppressive colleagues in their draft of the new national curriculum. It was, I thought, a stunning example of "problematizing the existential situation." They wasted no time in ranting; they addressed what they thought were matters it was within their power to re-define. The order of the day seemed to be that they would seize the opportunity to think very hard about what they were doing. I heard nobody say "But we must do what they say!" The energy went into thinking "If we are to do this, here's how we must go about it in order to be true to what we know is possible and just."

These free-born English women and men knew how to act. The oppressions felt in a democracy are different from those suffered in a totalitarian state, and we have different ways of confronting tyranny, the administrative tyranny, for instance, of Margaret Thatcher. We have ways of transforming our society which are neither violent nor millenial. That is an obvious point which we must tramp around and around, if freedom is not to be equated with consumerism. Teachers must work work work to see to it that cultural literacy is not equated with lists of facts to be digested. Literacy without conscientization can transform neither human beings nor their world. In liberation pedagogy, reading the world and reading the word are correlative and simultaneous. We have no more important a mission, no more creative a task, we teachers of English, than assuring that unity of literacy and a "consciousness of consciousness, intent upon the world." Paulo Freire has the last word:

> Human beings did not come into the world only to adapt themselves to the situations they find. It is as if we received a mission to re-create the world constantly. This is human existence. By being historical beings, we are creative beings.